Anthony Harris

The Sacred Virgin
and the
Holy Whore

SPHERE BOOKS LIMITED

SPHERE BOOKS LIMITED

Published by the Penguin Group
27 Wrights Lane, London w8 5tz, England
Viking Penguin Inc., 40 West 23rd Street, New York, New York 10010, USA
Penguin Books Australia Ltd, Ringwood, Victoria, Australia
Penguin Books Canada Ltd, 2801 John Street, Markham, Ontario, Canada l3r 1b4
Penguin Books (NZ) Ltd, 182-190 Wairau Road, Auckland 10, New Zealand

Penguin Books Ltd, Registered Offices: Harmondsworth, Middlesex, England

First published by Sphere Books Ltd 1988

Copyright © 1988 by Anthony Harris
All rights reserved

Made and printed in Great Britain by
Richard Clay Ltd, Bungay, Suffolk
Filmset 10/11½ Monophoto Baskerville

Acknowledgements

For help in the writing of this book I would like to thank: Ian Wilson, Dr Frank S. Pidcock, Theresa Mary Morton, C. F. Kaufmann, Penelope E. Morgan, Dr Oliver Scott, Bishop of Hereford, Don Cupitt, Andrea Reid, Pamela Willis, Professor M. H. Kaufman, Catherine Chandler, Linda Woolley, Alasdair Maclean, Alistair Smith, John Murdoch, Dr Jean de Grouchy, Janet Morley, Sara Maitland, Sister Hannah, Pauline Hallam, Xavier Harris, Barbara Chandler, Fionna Gilbert, Rev. F. O. Edwards, SJ, Miriam Stead and Abigail Chandler. I am indebted to the staffs of: British Museum, Egyptian Room; Ealing and Acton Library Services; British Library; Royal Society of Chemistry Library; British Journal of Photography; Royal Library, Windsor; Salesians of St John Bosco; QED, BBC Television; The Cathedral Library, Hereford; Museum and Library of the Order of St John; Victoria and Albert Museum, Textile Department; Shirley Institute; National Gallery: Musée d'Histoire de Marseille; and the curators and citizens, Vienne. I am also grateful to the staffs of the Society for the Promotion of Christian Knowledge; Catholic Truth Society; and the Archives and Library, Society of Jesus, London.

Permission to quote material was given by Ian Wilson, from *The Turin Shroud*, Gollancz, and *Jesus: the Evidence*, Pan; Marina Warner, from *Alone of All Her Sex*, Weidenfeld; André Deutsch from *Pope Joan* by Royidis translated by L. Durrell; Basil Blackwell, from

Records of Christianity by D. Ayerst and A. S. T. Fisher; Catholic Truth Society, from *More Meditations on Mary* by M. Nassan; Penguin Books, from *Josephus, the Jewish War*, translated by G. A. Williamson, and from *History of the Church*, Eusebius, translated by G. A. Williamson; Methuen from *The Messiah Jesus*, by R. Eisler, translated by A. H. Krappe.

All quotations are fully acknowledged as far as possible, either in the text or, identified by text reference numbers, in the Notes and References section at the end of the book.

Illustrations

The courtesy of the trustees of the British Museum and Musée d'Histoire, and the British Army Military Museum is gratefully recorded. Thanks to the Rights Staff at André Deutsch in attempting to track down the artist of the portrait of Pope Joan used on Royidis's *Pope Joan*, translated by L. Durrell, to no avail. I particularly acknowledge the help given to me by Ian Wilson in the finding of photos for reproduction of the Turin Shroud, and della Rovere's *Deposition*; and permission for their use is acknowledged, from the Salesians of St John Bosco, and the British Society for the Turin Shroud. I must also thank the Trustees of the National Gallery for a beautiful photograph of the Virgin and St Anne; the other works of da Vinci are reproduced by courtesy of gracious permission by HM the Queen, from the Royal Library, Windsor. See page 402 for full list of picture acknowledgements.

Contents

Introduction   Fertile Ground

This book is an account of an investigative odyssey which led to astonishing conclusions concerning the origins and developments of Christianity, but which also cleared away, like a mist, the myths surrounding the founder of what we call Christianity, and the women closest to him.

The facts are well documented here, and their implications fit a clearly defined hypothesis concerning the most dynamic person in history. However, the hypothesis also implies that institutions which often bear his name have knowingly suppressed the truth, even to the extent of creating myths which help the vested interests of these institutions. The myths have been, sad to relate, perpetuated by terror and force of arms.

I did not set out to find the wonder or the terror. Indeed there was no clear beginning of the paradoxes which led me to undertake this labour, though my involvement, or victimization, goes back more than three decades. There came a time, however, in the early 1980s, when a decision to embark on the odyssey could no longer be put off; the pressure of mystery and puzzle had grown too great to be ignored.

Even after a few months of a disciplined and structured full-time assault on what seemed paradoxical in Christianity, it was clear that, so revolutionary were the scenarios which presented themselves, I would have to remain objective as far as possible, despite the excitement of the chase, and the thrill of discovery. This meant jettisoning my own theories, and other people's, when they did not fit the facts. As a result, I can say that what I discovered was not sought, but I feel privileged because of it. Even now I am prepared to test my hypotheses in the light of new facts, but it will be reason – not mere opinion, or prejudice – which must act as the criterion.

This is an introduction, and part of it is to explain my methods, but what of my motives? I do not find I have a clear answer; I do not know why as a child, for example, I found the Christianity I was taught was so alien, or why I revolted against it. I suppose I might one day, but in this very confusion there is a pattern, for it was a natural reaction – that is, my protest came out of something in me as a child. What I was being told did not fit in with what I saw, heard, felt and tasted. But a child is vulnerable, and it takes a long time to put away the trust of a child and build up the scepticism of an independent adult. By then the damage can be considerable, but luckily for me I was not hurt, for I was brought up in the easygoing atmosphere of a Protestant English town, Gloucester, where Christianity was taught in so haphazard a manner it left my mind free, but puzzled.

I believe my childhood recollections do have a part to play, because up to the age of twenty at least, most of our reactions are, for the want of a better word, *natural* – they are real in a very human way, unstructured perhaps, but welling up from an essence of what we are as human beings. I am really trying to say that these spontaneous responses of ours should not be ignored. Someone else put it rather better, in the saying 'Out of the mouths of babes and sucklings comes forth wisdom.' I think part of wisdom is a persistent scepticism, even about one's own scepticism.

The investigative work I began in the early 1980s came out of a series of paradoxes and puzzles during my younger years, and it is clear that naïvety, far from being a liability, was in fact a strength, for it kept me outside a dogmatic prison. When it was time to put resources and effort seriously into the investigation of these paradoxes, I found that over the years they had built up in me the curiosity and sense of adventure that was necessary to push the work through to a conclusion, but I had no idea that the result would be of any interest to other people. I thought there was nothing new to be found out about a crucified Jew, but I was proved wrong. I thought dogmas would be seen to be just that, aberrations, but some of them have proved to be worse than mistakes – they have emerged as impudent lies – while others took on the status of scientific fact. I had no idea that as Christianity as it is taught came crashing down around me there would rise up a far more beautiful and believable edifice, of a kind whose roots stretched back far beyond the vengeful god of the Jews – a temple, as it were, which contained within it all human knowledge without suppression or contradiction. But getting there was a journey through terror and horror, of what appeared to be a conspiracy on an unprecedented scale, of a lust for power which was absolute both in intent and in its pitilessness. Yet there were also moments of considerable calm and attractiveness.

I began my report of the investigations with a specific question, about a specific woman, doing a specific thing which seemed inexplicable, and followed the current from then on, but in this introduction I have tried to bring into focus a few of the puzzles and experiences, not all by any means, which built up towards a decision to embark. As I have since learned during the odyssey, they were puzzles and paradoxes which had mystified a great number of other people too, some of whom had been murdered, others tortured, many sent mad by a hierarchy which insisted there were no puzzles, there were no paradoxes. But there are.

A Pagan Confession

At school we assembled in the mornings and sang songs about a strange God who came from the East. I pictured him as looking like the Indian carpet sellers who came to our house from time to time. Later, when I heard he lived in the sky, I saw him with a turban on a magic carpet. I don't think my teachers would have been very happy if they had known how the creed they were trying to put over to English children not yet ten years old appeared so alien. Indeed, the tales I heard from my grandfather of a thunder god making thunder with a hammer were much more to my taste, and when I heard that the wave of water which came hissing up the Severn every spring was really a goddess called Sabrina, I was hugely impressed.

It would take a book in itself to elaborate the sheer irrelevance, the boredom and the foreignness, of Christianity as taught to me in the Protestant schools I attended. It would also take a book to get over the sense of delight things natural and rural gave me. Luckily, when my family moved from Gloucester it was to Hereford, another cathedral city, another beautiful part of England. But something had changed. The Severn rushed through the black soil of Gloucestershire, but the Wye meandered through the scarlet earth of Herefordshire. I had moved to a land of scarlet things. The impression was overpowering. There were red cows on green pastures, red apples, and where the streams and rivers opened the earth the red undergarment was revealed. Even the cathedral was crimson, and on a summer's eve it glowed like a rose by the river, where in spring the fish were red, the salmon of the Wye. And so was my first girlfriend, in that she had deep russet hair.

I had reached the age of seventeen without once taking anything Christian seriously. I read out the lesson as prefect at morning assembly, and felt it had nothing to do with me at all. But there was magic in the countryside, and some of that awe was even reflected by the cathedral, which I passed twice a day. I went in there from time to time, drawn by its warmth, its red sandstone, its ancientness, curiously like the countryside, an anagram of stone. Inside it seemed female, receptive, an abode of secrets, but any power it had came from its echoes of nature.

Then when I was about eighteen I came across a naked Lady deep in the Herefordshire countryside. It was a summer's evening, the shadows were already lengthening, the air seemed iridescent with the redness of the soil and the reflection of cider apples. I stood there not believing my eyes. For there on this little English church, nearly a thousand years old, was a tiny carving of a woman displaying herself to the fields.

I was intrigued. She seemed so mysterious, and yet I already knew her. Furthermore, I wanted to know why this little Lady was under the eaves of a Christian church; after all, my ancestors had put her there, so I had to respect that. She was surrounded by fishes and lambs, all Christian symbols, so was she a Christian symbol too? And if not, why not?

Enquiries over the years about her and her sisters always elicited the same response: she was, it seemed, this Lady of Kilpeck, the Eve of the Eaves, a 'fertility figure'. Seasons passed and she watched yet more green fields turn gold under the sun, saw the poppies bloom, the apples ripen, and the hoar-frost melt on the tips of oak twigs. Nothing had changed for her in a thousand years; she had outlasted frost, wind, rain and vandals who cut down her many sisters and defaced the rest.

I don't mean to imply I made pilgrimages to Kilpeck, but it was a long time ago when I first met the Lady there, and I don't like to pass the church by when I am in the vicinity, which, alas, is not very often. But as time passed I learned that the Lady of Kilpeck was in fact a little goddess, and she in her rustic naïvety was the same goddess who had occupied the splendour of the Parthenon, for Eve of the Eaves and the Great Athene were the selfsame goddess, the Great Goddess in different guises.

The technical term is aspect. How many and how rich are those aspects! Venus in marbled wonder stood above the Roman crowds while, called Aphrodite, she was worshipped in Greece. Diana strode the woodlands, and Demeter softened the lions. Astarte's shrine in Babylon was veiled and scented, atop a great citadel, while in Egypt the beautiful Isis fed her child in the magnificence of her sanctuary in Alexandria. In every Roman home a candle was lit before the shrine of Vesta, goddess of the hearth. These are all aspects of the same Goddess, virgin, mother, warrioress, prophetess, protectress of children, even the earth itself.

Eve of the Eaves, then, is not a 'fertility figure', she is fertility itself. What she ultimately represents had apparently exercised the deepest emotions of men and women since the mists of time. There are carvings of her – some crude, some of the highest art – dating back millennia before the first city, and wherever there is a hamlet, a village, a fort, a city, we find her sisters. Sometimes the lovers of the Great Goddess were simple pastoral folk, sometimes the sophisticates of imperial courts. Sometimes she is fashioned only in wood, but then she appears also in gold and precious stones. Her abode can be a cave, a hut or a lofty airy palace, patrolled by bearded Assyrian guards, attended by retinues of priestesses, phalanxes of priests. Her vestments are of the finest silk or simple homespun. Her artists are sometimes rustic, like the mason who carved for Kilpeck, and yet often too, hands directed by artistic genius fashioned her form, in Rome and in Greece, Tyre and Babylon. She is found near rivers and in deserts, in forests and on mountains; she is the protectress of mariners. She is of the earth, water, air and the heavens. And yet today all over Europe, her shrines have been desecrated, her statues overturned, her sanctuaries despoiled . . . her very memory, it seems, has been erased from the face of the earth.

But I found that for me this was not true, since I knew her in the magical moments of my youth and my childhood. I found her because by some lucky accident I was born and grew up where the rhythms of her pulse were strong enough to feel, and her complexion was unsullied. Of course, I have since found out that I am not alone in realizing something has happened, as armies of scholars piece together what has been a terrible event in human history. But that was not enough for me, because her remains were merely being dug up, codified and labelled. Where was the regret and the sense of loss? Indeed, where was the respect that should be accorded to her dignity? Traumatically, I realized her death was being accepted as a fact.

As I worked through the literature, I found author after author cataloguing her ancient shrines, yet without any regret. It takes a poet such as Robert Graves[1] to point to the heart of the matter: 'Ancient Europe had no gods, the Great Goddess was regarded as immortal, changeless and omnipotent.' She was many-titled, and the beliefs about her were scattered all over the ancient world from time immemorial. Changeless, omnipotent and immortal? Sounds like the Christian and Jewish God, but the sex is wrong. He also points out that the Great Goddess was recognized to have a triple aspect, or trinity, in her very essence, which is given real flesh in the passage of a girl's life from virgin, to mother, to prophetess in old age.

Graves lived his life in veneration for the Great Goddess, and his form of respect was poetry. It matters little if his poetry is good or bad, the fact is he seemed to realize something important had happened to the Great

Goddess, whom he knew as the Muse. He was regarded by many as eccentric in this view, perhaps because he never got very far in finding out what had really happened to her, but his loyalty and dedication to her had one effect at least. It made me see that my unformed notions, suspicions, even longings, were not simply idiosyncratic, but part of a living, common human experience, which was religious. This appeared to me at first a shocking discovery, since all I knew about 'religion' was the aridity, the sterility, of Protestant Christianity. Obviously my ideas of religion needed a revision.

It was at this stage that I discovered Roman Catholicism, at about the age of twenty-two, for a friend of mine, a sincere Catholic, began to entice me into the mysteries of Benediction and the Mass. Here was something very different. There was something alive in a Catholic church, seldom found in Protestant ones, though this 'presence' is not uniformly absent from the latter. The candles, the statues, the ringing bells, the sweet-smelling incense, were all very attractive; there was some of the richness of the countryside here, some of the mystery, but there was something which provoked my ire too. To me the services seemed an echo of the female, of the unimaginably ancient – indeed they are culled from the rites of Isis, Venus and Athene – but the men at the altar were not only a distraction, they were somehow out of context. Or was it because they dressed as women and there were no women there? I think too that there was a sense of alienation, for these men were talking about a creator who had supposedly formed me and was on that piece of stone, but they were separating me from this deity. I could only go to what was arguably a presence of the utmost intimacy, the Being who had allegedly made me, through these strangely dressed men. My revolt was absolute. I thank the Protestant upbringing for this piece of common sense, and also a certain Jewish input, through Jewish friends, who have no such barriers between themselves and their God.

Yet though the rejection was entire, the fascination remained, for here in Catholic churches were images of two women. One was a virgin mother and the other a whore, both aspects being figures taken directly out of the Great Goddess tradition, though I was to discover that Mary Magdalene was never a whore, and the acolytes of the Great Goddess were not prostitutes – not in the way we use the words, anyway.

These experiences, confused and yet very much alive, were to receive a further jolt of energy when I went to Trinity College, Dublin, which was then a Protestant enclave in a Catholic city. The Protestant churches of Dublin and its cathedrals are usually architecturally finer than their Catholic counterparts, a legacy of the time when Dublin was a colonized city, a colony of Protestant England. If I felt the deadness in the Protestant churches in England, then the Irish ones were even colder, for women's images were largely absent. But the Catholic churches were not only full of people, they were shrines of Mary Magdalene and Mary the Virgin. Millions of candles were burned before the statues of these two women, and people on their knees kept vigils through the night before them.

The power, then, to which I was sensitive was the female imagery, that was what I felt instinctively was authentic. And that meant I could not be a 'Catholic', for over the altar was always to be found a crucified man, usually handsome, usually muscular, and he was attended by men, always. It all seemed so odd, so contradictory: they were worshipping a man, but could not let go of the women. I can't say I felt any sense of loss in not knowing this male god. The power of the two Marys drew me as if by magnetism, but I was content to leave it at that.

I could make neither head nor tail of it, but from time to time I returned to the problem, usually by chance, as I went into churches for the architectural beauty, and was confronted by an image of a blood-spattered man. This was perhaps the oddest image of all, for we are told that two thousand years ago a man was crucified in Jerusalem and that he spilt his blood to save us all. The remarkable thing about the claim is not that blood can save, for that, after all, was the commonplace of the Great Goddess cults, where ceremonies involving blood, sometimes menstrual, were part of the fabric of social life. The confusing claim is that a Jew had said it, a male Jew, and in doing this he was supposed to have been fulfilling the Jewish religion for mankind. It is difficult to construct a more self-contradictory statement. For one thing, the Jewish religion was based on eschewing blood. They bled their animals, while contact with a menstruating woman made a man ritually impure. If a priest came near one, he had to go through ceremonies to cleanse himself before going up to the altar, where sheep's blood was offered up. Indeed, women were not allowed in the temple, except in the outer court, and even this was denied when they were menstruating. Yet here was a Jewish man who was enjoining his followers to drink his blood, thereby breaking one of the central taboos of his religion.

Where did he get the idea? He could not possibly have got it from his Jewish background, not the one that is taught in Christian seminaries worldwide. Where, then, did it come from? It doesn't seem to be an idea that would come easily to a man anyway.

These are perplexing mysteries, but there are more, for nearly 2,000 years before that, a wandering herdsman announced that there was only one God. Given that everyone knew there were many deities, it seemed a curious stance to take. But to pile paradox on paradox, the real oddity was that this herdsman said the God was male.

The pastoral innovator was Abraham, and he founded the Jewish religion. It has hardly been a shattering revelation for mankind, since the more powerful and numerous peoples surrounding these struggling nomads knew that if there was one deity it was the Great Goddess, and they simply ignored the Jewish initiative, and enslaved the Jews into the bargain.

The Jewish male God, then, would have passed in to a sideshow of history but for the claims of Jesus Christ, or what pass for his claims. He said (so Rome teaches) that the Jewish religion had to be fulfilled, and he fulfilled it. Hence, if the new religion was taken up by energetic and clever people, like Romans and Greeks, the Jewish experience of a male God would be rescued from oblivion. This, as we know, has happened, for with the growth of Christianity, not Judaism, came the destruction of the Great Goddess religion, which mankind in every culture had thitherto subscribed to. It did not, however, proceed by argument, but by force, torture and despoliation.

Arguably, then, the great male religion which straddles the world, with its offshoots in Judaism and Islam, is a cultural oddity, something that was foisted by force of arms upon mankind, emerging abruptly and without preparation in the evolution of human thought. It is not the ethics which are of consuming interest, but the sex. What really happened – how could the living force of the Great Goddess be suddenly ignored by a person who called himself the Son of God? I did not know, and it seemed transparently obvious that no one else did either.

Our ancestors made no abstraction of blood in religion, for it was obviously magical and holy, none more so than the blood of women, for though men died when they bled, women did not. When they did not bleed they grew children. When they did not bleed any more, they no longer bore children. Clearly, their blood was intimately, indeed inseparably, linked with birth. A provocative thought is that here perhaps is the true origin of the notion of the 'born-again' effect of drinking Christ's blood; and since it was his teaching, it is plausible to suggest that it was this tradition he was fulfilling. And this tradition is none other than that of the Great Goddess, not of the Jewish sky God, who was male, vengeful, and could not be pictured. The Great Goddess, however, was already incarnate; she was the mother anywhere who had once been a virgin, and who one day would be the spirit, as it were, of her former fecund self.

Our ancestors had no difficulty with this; they depicted the Great Goddess as a woman. Today, after 2,000 years of Yahweh in the West, we call them fertility figures, which is a condescending term for a Goddess who once had more shrines than there are Christian churches, and who had a lot more functions than fertility, since she was also Goddess of just about everything human. As a result, she had many names, but her fleshly connection with ordinary women was not for one moment questioned or doubted. The notion of an incarnation is as old as that of the Goddess cults, and in the Middle East alone that goes back for 10,000 years.

It could not, therefore, have been the Jewishness of Christianity which aided its spread, since as a world religion Judaism had been a singular failure – very few converts were made, and to the sophisticated Roman, Egyptian, Persian or Greek there seemed nothing special about an abstract sky god who did not even have statues. It can be argued too that the moral tenets of Christianity were not all that different from the best of pagan religions.

The promise of rising from the dead was, however, certain to prick up the ears of educated and uneducated alike in the Roman Empire. Christians could tell of Lazarus being so raised. To Egyptians this sounded like Isis raising Osiris; to Greeks like raising Persephone from

Hades. There seemed none the less a confusion: the sexes
were all mixed up. As for Christ rising from the dead,
there was not even much new in that – heroes and
heroines came back from Hell, Hades, the Underworld.
As for the peasants, they had known all their lives, as
their ancestors had done for at least 10,000 years, that
the Mother Goddess killed and she gave birth. She killed
the seed when she made it open and grow. She killed all
living things but they returned to the earth and came
forth again in new life. Blood that was spilt in her service
could never be wasted. Resurrection as an idea was not
new, it was one of the oldest of mankind.

The speed of conversion, we may legitimately conclude, could not have been so great if the seed-corn of
the early Christian missionaries had not fallen on fertile
ground. That ground was the body of the Great Goddess.

Christ's promise was not unique, but what Rome did
was to make this promise its own property. You could
not, according to the new priests of Rome, attain 'salvation' except through a male priest. This was a very
new idea, and the free gift of blood that Jesus gave appears very quickly to have had sanctions attached to it.
Was this Jesus' intention? Or was a gift of love simply
that, a gift, just as Isis gave freely at any of her 10,000
shrines, a religion uncentralized, undogmatic?

The Virgin and the Magdalene

As I ploughed through the standard histories of the
Church, my suspicion grew that there was something
fundamentally wrong with the received picture. Perhaps
it can be summed up by the term 'the Church'. History
after history spoke of 'the Church', even in the first and
second centuries, as if there existed a central and unified
Christian organization in much the same way as the

Roman Catholic Church exists today. Close examination, however, does not support this assumption; rather there appear to have been several Christian theologies, engaged in a fight for supremacy. The one which triumphed was the Roman Catholic Church of Rome. I felt, though, that to identify this body with the earliest collection of vehemently fractious religious power groups set in Rome, Alexandria and elsewhere was a crucial mistake, and yet a feather in the cap, as it were, of the Roman Catholic view of history.

The first official historian of 'the Church' (how easy it is to fall into the error of using this phrase) was Eusebius,[2] born AD *c.* 260 in Caesarea, the Roman military and commercial port of Galilee. He became Bishop of Caesarea in AD 314 and made a strong impression on Constantine, who was then eighteen. The young Emperor was Eusebius' patron, protecting him, even making him his moderator at the Council of Nicaea. It is Eusebius we have to thank for telling us that Constantine had a holy vision which caused him to underwrite the Nicene Creed, which establishes God as Father, Jesus actually going to Hell, and the complex notion of the Trinity. The 'Church' was in honeymoon with the Roman Emperor.

Eusebius can perhaps be thought of as the first pro-pagandist of the Roman Catholic Church. In his history everything appears to have sprung fully formed into the waiting world, with bishops, deacons and a recognizable Mass. To accept Eusebius unequivocally is to suppose all this was more or less in operation within a decade of Christ's dying. Gibbon, in his *Decline and Fall of the Roman Empire*, takes a rather more believable line, pointing out that in the first three centuries there was no central church. Various sects, all but one later to be termed heretical, were busily consolidating their own positions and trying to escape persecution from the Roman Emperors.

What Nicaea decided was that only one kind could

flourish and, curiously, it was the one which gave most power to the hierarchy. Some of the 'heresies' were egalitarian, with the Last Supper being celebrated by lay people in their own homes. This is similar to what Jesus did, but it was not the way to exploit power, which demands centralization and a recognized authority. It seems a plausible hypothesis that the creed established at Nicaea was one dictated by power politics, not theology; the patristic Roman Church was going to claim sole right to remit sins and assert that through its sacraments alone (entirely controlled by its priests) could a soul gain salvation. In other words, if you were damned by the Church, you were to believe God damned you too. An odd idea really, when one remembers that Jesus said, 'Where two or three are gathered in my name, there will I be too.'

It seems that women were to be left out, for Mary Magdalene, despite anointing Jesus and carrying his body from the Cross, is not mentioned by Eusebius, while Jesus' mother is mentioned only to prove she belonged to the same tribe as Joseph, but he even fails in this attempt. So why did he attempt it? Was there something in Mary's real genealogy which the Church wished to suppress or misrepresent? As I was to discover, Mary's ancestry is acutely embarrassing to Roman theology, and that it still exists in the New Testament may probably be the bequest of heretics, in the sense that they were so numerous that their copies of Matthew could not be vaporized.

In addition, Eusebius asserts that the risen Christ was first seen by Peter, but the Gospels strongly assert Mary Magdalene was the first witness. Already the Roman Church was putting commentary above the Scriptures, a very dangerous development when so many Christians could not read. Even more alarming is the way the doctrine of Hell is introduced, on the basis of a clearly forged letter, allegedly written by Jesus! The political point may very well be that the Church realized it is no good having the keys of Heaven and Hell unless there is a Hell to save frightened supplicants from. This also throws light on the Nicene Creed, for Eusebius was notary of it, and it is there that Jesus' descent into Hell is for ever enshrined.

Eusebius is also one of the seminal influences in the developing doctrine of 'heretics', whereas they were just other Christians who did not share Rome's viewpoint. He becomes obsessed with a man called Simon, a Samaritan, against whom he raves, but the only sin Simon is guilty of, it appears, is his predilection for having women in his entourage. To the Roman scribe, however, this is the mark of the devil, for a flesh-and-blood girl, Helen, is called by him an 'emanation'. Her presence is particularly important in understanding Simon, for she has all the marks of an acolyte of the Great Goddess. Indeed, her role is very similar to Mary Magdalene's, which is probably why Eusebius fulminates against her and, without giving any justification, talks about Simon's 'vicious' use of women and his being the father of vices. He does not say what they were; we are expected to use our imagination.

Simon, beneath this attack, emerges as a true follower of Christ, even going to Rome before Peter. It may be that Peter was then able to take up some of the work Helen and Simon had done in preparing ordinary Romans for the new religion. Scant thanks they get from Eusebius, who has clearly seen the danger to his own patristic political needs in entertaining the value of a priestess.

But the main thrust at Rome was to repudiate sexuality altogether, not venerate it as the Great Goddess rural cults did, nor incorporate it into religious temple life as happened in the cities of Egypt, Assyria, Persia, Rome, Greece and Palestine. Millions of men locked themselves into a sexually void monastic habit, homophilic and homotheocratic. Males worshipping a male. At the same time, millions of women went into convents, the virgins of the new order. In medieval Europe the houses of Benedictines, Franciscans, Dominicans, Carmelites and so on culled off the most educated and highest-born. Isis had never taken the loins of so many men, nor had she shut up so many wombs. Aphrodite must have looked on appalled. The psychological damage monasticism implied is impossible to quantify. The Church was saying that the best Christian was one who had no sexual activity – the best woman was not even a mother or a wife, but an enclosed virgin; the best man was a eunuch.

Theologically, new notions of childbirth are even developed today, boding no good for women. That the Messiah should come by a virgin into this world is not even original; but this Jewish girl who bore her child in cold and squalor is, in Catholic theology, for ever a virgin, intact even after labour. This contrasts unfavourably with the natural development of a woman's life as signified in the triple or Trinity aspect of the Great Goddess (virgin, mother, prophetess or wise old lady). The serious imputation for women's lives of this shift in Church thinking has been noted by other writers, among them Marina Warner:

By defining the limits of womanliness as shrinking, retiring acquiescence, and by reinforcing that behaviour in the sex with praise, the myth of female inferiority and dependence could be and was perpetuated. The two arms of the Christian view of woman – the contempt and hatred evident in interpretations of the Creation and the Fall, and idealization of her more 'Christian' submissive nature – meet and interlock in the advocacy of humility for the sex. The Church can therefore continue to deny women an active and independent role in its ministry. The priesthood is closed to women because they are considered a secondary image of the maker, too gentle and timid by nature,

and destined to serve either their husbands and children as
wives and mothers or priests and children as nuns.[3]

Body of the Goddess

Christianity, then, appears to have fed on the body and
drunk the blood of the Great Goddess and, though
claiming to worship the same God as the Jews, actually
turned its back on the Jewish celebration of love of man
for woman. But even more sinister moves were afoot. The
Council of Ancyra, AD 314, was the Pope's anticipation
of real secular power, to come at last with the ascent of
Christianity through its adoption by the Emperor
Constantine. The documents we have of that Council
reveal a preoccupation with women, especially as acolytes
of Diana (which means in effect any aspect of the Great
Goddess – Demeter, Artemis, Isis, even Athene). However, there is a new slant: paganism is now equated with
satanism and diabolism. What is perplexing is that
women were the energy of early Christianity, but now
they are identified as a threat to the Church. The key to
this conundrum lies in the equation the Roman Church
(that is, the bishops and the Pope) made between their
hierarchical power and Christianity. Manifestly the two
are not the same, but the Pope was going to make them
the same. Few developments more clearly point to the
difference between fundamental Christianity, with its
love feasts and equality of women, its lack of dogma and
its subsuming of the old fertility concepts, and the power
hierarchy of the burgeoning Church of Rome.

What these clerics of the Pope were calling witchcraft,
diabolism or worship of Diana within the Church was very
probably an older form of Christianity. The give-away
element in the recommendations of the Council is the
enjoinder to eject the malefactor from the parish.[4] In
other words, the 'enemy' was within, and apparently it

was a feminine, fundamental, non-dogmatic Christianity.

In order to underpin its power, the Church needed not only the secular arm which it received from a Roman Emperor, but a concept to bind people to it, explicitly, from the cradle. The concept chosen was Original Sin, and it was developed by a brilliant man, who seems to have terribly misused his gifts. He was Augustine, a North African, who was born at Thagaste in AD 354, and died a bishop at Hippo in 430, as the Vandals were attacking the city. Augustine was a late convert to Christianity (he was thirty-three) but he recognized early the danger posed by the Great Goddess to a proselytizing new religion. He waxes vehement and sustained against devotees, priests and priestesses of the Great Goddess in his *City of God*, but conveniently forgets that he has had the best of both worlds, for all his young manhood he enjoyed the embraces of a common-law wife, only to cruelly repudiate her and his love for her later.

Augustine was certain that even a child in arms came from its mother's womb steeped in sin, and only the Roman Church could save the babe. A frightening idea, and many Christians rejected it – but in order to have power an institution needs a hold over people: what better than the keys of Heaven and Hell?

Julian, a bishop famed for his good acts – he even sold his estates to feed the poor – hated Augustine's insistence on Original Sin, but curiously his twelve-volume treatises have been destroyed, and his numerous letters have barely survived. However, Augustine's attacks on the Bishop Julian of Eclanum in southern Italy have been lovingly preserved.

Really, really: is that your experience? So you would not have married couples restrain that evil – I refer, of course, to your favourite good? So you would have them jump in to bed whenever they like, whenever they feel tickled by desire? Far be it from them to postpone this itch till bedtime: let's have your

'legitimate union of bodies' whenever your 'natural good' is
excited. If this is the sort of married life you led, don't drag up
your experience in debate.[5]

His hatred of the flesh appears to know no bounds; on
noting that when Adam and Eve had disobeyed God
they covered their genitals, he sermonizes (Sermon 151)
'That's the place! That's the place from which the first
sin is passed on!' The new Church had abrogated sole
power to free a child from sin, but also invaded the marriage bed, for even to make love was now a sin.

The Roman Church had the appearance of veneration
of the Great Goddess, in that Mary was venerated, and
Mary Magdalene honoured. Indeed, in the first three
centuries women were most active in the Church, their
husbands often being pagan. Roughly contemporaneous
with Augustine was the brilliant Jerome, translator of
the Bible. He recognized that freebooters were scrambling
on to the Christian altar to gain secular power, and also
to get near beautiful women. He, however, loved women,
and in his letters there are heroic and touching accounts
of these early Christian women, who lived a life of service
in their communities.[6] But as soon as their men became
Christian (that is, Roman Catholic), these women lost
their freedom of action, for they were to take a secondary
role, as St Paul had enjoined, though other Christian
sects ignored him.

The early misogyny of the Church appears to have
been a development of the experiment with which the
Jewish priests had been grappling for two millennia.
Arguably it suited Jewish political purposes to eschew
the Great Goddess, and so demarcate themselves from
their more powerful and numerous neighbours. But
Jewish misogyny never went so far as Rome's; there was
never that obscene taint, and the Jews saw sex between
husband and wife as a generator not of sin but of life.

The theme which emerges from this is that once the Roman Church secured military help from the Roman Emperors, it enacted a series of decrees which gave itself total spiritual power over every living human being. The notion of hell-fire was promulgated, and along with it the argument that sin came into the world via women. The hateful misogyny of Augustine triumphed over Jerome's more moderate views, simply because if women were to take an equal place the doctrine of their sinfulness would be undermined, and sin was the weapon of terror which the Church used to coerce people. After all, according to Rome, only through Romish priests could you be saved. In parallel with these developments was the libelling of previous Christians as heretics who had kept close to the one force which threatened Rome spiritually, the Great Goddess cult. The eventual supremacy of the Roman viewpoint, however, was not attained by reason, but by skulduggery, and this even went as far as forging documents in the eighth century, so that the Church could usurp power over huge tracts of Europe. Rome was not only a spiritual centre, but a centre of secular power as well.[7]

By the early 1980s the impression I was left by my intermittent forays into patristic Christianity over three decades was that many Popes had been interested in one thing – power – and what we call 'Catholicism' today emerged from their colonizing politics. Central to this lust for power was the need to separate people from their roots and instil fear of sex and women, because by those means the unstructured, uncentralized Goddess cults could be broken.

This was a problem in political terms, for if the institution was to be the force which its leaders insisted it could be, its dogmas had to be suitable instruments of power. The teaching of Original Sin, and the associated dictum of its being passed on by women from Eve, is a powerful theme; if people believed it, they were also told they could only be cleansed by its promulgators, the hierarchy in Rome.

It may be jejune to miss the obvious; practical power politics dictated the dogmas, not the necessities of theology alone. As an exercise in power politics, both psychological and secular, it seemed to me the Roman hegemony had few equals, but as a religion it was a disaster. I think my conclusions can be credited with a fair amount of objectivity, and indeed countless other commentators have come to the same conclusions, though by markedly different routes.

I was intrigued by the misogyny, and repelled by its ferocity, for the Church had used sex as Fascists use race – or, at least, I had uncovered sufficient material to argue this view, unpleasant though its implications were. I had no intention of pursuing the subject; there seemed no end to it, and nothing could be done about it. The religion that had shaped much of western Europe and the world had a wound, a self-inflicted one, and now it was gradually to die. As people in their millions forsook its altars and its churches, no longer willing to tease themselves with its conundrums, its unnaturalness, its political claims, it would, I felt sure, bleed to death.

But I noticed now that women were beginning to demand again their ancient right to be priestesses. I did not understand why they felt it so necessary to ask male hierarchs for a right which is inherently theirs, but they were responding to something just as Mary Magdalene had done, and Peter too, who in his simple love had no intention other than to do what he had been told, to spread the Word. There was, then, a possibility for regeneration, even development, for what is 2,000 years in the annals of the Great Goddess? A mere interim – Isis had presided over Egypt for more than twice that time,

while in her other aspects the Great Goddess went back
beyond recorded history to the dawn of human history,
tens of thousands of years ago. Her figurines and rock
paintings are still being uncovered.

Women at last before the Christian altar: I thought, at
least it will be interesting, and the frocks will be on the
right sex . . . but I paused – would this really be the first
time? Was it really conceivable that women with the force
and magic of Mary, Christ's mother, and of Mary
Magdalene, had not already been priestesses? If holding
a wafer is a priestly function, what function were the two
Marys performing as they held the bleeding body of
Christ in their arms when they took him down from the
cross? If it is a priest's function to sip wine that is blood,
what function is it to be covered by the real blood as
these two women were? The question is rhetorical, or so
it seemed to me, for the real must be greater than the
symbol, and all the Church has is the symbol, while these
two women had the flesh and blood in their hands;
indeed, one had borne the Christ in her own body, fed
the Christ with her milk, while the other had anointed
her Christ with her own hands, shed tears on his body,
and draped her hair over him. In the face of the realities
of the experience of these two women, the claims of
Roman monopoly suddenly seemed more than ever
inflated, and the substance of their rites meagre.

And if these two women were priestesses, were there
others who had been made 'unpersons' by propagandists
such as Eusebius, and woman-haters such as Augustine?
This was a specific and objective question; I wanted to
find the answer. The odyssey had begun, but it was to
lead to more than the answer to this problem – to the
uncovering of pitiless persecution, 'gendercide', a Vatican
conspiracy, and to the beguiling priestesses of the Great
Goddess.

Part I

Sins of the Fathers

Mystery of the Priestesses

In the ninth century a learned and beautiful young Saxon woman went to the south of France, where she visited all the known shrines of Mary Magdalene. The young woman's name was Joan, and she was something of a paragon, fluent in Greek, Latin, Old English, what passed for French at the time, and various German dialects. She was also a devout Christian who stood before the altar and celebrated Mass. Eventually she became Pope John VIII, and was murdered in Rome.

This story intrigued and horrified me, for this blameless scholar, caring priestess and brilliant woman stood head and shoulders above scores of the occupants of the Chair of Peter, and yet for several hundred years she has been made into an 'unperson', as if she had never existed. Yet there is little doubt she *did* live, and little doubt she became Pope.

I wanted to know how she became Pope, and why she was murdered, and why she had been so badly treated since. I felt – and it was purely an instinctive reaction – that a key to her life, even to her character, would be found in her pilgrimage to venerate the shrines of Mary Magdalene, for Mary too was a dramatic woman, very close, intimate even, with Jesus Christ.

I looked forward to making Joan's acquaintance, for she was clearly a romantic figure, full of verve and courage, to have achieved what she did. There was the triple mystery too: how she had become Pontiff, why she was murdered, and why she venerated one of the most controversial figures in Christianity.[1]

Joan is entered in the official 'Lives of the Popes' published during the office of a Borgia Pope, Sixtus, in 1479. Sixtus' secretary wrote the 'Lives'.[2] If she did not exist it would surely be a strange thing for a Borgia, whose chief interest in life was power, to have allowed the inclusion of a woman in the papal lists, because in a sense it weakened the papal succession, which prided itself on being wholly male. And assuming she did exist, the best thing would have been to ignore her altogether, but if there were too many documents relating to her life, that would not have been possible, so they did the next best thing – she was written up as some kind of witch.

This begs more questions, for Joan was elected because her predecessor, Leo IV, a much respected Pope, wanted her to succeed him. If this saintly and Christian Pope wanted her, how could she be a witch?

The simple conclusion is that Sixtus made the best of a bad job, and had her included because he could not get away with leaving her out. It is testimony in itself of her existence that her memory had survived from the ninth to the fifteenth century, for these were times of papal mayhem, when the occupant of the Throne of Peter changed so fast it appeared a lethal game of musical chairs was being played. Pope murdered Pope; they assassinated rivals, tortured one another; eyes were gouged, for often several claimants danced about the Throne all saying they were Pope.

Currently, Joan is regarded by Rome as having never lived, never been a priestess, never been Pope. When she became Pope, Europe was being divided by Charlemagne's heirs into smaller packets, and the Papacy was extremely powerful politically – and hence in military terms also – because of its insistent claims to represent God on this earth. A deal had been struck between the empire-builder, Charlemagne of the Franks, and Rome, that in return for a Papal state the Pope would proclaim Charlemagne the Emperor recognized by none other than God as rightful ruler of Europe. The Pope who made this astute bargain was Leo III, in AD 800.

Arguably, Charlemagne had more justification in claiming right to rule than the Church had in speaking for God, since, after all, his grandfather, Charles Martel, had at least turned back Semitic invaders from Europe in 732. If he had not, there would have been no Christendom, except perhaps in England, Ireland and the Eastern Orthodox countries. With Charlemagne, Europe had, at last, a focus for some kind of unity, and his hegemony included France, Belgium, Holland, Germany, Italy, Austria, Czechoslovakia and Poland. This vast and populous territory was known as the Holy Roman Empire.

Charlemagne was technically illiterate, but he supported learning and gathered around him the best minds of his day. One of these was Albinus (Alcuin), who was born in York *c.*735. Charlemagne met him in 782 in Pavia and was so impressed by his learning and ability that he gave him much power in Church and administrative spheres. He was also tutor to the Emperor's and other Frankish nobles' sons. This English connection enabled Charlemagne to call upon the missionary resources of the English Church, for the Saxons of Germany had not yet been sundered from their goddesses and gods. Clearly, if their culture could be broken, they would be more vulnerable to Charlemagne's empire-building.

To this end the Popes were very helpful, providing Anglo-Saxon missionaries from England to talk to their German cousins. Among these was Joan's father, a well-educated priest. He and his wife Judith – for priests could marry in those days – came from Yarmouth, and met Charlemagne at Paderborn. They were commissioned to evangelize in the forests of Germany, along the precipitous banks of the Rhine, where other priests from France were at work, descendants of the Merovingians, a Frankish clergy which Charlemagne and the Popes neither trusted nor could control. These wandering missionaries baptized in the Name of the Father, the Daughter and the Holy Ghost, a habit which would make few friends in Rome.[3]

The Pilgrim

In 814 Joan was born of Judith, though it is not certain whether at Ingelheim or Mayence. Her father baptized her in the waters of Meinengen, we are sure, in the name of the Father, the Son and the Holy Ghost.

The little family was itinerant, and Joan a precocious child, picking up the offices of the Church in English, Greek and Latin, and even able to speak the tongues of the Germans. She showed a great love of the Cross, and the Rosary, while her father, once a pupil of one of the best scholars of the time, Scotus, educated her well.

Joan's mother died when she was eight. There followed a stay at the Nunnery of Bittelfield, but her father was soon off again on his missionary travels, while Joan continued her education. With the empire of Charlemagne now again plunged into war after his death in 814, Joan must have seen more suffering and warfare than most people do in a lifetime, for the river banks of Germany were often heaped with the dead, and through these melancholy plots Joan would walk, as her father confessed the dying and, more often, baptized the pagans, trying, in his belief, to save them.

Active in the environs of Frankfort and the forests of Vistulia, the pair were often reduced to hunger and cold. Itinerant, as Jesus had been, Joan came to see the suffering of life, the deprivation of the peasants and serfs, the richness of the nobles. She became well versed in points of logic which she would dispute with all and sundry, and spent her nights in the great halls of the nobility, or by the fire of a woodsman or hunter.

In Joan's sixteenth year her father died, while the guest of a hermit, Arculfo, in his poor abode by the River Meine. After many adventures,[4] Joan eventually came to the convent of St Blittrude's, at Mosbach, where even though she had no dowry she was accepted. This speaks for her learning and personal charm, for in those days a place in a convent was not easily come by unless the girl had something to offer. Joan became librarian and calligrapher, copying out the priceless tomes of the abbey library, so that copies could be used by missionaries. In this she was diligent and, of course, she increased her already wide range of knowledge. She was joined in the task by a young Benedictine, Father Frumentius, scholar and skilled illuminator. It was their task to prepare a copy of St Paul's Epistles, to be used for missionary work. At that time the rule of St Benedict allowed nuns and monks to inhabit the same premises.

There was now a significant change in Joan's life, for twelve days' journey away was the Benedictine monastery of St Fulda's. It was much larger that St Blittrude's – sixty monks alone were engaged in making copies of the Gospels. The Abbot invited Joan because of her learning, and so there can be no question of scandal between Frumentius and Joan, but what is astonishing is that Joan took the male habit of a monk. She might initially have done so for protection when travelling, but she was to all intents and purposes a monk at St Fulda's. Curiously, many women hid their sex in this way, as if following a kind of tradition. I say 'tradition' for two reasons. First, if it were mere protection, then why didn't all the nuns do it? Second, St Thecla, one of Joan's favourite saints, also took the monk's habit, as did other holy women,

Saints Eugenia and Matrona. Royidis, Joan's biographer, is so impressed by this that he speaks of their white bodies, like angels' wings, under the black cloth of the Benedictines.[5]

Joan was now a young woman with a growing reputation for learning and piety. She had attracted the attention of leading Benedictine scholars; curiously her adoption of the male habit went without comment. Physically she was typical of women of Anglo-Saxon descent at the time – blonde, blue-eyed, strongly built – but even in the convent she was unusual in her piety, while her visions of the saints, especially St Thecla, were already marking her out as possessing that strange mixture of practicality and mysticism which identifies a Christian woman of action.

She had charisma, learning, and physical hardiness, as well as a very sharp mind. It is understandable, then, that Frumentius came under her spell. That he loved her deeply is transparent, but this love was spiritual, not carnal, though Royidis makes the mistake of assuming otherwise.[6] His error may partly be explained by his own infatuation, even though he cites correspondence from the monk which reveals his ardour to be spiritual, likening Joan to the Rose of Sharon, in an anticipation of the best troubadour tradition of physically unrequited love.[7]

Joan lived in dangerous times. When Charlemagne died in 814, his son Louis I (the Pious) became Emperor and reigned until 840, when Joan was twenty-two. Louis was succeeded by Lothair I, but his brothers contested his reign and, after a battle in which he was defeated, he had to give up some of his lands. The result was that after 843 Lothair ruled Italy, Lewis ruled Germany and Charles the Bald had France. Relationships were not good between these three and, owing to this central weakness, many small states arose in what had been the

Holy Roman Empire, while its borders were threatened by frequent raiders, including Magyars and Vikings.

Despite the uncertain political climate, Joan decided to leave Germany and travel to Athens, a pilgrimage which was to take her to Geneva and Toulon. Why did she decide to undertake this perilous journey, rather than stay behind the safe and mighty walls of Fulda?

First she went to see Agobardo, Archbishop of Lyon. He was born in Spain in 779, and so was in his early sixties when Joan saw him, at the age of twenty-eight, in the year 842. The Archbishop seems to have been taken with Joan, and he gave her sandals and money to continue her work. She brought in tow her devoted Frumentius, and went on to the oldest nunnery in France, at Arelas, founded by the very strict Caesarius of Arles, Bishop from 502. Here Joan stayed for a while, before what was perhaps her most important trek of veneration. She prayed and meditated at the Shrine of the Magdalene, and experienced a profound mysticism, and a premonition of her death, a travail she would undergo for the love of her Saviour.[8]

After this experience Joan went into seclusion for several weeks, and then undertook a pilgrimage by donkey to the shrines of Mary Magdalene – for there were many in southern France, including those at Aix-en-Provence, Marseille and indeed Arles itself.

Joan's choice of pilgrimage is remarkable – what was it about Mary Magdalene which was so important to her? We know that Joan had a special devotion to St Thecla, a woman who renounced her would-be husband and took a male habit, and that it was firmly believed at the time that Mary Magdalene had actually lived in France, landing at Marseille from the Holy Land, but what was the central element of Joan's devotion to this woman who, along with the Virgin Mary, was the closest to Jesus?

After this, Joan went to Athens, where Mary Magdalene's statues stood in the shrines once sacred to the
Great Goddess. There Joan lived off alms, and taught
the Scriptures, gaining such fame that many mystics
visited her, and she was cultivated by the Patriarch of
Athens, Bishop Niketas. In the process she no doubt
learned much of the Greek mind, and how to reconcile
to some degree the divergences between Roman and
Byzantine theologies, but still the question remains, why
this devotion to Mary Magdalene?

By the age of thirty, Joan seems to have learned all
she wanted and, like many religious leaders, she made
a break to be spiritually free and pursue her devotions.
This meant that Frumentius was left behind, for now
she had her eyes set on Rome. Once in Rome, she
began to teach theology as before, quickly gathering
around her young students who were attracted by her
brilliance. Just as in Athens, she impressed the older
and the more powerful. She became Pope Leo IV's
secretary. This Pope split his favours among the descendants of Charlemagne, one of whom, Lewis II,
suspected him of intrigue with Byzantium. This may
have been true; if so, it suggests a reason why Leo
found Joan so useful, for she knew just about everything there was to know about the Orthodox Church,
in terms both of theology and of persons, for she had
met and held discourses with all the notable bishops
and patriarchs in Athens.

Leo IV was a saintly man, but no fool: he was more
than a match for the machinations of Charlemagne's
brood, yet at the same time much interested in theology
himself. Despite the later doubts of St Bernard of
Clairvaux regarding the Assumption of the body of the
Virgin Mary into Heaven, Leo instituted a vigil on the
feast day of this event, 15 August, while his successor but
one, Nicholas I, 'placed the Assumption on par with

Christmas and Easter – tantamount to declaring Mary's translation to Heaven as important as the Incarnation and the Resurrection'. [9]

This abrupt change in Roman theology took place after Joan's pontificate, and though that does not prove that the reason for getting rid of her was connected with the dehumanization of a woman and a mother, it does not discount it either. The change must have reflected a strong current of thought in the hierarchy. Leo's initiative in the matter was cautious; indeed it may have been muted by Joan's influence, if she recognized in the process of spiriting Mary from the face of the earth a not-so-subtle danger for women. If the highest ideal of a woman was to be a virgin, and the mother of Jesus had her hymen intact even after parturition, then what hope could there be for ordinary women? Perhaps it was this which drew Joan to Mary Magdalene, for she was a woman of the earth, and so must Mary the Virgin have been a woman of the earth.

Joan, then, represented an obstacle to the formulation of more anti-women dogma. The importance of such dogma lay in increasing the psychological hold of the Church over Christians (or so I thought at this time), in that they made the aspirations idealized by the Church unreachable by any human being; this would imbue a sense of hopelessness, which in turn might arguably be expected to bring the distraught and the anxious to their knees before the beneficence of the male priests of Rome. In short, it made the Church more important.

The theme of power and the Church is something which clearly needs to be examined in greater detail, but already Joan appears as an obstacle to the realization of greater power. If the secular interests represented by the claims of Charlemagne were enhanced by the Papacy in return for recognition of Rome, we might expect that Charlemagne's heirs would have supported moves against

Joan. As we shall see, this turns out to have been the case, though to appreciate it we have to draw close to a spectacle so savage, and so blatantly un-Christian, one wonders how these prelates had the gall to call themselves after Christ. But then the lust for power, as has been observed, is a corrupting influence.

On Leo's death, Lewis II tried to instal his own candidate, the excommunicate Anastasius, as Pope. At this point we have to choose between the records of the period, for we not only have an anti-Pope, but on the Roman stage at the same time there were two Popes, John VIII (who is Joan) and Benedict III. Nicholas Cheetham, in his history of the Papacy, suggests that although there is a plenitude of historical material, there are few bibliographies.[10] In order to get through the mountain of conflicting reports, he has had recourse to secondary sources. This raises the serious historical question of how much we know about this period, after the various factions have edited and censored accounts. Royidis, who spent many years of his life studying primary sources and manuscripts, is in no doubt that from many records Joan has been expunged, while in others she has been labelled a witch.

Cheetham recounts that Benedict was confronted by the anti-Pope Anastasius with armed Franks, who, 'it was alleged, damaged some very holy icons' at St Peter's. In the Lateran Basilica the Franks and their anti-Pope dragged Benedict off the throne, and then they imprisoned him. Anastasius used his Frankish warriors to threaten the clergy, trying to make them consecrate him as Pope, but they refused, and so Benedict was reinstated and Anastasius banished to a monastery.

It is my contention that Benedict III is actually a composite figure, Joan's reign being conveniently subsumed into his. The fact that Joan was a Benedictine may be immaterial, but it would have provided a convenient starting point if one had been trying to rewrite history with an acceptable – that is, male – Pope.[11]

If Joan was fresh air in a torrid evening of the Papacy, the storm was about to break, for after John VIII (the man) died or was murdered, there came thirty-five Popes between 882 and 998. In the period 896–904, a mere eight years, there were ten Popes, one of whom was strangled, and two died in prison. The later ninth and tenth centuries were times of much papal in-fighting, with claimants murdering one another in a scramble for power, backed by the arms of robber barons of French and Italian extraction.

In order to reconstruct events, it must be noted that Anastasius had clashed with Joan, and 'orthodox' history was written by Anastasius. Joan had bested him, ex-communicated him and exiled him as Abbot in Trast-evere, which was a mistake as it gave him a power base from which to make his come-back. We also know that murder was not foreign to his family, his cousin having tortured to death the daughter of one Pope and the wife of another. Within three years Anastasius was writing the official papal histories, in the Lateran Basilica, for the rigid Nicholas II. That an excommunicate should have been at the side of the Pope is disturbing, but even more so when one remembers it was Joan who excom-municated him. Furthermore, Joan was a Pope who attempted to bridge the chasm between Rome and Constantinople, as her predecessor Leo had also tried to do. Nicholas was interested only in establishing his supremacy as prince of all Christian prelates, bishops and metropolitans. The suspicion that the ever-scheming, ever-surviving Anastasius may have terminated Joan's pontificate is a plausible one; in those days, as we have seen, such an action would not have been unusual. I put forward the hypothesis that the account of Joan being torn to pieces by a Roman mob, as given by Royidis, is indeed a factual statement of a death by violence. That she was pregnant I would repudiate. This means that the murder was political, and I point the finger of accusation at Anastasius. Through him, not only was the conservative Church rid of a woman, but Lewis II had at last on the Throne of Peter a man after his own heart, Nicholas.

It is possible, then, I observed, to fit Joan into the orthodox accounts, and see why she was murdered, again on orthodox considerations of the power politics which passed for theology in Rome. But I sensed something more. Can we really suppose that Leo did not know his brilliant secretary was a woman? And if he did know, why wasn't his initiative taken up by later Popes? In other words, was there a deeper reason behind Joan's murder? And are there any indications of what that might have been?

On the face of it, the stock answer is that she was a woman, but if we swallow that a pit is opened at our feet, for it means the Rome loved by so many puts the importance of gender above that of truth. Can that notion be seriously entertained? This is the tacit assumption behind the all too cavalier treatment of this woman, who was also an outstanding Pope. As I have said, I sensed something very dangerous here, but I hoped to ignore it, because I had become subjectively fond of this ninth-century woman; courage like hers is, after all, not very common. I emphasize this because my interest *was* purely subjective – I found her romantic, a fascinating woman of action yet one of visions and insights, a warm and loving human being who was also a great scholar and, clearly, a very great Christian. She was a priestess of Jesus Christ, murdered and then forgotten about, even sneered at. It didn't seem fair.

There was, I realized, one resemblance between Mary Magdalene and Joan: they were both obviously priestesses. If Joan in holding Mass was a priestess, when she held a wafer in her hands and drank wine from a chalice, then how much a priestess is Mary Magdalene, actually holding the body in her arms, and having the real blood pour over her skin and limbs at Golgotha? I wondered if that thought might have crossed the jealous minds of the power-seekers in Rome. Probably it did, for they were not lacking in insight when it came to what they loved, though they did not share this notion – or if they did, they kept it among a very select few.

There is also the curious mention in the accounts of Joan's life of her having been pregnant when she was murdered. In some descriptions, this is given as sufficient reason for her killing. This is a grotesque and cruel line of thinking, but again it underlines the sin she appears to have been guilty of, her sex. Actually, the chances of her having been pregnant are remote, for we know that Joan took to heart the enjoinder to celibacy and chastity of a follower of Christ. Though I did not see why a person had to accept this, the fact none the less remains that in her time virginity was an ideal, and so Joan, with her heroic sense of sacrifice, would have lived up to it.

The ambivalences appeared very rich indeed, and I was nowhere nearer understanding why she might have felt so close an affinity with Mary Magdalene. A brilliant woman, an unsung martyr of the Christian faith, has been extirpated from the annals of the Papacy. She venerated the woman we know as Mary Magdalene, whose bones are somewhere in the south of France. When she visited those shrines, Joan set out on a course she feared would lead to her death. Part of her religious upbringing, indeed her early pastoral life, was spent in

the company of Frankish priests who called the second
person of the Trinity 'Daughter'.

Part of the fascination and mystery of Joan is that,
despite being a devout Christian, she took to being a
priestess before the altar at the centre of Christianity, in
an all-male hierarchy. A partial explanation of this is
that she saw in Mary Magdalene the role of authentic
priestess, in that in her arms was the true body, not the
symbol. It could be that the claims of Rome for male
supremacy are in fact contradicted in the Gospel accounts
of what this woman, Mary Magdalene, actually did.

I could summarize well enough, but the questions still
remained. In particular, what had Joan learned in the
south of France, or what had she heard to cause her to
go there, and then learn? What was it that made her
become priestess? And in that question was the one that
naturally followed: had other women learned something
from Mary Magdalene which had given them the insight
to see that they could be priestesses? In short, were there
other women of the wine?

The question was apposite and legitimate, and one that
could be answered by objective research, but before I
buckled down to that, it seemed to me that there was at
least one other great priestess of Jesus Christ – his mother,
Mary. The deduction, I think, goes something like this.
A Roman Catholic priest offers up as sacrifice a wafer,
and a chalice of wine; these are the 'transubstantiated'
symbols of the living Christ. But of course they are also
merely bread and wine. The offering Mary made was
the fruit of her womb, her child, and it was her child on
that cross – real flesh, real blood. In short, she held in
her arms (along with Mary Magdalene, at Golgotha, the
Place of the Skull) bone of her bone, blood of her blood,
flesh of her flesh. If these women are not priestesses, then
who shall be priest? I did not know, for I am not a professional theologian, merely an investigator, with ques-

tions to ask which may well be far too large for an answer. Yet what I did know, as any other person might observe, was that this is a paradox, and it is a gnawing one. I wondered if there were other priestesses of Jesus Christ. I soon found there had been, but they too had been murdered, though in their cases death followed humiliation, torture and the killing of their kinsfolk. Moreover, their murders were committed on the orders of Popes.

These murders began in 1209, in the towns, olive groves, vineyards and hamlets of southern France, and lasted four terrible decades. The people who lived here were the Cathars, and they inhabited some of the places to which Joan had made her pilgrimages.

Women of the Wine

In the Languedoc region of southern France not a hundred miles west of Marseille, the Cathars had a virtually independent state, just as the Merovingian kings had done. They did not believe in a separate sacramental priesthood of men, but followed both men and women as priests. St Bernard had attempted to restore them to the fold, remarking that: 'No Sermons are more Christian than theirs, and their morals are pure.'[12] St Dominic, from whose order of preaching friars the Inquisition was to spring forth, also went to preach, but was ignored. The problem was that the masculine priesthood of Rome was unacceptable to Cathars.

The central position held by women in the Cathar church is as important as any other doctrinal difference between the people of Languedoc and the prelates of Rome. The actual weight the issue held has been underemphasized in the past. In all Christendom, only one area had women priests, and that was to be sacked; it was also an area where Mary Magdalene was venerated. And we must note with growing suspicion and dismay that the body of men who were later to mutilate and burn women as witches, the Inquisition, not only burned all Cathar records, but in some cases Dominicans persuaded men to burn their own private collections, as happened in 1234 to Robert de Montferrand, who had a library of Cathar literature collected over four decades.[13] What we know has come down to us from enemies of the Cathars, the shock troops of Orthodoxy, the Inquisitorial Dominicans.

But the records do not give a coherent picture; indeed professional historians find no explanation which is wholly convincing as to why the Popes destroyed these women. St Bernard is quoted as saying that the Cathars hated the corruption of Roman priests in the Languedoc, but venality was rife everywhere, so his explanation makes little sense. Other arguments seem to rest on the Cathar nobility being different because they were different, which is no answer at all.[14]

It seemed to me that the mystery of the region and its history might be uncovered, or at least limited, by considering what facts we have. A devout Cathar woman was called a 'perfect', *parfaite* in French. She did not marry, was chaste and dressed simply, even though most such women came from the nobility. The *parfaites* ministered to the poor and held services; being preachers, they were itinerant, though they had houses where they congregated. In all this they were living heroically the life of Christ. Some of them took it a step further, as we shall see. Acceptance as a *parfaite* was a lengthy process. Even after two years of instruction, Dulcia de Villeneuve-la-Comtal was still not accepted, while the *parfaites* who fled to Montségur during persecution left behind Raymonde Jougla to continue her studies. The final vows were more often taken by women than men, for they were extremely strict, more ascetic and confining in matters of personal freedom than even the most austere

Catholic nunneries. Clearly, the spearhead of the Cathars in a theological and spiritual sense was formed by women.

A Cathar *parfaite* carried a copy of the New Testament at all times, as did the 140 women priests who were burned to death at Minerve. She had renounced the cross of baptism, along with rich foods and vestment. Her prayer, like that of male 'perfects', was the 'Our Father'. The Roman Mass was not celebrated but something was, details of which have been efficiently destroyed by the Inquisition, as we noted earlier. The *parfaite* was expected to preach and to travel with companions to do this work. She renounced all earthly goods, all secular position, marriage and sexual relations. She was, in other words, like Mary Magdalene and the other women who followed Jesus.

The renunciation of the cross, we may reasonably conclude, was not the repudiation of Jesus, since the whole life's work of these women was to spread the New Testament, in which there is no mention of Popes, nor secular institutionalized Church, but insistence on a simple Christian life. It seems that by renouncing the cross, the Cathars were rejecting the claims of the Church of Rome. The Cathar woman was freeing herself from the spiritual fetters of patriarchal Rome, and coming closer to the real roots of Christianity, at the centre of which was the Crucifixion, movingly described in the Gospels she carried with her wherever she went. We may, therefore, safely assume that the construction placed by the Inquisition on the repudiation of the cross, as repudiation of the Crucifixion, is false witness on the part of the Dominicans.

Innocent III (1198–1216) proclaimed the Crusade against Languedoc in March 1208. He advised his legates to proceed with cunning, for they hoped to separate the Toulouse nobility from the Cathars. They failed in this,

partly because Innocent's men were fanatics and partly
because Raymond, the titular lord of the region, was pro-
Cathar. French nobility, hoping for loot and papal
preferment, turned up for their forty days at Lyon on 24
June 1209, the feast of St John the Baptist, patron saint
of Lyon. There were Burgundians, northern French
aristocracy and some Milanese present, but there was
also among those joining the crusade a fortune hunter,
Simon de Montfort. A tall, muscular man, well past the
flush of youth, he was at first a mere captain among
captains, but later he became the undisputed leader,
truly Innocent's butcher.

In the summer of 1209 Béziers was taken and burned.
Men, women and children who crowded into the church
of Madeleine (Magdalene) were put to the sword,
Catholics and Cathars alike. In the decade that followed,
Simon buried people alive, mutilated them, and had
priests tied to horses' tails and whipped through city
streets, then hung on gibbets. He regarded himself as an
instrument of God, and was fanatical, merciless, but
brilliant in military tactics. Like an SS general, he did
his job because he believed he was in the right; at the
same time he was being noticed by those who counted
for preferment. However, he was not to reap the fruits of
victory, for after nine years of bitter fighting, the burning
of *parfaites* and the sack of countless Languedoc towns, he
was shot in the head on 25 June 1218, outside Toulouse,
and the missile was fired by women of the Toulouse
bourgeoisie.[15] The actual object which struck him was a
large piece of masonry from a trebuchet, a kind of
catapult.

Innocent, taking time off from the burning of women
in the Languedoc, held a remarkable Council in Rome
in 1215, at which 400 bishops, 800 abbots, 71 archbishops
and more than 2,000 assorted ecclesiastics attended, all
of them male. Innocent began his address to this

assembly, which was to celebrate the wars against heretics, with the text of Luke 22:15, 'With desire I have desired to eat this passover with you before I suffer.' The Council then went on to draft seventy canons on Church discipline, to be included in Canon Law and hence binding on Catholics, at the pain of excommunication (which was usually the prelude to something worse). The doctrine of transubstantiation was also approved; from now on the blood and the body of a male Christ would be on the altar, from wine and bread.

The increasing legislation of faith, the adumbration of new dogma, the elevation of the Virgin Mary to a historically unrecognizable figure could be viewed, I felt, as a need for the Church to bolster its own power – but against what? The facts are that the simple truths of Christianity, those of redemption and love, were being encrusted with dogma, set about by a thicket of laws. If you disobeyed the injunctions of Rome, you faced torture, and death by burning. If you were a woman, you did not even have a say in the drafting of dogma and laws. The Church was not only a religious body, it was a secular and a military one. The Popes who cut and dried the beliefs of men and women also cut and dried their bodies through their soldiers and their allies.

During the actual fighting of the Albigensian Crusade, burning of heretics was brisk; it was carried out by Simon de Montfort: 140 at Minerve, 300 at Lavaur, 60 at Les Cassés. In the spring of 1211 de Montfort persuaded the crusaders to reject Raymond VI's peace offers, and so prolonged the killing for another eighteen years.[16] When the organized Cathar resistance was broken militarily, the remaining Cathar 'perfects' found some kind of safety in perpetual flight, moving from one safe house to another, until they were denounced.

Innocent III was succeeded on his death by Honorius III (1216–27), but Innocent had seen the majority of his suppression of Languedoc completed, even though at times it seemed that the courage of the Cathars might prevail against overwhelming resources. The Cathar cause was now led by the nobleman Raymond VI, who, though he was no Cathar, was intent on protecting them. He achieved a remarkable victory at Naziège against the crusaders, killing most of the knights in their army. He died when the balance was still to be decided and his son, who had Plantagenet blood on his mother's side, took leadership, becoming Raymond VII.

By this time Avignon and Marseille, though not parts of the Languedoc proper, had volunteered their services in the Cathar cause, producing a stalemate. The French King, Louis VIII, supported the Pope and entered the lists. By November 1228, Louis had captured Avignon and reduced the number of other strongholds. Raymond offered his surrender. Under terms presided over by Honorius, Raymond paid a huge fine of 10,000 silver marks, plus 4,000 for the building of churches, and 4,000 towards the foundation in Toulouse (which town he was allowed to keep) of a university for the defence of patriarchal Catholicism. Louis came away loaded with booty, including the county of Foix. The treaty was formally signed on 12 April 1229 in Paris. The French King betrothed the nine-year-old Joan of Toulouse to a member of his court, while Raymond was made to beg for papal forgiveness in front of the partially complete Nôtre Dame in Paris.

Raymond VII, as part of his peace treaty, was required to inform on and arrest his own Cathar subjects. Catholic bishops in Languedoc paid for their own network of spies. It seemed to work: Raymond du Fauga, Bishop of Toulouse, surprised nineteen Cathars, men and women, in a forest, and burned them all. The forests, apparently, were to be the catacombs of the Cathars. But the Pope, (now Gregory IX) was not satisfied with the piecemeal forays of his bishops in the Languedoc. It was felt that a more persistent and full-time organization was needed to root out Cathar women. In March 1233, Gregory ordered a general Inquisition throughout the Languedoc; he gave the task to the Dominicans.

Father Pierre Seilha, who had witnessed the Dominicans' failure in the Languedoc and their humiliation in argument at the hands of Cathar women, was appointed Inquisitor. His partner was a cruel lunatic, Father Guillaume Arnaud. In Moissace they burned 210 Cathars. Inspired by the two inquisitors, the Bishop of Toulouse led a mob, on the feast of none other than St Dominic in 1235, to the house of a venerable Cathar noblewoman, where they dragged her from her bed, and burned her to death outside Toulouse.

The depth of their cruelty is well attested by the historical records. The Inquisition condemned even the dead, ripping the rotting corpses from their graves, then parading them through Languedoc cities before consigning the remains to the stake.

Raymond VII of Toulouse could do nothing to stem this tide of infamy, for if he openly confronted the Pope (as represented by the Inquisition), he would face another Crusade. He took the only possible way out; he appeared to support but did next to nothing to help the Inquisition. Based in Toulouse, Raymond's seat of government, the Dominicans pursued their task with a zeal that was only to be matched by that of the witch hunters, and by the Jew hunters of the Third Reich. In two years from 1241, Father Pierre Seilha imposed solitary confinement for life in leg irons on men and women, who were to be fed with bread and water only, in the depths of unsanitary, dark and airless dungeons. This punishment, mitigated in some cases by not confining them in irons, was imposed on 732 Cathars in Toulouse alone. In this period the Inquisition 'processed'

600 towns and villages in the Languedoc, causing an unimaginable amount of human suffering, particularly for women, who became the chattels of their gaolers. Cathars who refused to take 'penance' – which meant being locked up and maltreated, starved and bullied (and worse) for life – were burned.

The Cathar Arnaude de Lamouthe had only survived the war by being constantly on the move. When the Inquisition threatened her and her family, she had already been hiding for several years from the Dominicans in a hut in Lanta, a mere half-day's march from Toulouse, with her mother and her sister. She then moved to a cellar, where her sister died; Arnaude buried the corpse and moved on. From 1234 to 1237 she changed her hiding place every few weeks. It is a story of almost unsurpassed bravery and persecution. One falters trying to gauge the suffering this woman and her mother went through, on the run for years, moving from pit to cellar, hut to forest, field to farmhouse, every few weeks; dependent on the local Cathars to help with food as the armed thugs of the Inquisition beat the bushes, burned the ricks, threatened the villagers to discover Arnaude's whereabouts. In 1243 she was arrested in a wood, and more than a hundred names were wrung out of her wretched, suffering body.

At this stage a sense of numb horror pervaded my thoughts in this investigation.

I found that a woman had been Pope, but she was torn to pieces by a mob in the pay of a bigot. This Pope, Joan, had dressed as a man, led a life as near as possible to that of Christ's, and made a point of a pilgrimage to southern France, where Mary Magdalene may have lived. She went there after being in contact with priests, entirely independent of the Roman Church who blessed in the name of the Father, the Daughter and the Holy Ghost.

In the same region, women priestesses were butchered under a Crusade called for by a Pope who gave the killers absolution, and later, again under orders from Rome, a gang of Dominican priests set about torturing the remaining few women priestesses of the Cathars.

The odd thing was that these women were said to have possessed the actual flesh and blood of Jesus Christ. This is to be contrasted with the accusations of the Inquisition, which insisted that they worshipped a demonic head. This was, with remarkable lack of consistency, tied in with the Johannite heresy, which was worshipping John the Baptist as true saviour. This man lived contemporaneously with Jesus, and had his head cut off.

Other heretics abounded in Europe, but none of them at this time was visited with such savage repression, which was so extreme as to represent genocide of the *langue d'oc* speakers of the region. The thread running through all this was a virulent hatred of women, which seemed, in a way as yet unclear, to be connected with the association of a 'reformed prostitute' with the area. She was Mary Magdalene, whose hands were stained by Jesus' blood as she helped to take him from the cross. Sensing that women were so intimately involved with the region, I had begun, purely for convenience, to call the mosaic of facts and stories 'Mary Magdalene's Church'.

I was still surprised by the enormity of the crimes against women Christians committed by the men of Rome. It seemed to be far more than misogyny, but what it meant I had no idea. Whatever it was, it was so powerful that it led to the setting up of a permanent body, the Inquisition, which was to make a career out of torturing and then destroying women in the Languedoc and, as I was later to learn, all over Europe.

Terrifying is a word clearly appropriate for these Dominican priests, but they also appear to have been

crazed, for early on in the very first trials of the Cathars
they revealed an obsession with a head which they could
not find, but were convinced the Cathars possessed. I
saw this as a chilling development, because Christ died
at the Place of the Skull, attended by two women who
were covered by his (real) blood. The terror of the images
was compounded, not mitigated, by the fact that it was
women whom these priests were torturing to death,
women priests. The Inquisitors lapsed into a kind of
compromise, saying the Cathars were worshippers of
John the Baptist. But if the head these women worshipped
was John's, how could it be demonic, since the Baptist
was a Saint? And the Cathars believed Christ, not John,
was their Saviour, for they carried copies of John's Gospel
with them wherever they went. At times it seems the
Inquisitors were seriously entertaining some confusion of
John the Baptist with John the Evangelist.

All this was perplexing enough – even embarrassing,
in the sense that these mysteries had lain unsolved for so
long, and now I had stumbled upon them – but on top
of this the Cathars' end came not, as you might reasonably
expect, when they were crushed for ever by soldiers and
priests, but with yet another mystery.

The mystery was in the fall of Montségur, the last
Cathar fortress, a citadel remote and splendid towering
over a precipice in the Pyrenees. The French King's
forces, under the command of his captain, one d'Arcis,
captured the stronghold in the spring of 1244. But it was
no ordinary siege, for author upon author has asserted
that something was taken out of Montségur by four
Cathars during an inexplicable truce. Ian Wilson thinks
it was the Turin Shroud, an interesting idea in that the
French captain was allegedly an ancestor of the Bishop
d'Arcis, who fulminated against the relic's genuineness;
Baigent and his co-authors felt it was some kind of secret
which implicates a shadowy organization and a new kind

of church. The mystery, then, is not of my making, for though sober historians, as befits their professional habits, do not speculate on what was taken, they are certain that something was.[17]

After the four *parfaits* made good their escape, the Cathar priestesses and their menfolk were burned in a public cage, a holocaust of Christians. Along with them some mercenaries burned too, even though they had been offered amnesty. Their sacrifice was instrumental in the saving from the ruins of Montségur of whatever it was the *parfaits* took with them.

This object had to be something so holy and sacred that even hard-bitten fighting men, with no allegiance to the Cathar cause but their pay, would go to an agonizing death for its preservation.

What was the sacred object? I found a plausible answer, but in doing so I uncovered an even greater mystery.

Knights of a Special Lady

Surveying the world from Rome, the Popes of the eleventh century were chagrined to observe that the Holy Land, once at least nominally Christian, was now in the hands of the infidel Saracen. It was on their agenda to recover it for the Faith, but for that they needed soldiers and money. In the event, Frenchmen rallied to the Pope's call for a Crusade, and eventually took Jerusalem, the leaders being given titles to Palestinian lands.[1] Jerusalem and other holy places could now be centres of pilgrimage, or such was the pious hope.

The nobility of France, uncoordinated in their rule of Palestine, were in reality living on borrowed time. They were simply warlords who had captured some strong areas, and they did not control the ports or the sea lanes. The Muslim threat remained, and was eventually to push them all back into the Mediterranean, and thence to France. In the interim there was a strange development. In 1118 Baldwin I, King of Jerusalem, received Hugh de Payens, a nobleman from Champagne, and eight other knights. They were given accommodation over the foundations of parts of the Temple of Solomon, and so became known as Templars.[2] Ostensibly the duty of these nine men was to guard the pilgrim roads so that Christians could travel to the Jordan, where Christ was baptized, and to Bethlehem and Nazareth. But though armed guards on such routes were more than necessary, it is difficult to understand how nine thousand men could have carried out the task, let alone nine. Furthermore,

the Templars did not increase their numbers during the
first nine years. Nevertheless, by November 1128 a
Church Council in Troyes welcomed the men at the
Court of the Count of Champagne. The Order of the
Knights Templar was now officially recognized, but there
were some odd facts about them. For one, they were subject to the Pope alone, which meant they were virtually
uncontrollable. Another oddity was that although each
Knight was sworn to poverty, the Order appropriated
all his worldly possessions and so became very rich very
quickly.

The Kings of Jerusalem, short of manpower, welcomed
the Templars, now a growing organization, ceding them
castles and the right to build castles, for which they
employed Muslim architectural skills. The Templar
militia were the best Christian soldiers, perhaps the best
soldiers in the world at that time. They did not retreat,
they fought to the death, and the Order had a rule that
none of them would ever be ransomed. Indeed the
Templars, although profligate of their blood, were tight-
fisted with their money. Within a few generations they
had scores of castles in Palestine (now called Outremere)
and France, and lands in Spain, England and Scotland.
They also had a powerful fleet. Their early acceptance,
though partially explained by the need for more soldiers
in Outremere, also rested very much on the support of
Bernard of Clairvaux, who championed them with vigour
in their early days. His protégé, Innocent II, was so taken
with them that he ratified the Order by Papal Bull in
1139, although the Holy See was to destroy the Order
after the fall of Montségur. Clearly something happened
which was to sour the relationship between Pope and
Templar, and it appears to have become important after
the destruction of the Cathars.

The links between French nobility, especially in
Languedoc, and the Templars were strong from the very

beginning. For example, the Counts of Toulouse held Tripoli, but its borders were guaranteed by Templar strongholds. The Templars were greatly feared, for they controlled much land, many fine soldiers and castles, and possessed a Mediterranean fleet, in addition to being bankers, financing trade between Palestine and Marseille. All this meant that the Templars were effectively free to think and do anything they liked: nominally, the Pope was their master, but they obeyed their own Grand Master in Jerusalem. There is no evidence to show that he checked with the Pope halfway across the Mediterranean to ratify his decisions.

This ambivalence was clearly shown when the Templars failed to intercede openly in the Albigensian Crusade – which, as austere Knights of the Pope, they might have been expected to do, hacking down Cathars with the same efficiency as they struck down Muslims. The reason is clear, for many of the French members of the Order were of Languedoc blood. Many Cathar families gave their sons to the Order. Passing into the Order meant vows of chastity, poverty, and above all obedience, and obedience is a prerequisite for secrecy. As the women of the Cathar nobility entered the houses of the *parfaites*, the young men entered the Temples of the Knights. Given these relationships alone, much light is thrown on the destruction first of the Cathars and then the Knights Templar by the Church militant. Some Inquisitors may have indeed thought they were destroying the same thing, whether they burned a Cathar woman or a Templar.

Further connections are revealed by the donations of money to the Templars by the Cathar Lords Bertrand de Blanchefort and Raymond-Roger Trencavel. Bertrand actually joined the Templars even though he had a wife, Fabrissa; Cathar *parfaits* were enjoined not to use their marriages sexually, and so he could still claim to be chaste. Furthermore, the Preceptor of the Toulouse Temple at the commencement of the Albigensian Crusade was a Cathar of the Trencavel family,[3] and we know that Champagne and Albedune Templars provided safe houses for Cathars. If something was taken from Montségur, there was only one organization capable of safely transferring it and giving it refuge – the Knights Templar. It is a plausible, though speculative, idea that the Cathar relic could have been transferred from Montségur to Acre.

Jerusalem was retaken by the Saracens in 1244, but the great Templar fortress, Acre, did not fall until May 1291, the Grand Master fighting to the last with his Knights, preferring death to surrender. The Templar treasury and many officials, along with the non-combatants, including women and children, were transferred to Cyprus by the Templar fleet, for the fortress abutted the Mediterranean. Amid scenes of fire and desolation, as the galleys plied in the frothing sea, now no longer blue but the colour of blood mixed with fire, and the flames of the dying castle licked into heaven, Acre fell – literally, for the walls collapsed on Muslim and Templar alike. But the galleys did reach Cyprus, whence the Templars took their wealth, relics and records via Marseille to Paris, to their new head-quarters, the fortress Preceptory of Villeneuve de Temple, opposite the King's palace, the Louvre.

We have already noted that Bernard of Clairvaux championed the Templars. He was cool about the new dogma of the Assumption, the bodily transference of the Virgin Mary into Heaven. Perhaps he knew something which induced that ambivalence. The Pope too may have heard that the Templars guarded a secret which gave them their arrogance. Did the cooling of relations between Rome and the Templars have anything to do with the Montségur relic? They appeared to believe no one could touch them, even snubbing the French King, Philippe the Fair, when he applied for membership. Did they suppose the Pope would protect them? If so, they were sadly mistaken, for whatever hold they may have thought they had over the Papacy was taken from them by force of arms. Philippe moved against them in the early hours of Friday 13 October 1307, arresting Templars all over France and confiscating their preceptories, including that of Villeneuve in Paris.

The tortured voice of Aimery de Villiers gives us an insight into the methods of Philippe's Inquisitors: they had prearranged questions which had to be answered satisfactorily if the torture was to stop. What confessions did torture wring from these men? The Inquisitors wished to establish idolatory, and from the mouth of Brother Raoul de Gizy, the Champagne Preceptor, they got this:

INQUISITOR: Now tell us about the head.
BROTHER RAOUL: Well, the head. I've seen it at seven chapters held by Brother Hugh de Peraud and others.
INQUISITOR: What did one do to worship it?
BROTHER RAOUL: Well, it was like this. It was presented, and everyone threw himself on the ground, pushed back his cowl, and worshipped it.
INQUISITOR: What was its face like?
BROTHER RAOUL: Terrible. It seemed to me that it was the face of a demon, of a *maufé* [evil spirit]. Every time I saw it I was filled with such terror I could scarcely look at it, trembling in all my members.[4]

Note how the Inquisitor leads the witness. He does not ask 'What was done', but says, 'How did they *worship* it?' This would be disallowed in cross-examination in any decent court. Note, too, that the structure of the whole deposition has an unreal or prepared air about it. This cannot be a true account, for how could men like the Templars worship a terrible face like a demon's? Is it not more likely that they were 'worshipping' a carving or icon of Christ – even a relic? In which case the word should be 'venerate' not 'worship'. To misrepresent is a sure way of damning someone, for the facts are not in dispute, merely the interpretation.

The thread that runs through the confessions, clearly implanted by the Inquisitors, is worship of some kind of head. This may be a subtle traducement of the Cathar ceremony where a postulant's head was touched with the Gospel of St John. Misrepresentation of fact is one of the safest methods of bearing false witness, because one can swear on a basis of fact. Ian Wilson, in his painstaking history of the Turin Shroud, points out that the association of the Templars with a sacred head was not current until the beginning of the thirteenth century, that is, when the Albigensian Crusade was under way.[5] But there was nothing demonic about this veneration; rather there was a fertility element:

Some of them [the Templars] or most of those who attend the Chapters, say that this head can save them, that it has given them all the wealth of the order, that it makes the trees flourish and the earth fruitful.[6]

The reference to trees and earth is a direct one – what was its source? The solution to this comes from a witness who was not under duress, the Abbot of Lagny, who averred that priests had little more to do in the Chapters of the Order than recite the 67th Psalm. What is remarkable about this Psalm is that it addresses the fertility aspects of the godhead: 'Let all the people praise thee, then shall the earth yield her increase' (Psalm 67:5, 6).

Wilson refers to confessions where Templars

. . . thought it [the mysterious head the Inquisition were so interested in] was their Saviour, the speculation of others, obviously uninitiated, that it might have been Hugh of Payens, the founder of the Order. It explains, too, why copies of the Templar head were never found – without identification marks they were not recognized for what they were.[7]

The real explanation, one might be forgiven for thinking, is that copies were not found because the grizzled, bearded head that the Inquisition were after did not exist save in their imaginations. Moreover, Wilson, in adducing this damning evidence, is trying to prove the Templars were 'worshipping' a folded cloth, namely the Turin Shroud, folded in such a manner that only the head could be seen. If they had such a cloth, why was it folded? And further, there is nothing heretical about the image on the Turin cloth, and the Templars could have displayed it with the same pomp and ceremony as the de Charnays and the Savoy Dukes were to do. The Turin Shroud is so orthodox, so clearly masculine, that all the Grand Master would have had to do would have been to show the Inquisitors the object of Templar 'worship' and the case against them would have fallen flat. In any case, there is nothing about the Turin Shroud which has anything to do with fertility. Finally, it is a two-dimensional image, while even the young and uninitiated Templars were convinced that an actual head was vene-rated, even if they were not too sure whose head it was supposed to be. I can, however, agree with Wilson that there is little convincing evidence of satanism in the Templars.[8]

What we find out about the head is particularly im-portant because it links the Cathars with the Templars in matters of religious practice. Item 58 of the inquisitorial charges reads: 'That they bound or touched the head of the said idols with cords, wherewith they bound themselves about their shirts, or next [to their] skins.' During the reception or initiation of new Templars it was alleged, in item 59, that this was part of the ceremony, and item 60 asserts: 'That they did this in worship of their idol', and that they had to wear the cord all the time (item 61). Item 46 asserts that a man's skull was the idol, and that it had three faces.[9] This is inquisitorial fantasy at its most exaggerated, and the insistence of the Inquisitors in keeping the notion of femininity at bay from the idol is noteworthy. The cord symbolism is significant, for the Cathars too had cords to show their reverence for Jesus and Mary. The cords were confirmed, without torture, during the examination in England of the Templars of Garway, the church a few miles from Kilpeck in Herefordshire.[10]

The Templars, like the Cathars before them, were caught between the crushing stones of a giant mill, pushed around as if by a blind and demented quasi-Samson. The need for conformity was the energy that motivated the giant, and the stones were the armed men of the King and the persistence of the Inquisitors. Yet for all the force brought to bear on these hapless men, no martyr to a satanic or heretic creed was found, for though they died, the Templars died professing love of Christ. And for all the powers of the forces arraigning them, the Templars were not shown one grizzled head of John the Baptist, or even one little demonic idol.

Fire, iron, cords and whips were used on the Templars without let; Bernard de Vado recounted:

So greatly was I tortured, so long was I held before a burning fire that the flesh of my heels were burned away; and these two bones, which I now show to you, these came away from my feet. Look and see if they be not missing from my body.[11]

The words of Aimery de Villiers de Duc give an indication of the dependability of Templar 'confessions':

I confessed to some things because of the torture inflicted on me by Guillaume de Marcilly and Hugues de la Celle, knights

of the king; but they were not true. Yesterday, when I saw
fifty-four of my brethren going in carts to the stake because
they would not confess to the sins imputed to us, I thought that
I should never be able to withstand the fear of the fire. I know
in my heart that I would confess to anything. I would confess
that I had killed God, if they asked me.[12]

The tortures did not, however, extract what the Inquisitors wanted to hear; and if some men gave way,
they never went so far as to repudiate their Christianity,
despite all manner of suggestion made to them.[13]

Relic of a Small Woman

What is astonishing in these trials is that *the Inquisitors
actually knew what head it was*, that it was never grizzled,
monstrous or demonic, nor even male. They had the head
and did not exhibit it. Indeed, they did not dare to. As
we have seen, they had to force the Templars into con-
fessing to non-Christian practices. That these men died
saying they worshipped something especially Christian
should have alerted other writers to the truth: there was
a head, and it was Christian.

The Inquisition records reveal that among the
Templar belongings found in the preceptory of Villeneuve, where the struggles against the King's men were
fiercest, was a hinged casket in the form of a woman's
head.[14] Inside the reliquary were two pieces of the skull
of a woman, with an identifying label which bore the
inscription 'Caput LVIII' and the sign of Virgo. Caput
LVIII means simply 'head 58'. It is significant that in
some accounts of trials this head is not mentioned, but
'Caput LVIII' is used merely as a 'heading' to questions,
as with the transcript regarding the cords discussed
above.[15]

Here then, in the Villeneuve Preceptory, was a real
head – the pride and joy of the Cathars, from whom it

was reverently received for safekeeping by the Templars after the fall of Montségur. But the Inquisition ignored it. Here was the head and they pretended it did not exist, opting instead to talk about male heads with beards, with strange-sounding names, and with demonic or (preferably) satanic affiliations, none of which they were able to prove. One confession reads that the Templars worshipped 'a human head without any silver or gold, very pale and discoloured, with a grizzled beard like a Templar's'.[16] Why on earth would any witness say a head had no gold and silver? Were heads usually so accoutred? Were the Inquisitors so used to seeing human heads with gold and silver that they had to be told the head at Villeneuve did not have any? I suggest the head was the Villeneuve reliquary, and its record was traduced by inquisitorial process to that of a bearded male head.

Here, it seemed, was a real mystery, for the skull bones were clearly of crucial significance to both Rome and the Cathars and Templars. The 'heretics' were convinced they had the flesh and blood of Christ, and so the reliquary contained the bones of Christ. If that had been so, the claims of Rome would have been destroyed. The most realistic conclusion was that the Popes knew there was something threatening in the Cathar headquarters in Languedoc, and attacked them at the first opportunity, but an accident of history meant the head was safely guarded by the Templars. As soon as they were weak enough, they too were attacked. Moreover, the Church's policy was annihilation of both Cathar and Templar; even recantation meant lifelong incarceration for the heretics. All that scurrying about in the south of France had a real purpose – finding the tell-tale reliquary.

If the 58 is merely a number, where are Caputs 1, 2, 3 . . . 57? None has been found. This suggested to me that the 58 is a code. The fact that its two digits add up to thirteen, the number of lunar months and the number of menstrual periods in a year, is relevant to the fertility overtones of Psalm 67, but why 58?

I was at the point of dismissing this, for it appeared far too speculative. But then the Inquisition had not dismissed the relic, they had done everything they could to make out it did not exist. If by a more sanguine approach they could have rendered its implications harmless, surely they would have done so.

The reliquary, then, had to be of Christ: such a view fitted the facts most closely. Yet if that were the case, consistency demanded that a realistic interpretation of the cipher on the reliquary had to be formulated. I still needed a working hypothesis to explain how the cipher referred to Christ and to a woman at the same time. To say the least, it was an intriguing puzzle, but its difficulty or strangeness was no reason for walking away from it, or closing my eyes to it.

Number lore is a very ancient science or art, but its foundations are extremely prosaic. Five, for example, is taken to represent a woman because she has two arms, a head, and two legs. When standing with her feet apart, and arms outstretched, she fits into a perfect five-pointed star, the pentacle of the Great Goddess. A six was used to denote maleness, as in the Star of David, because of the phallus. It is not surprising, then, that five is often encountered in the Great Goddess cults.

Eight, similarly, is a female motif. For example, the Great Goddess in Babylon had a temple which was a citadel of eight towers, at the top of which was her sanctuary. It is not so clear that eight is a female sign, until one realizes that it is made up of five and three. Five is obvious, as we have seen, but three is even more persuasive as a symbol, for in the Great Goddess cohered the three main stages of a woman's life, virgin, mother and old lady (often, in this last stage, a prophetess). The Goddess was therefore known as the 'Triple Goddess'.[17] The addition of five and eight gives the number of menstrual or lunar months in a year. The moon waxed and waned in a menstrual month, and so the Great Goddess was always associated with the moon, and covens or colleges of priestesses were made up of thirteen as a result. Jesus Christ had such a coven of thirteen, Christ and twelve apostles.

Five is also used to represent a rose; in heraldry, a five-petalled flower is drawn. A rose, of course, is the universal symbol of love, and it is a visual analogue of the female sex. A red rose is a particularly powerful symbol, for it has both the sexual imagery and the colour of blood; the Great Goddess colour is crimson. The Goddess cults did not draw a clear distinction between worship of the Goddess and sexual love – indeed religious experience was considered clearly present in sexual matters. The love of the Goddess, then, was conjoined in the everyday facts of amorous love, married love, pregnancy and childbirth.

Rose of Sharon

My analysis of female motifs in the Templars so far does not begin to uncover the riches which are there. The Order was founded in 1118, by nine men, of whom nothing was heard for nine years. The date contains a trinity, three ones, and the female number eight already discussed. The trinity refers in the Goddess tradition to her own trinity, incarnate, as it were, in the life of women, virgin, mother, prophetess (wise old women, called by the Church 'witches'). Nine is three threes, a cipher of this trinity, and also the number of months of pregnancy. The dates and times chosen by the fledgling order are certainly remarkable for these coincidences, if that is all they are.

The Knights wore surcoats of white, with a splayed crimson cross. This cross had its arms like the petals of a red flower. Arguably it can not have been a cipher for a rose, because the symbol of a rose has five petals, but four is derivable by addition from thirteen, another mystic number of the Goddess cults, as I have noted. The white signifies purity, as in lilies. The red of the cross signifies the blood of Christ. This dual symbolism echoes the Song of Solomon 2:1: 'I am the Rose of Sharon and the Lily of the valleys.' This neatly fits the fact the Templars began in the foundations of Solomon's temple in Jerusalem. Hebrew poetry is not only allusive, but usually says the same thing twice, in other words we are to assume an equivalence between rose and lily. The lily is usually depicted in heraldry as a three-pointed glyph

ψ , while the rose is five-petalled. Oddly these give the numbers three and five, which by addition render eight. Again one is struck by the uncanny connections with the number ascribed to the skull bones of the small woman, fifty-eight.

But there is much more to the rose symbolism; the rose is universally recognized as indicating carnal love, while the Lily represents platonic love. Christian exegesis often entertains the notion that the Rose of Sharon is Christ, though some commentators think it the Church. Following the more persuasive former interpretation, we may see again a plausible blood symbol.

The Rose, being ciphered as five, is related to the pentacle, the five-starred cross of a woman with arms and legs stretched out. Troubadour poetry, and poetry in general, unblushingly uses the rose as a motif for a woman's sex. But the glyph for the lily may in fact be a visual pun on a woman's groin γ . The author of the Song of Solomon has, then, got most of it right, but a rose is a more experienced stage in a woman's life than the more virginal lily glyph. Chivalry is redolent with the use of roses and lilies, and of course the Templars were pre-eminently the Knights of Chivalry. They were accused of spitting on the cross, but if the cross in question was their own four-petalled one, then it sounds as if these were kisses being traduced.

The odd thing about the lily glyph is that, reduced to essentials, it is also in the form of a cross ⅄ or four-pointed star, the kind seen on the backs of priests when they are wearing ceremonial garb in the Roman Catholic Church. They appear to be blissfully unaware of its deeper meaning, or rather its double meaning of sacrifice, the cross, and femaleness, the lily glyph.

Another form of the lily cross as distinct from the rose cross is the Y cross, a shape upon which a person can be nailed. It has a clear graphic relationship with the lily glyph and its cross, but is a more modest glyph of female sexuality, and could be found in the costume of the ladies of chivalry. Here it took the form of a girdle, tied round the waist, low-hung, so that in the front it formed the two arms, as it were, of the Y cross, the central element being made by the hanging tassel of the girdle. Sometimes it was a single cord, tied in a knot at the front, just above the cleft of the legs or pubic arch, though often it was an embroidered sash, with a buckle of jewels.

And who were the ladies who wore such girdles? They were usually aristocratic, wilful, amorous, like spirited young women anywhere. They had names such as Alicia, Alienor, Beatrix, Hélouise, Jeanne (the French form of Joan), Marie, Mathilde, Mélisande, Sybelle and Yolande. We have a vivid picture of these women from Gautier, a French doyen of chivalry, who tells us the Church looked on with some misgivings as they flew the falcon, and ran their estates.[18] He tells us about one in

particular, Aelis, who lived in the Chateau La Ferte-
Henri. Her plaited hair is like spun gold, her eyes are
blue, her complexion perfect, her cheeks 'pink as the Rose
in May', her bosom 'white as the February snows'. With
perfect white teeth, beautiful hands and delicate feet, she
is clearly absolutely gorgeous. What Gautier does not tell
us is she wore the Y girdle, an ancient sign of the tree of
life. The other point missed by Gautier is that these
wilful, active, aristocratic ladies, despite their over-
idealization in chivalry, were the same women who threw
themselves at the spears and swords of the Pope's soldiers
rather than renounce their Cathar faith, while their
brothers, fathers, sons and husbands formed the back-
bone of the Knights Templar.

From this analysis the Knights Templar were becoming a more readily understandable order, in the sense
that if they really did believe, for whatever reason, that
their Saviour was a woman, then their ardour becomes
patent. They fought against the male monotheists the
Saracens in Palestine, and then against the Roman
Church, refusing to attack the Cathars. Their chivalry
and valour was not motivated by the inexplicable cult of
chastity because sex was wrong, which the Church
promulgated, but by the fidelity of true lovers, lovers
that is of the Great Goddess. They were drawing not
only on an inspiration of the blood sacrifice of Jesus and
the Cross but also on the great themes of the Goddess
cults. And was part of that energy issuing from the lost
Church of Mary Magdalene? The woman closest to
Christ, who had come to the south of France? I did not
know, but the allusions were clear.

As the Cathars and the Templars were being destroyed
by an all male Church hierarchy, legends and stories of a
great and melancholy loss were rife across Europe – the
romances of the Knights of Camelot, from which something, symbolized by the Holy Grail, had been lost.[19] I

wondered if there might be something in this literature which would either illumine, or be illuminated by this strange belief that the Templars possessed the 'flesh and blood' of Christ, a belief they were apparently willing to die for.

The deluge of books on these romances, now numbering thousands of titles, suggests some very deep response in the human psyche, which would seem difficult to understand if the story were only about a cup or platter. Equally impressive is the fact that no one has come up with a satisfactory explanation.

There are two explanations for the Holy Grail: one that it was a cup or platter used by Joseph of Arimathea to collect blood from Jesus when on the Cross, or that it was an item used at the Last Supper, with sacred blood in it. The two traditions are not exclusive, because something used at the Last Supper could also be used at the place of crucifixion. The blood relationship, as it were, is seen more clearly in the French medieval word, *Sangreal*, used synonymously with *Saint Graal* (Holy Grail). *Sang* is literally blood.

The problem here, however, is that it is difficult to conceive that such legends have arisen from a preoccupation with a cup, even if it was used at the Last Supper or at the Cross. A clearer picture might be obtained by equating Christ's presence with the blood of the Last Supper. In other words the deeper meaning of Holy Grail is the actual chalice of holy blood, and that chalice is Christ. Since the Templars had possessed, or believed they had possessed Christ's bones, the pieces of skull belonging to a woman, the later traditions of the Grail are seen as statements of fact, namely that the Grail had been lost; indeed, stolen by the Inquisition. But the earlier legends relate to the loss of Jesus.

The Holy Grail in the mystic sense is paradoxically the most real of the legends, for it arguably refers to none other than Jesus, a woman, and she was lost, and so must be found. The later romancers, that is those writing after the Templar débâcle, were possibly all adding to the loss of the most holy relic in Christendom, the skull bones of Jesus Christ.

The Grail legends are also suffused with alchemy, and here I found a direct link with the Great Goddess concepts of change and blood.

Alchemy, which gave rise to chemistry, received a boost from the Templars because they brought back with them lore from the more chemically advanced Saracens in Palestine. These reclusive men and women often wrote in a script, copying the Hebrew language in leaving out vowels, which was a mixture of their own language and Greek and Latin. Much of the alchemists' preoccupations concerned Calxes, which in their script was CLX, which when heated turned from red powders into silvery liquids, and vice versa. Mercury is the prime example, though lead can also be made to do similar tricks. The symbolism hardly appears to need teasing out, once one recognizes the Great Goddess motifs of the relationships between the silvery moon and menstruation. In their laboratories the alchemists could mimic the lunar passage into blood, and back again.

Indeed the alchemists regarded Isis as the first alchemist, something which sober historians find puzzling, even apochryphal, but at the same time they are sure the alchemists knew a great secret which was never written down. The puzzle may not be so hard to unravel now. Imperfectly perhaps, these alchemists, not all of whom were men, understood that the roots of Christianity were older than Roman Catholicism, just as, apparently, did the Knights Templar.[20]

The mystic connections between Templars, chivalry and alchemy are apparently based on a tradition of the femality of Christ, a kind of a secret sign language which has long lost its original meaning and has fallen into the formless inconsequentialities of the arcane and the occult, but if we were to dig deeply enough into these subjects we would find a basis in human experience. Indeed the symbolism goes further, but perhaps suffice to say that the wine chalice used in medieval times was also called the flower cup, which could be a loaded reference to the five-petalled rose which we know as the rose of chivalry and heraldry. But the Rose is also a symbol of love. That it is blood-red can be seen to allude not to romantic love but the love of the woman who died on the cross. Curiously the cipher CLX crops up again here, for chalice in Old French is *calice*, Old English *celic*, and Latin *calix*. The link between x and ch, ce and c is pronunciation, for x, chi, is the Greek for the sound ch in chalice. *Calix* is in fact a Latin cup, often confused with calyx, the outer whirl of petals of a flower bud. Oddly, the Church has eschewed the rose symbol of love, though the builders of cathedrals were not so coy, using the rose window as their song of veneration for the true Christ. There wasn't much the Church hierarchy could do about this for masons were a law unto themselves, as you can see to this day at Notre Dame, where windows have the five petals of the rose.

Had the Church embraced the rose it might have impaled itself on the thorn that is always there, in this case admitting to its own confusion,[21] for to them pentacles were sin signs, as can be shown by cutting across an apple and revealing the perfect five-pointed star of this roseaceous fruit. The Church needed Eve's apple to prove sin and so couldn't admit to the rose of love, even though the symbol is perfect – for a woman Saviour.

Of course all this cannot be proved, except that the allusions are too close to be the result of mere chance. There might be another reason for them being so related other than the femality of Christ, but the fact remains that chivalry's death did clear the way for killing women as witches, and the death blow to chivalry as a mystic force was the destruction of the Templars. Naturally with the improvement of means of warfare the knight was a lost figure, but his ideals need not have died with him – that required the suppression of those ideals which were deeply connected with a reverent sense of the dignity of women, something which the misogynist Church would not welcome. None the less, the sheer poetic force of the chivalric symbols is feminine in essence, which supports in an allusive manner, and with great beauty, the construction put on the meaning of Caput 58.

Arguably, the Inquisition knew that this relic existed from their torturing of the Cathar women, but until the Templars lost their castles in Outremere, Palestine, they were virtually untouchable. However, once their last fortress in Outremere fell in 1291, many of the Knights came back to mainland France, though they still had island bases in the Mediterranean. These too they eventually lost. And so, some sixty years after Montségur, the Templars were vulnerable if the Pope agreed to a move against them. King Philippe of France owed them money and they openly treated him with contempt, so it was to his interest to remove them.

The dawn arrests of Jacques de Molay, Grand Master of the Templars, and others at the Villeneuve Preceptory had been so swift that the revered relic, known as the head of the Virgin, was not safely hidden. The tortures of the Templars led them to make confessions which they later recanted. The trials dragged on for seven years, proof in itself of the weakness of the French King's case. But he had his way on 19 March 1314, when four of the last Templars, including the Grand Master, were asked on a public scaffold in front of Notre Dame to reiterate their 'confessions' before the Pope's emissary. Two did and were then incarcerated for life, but Jacques de Molay repudiated his testimony and said his only shame was that torture had forced from him statements grievous to his Christian beliefs. His companion, Geoffrey de Charnay, took the same line. The Pope's emissary was stunned, clearly anxious that a miscarriage of justice was now public, but Philippe pushed the execution forward, having the two men roasted to death over slow fires on the Île des Juifs (now a part of the Île de la Cité). These two lovers of Christ asked to be tied facing the Cathedral of Notre Dame (Our Lady). We are now perhaps in a more privileged position to understand the meaning behind this request. They died with great fortitude, like the Christian martyrs of old, in whose direct line, we suggest, they were.

I must confess I baulked at these implications; the issues appeared loomingly large, not what I had anticipated at all. I felt out of my depth. But gradually the excitement subsided and more practical considerations came to the fore. All I really had before me was a plausible, if disturbing, hypothesis to explain the demise of the Templars, but the hypothesis rested at this stage on the very involved cipher analysis of a relic which appeared to terrify the Papacy and gave women Cathars and Templar Knights the courage to face death. Not all these people could be deluded. Then there was the Templar legend of the dead woman sexually taken in her grave, the origin of the skull and crossed thigh bones motif which is found in Templar lore. If the skull is identified with Caput 58, then the legend was independent evidence of Christ's female gender. It would not be the first time a nugget of truth was found in a legend. The full story identifies the lover of the woman as a Lord of Sidon, but of course Sidon can stand for Sion, which is usually a reference to the Temple mount in Jerusalem. The Grand Master could be so termed, but then so could Pontius Pilate, for he controlled Jerusalem from the fortress of Antonia, whose steps still exist. The Lady is called the Lady of Maraclea.[22] The story has come down to us with an obscene taint, but what if it referred to the veneration of the body of Christ? Had her body been removed from the tomb by a lover or lovers, where love need not carry any sexual overtones? Had then the Church destroyed the force of the story by making it obscene, just as they had with the Templar veneration of a head? Possibly, possibly not, but the way forward was clear enough.

Was there something that the Church did which would support or demolish the hypothesis that seemed to emerge naturally from investigation so far? After all, if the hypothesis were so difficult to sustain it might mean that the Church could simply ignore what the Cathars and Templars were saying; simply live out the storm, as it were; let it die a natural death. But the Cathars and Templars were not allowed to die a natural death, so the question reasserts itself: did the Church do something after the killing of the Templars which reinforces the suspicions so far raised?

Couched in these terms, irrespective of the controversial nature of the material, the problem resolves itself into a set of objective tasks. For example, if there is anything in the notion that Christ was female, then there should be clear evidence, in the policies pursued by the Popes, that they knew, or feared, this to be the case, and would take steps to make sure that no one else did. And what would be the most clear expression of this, apart from denying women the altar? A proof of Jesus being male? Yes, that would do, for if the proof were sound, then the cruelties of the Church to the Templars and Cathars might be explained on some other grounds, though that seemed unlikely; if, however, the proof were unsound, indeed a fraud, even an impudent forgery, then 2,000 years of dogma would have to be revalued.

Was there such a test case? I looked around and found one, something blatantly male, which at the same time was offered as a proof of the resurrection. Strangely, it came into history through a Pope who employed Joan's annalist; even more curiously, its antecedents can be traced back to a man who died in torment in front of Notre Dame, the Templar de Charnay. I am of course speaking of the Turin Shroud.

— 3 —

Mary's Child?

Most people in the world, with the possible exception of some aboriginal tribes in the Upper Amazon and Communist communes in outer Mongolia, have heard about the Turin Shroud and seen its pictures in books, magazines and on television. There are Shroud societies in virtually every country in the world. Within this global interest is a central caucus of enthusiasts who insist that the shroud is the actual burial cloth of Jesus Christ, that the image on it shows Jesus Christ, and that in any case, it is a 'photographic' image. Can these claims be substantiated? There is more at stake here than a pious wish to see Jesus Christ. For one thing, if the Turin Shroud is authentic, then Isaiah is wrong, but Isaiah is taken as the prophet of the Virgin Birth, the announcer of the Redeemer by the Catholic Church. For another, the shroud, or something like it, emerged to take its place in history in 1355–6 soon after the suppression of the Cathars and the Templars and the beginnings of the witch trials, all issues involving women in some religious function or other. It seemed provocative that a macho male Christ should be foisted on the world at this time.

The image is on a piece of badly stained and burned linen, kept in a casket under several locks, behind the High Altar of the Royal Chapel in Turin Cathedral. It shows, when stretched out, a handsome muscular man with long hair and fully bearded, powerfully built, about six feet in height, totally unlike what the scriptures of

Isaiah and some very early Church Fathers' report.[1] It is possible to technically analyse the physique, which I did, and found it to be a relatively rare one; only four men in fifty have it and it is often found in the super-athlete class.[2] How was this image made?

Image Theories

One explanation is that the image was formed by direct contact with a dead body, the idea being that the sheet was laid down, the body laid on it and then the cloth remaining was folded over on top. The sheet is certainly long enough for this six-foot athlete, but there is a technical difficulty, for if you do get a contact image from a living body by pressing a cloth on to it, the image is very distorted, so the contact idea is rejected even by shroud enthusiasts. Tests made with USAF airmen with a wrap-around cloth showed that contact was made, as you would expect, at top of the head, forehead, chest, hands crossed over loins, knees and feet. However, the experimenters simply ignored the absence of the image of the top of the head on the shroud, which their experiment proved should be there. Ian Wilson[3] reports on these experiments and, recognizing that the contact hypothesis cannot work, postulates that in some manner the shroud was placed over the body with mathematical flatness, both back and front. Apart from the impossibility of this in a burial, how would the image be transferred to the cloth?

Several writers waxed eloquent on a vapour theory, where body fluids evaporated and formed an image on the linen. This idea at first has its merits, for sweat does contain minute amounts of lactic acid which can reduce carbohydrates, and which might come out as a stain on the carbohydrate of linen cloth. Curiously, the published hypotheses simply ignore this most promising material and pin hopes on inert materials like urea, which would not evaporate substantially, or vague 'ammoniacal vapours' from decomposition. There is, however, an unanswerable objection to the vapour theories: diffusion is a random process and so would produce a very hazy image. Yet this objection is topped by an even more compelling one: the image density. Light and shade on the cloth would be related to the source material, that is the body, its nearness and contours, in a very complicated mathematical fashion, but the work with USAF volunteers showed that the relationship was simple. Besides, in a cold tomb, the period of Friday evening to Sunday morning is not long enough for severe decomposition to occur.

Faced with the failure of vaporization and contact, shroud apologists have actually invoked nuclear explosions or even radiation.[4] They have seen the tragic 'flash' photographs of vaporized objects in Hiroshima and wonder if there was an explosion in the tomb, but they forget that nuclear energies would vaporize the cloth. Also, radiation obeys physical laws, which could not give the image found on the Turin linen. When one weighs the evidence – and the extreme enthusiasts are willing to go against all logic – it is probably best to say no more. Even at this stage the suspicion emerges that the real issues surrounding this linen are: who created the image, and why?

The Too Perfect Corpse

The face of the man on the Turin Cloth is in repose, but men who have died through violence do not wear such expressions, even if they have gone to their deaths willingly. The fatal reflexes are such that the face bears a rictus. Furthermore, the hair of the man on the Turin linen is hanging down as it would if he were standing.

The image, then, is not of a man crucified, nor yet of a man lying down.

These discrepancies caused me to examine the wounds. The Roman *flagellum* was barbed, either with iron or bone, so the flesh would be torn, lacerated, but on the Turin man there are simply indentations. There are about 120 of these marks, which suggests a three-thonged whip, which does not accord with Roman and Judaic usage: two score strokes less one, with a two-thonged whip. The blows do not overlap, but form an artistic pattern.

There is also a problem with the blood marks, or rather their depiction, for there is too much blood if the body had been washed according to Jewish custom, and too little if it had not been so washed.

Even if the body were cleaned, we still cannot find an explanation for the beautifully artistic form of the rivulets of blood on the head. If this is a dead body, why should it bleed in this fashion after death? And if the body were not cleaned, where is all the blood matted with a mixture of sweat in the beard and hair? If not cleaned, where is all the blood on the body from the gaping tears that repeated whipping with a *flagellum* with tipped ends would produce? Are we to assume that after some parts of the body were cleansed and the hair washed, perfect rivulets of blood flowed down on to the forearms from the nails in the arms and from the thorn wounds in the head? The skin of the skull bleeds profusely even with minor perforations, yet there is only one clear stream of blood on the head of the Turin man. Was there only one thorn? This lack of blood should be contrasted with the matted scalps of people who have been brutalized, so easily is blood shed from the head.[5]

If we put ourselves in the place of a putative artist commissioned to produce a shroud, we would probably decide to make it look as 'acceptable' as possible. A tangled mass of undifferentiated hair and blood and a body torn by a whip is the truth, but it looks nothing like the image on the shroud. Then there is the problem of the body having been 'perfectly' crucified. The terrible deformation of muscles in face and body caused by crucifixion are, again, like the actuality of real wounds and suffering, absent.

Real evidence of crucifixion is extremely distressing, for at the Giv'at Ha-Mivtar excavation in Jerusalem, the bones of a crucified Jew were found. He was of slight build, mature but not old, and in his case they had crucified him by putting the nails behind his wrist between the two main arm bones of the forearm, namely the radius and ulna, for scratch marks are shown. As for his feet, they had smashed one nail straight through both ankles, so twisting him into a terrible shape, so unlike the beautifully uncontorted open pose of Christian iconography. In short, we see in the shroud the artistic convention during the Renaissance, not the terrible reality of a human being done to death on a cross.

To date the shroud has been exhibited four times this century, but the explosion of interest can be dated to 1931 when the professional Turin photographer, Giuseppe Enrie, used special film, orthochromatic, and a yellow filter, to enhance on a black-and-white print the beige and faint carmines of the image.

It was also on view, in 1933, by the express wish of Pope Pius XI, who believed that the image was not the work of man but was mysterious; this, he felt, 'is demonstrated'.[6] As we have seen, it is not demonstrated; indeed the weight of evidence is that this shroud is a work of art of great ability, but not beyond the competence of many Renaissance artists. In 1973 the shroud was exposited for television, and samples of cloth taken. The samples, however, did not show traces of blood, only

iron oxide.[7] By an irony of history, the shroud was exhibited for a longer period of time, forty-two days (beginning 26 August 1978) than reigned Pope John Paul I,
whose election, reign and death occurred within this
period; indeed his reign was only thirty-three days and
some commentators feel that he was murdered.[8] As
shroud investigator Nickell points out, the commission
set up to examine the shroud was subject to severe re-
strictions, no carbon-14 dating, for example, in October
1978. The Commissioners were nearly all shroud apologists and there was a distinct lack of women. Moreover,
the one woman who had been in the preliminary examination in 1969 and was also in the Commission of
1973, Professor Noemi Gabrielli, a retired Professor of
Art, and director of Art Galleries, Piedmont, insisted that
the shroud was not genuine but a work of art, and that it
is not the Lirey cloth (which we will discuss later). It is
noteworthy that this scholarly and erudite lady has been
attacked by shroud apologists. Nickell is incensed by the
unjust treatment she received, pointing out that much of
the criticism against her was based on her sex.[9] In any
case most of the people involved in the Shroud of Turin
Research Project founded in 1977 were, Nickell reports,
not unbiased scientists but members of Christian
churches, with only one self-confessed agnostic.[10]

One scientist who fell short of absolute belief was
Walter McChrone, a microanalyst who found that the
shroud image was partially due to ferric oxide particles.
He was able to show that image density could easily be
controlled by rubbing jeweller's rouge (ferric oxide) with
his fingers on a cloth.

If the carmine stains on the shroud are blood, they are
a very strange colour, because blood even a few years old
tends to be black, not red or even carmine. Perhaps the
most indicative evidence that blood was not on the
shroud and never had been was provided by neutron

activation analysis, which is extremely sensitive; results of tests for the elemental composition for blood seem to have been negative. Blood of course contains iron, and the presence of iron oxide on the shroud might be thought to substantiate blood, but the distribution of the iron oxide particles is not related to the blood stains, but to the whole image. McChrone was also able to detect vermilion, mercuric sulphide, a common pigment in the fourteenth and fifteenth centuries. He felt that the artist had, therefore, used iron oxide and vermilion in at least part of the image-making process. By April 1980 he was confident he had found traces of madder rose too. We know from art history that lake colours such as madder rose were often used in conjunction with vermilion to depict blood. McChrone, who was indefatigable in his analysis, was also able to show the presence of a binder in the fibres of the image area and suggested it was collagen tempera, a common if not universal medium for pigments, certainly in fourteenth- and fifteenth-century Italy and elsewhere.[11]

Nickell prepared iron oxide paints in tempera, according to twelfth-century recipes and medieval artists' recipes in general, and subjected them to forensic tests for blood; they yielded similar results to those obtained from the shroud.[12] In other words, the blood tests used on the shroud were not specific. To this date the presence of blood on the Turin cloth has not been substantiated.

The difficulty now is to demonstrate how the yellow-beige image is formed. Many tests, including those of the Shroud of Turin Research Project scientists, lead us to the conclusion that there is no pigment in these areas, that is the non-blood areas. However, using the medieval pigment mixes, Nickell showed that linen fibres will be partially degraded by them, and the surface of fibres damaged. A chalk or powder form of pigment, including Venetian red, when used on linen and then washed off, causes a yellowing and damaging of the fibres on the surface to which the pigment has been applied. The reason for this is that iron salts can act as catalysts to the oxidation of flax, of which linen is made, for it is basically a cellulose material which will oxidize and therefore yellow, just as the yellowing of paper occurs with age. The plausible hypothesis, put forward by Nickell and his co-workers and tested by them[13] is that the image was built up by using a chalky pigment containing Venetian red, and which through the circumstances of time has been washed out. In support of this idea we may note that the Turin Shroud may have been washed after the fire, but this is not certain – certainly water was used to put out the smouldering for we can see the water marks to this day. However, possible as the tempera Venetian red hypothesis is, we still have to answer the question of who made the image and why?

When directly confronted with these questions, the shroud enthusiasts attempt to push back the origin of the shroud to as near Christ's birth as possible, but cannot manage to get past the fourteenth century. Ian Wilson suggests that prior to 1355 the shroud, if it existed, was folded up to show only the head, so that it could have been mistaken for a mandilion[14] – although mandilions' heads are haloed and the shoulders clothed, whereas the Turin man has no halo and wears only a loincloth. Mandilions are formalized works of art depicting Christ's head and shoulders with no attempt at anatomical veri-similitude for they stem from the legend that as Christ was being led along the Via Dolorosa to his crucifixion, a woman named Veronica wiped the blood and sweat from Jesus' face with her veil, on which the imprint of his features remained. The mandilion in the Tretyakov Gallery is typical.

Drawing these findings together, it appears that the image was formed by using Venetian red chalk and powder. It was applied in such a manner that those areas nearest to the artist were more thickly coated than those at a distance. If the artist did apply pigment like this, then he would have formed a 'negative', which fits in with the findings of the USAF experiments. Does this technique work? It has been used by the artist Susan Hilton who, when at the Royal College of Art, produced for a television programme a beautifully haunting 'Turin Man' head[15] which withstood all the tests carried out on the shroud as to lack of evidence of brushwork (use of powdered pigments) and image density scans.

As a further test of the Turin Shroud's status there is the question of the linen upon which the image is made. Technically it is, by the direction of the twist of the threads, what is called a Z Z fabric.[16] I asked Linda Woolley of the Department of Textile Furnishing and Dress at the Victoria and Albert Museum if such was common in the first-century Judea or thirteenth-century Europe. She replied, 'It would be likely for a linen of the first century to have S spun warp and weft, although again Z is not out of the question,' the reason being that 'linen thread had a natural tendency to S spin.'

There are of course other tests to be performed. When this book went to press the carbon-14 dating tests had not been done; however, in anticipation of the results, the following points need to be observed: 1) it is not uncommon for wide divergences in dating to be obtained on similar samples from different laboratories, and so the results of one laboratory or team are insufficient – although even without the inherent variation in results of this method, it is ordinary scientific practice that more than one test should be carried out by different workers since otherwise there is always the legitimate doubt that an error has crept in; 2) the actual image on the shroud is caused by damage to fibres, not the presence of a pigment, so the actual date of the 'image' cannot be obtained; 3) the pigment iron oxide contains no carbon, so even if the image were actually of this substance, rather than being fibre-damage patterning, it could not be dated by the carbon-14 method; 4) furthermore, so clumsy is the method that it involves destruction of the entire sample, so image and cloth could not be separately analysed; 5) if, after the above provisos have been noted, the dating should show first century, then it merely means that the flax was of the first century, although contamination is always possible, in which case average values are obtained; 6) if, however, the dating of the cloth is later than first century it cannot be the shroud of Christ and must be a fraud.

On balance, the Turin Shroud does appear to be a forgery. The theological point it makes is unavoidable: Christ was a tall athlete, of stunning good looks. Why should the Church, or a section of it, wish to promulgate such an image in direct contradiction to the prophet Isaiah who said that a virgin would conceive; and that Christ would be without beauty, an afflicted person. If his prediction about Christ's lack of beauty can be ignored then why not his Mary prophecy? The point could not have been missed, but the risk was taken. Clearly the stakes must have been, and still are, very high indeed.

Scandal of the Lirey Shroud

It must be noted that the Turin Shroud was not even in Turin until 14 September 1678, when it was taken there from Chambéry by the then Duke of Savoy, Duke Emmanuel Phillibert, who had moved his seat of government from Chambéry to Turin. We can be certain that the cloth so egregiously exhibited from that date to this is the cloth taken from Chambéry, and there is evidence that it had been previously exposited with great pomp and ceremony at Chambéry in 1502, but before that date we have no objective evidence which can lead us to be certain that prior 'shrouds' are in fact the Turin Shroud. Faced with this disturbing fact, people who want, against all evidence, to insist that the Turin linen is the burial shroud of Jesus Christ, have had to acknowledge it as the same cloth which was produced in the most dubious of circumstances in the little village of Lirey in France. In 1355 or 1356 (even the apologists cannot date with certainty) this cloth was exhibited by the de Charny family and caused so much scandal that their bishop, Henri de Poitiers, had to threaten them with severe ecclesiastic sanctions if they did not desist.

Who was the person who suddenly produced the burial shroud of Jesus Christ in the little wooden church of the de Charny estate where now stands the village of Lirey, ten miles south of Troyes, 100 miles south-east of Paris? Her name was Jeanne de Vergy and her husband was Geoffrey de Charny, whom we will call for convenience Geoffrey I. We know that Geoffrey I died at the battle of Poitiers, fighting against the English led by Edward, the Black Prince, in September 1356, four months after the consecration of the little chapel on 28 May. We do not know if Geoffrey was alive when his wife first put up the image. We do know that they were not a rich family, otherwise the church would not have been wooden. If Geoffrey was dead and the exposition was late 1356 we can attribute a very human motive to Jeanne's action. The family, having lost its Knight father, faced poverty, so Jeanne, a young war widow, decided to exhibit the shroud to make a living. Whatever the reason it was very successful, for pilgrims came, and gifts were made. It looked promising, but Jeanne had to desist when Bishop de Poitiers demanded verification of her claims. Jeanne stopped showing. The shroud was not seen again for a third of a century, and this time the new Bishop d'Arcis found the de Charnys even more bold.

The de Charnys were a strange family, as this passage written by Geoffrey I shows: 'He [the new knight] should also be girded by a completely white belt, signifying he should live in chastity.'[17] And this from a man who was married to a young wife, Jeanne de Vergy. Indeed, Geoffrey's knightly obsessions led him to found a new order of knights, the Order of the Star, wherein suicidal bravery was expected of the members. This order foundered, and along with it the fortunes of the de Charny family. The ladies and knights of the de Charny line were not reduced to being charcoal burners like the famous noble couple of Chivalry, Girard and Berte. Instead it appears they became relic expositors.

Ian Wilson, seeking to find the shroud in antiquity, makes a convincing case for relating the Lirey de Charnys with the Knight Templar de Charny who was burned at the stake on the Île de Juifs in 1314,[18] an incident mentioned earlier in this book. If the relationship is true, then perhaps it could have been the Templars who gave a painted shroud to the Charny, de Charnay, or de Chargny (the spelling varies) family. The Knights Templar controlled vast resources and riches so they could have afforded to ease the de Charny poverty with a Templar artifact. Shroud apologists insist that the Lirey painting is none other than the Turin Shroud, but as the story unfolds this earnest wish is found not to be supported by the facts.

Bishop d'Arcis, Bishop de Poitiers' successor, was hindered by the Church in his efforts to have the Lirey cloth given its correct status as an artifact and not a true relic. In his 1389 letter[19] to Clement VII he says:

. . . it is a wonder to all who know the facts of the case that the opposition which hampers me in these proceedings comes from the Church, from which quarter I should have looked for vigorous support, nay, rather have expected punishment if I had shown myself slothful or remiss . . .

Bishop d'Arcis, Bishop of Troyes, was risking his career, but he had come late to the Church, having been a trained lawyer, and in him we can detect that sincerity of office not infrequently found in the hitherto worldly who become priests, as shown on a larger canvas by Thomas à Becket, who turned his back on a wild, even profane youth when he took the Mitre of Archbishop of Canterbury, and died for being a turbulent priest. D'Arcis pleads to the Pope:

I would ask you then, most blessed Father, to vouchsafe to bestow your attention upon the foregoing statement and to take measures that such scandal and delusion and abominable superstition may be put an end to both in fact and seeming, in such wise that this cloth be held neither for *sudarium* nor *sanctuarium*, nor for an image or figure of our Lord's *sudarium*, since our Lord's *sudarium* was nothing of the kind, nor, in fine, under any other ingenious pretext be exhibited to the people or exposed for veneration, but that to express horror of such superstition it be publicly condemned, the surreptitious letters above spoken of being recalled, or more truly declared null and void.

But it was to be of no avail. Jeanne de Vergy's son, Geoffrey II, succeeded in getting from Clement VII a Bull which allowed him to exposit his 'painting', and the term is significant, for it is used in d'Arcis' letter, as a likeness for meditation, but not a true relic. There are two points here: first as the shroud apologists insist, the image at Turin is not a painting, but d'Arcis' predecessor, de Poitiers, Bishop of Troyes, actually said he had the confession of forgery from the painter of the Lirey Shroud.[20] Hence doubts of the link between the Lirey painting and the shroud at Turin appear to be well founded on this evidence alone. The second point is why did d'Arcis fail against the de Charnys while his predecessor succeeded? Jeanne, rebuffed in her attempts to

improve her situation with her relic in 1355–6, had
remarried after Geoffrey I's death. Her new husband was
no less than the rich and powerful uncle of Pope Clement
VII. Yet even with this patronage, the de Charnys were
able to get no more than a dispensation to exhibit as a
likeness, not a relic. At the same time, Clement enjoined
a vow of perpetual silence on d'Arcis, for what he was
saying was simply too embarrassing. Yet the ramifica-
tions do not end there, for Geoffrey II actually married
a niece of Henri de Poitiers, the dead bishop whose
evidence outsider d'Arcis, with his touching belief in
truth and objectivity, had hoped he would be able to
use.

This was a period in history when a good relic could
transform the material state of a church, and therefore
that of the aristocrats on whose land it rested. The process
was through pilgrims who, coming to a relic's resting
place, would dispose of money, jewels, *objets d'art*, in
veneration.²¹ An ordinary burial cloth was one thing, a
burial cloth with the image of Christ's body on it,
showing all the signs the faithful had come to expect from
the munificent Church art of the time, could transform a
family who controlled it.

Neither Bishop Poitiers nor d'Arcis had agreed to this,
which is surprising, for if there were any sanctity in the
claims of the de Charnys and their deans, it would have
been an acceptable source of income for the Church, and
a bishop could have basked in the glory of that source of
light and succour in his diocese. Henri de Poitiers had
threatened (1355–6) the de Charnys and they, frightened of the consequences, as Bishop d'Arcis says, of
'seeing their wickedness discovered' had hidden the
shroud away.

D'Arcis ends his letter to the Pope, Clement VII who,
we must remember, was a creature of the French King
and was based in Avignon, not Rome, with these

memorable lines: 'I am convinced I cannot fully or sufficiently express in writing the grievous nature of the
scandal, the contempt brought upon the Church . . . and
the danger to souls.' He wrote, perhaps, prophetically.

Geoffrey died, leaving a daughter, Margaret, who
prised the shroud from her own canons at Lirey, saying,
not unreasonably, that marauding bands of brigands,
including English soldiers, were a danger to life, limb
and linen. The cloth was installed in the castle of one
Humbert, her second husband, her first having been
killed fighting the English on 6 July 1418.

The Lirey Canons had in their possession a receipt for
the shroud, which also contained a promise that once the
troubles were over and marauding bands had vanished,
the cloth would be returned to them. It was a promise
never to be kept. Margaret had, in the offices of her
second husband, found a means of controlling the cloth
without Lirey Canons having any effective say. She now
needed an appropriate venue to exhibit in, and chose the
Chapel Buessart, on her husband's lands, which had a
meadow on the banks of the River Doubs, known as Pré
de Seigneur. It should perhaps be observed that the move
was undertaken prior to the disappearance of marauding
bands. In any event, a cult grew up, as the shroud was
exhibited in the meadow. Copies of the shroud were
made, amongst which was one called the Besançon
Shroud, destroyed in the French Revolution. Actually,
at this point in the narrative a massive doubt emerges.
The shroud called Besançon may not have been a copy
at all, for as Bishop L. D. Fox writes: 'In 1349 the Holy
Shroud had been in the cathedral of Besançon, and had
disappeared thence during a fire.' It is perhaps sheer
coincidence that a copy, or rather what is said to have
been a copy, reappears when the de Charny relic is being
exhibited in a meadow. In 1418 there are two shrouds.
Which one will history bless? The cloth of Besançon has

little chance of notoriety today because it no longer exists.

Margaret de Charny's entrepreneurial career was not without its setbacks, and her pluck must be recorded. In 1449 we see her in Chimay, Hainault, Belgium, where she exhibited her cloth, but on being challenged by the Bishop of Liège, she had nothing to show but Clement VII's Bull, which gave her the right to exhibit it as a likeness of Christ. Clearly, she was attempting to do more. How many times she pushed her relic we do not know, but she was unsuccessful, as late as 1452, in Germolles, France.

Peripatetic Margaret, now advanced in years, does not give up. She is in bad odour in Lirey, where the Canons there are still fretting about the cloth, for their revenues have drastically fallen, but receipt from Margaret's husband notwithstanding, they will never get the shroud back. On 22 March 1453, Margaret receives the deeds to a castle in Varambon and revenues from a Lyons estate from the Duke of Savoy in return for the Lirey cloth.

The Savoys liked relics. Their direct ancestor was Saint Louis, King of France (1214–70), who allegedly owned the true Crown of Thorns. The Savoy Duke's father became a Pope, Felix V. The Savoys now had an item befitting their connections and the family fetish for collecting relics.

And Margaret? She gained worldly possessions but was excommunicated[22] formally, by none other than the Besançon Ecclesiastical Judge on 30 May 1457. The charges included scathing terms of Margaret, describing her as 'the perfidious woman' who 'handed over and it is said, sold it [the cloth] to the Duke of Savoy'.[23] Margaret died on 7 October 1460, childless.

One can have some sympathy for the wives of the de Charnys. They were impoverished by strange mystic husbands. An early ancestor had died as a heretic, but we must presume that his family knew something of his true Christian beliefs, yet here we have Jeanne and Margaret expositing something they knew to be fraudulent and which was only given relic status through family intrigue and the machinations of the Pope – who was related to them by marriage. Behind this sad story is a deeper wound, for at one time the de Charnys had been their own people, had died for their beliefs, but heresy or rather the accusation of it, which caused the death of their Templar ancestor in 1314, had struck them hard. Can we see in the peregrinations of these two sad women, the first young and widowed, the second old and widowed, hawking a relic about, an attempt to reinstate themselves in the good offices of powerful French Kings and their creature Popes? The evidence strongly suggests that by Jeanne's and Margaret's time, the Church was, either through King or Pope, so powerful that existence without its blessing was well-nigh impossible.

For the Court of Savoy the relic was coming into its own. The Savoy church, Sainte Chapelle at Chambéry, where the relic was exposited, became a horn of plenty, except that riches were not flowing out, but flowing in. From venerators and pilgrims came sumptuous draperies, stained glass, sculptures, reliquaries festooned with jewels. With their 'relic' the Savoys appeared to have conquered both Heaven and Mammon, and carried the 'shroud' everywhere with them.[24]

The Savoy Dukes were becoming more important as the years passed, for Savoy is the strategic gateway to Italy from France. The Savoys were related by blood to the French throne, and any French king who wished to invade Italy – and there would be several – would find it convenient to be on good terms with the Savoy Dukes because they controlled several alpine passes. There were even intellectual developments at the Savoy Court, for the young and brilliant, but impoverished, theologian,

Francesco della Rovere, was to write his treatise on the
'Blood of Christ' (written 1464, published 1473) in which
he states that the Savoy linen had the true blood of Christ
on it.[25] This is one of those seminal meeting points in
history, for this once obscure General of the Franciscan
Friars Minor, some of whom the Savoy Duke Louis and
his wife Anne cultivated in their retinue, was to become
Pope Sixtus IV. With this man's approval of the linen
anything was possible.

The Borgia Connection

Father della Rovere became Pope Sixtus IV on 25
August 1471, and was crowned with a tiara by Rodrigo
Borgia. There followed, at the direct institution of this
advocate of the Savoy Shroud, a period of nepotism,
power seeking, simony and corruption which, even for
Popes of this time, was breathtaking.[26] One of his
nephews, Pietro Riario, was appointed to the sacred
college, made cardinal and, with the new benefices
disposed on him by Sixtus, had an income of 60,000 gold
florins, a level of wealth which is difficult to grasp today.
This young man threw himself into debauchery on such
a scale that he died within a few years. Had all the della
Roveres been of such mettle, Sixtus might have de-
spaired, but he had another nephew who was altogether
of sterner stuff, a giant in corruption, intellect and physical constitution. This man, Cardinal Giuliano della
Rovere, used his money to gain power and eventually
was to become Pope Julius II. In 1506 Julius was to give
the same status to the Chambéry Sainte Chappelle as the
church in Paris where the True Cross, the relic of St
Louis, King of France, ancestor of the Savoys, was
lodged.

Sixtus, like the Borgias, and we note one of them
crowned him, hired men like Botticelli, Perugino and

Ghirlandaio to produce sumptuous works of art, some of ostensible ecclesiastic value, some of a more personal nature. He was also a savage man, torturing his enemies before executing them. He was to be Pope for thirteen years, and in that time Leonardo grew from nineteen to thirty-two years old.

Della Rovere's theological position was that the 'Blood of Christ' was a primary redemptive agent, but only the Church could give it, in the Mass. Salvation at a price? Did Sixtus view his early (he had been just a priest and then cardinal) raptures about the Savoy linen with a new and shrewdly assessing eye when he became Pope? His treatise on the 'Blood of Christ' was published in 1473, so he was on public record as saying that the shroud was a relic and that it had real blood of Christ on it. *If* that was what a Pope said, clearly the matter of the Savoy linen should not be treated by half measures. The choice was that Sixtus could either let the opponents of the shroud have their day, in which case he was committing political and spiritual suicide, or elevate the shroud to a true relic and accord it all the pomp and veneration he could lavish on it. It is not perhaps too difficult to see what choice this ambitious man made.

Sixtus was championing a linen cloth which had been repudiated by two bishops of Troyes, and by other high-ranking Belgian and French ecclesiastics. The first exhibitor of the shroud, Jeanne, was the aunt of one of Sixtus' predecessors, Clement VII, who had forbidden Bishop d'Arcis to say the shroud was a fraud. All this was unedifying enough, but when the new and adolescent Duke of Savoy, Amadeus, embarked on a frantic rebuilding of the Chapel at Chambéry, it was clear which way Sixtus was going.

This Duke of Savoy, Amadeus IX, still in his teens was heir to Duke Louis and his wife, Duchess Anne, who had bought the linen from Margaret de Charny. Now their

son was spending vast sums to make a sanctuary for the
linen, and he asked Sixtus for his approval. Of course
the approval was given. Hadn't Sixtus written about the
shroud long before? And wasn't this boy's father the son
of a Pope, Felix V (1439–49)? With this kind of background there were possibilities. Could a dubious piece of
cloth be made into a true relic? All one had to do was
build chapels, issue Bulls and ignore what good men and
true had risked their careers to say. The only problem
may have been that perhaps the piece of cloth wouldn't
stand up to its new role. Was this cloth from the poverty-
stricken de Charny family really convincing enough for a
ducal sacristy, a centre of temporal and Church power?
Probably not, but on 11 June 1502 a huge and costly
procession of Lords temporal and spiritual solemnly
accompanied a linen to the high altar, where the piece of
cloth was exhibited as if it were the sacrament. This was
the Turin Shroud, not the Lirey 'relic', for there were no
artists in 1355 who could have produced it as we know it
today.

To reassure myself on this point, I asked the following
question of several art experts. Did they know of a likely
candidate who fulfilled the following criteria: 1)
portraitist, active at any time between 1244–1355; 2)
associated in some way with the Knights Templar; 3)
associated with Popes; 4) having anatomical skills in
portraiture comparable with those shown by da Vinci and
Michelangelo.

I chose the dates 1244–1355 because 1244 was the fall
of Jerusalem, when the Templars went to Acre, and 1355
was the first exposition of the Lirey Shroud. Alistair
Smith, Keeper at the National Gallery, London, said 'I
have thought about this for some time and no precise
artist comes to mind.' John Rowlands, Keeper at the
British Museum, reports: 'I am afraid I do not have a
candidate for you.' However, it was John Murdoch,
Deputy Keeper, Department of Prints, Drawings and

Photographs and Paintings of the Victoria and Albert Museum who removed any possibility that there could have been an unknown thirteenth-century artist capable of painting the image that we see on the Turin Shroud. He said:

The best answer really to your question is to say that even the idea of portraiture, let alone anatomy, belongs to the Renaissance. Images of people exist from the 13th Century and much earlier, but they have quasi-symbolic rather than a natural relation to the individual.

Even 1355 is too early for true anatomical work of great artistry. This suggests that the Bishop of Troyes, de Poitiers, who claimed that he knew the artist who did the Lirey Shroud, had seen a work of a formalistic nature, as he implied, lacking in verisimilitude so that no one could have acknowledged it, unless for blindly superstitious or self-seeking reasons. It really does seem that the Lirey painting is not a candidate for the Turin Shroud, and several experts have expressed this view.

The Turin Shroud is a work of art.[27] Who might the artist have been? I had no idea, but I did have a little book of Great Drawings from my student days. I flicked through it to see who, in the relevant time period, had sufficient ability and anatomical knowledge to set about creating a shroud. I found no answer on anatomy, but I did find a self-portrait of an old man, with the same dignified countenance as the younger man on the shroud. Given differences in age, they had the same kind of hair, moustache and beard, and they both had a similarity in the lines of the bridge of the nose. The drawing was done in red chalk, which only marks the surface of fibres. What, I wondered, did this old man with a nose so similar to the man on the shroud look like at, say, thirty-five to forty-five years of age? The man in question was Leonardo da Vinci, and the drawing, by his own hand, of himself. It is kept in Turin, at the Royal Library.

The art experts had no candidates because there were none during the time I mentioned, but when we come to the exposition in 1502 of the indubitable Turin Shroud by the Duke of Savoy before the mighty princes of Church and State, the Renaissance was well in existence, and Leonardo da Vinci was fifty years of age. When the Rovere-Borgia Popes were active he was at his zenith, though always poor. To revert again to John Murdoch of the Victoria and Albert Museum:

As for Leonardo, it was his intellectual participation in the scientific aspects of Renaissance culture that led him to make the anatomical studies that have caught your attention. The whole point about Leonardo was that he was rather a special case.

Leonardo and His Patrons

Born in 1452, the bastard son of a notary and a woman of no illustrious family ties, Leonardo grew tall, handsome, muscular and gifted. By the age of twenty he had moved from Vinci near Prato, and was a member of the Craftsmen's Guild of St Luke in Florence. His master was Verucchio, whom he surpassed as a draughtsman. He obtained, fitfully, commissions from very minor churchmen, but produced astonishing works of art. By 1489, at the latest, he was drawing anatomical works of an accuracy and attention to detail scarcely known before. He moved about constantly, seeking work in France, Milan, Rome, Florence. The never-ceasing movement may be the partial explanation for the paucity of the amount, not the quality, of his work which has survived, though as we shall see, much was destroyed by hands other than his own.

In April 1501, with the *Last Supper* (to be lost for

generations when the monks' refectory where it was painted became a stable) and the *Virgin of the Rocks* behind him, he was at work in Florence on a composition entitled *Madonna with the Yard-Winder*. In 1502 he was appointed architect and military engineer to Cesare Borgia, but he was soon back in Florence, and had the experience of seeing Michelangelo, with his great series of commissions for Pope Julius, go from strength to strength, even being asked his opinion on how Michelangelo's statue, *David*, should be placed. Everyone, it seems, praised Leonardo, but he did not get commissions on Michelangelo's scale, and those he did, such as the bronze horse and rider of Duke Francesco Sforza, were never completed. He also had to swallow having doubt cast on his ability to complete assignments by a Medici ambassador. In 1505 he received payment for his expenses in setting up the scaffolding for the painting of the *Battle of Anghiari*, the cost of which he had borne himself for at least a year. Then in May 1506 Leonardo was given leave of absence from his work in Florence to return to Milan. In the same year, on two separate occasions, in letters of 18 August and 16 December, Charles d'Amboise requested the Signoria of Florence, to whom Leonardo was still contracted, for an extension of his leave, which was granted. In July of the succeeding year, Leonardo was made Painter and Engineer to Louis XII of France. He was to die in France, in a Manor House at Cloux near Amboise, thirteen years later. This Manor House was the gift of Francis I of France, the monarch who, in 1511, made a pilgrimage to Chambéry with his wife, Anne of Britanny, to venerate a wonderful linen relic, whose august shadings and anatomical detail were clearly observable.

Pope Sixtus IV died suddenly in August 1484, his nude body on a table, but his collection of relics and his name

were to survive, for his nephew Cardinal Giuliano della
Rovere had learned much from his uncle. Using his influence and wealth, he succeeded in having his creature,
Giovanni Cibo, placed on the papal throne as Innocent
VIII. Nevertheless it was della Rovere himself who
carried a gift from the Turkish Sultan through Rome
from the Porta Flaminia, perhaps in a poor taste celebration of the Christian retaking of Granada in 1492.
The gift della Rovere carried was in a silver casket, and
was a spear, reputed to be the one which lanced Christ
on the cross. In July of that year Innocent was dead, and
the next Pope was a Borgia, Alexander VI.

To say the Borgia Alexander VI was a womanizer is
inaccurate, he was in fact more of a child molester, his
mistress being only a young girl. This unedifying spectacle, that of the unwedlocked union between a sixty-
plus-year old-Pope and a beautiful child, was compounded
by nepotism.

Alexander was to sell his soul in dissolving the marriage
of Louis XII from a good but deformed woman, now
Queen Jeanne, on the impudent grounds of non-
consummation, a favoured device, for it cannot be easily
or modestly disproven, by a husband who wants to marry
another woman for dynastic gain.[28] The new woman in
question was Anne of Brittany, so Louis thereby obtained
the Duchy. The instigator of this plot was Louis and the
legalizer of it was Pope Alexander. Part of the deal
involved Cesare Borgia's elevation to the Dukedom of
Valence; this appalling young man connived with Louis
for nothing less than a papally-blessed axis of Venice–
France to interdict Italy. In September 1499 Louis'
troops invaded northern Italy, killing and plundering.
The Fortress of Milan was sold, and Louis entered in
triumph on 6 October; beside him was Cesare Borgia. In
this same year, Leonardo, despite his procrastination of
the Duke of Milan's bronze statue, including the horse,

was given a vineyard by the said Duke. Leonardo left Milan after the French came, but before his patron returned. The sleek, womanizing Cesare Borgia, who rode into Milan with the triumphant Louis, was to hire Leonardo as architect and military engineer some three years later on 18 August 1502, the same year that the Savoy family opened their refurbished church at Chambéry, the occasion being the solemn exposition and laying to sanctuary of a shroud. Five years later, Louis was to make Leonardo his employee in the same capacity that Cesare had.

We are accustomed, perhaps, to see in Leonardo all the virtues of the Renaissance, happily untouched by the vices of murder, lechery, poisoning and bloody intrigues. But Leonardo mixed with the great at a time when 'If women do anything that displeases us men, we are at them with cords, daggers and poison' and 'We Italians are irreligious and corrupt above all others.'[29] It was a time when priests were polygamous, when they took to brigandage and murder, violating women for sport, against a background of extreme profanity in both aristocracy and commons. Here was a society where superstitious awe of relics was compounded with an eye for the main chance, no matter how basely achieved. In this heady atmosphere da Vinci, now at the court of Cesare Borgia, designed strange machines with scythes to cut off men's legs, produced plans for fortified cities in the Romagna for Cesare, and also drew studies of his master. In his rapine and drive for power Cesare was accused of having his mercenaries keep back forty women, young girls mostly, from the sack of Capua in 1501 for his own lust.[30]

Pope Alexander, Cesare's doting father, presided over a Rome both anarchic and lethal, where murder was so common it caused no comment. Indeed, Cesare was suspected of most deaths by poison and strangulation, for

he had about him famed doctors and mercenaries, as
well as engineers and painters. Yet the Borgias' hegemony, created as it was by playing off greater powers
than theirs, came to a rapid dénouement. Cesare and his
father appear to have contracted malaria during an
outbreak in August 1503. On 18 August in the evening
Alexander died. His body was profaned while it cor-
rupted in the sticky heat, and Cesare's downfall was certain when Cardinal della Rovere became Pope Julius II
after a short-lived and ineffective puppet implanted by
Cesare. Cesare was killed on 11 March 1507. Della
Rovere stayed Pope until February 1513. Leonardo
became the new architect and engineer of Louis XII of
France, the very King whose soldiers had ravaged Italy
and who had broken the giant clay model of his horse, a
project Leonardo had laboured on for sixteen years in
Milan.

Can Leonardo, always in straitened circumstances for
money, have remained untouched by the atmosphere in
which he lived? And who are we to judge him? He
showed a remarkable ability to survive civil wars and the
fall from grace of his patrons, who included a notorious
murderer, poisoner and lecher in the person of Cesare
Borgia, and a French King who completed the destruction of chivalry with iron cannon balls against the
cities of Italy. The patronage of such men may be fate,
but it was one which Michelangelo and Raphael largely
avoided. If, indeed, a Pope had commissioned da Vinci
to produce a burial shroud, it would have fitted the usage
of the age as closely as a silk glove upon the Pope's hand.
But which Pope might have used this artist?

The initiative for the commission may have first come
from Sixtus IV, the della Rovere who made his theological name with his treatise on the blood of Christ, which
he asserted was on the shroud owned by the Dukes of
Savoy. As we have seen he had strong motives for

elevating the status of a relic so useful against any suggestion of a non-Apollonian Christ, but at the same time a miraculous shroud would serve to stifle, at least in the uneducated mind, the increasing voice of humanism, so outstanding a feature of the Renaissance.

However, it may be that he was unable to impress Leonardo with the urgency of the task he had in mind. At this time, from the age of nineteen to thirty-two, Leonardo was in the position of the young hopeful. He was not to know his life would never realize the achievement of a Michelangelo; he had every reason to suppose he would be a great artist, rich and famous – but he was never to become that: well known yes, rich never, for Leonardo is one of those gifted men whose promise outruns their work.

By the time the Borgia Pope came to the papal seat, the position had changed markedly: Leonardo no longer had the promise of youth; indeed, he had achieved very little. Posterity would laud his genius, and wonder why such gifts had produced so little. We have seen that he became the employee of the Borgias, and then of the French King. The inescapable possibility is that any commission at this time would be welcome. Furthermore, the unprincipled Borgia Pope and his son would not be above using blackmail. There is the fact of da Vinci's pederasty, sodomy the charge, in 1476; he was not so much acquitted as let off, with the ever present proviso that the accusation could be revived, and re-examination made.

The other pertinent point to observe is that the interests of the Papacy have a way of making the politics of Popes very similar. The need for a Pope to keep the Church powerful is the same whether he is a della Rovere or a Borgia. In other words, the reasons which may have led Sixtus to approach Leonardo would also apply to Alexander. Timing and motive fits these Popes, but intriguing as this possibility was, as a hypothesis it required the demonstration that da Vinci had the skill to make the Turin image. Will an analysis of his abilities and his life survive such an objective test?

Despite his ability, or perhaps because of it, Leonardo never achieved the wealth that reasonably was his. The della Roveres and Borgias spent more on their fineries than Leonardo did during his whole life. Even his friendship with kings brought him no more than the modest house near Amboise, referred to as Cloux in many of his biographers' works. It is in fact Clos-Lucé, where there is now a museum of his engineering plans. The house at Cloux was the residence of Francis I of France, the king who went to Chambéry to venerate the shroud in 1511. By one of those coincidences, though an understandable one if our hypothesis is correct, Cloux was owned by the King's mother when he was a child; she was Louise, a daughter of the family of the Dukes of Savoy, the very family who exposited the shroud. This family did well out of the shroud, many, many more times the value of Cloux – which was not, it is interesting to note, Leonardo's to bequeath. Money problems had dogged him all his life.

He lived simply, almost to the point of poverty, listing his domestic utensils in his notebooks: '. . . one small candlestick . . . three pairs of sheets of four widths each . . . two towels . . . one basin . . .[31] He had also to find the money for the tools and the materials of his trade, pens for ruling, ruler, varnish, a very sharp knife, a piece of tapestry, book of white paper, charcoal,[32] and he specifically mentions a debt 'for the cloth'.[33]

This struggle against material deprivation, the total dependence upon patronage in order to practise his art, springs out from these melancholy, homely lists, as if demanding a comparison with the debauched lives of the della Rovere Popes and Cardinals who thought nothing of spending more on a banquet than ever Leonardo commanded for months of his existence, men who in high office behaved with such disregard of wealth that they gave courtesans silk slippers festooned with pearls.

That there was much anguish in this brilliant man's life there can be no doubt. His notebooks contain strange cryptic statements, for example, 'Alas! whom do I see? The Saviour crucified again?'[34] Certainly he could not speak out freely. He could not be sure of proving what he said, and no doubt the work was done *in camera*. In an age when Popes tortured and kings burned, a false word would threaten not only his livelihood but his very life.

This complex man ended his days on 2 May 1519. He died apparently disenchanted with his art, an anguish explained by the Vice-General of the Carmelite monks as stemming from a preoccupation with mathematics, yet this suggestion dates from 1501, a year before the celebrated exposition of the shroud at Chambéry.[35]

Leonardo's distaste is more likely to have come from a more disreputable reason if our thesis is correct, that da Vinci had created a shroud, had realized what was likely to come of it, and had been powerless to alter the course of events. Disenchantment is understandable; especially so, perhaps, when the visiting Carmelite wishes to discuss a picture of the infant Christ, near a basket of flax – from which linen is made.

We also find in his notebooks, which were composed in the last ten or fifteen years of his life, an entry on flax and death:

Flax is dedicated to death and human corruption: to death by the lakes with nets for birds beasts and fishes: to corruption by the linen cloths in which the dead are wrapped when they are buried, for in these cloths they suffer corruption.[36]

He poignantly observes:

Call not that riches which may be lost . . . As for property and material wealth, these you should ever hold in fear; full often they leave their possessor in ignominy, mocked at for having lost possession of them.[37]

Are these soulful observations general, or are they specifically related to a commission? The question has weight because his notebooks refer to past (such as the Milan Horse for Sforza) and future projects.

There is, then, evidence of anguish, even despair in Leonardo's final years. Having gleaned so much from his notebooks, I had hoped that even more detail would emerge to either prove or disprove the notion of his being the author of the shroud. As we shall see, the evidence is persuasive, even though some of his notebooks have been lost. More disturbing, some in the Vatican Library are not even authentic.

McCurdy[38] suggests that on Leonardo's death his notebooks passed to Francesco Melzi. This is supported by what we know of Leonardo's will, for he bequeathed to Melzi all his books and much else besides. Melzi died in 1570, and the break-up of the collection began, particularly when a tutor of the Melzi family took thirteen volumes of the notebooks to Florence to try to sell them to the Grand Duke, but nothing came of this, because the Duke died. The tutor, Gavardi de Asola, tried other avenues, but in the end returned to Milan in 1587, where Dr Orazio Melzi made him a present of the thirteen volumes. Indeed, Orazio allowed other people to filch the manuscripts and memorabilia of da Vinci from the Melzi villa in Vaprio, where much material was left neglected in an attic. Some volumes found their way as a gift to the Barnabite Order of Monks, of which a portion went to the King of Spain, Philip II; others went to

Cardinal Borromeo who founded the Ambrosian Library. However, two volumes have disappeared from history altogether: one went to Joseph Smith, English Consul at Venice, but was not traced further, while the other was given, either directly by Melzi or his agent, to Charles Emmanuel, Duke of Savoy! This manuscript, with unknown contents, has also vanished. Given da Vinci's penchant for writing about what he had done, as in the case of the bronze horse, with detailed and meticulous accounts, there is every reason to suppose he would have given a full account of his creation of the shroud. That by a sheer fluke one of his notebooks should have passed to the Duke of Savoy is difficult to believe, and then for it to vanish of its own accord strains credulity. The disappearance is further confused by conjectures, as McCurdy relates, of its being destroyed, 'perhaps burnt in one of the fires which occurred in the Royal Library at Turin in 1667 or 1679'. Civil discord apart, the Savoys have a remarkable propensity for fires, there being a similar spate of burnings in the late fifteenth century, and it may be speculated that perhaps during these conflagrations the Lirey linen was destroyed.

When manuscripts are lost in attics, we can reasonably suppose no more sinister reason than the disorder of time, the many mishaps of everyday life, but when manuscripts are housed in libraries and unaccountably disappear, with no one in control of those libraries ever once crying theft, a small suspicion is perhaps both rational and prudent. It is therefore disquieting to learn from McCurdy that the Vatican manuscripts are copies, that is, not in da Vinci's own handwriting; indeed, less than a quarter of the authentic da Vinci notes tally with the Vatican's collection. Facing these facts, McCurdy concedes 'some of the manuscripts have now vanished'.[39] Furthermore, we do know that manuscripts written by da Vinci in his own hand in mirror writing certainly disappeared while in the possession of an unidentified Milanese painter. These, as McCurdy points out, are very unlikely to be the same as the Vatican manuscripts.[40]

Masterpiece

Current studies show that the image was probably made with Venetian red powder or chalk, but the 'blood' was painted with a red pigment in tempera. The figure is tall, handsome and muscular, like da Vinci himself, rendered with great anatomical accuracy, unmistakably Renaissance rather than Byzantine or Gothic. This figure gives a powerful image even when the negative of a photograph of the Turin Shroud is made. Did da Vinci have the skill to do this work?

The use of red chalk or pastel of a Venetian type, with iron oxide in it, was a Renaissance invention – several authorities credit Leonardo with its first use, for he was well known for being, as A. E. Popham, Keeper of Prints and Drawings at the British Museum notes: 'an innovator in the technical means of drawing as well as of painting'.[41] Popham further observes that, towards the end of his life, Leonardo showed he had a grasp quite unique in using chalks on rough paper, 'almost with the effect of fine stippling. But in spite of the absence of definition, there is no lack of design or structure in such drawings.' This is a perfect description of the technical features of the image on the Turin Shroud.

Popham observes that Leonardo, in the anatomy notes in the library at Windsor Castle, is thinking of writing a book on human anatomy as early as 2 April 1489, while his studies on light and shade, now in the Institute de France, are dated in da Vinci's own hand, 23 April 1490. Da Vinci is certainly considering some important work, for he writes, 'I would know how much one increases when raising oneself on tiptoe.'[42] The remarkable thing is that the Turin Shroud shows a standing man with feet pointed down, as if on tiptoe. We further know that da Vinci was absorbed in studies of Christ's head (he did one in 1495, now in Brera, Milan), light and shade, and male human figure work. He was searching for ideal proportions and seems to have arrived at some: 'from the chin to the top of the head is an eighth part [of the height of a man], and 'the breadth across the shoulders a fourth part'.[43] The Turin image has these proportions, allowing for the difficulty in measuring proportions of a photograph. We know that da Vinci saw his own body as an important guide, 'take careful note of that part in yourself which is most misshapen [otherwise what you draw] will be the same and devoid of grace', and the only sure way of making good paintings or drawings was 'to work from nature, he who has not much knowledge of this often makes very great mistakes through relying too much upon his own skill, and not having recourse to the imitation of nature'.[44]

We are told by Vasari and other biographers[45] that Leonardo was taller, handsomer and stronger than most men; indeed Giovanni da Gavina, a contemporary, says, 'beautiful in person and aspect, Leonardo was well proportioned and graceful.' He also mentions that Leonardo wore a short cloak when it was the fashion to wear long ones. Was this penury, or was he showing off his beautiful legs? What we do know is that the Turin image is of a man in the prime of life, with long shapely legs, a powerful chest and a handsome dignified face.

When he was twenty-six, in 1478, Leonardo made a study of John the Baptist, heightened with white on blue paper, which is now in Windsor Castle. The model was very likely one of his friends, but the figure is very similar to that of the Turin Shroud image, and has a right arm from shoulder to finger tip as long as the right leg from hip to ankle, which is a distortion used to produce a dramatic effect. Curiously, the Turin figure has one arm much longer than the other, the right.

There can be little doubt that da Vinci had the requisite skill, the motive and the opportunity to take up a commission first broached by the della Rovere Pope, and consummated by a Borgia Pope. But how did he do it, if he used himself as a model? Again, the answer is found in his notes, but before we come to that there is the fascination of crucifixion details also found there.

The Gospel stories mention a crown of thorns, and a reed in Jesus' hand. In his 320 drawings, da Vinci's notebooks reveal only about a dozen of a botanical nature, three of them deal with brambles and three are studies of bullrushes or reeds.[46] Some of these were done in red chalk. One would have expected to find even more allusions to the theme, but as we have observed, many of da Vinci's notebooks have disappeared in mysterious circumstances, while the Vatican collection is at best suspect. The thorn and reed studies, though, are unquestionably his. The surmise is reasonable that these indicate his preoccupation with crucifixion details. What other material was lost? In this regard the carrying of the so-called lance that speared Christ on the cross by the della Rovere Pope's nephew in a procession, mentioned earlier, is intriguing. The Romans would have used a *pilum*, which would not make the leaf-shaped mark found on the Turin Shroud. By della Rovere's time, spears were of the ovaloid type in cross section and so were Saracen spears. Da Vinci kept to this contemporary pattern in his depiction of the spear wound – not the historical one.

How could da Vinci have used himself as the model? We know he fully understood the effect of viewing objects through linen, for he makes a specific reference to it: 'there is a fourth [kind of light] which passes through substances of the degree of transparency of linen or paper or suchlike things',[47] but he also knew about the use of mirrors, and waxes very enthusiastic about them, 'the mirror is master of painters'.[48] He actually wrote in such a way that one can only read the words by viewing them in a mirror. If we add all these factors together, we may reasonably conclude that Leonardo had the technical means for the commission. His knowledge of anatomy, of course, would not allow him to put nail marks in the centre of the hands; he had seen too much blood and carnage with the Borgias to be ingenuous to that extent. Yet he had to show the feet wounded, and for this he stood on tiptoe. But verisimilitude has its limits. Not too much blood, otherwise one cannot see the shape of the image. Apply a *flagellum* with pigment on the thongs and barbs, gently, to oneself. View the result in a mirror. Artistically arrange until the right pattern is achieved. The rictus of death, which would be present if the image were a photographic negative of a tortured man, is not there on the Turin Shroud.

The scenario seems to ring true: da Vinci has been asked to create a work of art which will make the viewer believe he or she is seeing the crucified Christ. A sombre and magnificent theme for the faithful to gaze upon. More than one observer, Popes among them, have remarked on the gravity of this man's face, and it is not the face of a tortured human being. Is it more like a man intent on a great work?

In the period 1490–1500 da Vinci did much travelling; a shroud commission would be convenient during these journeys for, unlike the Bronze Horse which Michelangelo teased him about – sixteen years and still not finished – the shroud linen could be wrapped and carried. Perhaps this is one of the reasons why a legend of a folded man-dilion grew up.

Linen itself was easily obtained in the textile trade, imported, then as now, to Milan. But with a desire for authenticity, the patron, or the artist himself, demanded linen from the Holy Land. Not difficult to arrange, since there was considerable trade with the Turks who controlled it (we might recall that a sultan sent della Rovere, the Cardinal, the 'true' spear that lanced the Christ of Golgotha). This attention to biblical detail would explain the pollen, claimed to be from the Dead Sea area and from Turkey, found on the Turin Shroud. These 'pollen' findings are challenged by Nickell, but given the amount of trade between the Middle East and Italy, including Syria and Egypt, it would be surprising if there were no Middle East pollen in the linen. The quality, then, of the linen itself, is merely a reflection of the social and economic conditions of Leonardo's Italy.

Curiously, the 'blood' on the Turin man appears to have been worked by a hand less gifted than the executioner of the rest of the image.

One arm is longer than the other, and we have already read how Leonardo was well aware of magnifying imperfections in oneself, yet he himself had trouble with his right arm, though we only know of this certainly towards the end of his life. The deformity, or rather, strange proportion of the arm in the Turin man recollects the work he did on the young John the Baptist, which we have already discussed. Canonical measurement and proportion is one thing, but artistic impact is another. John the Baptist leaps into life with his impossible dimensions. No one knew better than Leonardo how to use the workings of the eye to create effect. The objective opinion is that the arm is too long but the visual impression is perfect.

And why the negative image? The body of Jesus wrapped in the long linen was held to have impressed itself by image upon a cloth, just as the legend of Veronica's veil attests. But scores of artists merely painted a face, a mandilion, of often indifferent artistry, as we have seen. It was left to Leonardo, we suggest, to work the reasoning through. Whatever was impressed would not have the delineation of outline, for through 'sweat' such effects are not made. What would such an impression be? Da Vinci would have discovered very early on that in any case such an impression would be distorted. But what do you obtain when a body lies on a cloth? You can do it yourself; lie wet upon a sheet and see what you leave behind you. A series of fast fading wet patches, revealing points of contact, the general dimensions of the body, nothing more. What if you stand in front of a linen screen and view yourself in a mirror? There now comes into play the possibility of art; of using lights, of building up a non-directional image, just like a shadow, like the imprint of the vapours (as we would imagine) from a man recently dead. We have seen that Leonardo did many of his finest works using chalks and protecting a work with varnish. The most plausible material to be used for the image, as we have discussed, is Venetian red, a ferric oxide material. It can be applied as powder, chalk, or in suspension, perhaps with a vegetable dye. Such application will not leave directional strokes but will in time gradually come away from the fabric unless varnished. And we know that the shroud has had at least one dousing after a fire, so the natural process of ageing has been aggravated by water.

Leonardo paints dark those parts nearest to him, for that would be the result of contact, and light those far from him. This is the recipe of a photographic image. This is why the Turin Shroud photographs better as a negative than a positive. Also the inversion of left with right occurs, as it does in a photographic negative. However, the laws of light which control the dark and light in the original, and the corresponding light and dark of the image made by the artist or photographer, are the same. The technical problems which da Vinci had to solve were so brilliantly achieved that the negatives of some of his work are powerful works of art, with no loss of structure. That he understood the inverse relationships of shadow and light technically is seen from his work, but he also clearly understood the process. 'Among bodies in varying degrees of darkness deprived of the same light, there will be the same proportion between their shadows as there is between their natural degrees of darkness.'[49]

The painting process is basically the transformation of a 3-D image into a 2-D one, one which da Vinci is a master of, but what of the reverse process? The sculptor Leo Vala[50] has made 3-D images of the Turin Shroud face and they are quite good. This has been cited by some proponents of the shroud's authenticity as proof positive, but in this they are hoist with their own petard, since they appear unaware that Leo Vala did his first test on a painting, and by one of those strange coincidences, the painting he chose was da Vinci's *Mona Lisa*, who was young, very much alive, and the only mystery about her is her smile.

We have a rational hypothesis, with objective artistic techniques, which *does* explain the image in all its detail. We may, therefore, be allowed to use the 'flashback' technique: Leonardo is in his studio, a coarse screen to his left, behind which is a mirror, full-length. He can see himself in this mirror through the screen, and so can control the lighting in precisely the way he wishes to bring out relief and modelling, while to his right is the Turin linen. He studies, he applies his pigment and then, in a sudden inspiration, he stands on tiptoe, a wonderful way of revealing the feet of a man crucified. Later, he has two mirrors on his left, this time one forward and one rearwards; the screen is near the rear one. He can see his back in the mirror in front. Again, he stands on tiptoe, high right foot partially behind his left. There is the whole sole visible apart from the toes. He copies.

Today this work of art has been reproduced several
million times, and is on sale, or has been, in virtually
every bookshop and church.

Motives

Francesco della Rovere, in recruiting Leonardo, may
have been paying spiritual debts to Louis and Anne and
their descendants, for they had been kind to him when
he was no more than a friar. As Pope, he could afford to
be generous, self-seeking and prudent, all at the same
time. The notebook evidence suggests the work was
completed during the Borgia Pope Alexander's reign.
And what of the very young Duke of Savoy, Amadeus?
He laboured more than three decades to make a sanctuary for a true relic of the passion. If his Lirey Shroud
burned, would that not mean to him that it could not
have been genuine and its demise was a sign that the
way was open for the true shroud, coming from the Pope?
Perhaps, for in those superstitious and anarchic times,
the mind grasped at wonders. We will probably never
know if it was chicanery, or credulity heated by piety, or
a kind of spiritual pride, which led to the elevation of a
work of art by Leonardo, if indeed it were he, to relic
status. It was probably a mixture of all these factors.

Yet there is good reason for imputing different motives.
The Popes involved in this Turin Shroud were often at
loggerheads, especially since would-be Popes often fought
with the incumbent. It seems unlikely that there would
be a pious agreement about a gift of relic status to a
forgery. Or does it? For these men, despite their different
alliances, had one thing in common, the need to elevate
and maintain papal power. Nothing could be allowed to
diminish that. Could it be that in the Vatican there
resided the skull, Caput 58? A relic potentially fatal to
papal claims of spiritual hegemony? The shroud image

burst on the world after the murder of the Cathar women and the destruction of their Templar cousins, and we have seen that there are good reasons for entertaining the hypothesis that they believed they had the skull bones of Jesus Christ, which were the bones of a small woman.

This chain of connections, some tenuous, others flagrant, yet others strong as steel, entwine the Popes of the shroud period by a thread of urgent common purpose. Any question of Christ's non-resurrection or gender must never be allowed to surface. Indeed, active steps should be taken to prove the opposite: Jesus was a tall muscular Christ, of manly proportions. They even had the burial shroud to prove it.

The least one could say about the Turin image was its convenient emergence, an ideal 'relic' to support the claims of Rome in an increasingly sceptical age. In this welter of possibilities, there was one solid reassurance: whoever greeted Mary the Virgin and Mary Magdalene on Easter Sunday, it was not a six-foot homosexual Italian painter. Whom, then, did they see?

At this stage of my investigation I had no possibility of answering a question which had sooner or later to be faced, but it did occur to me that irrespective of my hypothesis on the gender of Jesus Christ, the Popes of the Renaissance showed a remarkable potency in controlling such gifted men as Leonardo. It seemed that there were more ways of control than merely threatening to burn a person to death. Galileo was broken, worn out by the inquisitorial process, while Giadarno Bruno was actually burned. The Catholic Church was terrified of science because, being an unnatural religion, unlike the Great Goddess cults, it had difficulty in keeping up with change. When Galileo asserted the sun was the centre of the solar system, not the earth, the Papacy was alarmed, because in their theology the earth had to be the centre. It is probably worth noting that wherever the Pope had secular power, science was held back, a fact conveniently ignored by many who cite the Papacy's munificent patronage of the Arts, which they confuse with the struggling hopes of rational men who were finding the courage and the methods to question dogmas, even through the fog of terror imposed by the Inquisition. It is an age-old practice of those who would retain power to pretty up their policies for consumption, so we have the melancholy spectacle of the best artists in Italy using their gifts to underpin dogmas, such as Original Sin, with their beautiful renderings of Eve bringing about Adam's downfall. Furthermore, if my analysis of da Vinci is correct, the use of artists could result in stupefying heights of mendacity and fraud. Perhaps the nearest equivalent we have today, apart from politics, is the advertising industry.

More specifically, an examination of the Turin Shroud reveals its fraudulent nature, and it seems plausible that da Vinci created it; but the authorship is incidental, the main point being that the shroud elevated superstition to a holy art form, and impressed an image of a six-foot muscular Saviour on the laity and clergy, which was taken up by lesser painters and sculptors of the Renaissance in their chocolate-box images of Christ. One wonders what effect these images had on young women in those hives of nunneries.

The Turin image perhaps would not be so provocative if there was no evidence that the physical Christ was a woman, and a small one at that. That hypothesis came out of material relating to the suppression of the Templars, and the connecting organization between Turin and that débâcle is the Papacy, the intrigue and terror being provided by the Inquisition.

I felt, then, that the hypothesis that the Popes really did fear the implications of a skull taken from the Templars had been strengthened. It appeared to provide a useful research tool, to pry into unopened caskets, as it were. The natural question now seemed to be, did the Popes who were implicated in the Turin fraud do anything else against women? The answer is dramatic and cruel, for these self-same Popes also promulgated in Bulls the decrees against women concerned with witchcraft. These decrees were to result in female gendercide.

Shaven Women

Misogyny can account for the initial policies of the Roman Church, but misogyny alone cannot explain what happened to the Cathars, the Templars, and the reason for the fraud of the Turin Shroud: and, I feel, it cannot explain the intransigence of the Roman Catholic Church today on the question of ordination of women. To understand what happened to the Cathars is, I suggest, to understand what happened afterwards to the Templars, and why the male image of Christ was made miraculous at Turin. Essentially, the muted suspicions of Rome about the female flavour of religion in the south of France flared into terror when the Papacy heard reports, probably from St Dominic himself, that the Cathars possessed a relic of a small-boned woman. It seems possible that the records have been so truncated and censored that only the Church's history of that period remains, but the existence of Caput 58 – the provocative witches' number 58 (thirteen by addition), a pious reference to Yeshu's (a Jewish variant on the name Jesus) own coven – shook the Papacy. For this could be proof of the non-resurrection of Jesus Christ, and, moreover, the proof that changed Christ's gender.

Partial proof can be taken from the scene of history: shortly after the Turin exposition the Church began to lose its power; for centuries since then it has been unable to command armies of suppression, and has had to suffer a diminution, much of it through its own doing. But there was to be one further development of the quantum

change of outlook from Rome on women, for having set
up the Inquisition to destroy evidence of the femality of
Christ, Rome was to use it without let on women in a
gendercide. If my hypothesis so far was correct, then
there should be in that onslaught on women evidence
that mere misogyny had been transcended: that a fear of
the truth of what the skull represented had taken over
the minds of Popes and Inquisitors. But I was unprepared for the new dimension of horror that I was to
uncover.

The attack against women took place in the guise of
witch hunts, and originated from the Papacy itself. It
was directed against any woman, high or low born, whose
religious observances differed from those imposed by the
Popes, no matter how loving and kind she might be, how
self-effacing, how chaste, how energetic in works for the
poor and the defenceless. The concepts for the attack are
historically inseparable from the destruction of the
Cathars and the setting up of the Inquisition, the ruin-
ation of the Templars and the veneration of a fraudulent
image exposited in Turin. The instruments of the terror
were directives issued by Popes, called Bulls. The Bull of
John XII was issued in 1320. John knew of the murder
of the Templar Grand Master in 1307, and was active in
mopping-up operations against the Templars. The Bull
of Innocent VIII, which followed in 1484, was more
stringent and far-reaching than John's. Innocent was a
close affiliate, even puppet, of the della Rovere family,
whose first Papacy was that of Sixtus IV, self-confessed
witness of the shroud before the Turin version existed.
The Bull of Alexander VI in 1501 came from the Borgia
Pope, who saw to it that the shroud image as we know it
today was exposited with great pomp in 1502. His own
son was raping young girls in Capua in the same year
that Sixtus signed a document leading to the humiliation,
degradation, torture and death of uncountable thousands

of women, young and old. The Bull of Alexander was dutifully enacted in the field, as it were, by another della Rovere Pope, Julius II, and apparently another twist of the screw was thought necessary, since another bill of torture was issued by Leo X in 1521. From scented seats, beneath perfumed canopies, these men put their often-kissed rings to the seal of documents as infamous as the worst that can be cited in human history, those from our own century included.

I suggest that this public decrying of 'witchcraft' had a deeper motive: the total destruction of any vestige of the female orientated religion, which I refer to as the Church of Mary Magdalene.

Even so, the Papacy had difficulty in trying to justify their new crusade on theological grounds, and their confusion is patent. As usual they sifted through the Old Testament to find a peg on which to hang their policies, and appeared to have found one in Exodus (22:18), where those 'holy' words, 'Thou shalt not suffer a witch to live' are enshrined in the name of a religion of love. But there were other obstacles to overcome. A witch to the ancient Jews might not be the same as a witch in southern France, millennia later. A second objection was that Christ's life was a repudiation of much of the Old Testament Law, stoning women to death for adultery, for one thing. But at the centre of the theological argument was the passage in John, 'If a man does not abide in me, he is cast forth as a branch and withers. And the branches are gathered, thrown into the fire and burned' (John 15:6). The jurist Bartolo cited this saying in 1350, as support for extreme measures against witches.[1] But the way it was used by the Papacy meant unquestioning belief in the Catholic Church. However, some factions, such as the Copts, the Church of Mary Magdalene, the eastern Orthodox Church and the Protestants, not to mention the so-called heretics, found this centrist assumption unacceptable, as their departure from it reveals. Rome takes its cue from the statement, attributed to Jesus, 'Blessed are you Simon bar-Jona . . . I will give you the keys of the kingdom of heaven' (Matt. 16:17-19). Why should anyone believe that this was said by Jesus, Yeshu bar-Joseph? My point is rather a simple one: the unarguably authentic sayings of Jesus do not suggest the foundations of a monolithic Church, nor yet the justification of torturing and killing people.

The Pope's political move against women was codified in a document, *Malleus Maleficarum*.[2] It was first printed in 1486, and in this form was the work of two Dominicans, Heinrich Kramer (1430–1505) and Jakob Sprenger (1436–95), though the manuscript was that of Kramer, who began writing and circulating his ideas from 1474. *Malleus* (hammer) went into sixteen German, eleven French, two Italian, and several English editions. It was used on the bench of virtually every inquisitorial tribunal for nearly two-and-a-half centuries, and was the judicial tool, the hammer, used for the destruction of hundreds of thousands of women.

Kramer, a German, was made Prior of the Dominican house in Schlettstadt, near Strasbourg, when still a very young man. A brilliant scholar, he quickly earned the titles of Preacher General and Master of Sacred Theology, and by 1474 he was appointed Inquisitor (for the Tyrol, Salzburg, Bohemia and Moravia). He also gained preferment as Spiritual Director of the Church in Salzburg, being highly thought of by the Archbishop. Sprenger's *curriculum vitae* is remarkably similar. Another *wunderkind*, he joined the Dominicans in his middle teens, but by 30 June 1468, when he was thirty-two, he was already Master of Theology, and on this date was made Dean of the Faculty of Theology of Cologne. A year later the Dominican General, Cassetta, appointed him Inquisitor for Mainz, Treves and Cologne.

These two young men, academically brilliant, very energetic and zealful, collaborated in the production of their masterwork, the *Malleus*. Its contents were informed by a fear, fascination and hatred of women, which today we can recognize as sexual longings transformed into sadism. Or were these two men in fact animated by a fear of something else? In their undoubted sincerity, their allegiance to Rome, was there not also a fear that the faith they lived by was under attack not by mere heresy, but by something deeper which struck at the very institutional roots of the Church? Perhaps, but we may note that these two men were dependent on the institution of the Church for everything they had, their learning, their position, their power and their faith. Against that, mere sexual frustration is small beer.

However, both Sprenger and Kramer might have passed their lives as provincial clerics had it not been for the Bull of Innocent VIII, whom we met earlier as the creature of Cardinal Guiliano della Rovere, who himself became Pope Julius II. Innocent, on 9 December 1484, speaking as Vicar of Christ to the City of Rome and the World, proclaimed the papal *Summis desiderantes affectibus*, which deplored witchcraft, and identified Sprenger and Kramer as Chief Inquisitors to destroy it. He called on all bishops to publish the Bull, and to render all help to the Inquisitors, even to provide the necessary muscle from local militia, magistrates and police. The Bull spells out unambiguously that anyone interfering with the Inquisitors faced excommunication and more terrible penalties, and that these processes would be without right of appeal

By the bitterest of ironies, the man who was to cause the deaths of millions was guilty of worse crimes than those which the Inquisitors were seeking to drag out of innocent people, by means of torture. Innocent VIII broke his vows of celibacy by having his mistress live with him. He had two children by her: one, a boy, was married into the Medici family; the other, a girl, was married to his treasurer. In his last months he sucked at the breasts of a wet nurse in a vain attempt to keep alive; even blood transfusions from young boys were tried, to no avail – except that the donors died.

The Bull of Innocent VIII is evil, but probably less terrible than the way in which it was translated into a living hell by quasi-judicial means, given form and substance by the two Dominican witch hunters. In their *Malleus* they speak of women in almost crazed terms. A woman is a 'delectable detriment' and a 'necessary evil', and when a woman is alone, according to them, 'she thinks of evil'. These were words from the flower of Dominican intellectuals, the preaching Order of the Church – but an Order which had been humiliated by the wits and real learning of the priestesses of the Languedoc. These hatreds were then converted into a process for revenge, for the *Malleus* is a practical book of recipes for degradation and cruelty. The *Malleus* advocates lying to a prisoner: 'for a time the promise [of freedom] made to the witch sentenced to imprisonment is to be kept, but that after a time she should be burned.' Many 'witches', unable to bear torture further, tried to commit suicide; the *Malleus* advises that guards should 'constantly be with the prisoner', so that she would not have the opportunity of putting an end to her misery. Neither youth nor pregnancy would save a woman. Girls of thirteen and fourteen were burned to death after prolonged torture, pregnant women racked until they died. That women were the target is proved by the victims, but in *Malleus Maleficarum* the learned Dominicans even demean their own scholarship with spurious derivations of the Latin *femina*, woman, saying that the word came from *fe* meaning faith, and *minus*, less.

The other pertinent point about the records of the

trials these priests held is that the documents were penned by clerks controlled by the Inquisitors. This is an unpalatable fact, for it means that we are left only with the persecutors' view of the matter, for the Inquisitors burned their victims' records as well as their bodies.

My suspicion that 'witchcraft' as such did not exist, but was invented by the Papacy in collusion with the Dominicans (and later the Jesuits) is confirmed by de Cauzon, a Roman Catholic, who avers that the Inquisition 'had invented the crime of witchcraft and ... relied on torture as the means of proving it.'

The Dominicans roamed southern France for decades, with spectacular trials at Toulouse and Narbonne. The procedure was oiled by allowing the French King to partake in the confiscated property. Lord Acton, in his letters to Mary Galdstone, affirms the culpability of the Papacy: 'No deduction can be made from her [he means the Church, which had mysteriously appropriated the female pronoun as far back as Eusebius] evil doing towards unbelievers ... and witches. Here her responsibility is more undivided, her initiative and achievement more complete.' Acton has his own irony in using a word like achievement, but there is an irony he was unaware of in the word 'complete', for that ultimate was apparently the aim of the papal policy: extirpation of any trace of the female centre of their religion.

These infamous policies led to the destruction of 30,000 men, women and children in Spain in 150 years, but the witch hunts went on there for 300 years. The German figure is between 100,000 and 200,000, with France having a similar number. In England the figure is about 1,000, primarily because the Inquisition was never allowed to 'process' the English countryside. In America, the figure is below a hundred and centred on a Protestant hysteria, but the theology was Roman. In total then, we know of a quarter of a million immolations, which does not include those who died under torture, who committed suicide, or those relatives who went mad and died by seeing their loved ones mangled before their very eyes. Also, the records on both Catholic and Protestant sides have been subject to censoring, so the figure has in reality no upward limit, save that of the technical efficiency of the killers. It would seem that a conservative estimate is that of the total dead, at least a million were women, and that the majority of this number were murdered by the Holy Office, by the Inquisitors.

Their technique was peripatetic: the Dominicans would travel around France from one Dominican monastery or convent to the next, threaten the local magistrates (if needed, since there was money in this processing, as they called it) into compliance, and then set about mangling innocent people, and then killing them. In the hundreds of trials cited by historian Hope Robbins there is a curious feature: the accused are always guilty, and the accused never escape. Without material exception, they are all murdered, by burning usually, but a great many died under questioning. The priest would sit watching these women being mangled, their breasts torn by spikes on walls, their eyes gouged out, their private parts burned, their bones squashed, and would ask the questions; the answers would be written down when what was wanted was heard. Then, after saying Mass, these priests, with papal blessing, would go on to the next village. It was a brilliant exercise in terror, control and murder, and it was organized by, sanctioned by, and blessed by a succession of Popes. It is difficult to see any other motive but doctrinal.

Both Old and Young

The hypothesis of doctrinal motive is certainly strengthened by the fact that papal authority sanctioned the oppression and, in effect, gave *imprimatur* to the hand-book which the women-killers used, the *Malleus*. It is this book which is responsible for the similarity of the trials, as they are called. Women were arrested, shaved, examined for 'devil's marks', a process which always gave positive results, then further tortured until they confessed (though by this time many already had) to weird practices of a set order invented by Sprenger and Kramer. As a result of their confessions, these women were burned.

As noted earlier, no one escaped. If a woman stead-fastly denied the obscenities attributed to her, she was burned as obdurate; if she confessed, she was given absolution and then burned. But what is remarkable is the pattern of events; and this question arises: why did the Inquisition create the vile charges they used again and again? Can we discern a motive for their actions in the actual form of accusation?

As I began to examine the transcripts of the trials a two-fold emotion almost choked me. First, the revulsion at such cruelty, and second, a growing, even dangerous, feeling that the charges produced by the Inquisition were a ghastly parody of the arrest, trial and crucifixion of Jesus Christ. Of the former emotion, that is perhaps a personal response, subjective in its very nature, but the second could have arisen by recognizing an objective pattern; if so, it should be demonstrable.

A woman would be arrested, then stripped, as required by the Dominican authors of the *Malleus*; this was done so brutally it was a torture itself. As one observer noted, the disrobing was done 'without regard to humanity or honour, not only to men, but to women and virgins, the most virtuous and chaste . . . even to their pudenda.' The Inquisition must have known that their Lord and Saviour had been stripped.

The woman was then shaved on every part of her body, the reason being, according to Sprenger and

Kramer, to discover magic amulets or charms. They even averred that the devil was able to hide in a woman's hair. There are two themes here. The magic power of hair is certainly a part of the Great Goddess tradition, for acolytes of the Goddess were often shaved voluntarily; this is a tradition similar to the shaving of nuns' heads. The second concerns the devil's marks, 'even in the secret parts not to be named', which had the remarkable property of giving no blood on mutilation, and of being insensitive to pain. The marks were the invention of the Inquisition, but provided a means of identifying virtually any woman as a witch, as I was, sorrowfully, to come to understand. But why had the Inquisition chosen this particular cruelty, apart from its certainty of a positive result?

It was with more than a little hesitancy that I approached this question, for it meant entering the minds, however transiently, of men who had coldbloodedly set out to destroy thousands of women, piecemeal. First, it is a matter of common knowledge through observation in physiology that heightened states of terror and hysteria induce lack of sensitivity in parts of the body. Second, there are parts of the body which are insensitive to pricking, on the back for example. Third, terror induces blanching of the skin, because the blood supply is withdrawn to deeper organs. Fourth, healthy young women clot very easily, while old women do not bleed well anyway. Add all these factors together, and the torturer can be certain that if he applies his bradawl sufficiently often, he will, after say a hundred or so deep, bleeding lacerations of breasts, thighs and even more delicate areas, come across one which will not bleed. One is sufficient.

At this doleful point it occurred to me that the Inquisitors must surely have been aware that the sport they were having with women for hours on end bore a staggering similarity to the sport that the Roman soldiers, and the priests before them, were said to have had with Jesus Christ. Like Jesus, many of these tortured women would say nothing. I think the impressive point of this parallel was that it implied something odd about the inquisitorial mind. As religious historians they could not miss the parallel, which shows a remarkable indifference to Christian love. But suppose, as in the case of Kramer and Sprenger, that they were privy to some information given to them by Pope Innocent, the della Rovere puppet? Suppose they suspected they were dealing with defenceless creatures more like Jesus than anyone could dare to say?

If the aim was to bolster the obvious masculinity of the image of Christ so dear to the Papacy, then enemies of Christ had to be as unlike this tall, muscled, lustrous-haired God as possible. Indeed in a forged letter, the infamous letter of Lentulus, which figures very largely in papal claims of a perfect-bodied Christ (to which I will revert later) Christ is described as being without spot. The odd thing is that in suppressed copies of an 'apochryphal' writing of St John the Divine, we are told that he, John, when embracing Jesus – as in the Last Supper, a story also found in the canonical Gospels – is bewildered to find that parts of Christ's breast are hard, others soft. This would seem to suggest that Christ suffered from a skin affliction of some kind. Here we have a duality. The Popes, who probably knew about the real physicality of Christ, sought to destroy any belief in it by foisting on the Christian world the image of a male Christ with a perfect body, yet in the act of making the witches appear as unlike this image as possible (in seeking proof of their guilt by use of the 'pricking test' and other denigrating tortures) ironically the Inquisitors were straying very close to the historical truth. I am not suggesting that the rank and file Dominicans, as they ordered girls to be stripped and whipped, their bodies stretched and then pierced with iron points, knew of the fears of their Popes, or indeed of their superiors; they were devout and zealful, and like other black knights centuries later, would do exactly as they were told.

Provocatively, then, the Inquisitors chose the 'pricking test' as a criterion of witch-hood. As the bradawl was applied, sooner or later a devil's spot would be discovered. It was remarkably efficacious, which might have been sufficient a reason for the efficient Dominicans.

There are numerous accounts of women being sent half mad by the probe of steel into their bodies, but here is a less harrowing story, an account of what happened in an Ursuline convent, in Aix-en-Provence, the town which strongly claims to possess the authentic relics of Mary Magdalene. Here a young woman appeared to be infested with devils. The Inquisitor said to her, 'Is it true Madelaine [de Demandda] thou art a witch?' The girl confessed that a young priest, Father Gaufridi, 'had stolen her most beautiful Rose'. The Inquisitor kept at her for several months, and her persistent story eventually led to the long torture of the priest for over a year, until he was finally burned to death on 30 April 1611. Madeleine was seen as a victim, and though persecuted and imprisoned for many years, she lived to a ripe old age, but the Inquisition had got out of her confessions of witchcraft, and had even found devil's marks on her feet, and under her left breast. There were rationalists at the time who concluded that this girl had fallen in love with an older man, had had a carnal relationship with him, but as she could not reconcile her loss of innocence with the life of a nun, she had therefore blamed the priest. However, the Inquisition had forged ahead, proving the unbelievable by torture of the unprotected.

The devil's marks, then, appear to have been a convenient excuse for terrorizing women and proving that any one of them was a witch. The overtones of connection with Christ are there, but they are allusive rather than certain.

Fertility and a Kiss

Another common feature of the trials was to prove the witches' Sabat. Certainly, rural people did meet in forests and perform fertility rites. There was dancing before bonfires and no doubt some sexual frolics. It may be that a woman wore a dildo, or artifical lingam, for ritualistic penetration of acolytes, at least this idea is put forward as explaining the coolness of the generative organ of the so-called devil. However, these simple fertility rites were traduced by the Inquisition into events of child sacrifice and devil worship.

The Sabat also featured the *Osculum Obscenum*, the devil's kiss. This invention reveals Kramer and Sprenger at their most cunningly inventive. The kiss was an act of satanic love, for the witch was said to kiss the devil's anus. What is curious about this accusation, apart from its inventiveness, is that it has no conceivable place in any Goddess ceremony. The Great Goddess mysteries certainly involved a loving veneration of the generative organs, for it was argued that this was their due, since from them new life came. To a woman brought up on the down-to-earth, yet compellingly beautiful, ideas of the Great Goddess, anal kissing would be sacrilegious in a religious ceremony. Certainly, it may have been practised as a private domestic vice, but since the part was sterile, it could not be venerated. Furthermore, the confusion of apertures was hardly something most country folk might reasonably be expected to make. The Inquisition, then, is exposed as a factory of obscene ideas; they could have easily proved quasi-idolatry in members of the old religion, but they were not interested in that;

they invented their own crime, based on their own fantasy.

However, if the notion is entertained that the political motive behind the witch trials was to do as much dirt as possible to women whose religion was outside the Church of Rome, and then physically destroy them, the fantasy begins to make a chilling kind of sense. Judas Iscariot betrayed Christ with a kiss, as these women were made out to. But the connections with Gethsemane and the Sabat may go even deeper. If the Popes feared even the legend of a female Christ, and if there were people who had heard, however distortedly, the teachings of the Church of Mary Magdalene, then in the Pope's fight for survival, no infamy was too great to heap on the heads of these women. Certainly, a sincere though woman-hating cleric in the Dominican order could be induced to torture, with free conscience, women accused of doing something so evil as mocking Christ by kissing the devil. The act was obscene in itself, but it was also theologically loaded with the image of Judas, the great betrayer. Who but the Keepers of the Keys knew the real reason for the charge?

It seems, then, that the Inquisition had invented their own rituals, often with grotesque homosexual overtones. One begins to wonder about Sprenger and Kramer, both young, both gifted, both charged with almost superhuman energy. Were Sprenger and Kramer covering up a secret of their own? Possibly, but that would explain only the obscene kiss, not the shaving, not the looking for spots, or the swimming trials.

In swimming trials, women were ducked; if they drowned they were innocent, if they did not, they were witches. Is this a parody of baptism? And what of those 'familiars' that witches were supposed to have? Old ladies have pets in their loneliness, although most witches were young and nubile – still many girls have pet dogs and cats, doves and singing birds, though it must be admitted there is not a great fan club for toads. There is, however, abundant literature on animal totemism.

Certainly, many so-called witches knew the medicinal power of mixing herb extracts in oil and water, and so obtaining an ointment, but the crazed Inquisition charged that these sweet-smelling unguents were magic pessaries for flying, and others for killing. What little knowledge we have of real ointments used by 'witches' suggests they were indeed medicinal, though some produced deliria, and yet others may have had aphrodisiac effects.

That the Inquisitors should have been obsessed with flying and imputed this to special ointments again echoes the Gospels, for Mary Magdalene had anointed Christ with ointment, and he had later ascended into heaven. Even the hair motif is there, for Mary Magdalene washed Christ's feet with her tears, and dried them with her hair. It appears that the inclusion of Mary Magdalene into the embraceable figures of the Papacy was not accomplished without some difficulty.

Witches, too, were said to have a special witch's hat, although this seems to have been the headgear of women who worked on the land, rather than some ceremonial item. But the notion of a woman wearing headgear is itself interesting. Women had to cover their heads in church. Why? Paul insists they do, but again, why? The priestesses of the Great Goddess cult in ancient times wore veils. Is there here a recognition of that fact? And what of the crowning with thorns? Another clue to a distorted tradition?

The compelling conclusion appears to be that the inquisitorial mind had concocted a series of weird rituals which had no basis in fact. However, that this creative energy had a political or doctrinal impetus does fit the facts. What is so staggering is that they need not have done this. The rituals of the old Mother Goddess religion were heretical enough to warrant, in the eyes of Rome, suppression. The fascinating possibility emerges that Rome simply dare not charge people with practising Great Goddess rituals because they were, from Mary Magdalene's Church, so obviously Christian.

Rural adherents of the Great Goddess in France, Germany, England and elsewhere may have opted to recognize this, in repudiation of Rome. They may have seen in the crowning of thorns, not a barbaric act, but the fitting of a plait of rosebriars or other flowers. They may have seen in the scarlet cloak, the time-honoured idea of the redeeming power of blood, the figure of the Great Goddess herself. And the reed? The floral sceptre of the Great Goddess's sovereignty over all life – and death. If so, the ritual copulations were not done with a dildo, and one can only estimate how many country marriages were being sanctified in sacred groves in the forests.

Rome had a double problem with these adherents of the Great Goddess: some of them were undoubtedly more Christian than the Pope; while others had repudiated the Christian message as couched in dogmas from the Lateran, in favour of their old religion, and so had been denied the fulfilment by Christ of the Great Goddess truths.

The Church of Mary Magdalene, however, was not a centrist church, and in not being bolstered by soldiers and magistrates, was destroyed, though it took many centuries. If this reading of the persecutions of witches is correct, some of the original ideas from Mary Magdalene's mouth had survived even the Cathars' and the Templars' downfall.

The witch emerges as a Christ figure, as the Inquisition in their mania had made her, for in their attestation they treated her as a queen. In their description of her, they saw her as being speared by a cold object, wearing the red cloak of shame and lust; they cut off her hair as if to banish any idea of crowning, and they mocked her with their questions. The treatment of witches had a parodic, overheated symbolism in it, allusive of the trial of Jesus. Jesus was taken from the priest to the secular arm, that is from Caiaphas to Pilate, just as the witch was taken from the Inquisitor to the secular arm, for the Dominicans would never dirty their hands by actually cutting the flesh, breaking the bones, or raping.

Jesus did not have answers to all of the questions, just as the witches did not, and for the same reason: for of the charges offered, Jesus and the witches were innocent. Jesus was stripped and beaten, and so were the witches. The parallels, we may think, are too exact for sheer chance. Perhaps the most bizarre aspect of the trials was that the Inquisition acted the part of the devil they said they hated, behaving in many ways worse than the tribunals which destroyed Jesus. There is the dangerous, the horrifying, yet objective possibility, that these men, ostensible lovers of the Christ God, were carrying out a parody of the destruction of their true redeemer, the small and disfavoured woman who died on the cross in Golgotha. The irony is so biting, so unexpected, that it is almost suffocating. The Church's successful extirpation of organized worship of the Mother Goddess was enacted in the hamlets and villages, and sometimes the towns, of Europe, day after day, week after week, for two and a half centuries, in harrowing detail similar to the immolation of Christ. Frighteningly, the Church had chosen women to play the role of victim.

These horrors are the historical evidence of a misogyny so virulent that the like had never been seen before, and with the destruction of the Church's secular power, has not been seen since. It is a phenomenon which arguably fed on the patristic prejudice of the Church fathers, a tradition begun with the Temple Jews, but it was a Christian hierarchy which developed it to a stage when not even Caiaphas the High Priest and his clique could have supported it. True, the destruction of the Great Goddess was politically necessary if the Roman Church hierarchy was to maintain its centralized power, but even that is insufficient to explain the witch annihilation, and the crusade against the Cathars. Rather the response was so savage that it can best be explained by a Papacy fighting for its life and so no holds were barred. The mortal struggle arose, I have suggested, because the Cathars possessed proof not only that Jesus Christ was a woman but had not been assumed into heaven bodily. The gender of Christ, then, was inextricably linked with the central dogmas of the Church. If the femality of Christ were admitted, then a process of deconstruction of what the Roman Church had built would begin. Fortunately that does not mean the truths of Yeshu were under threat, only the claims of a centralized, dogmatic and violent hierarchy. Yeshu's truths and the Church of Rome's dogmas are not, it would appear, the same thing at all.

This at least is a pleasing discovery. Once the real teachings of Yeshu are seen as distinct from the power politics of Rome, her bequest is salvageable.

In conclusion to this terrible episode of the witches, I had again found support for the seemingly insupportable, the femality of Christ, at least in the sense that the Popes acted as if they feared Christ might be a woman. Perhaps it is best to try and summarize the strengths and the weaknesses of the case so far.

1) Traces of the Great Goddess religion appear everywhere one looks in the actual symbols and many ceremonies of the Roman Catholic Church. However, there is a central paradox, that of a Jewish man suddenly appearing in history, teaching that his blood was capable of saving people in some way. In order to bolster this

apparent *non sequitur*, the Roman Church had developed terrifying doctrines, such as the taint of sin passed on from woman to child, so that a babe at the breast was reeking of it.

2) There appeared to be evidence of a tradition associated with Mary Magdalene, Christian in origin and intention. I called this the Church of Mary Magdalene, and it was in some way connected with Marseille and the south of France.

3) Pope Joan in the ninth century made a pilgrimage to the Shrines of Mary Magdalene, for she had heard of the Magdalene tradition of the daughter of God through Frankish priests who baptized in the name of the Father, the Daughter and the Holy Ghost. Whatever she taught on this has not come down to us, for she was murdered, and called a witch.

4) The Magdalene Church flourished in the Languedoc, and despite papal oppression, it survived as the Cathar religion. This could not be suffered by the Papacy because the Cathars were openly saying they had the bones of Jesus Christ, which meant that the central Roman dogma of resurrection of the earthly body was challenged. It became papal policy to recover the bones and scotch the rumours. They mounted a so-called crusade, the Albigensian, and killed the Cathar women priestesses. Even when the fighting was over, Rome continued its oppression by creating the Inquisition, which burned thousands of Cathars, until Catharsism was extirpated.

5) Even with the fighting forces of the Cathars liquidated, Christ's bones were not found, for the relic had been safely secreted by the Knights Templars. Realizing this, the Popes decided to destroy the Templars, and succeeded in purloining the skull bones, Caput 58. It has not been seen since outside the Vatican.

6) Contemporaneous with the liquidation of the

Cathars and Templars there was a ploy to 'prove' that Christ was male, and using the best artist available, one whose personal circumstances made him pliable, a forgery of Christ's burial shroud with an image of a provocatively male Christ was exposited in Turin.

7) The result of the Templar débâcle was the death of chivalry, which suited the Church's policies because it prepared the way for gendercide in the witch persecution. With this accomplished, all trace of the Magdalene Church would be wiped from the face of the earth.

However, I had found that this last goal had perhaps not been as conclusive as the Roman Church would have hoped, because I had come across evidence that possibly the tradition of the Magdalene Church still survived, albeit in a much altered form; but this was not the time to pursue the leads, for the existence of the Church of Mary Magdalene rested on a much more fundamental idea, the hypothesis of Christ's female gender. Obviously this was more important and had to be faced. It was one thing to discover data which suggested that certain people felt sufficiently strongly about the idea of Christ being female to have died for it, while others, the hierarchy in Rome, were so fearful that they persecuted anyone who seemed to suggest that this could be so, but entirely another to tackle the problem in the life of Jesus.

Perhaps the key to the mystery could be found in the observation that the doctrines and images of the Roman Church were aggressively male. If indeed there was anything in the notion of Christ's female gender, then it meant that the historical Jesus had been purposely repressed by the hierarchy at some point in its development. As the evidence stood at this juncture, real concern was shown by Rome at the claims of the Cathars, though there was a suggestion in Pope Joan's pilgrimages that rumours may have been rife much earlier.

My task was very quickly concentrated down to a very

simple question indeed: if the Turin image was not that of the authentic Christ, not even in the tradition of the afflicted Jesus of the prophets, who then was Christ? But whoever Christ was, male or female, there were already grounds for a rejection of the six-foot athlete, an image that seemed to obscure his or her reality. In short, who was the real Christ behind the image? No matter what the implications, that question deserved an answer.

What Did the Real Jesus Look Like?

It is often said that there are no physical descriptions of Jesus in the Bible, but strictly speaking this is not true. Certainly we are not told that he was a head taller than everyone else, as in the case of King Saul, but as we have already noted Isaiah said that the Redeemer would be physically unattractive and might have some kind of serious physical affliction.

The Gospels themselves give several hints, especially the passages where he escapes through a crowd, which imply smallness of stature, though something else is obviously involved too – some change of appearance. Then there is the case of his sweating blood when praying in the Garden of Gethsemane. Is this a clue to his affliction? And what of his transfiguration when on a mountain top? He turned white. What does that mean?

I felt that since such details were obtainable from a cursory study of the Bible, a prolonged assault on the archives would yield even more, and that there was a chance that the physical description of Christ would emerge. After all, it is easy to estimate the height of someone from a piece of leg bone, and determine their sex from skeletal parts.

However, I tempered my optimism by observing two very daunting facts. One, the early Christians, Roman, Arian, Docetist and so on, were uniformly persecuted for at least three hundred years. They persecuted one another and they were savagely attacked by Nero and other

Roman Emperors. As a result their records were destroyed and their character traduced in government
documents. On top of this was the second fact I had
discovered, that official Church records could not be
trusted automatically; consequently, what did exist had
to be carefully scrutinized for bias.

The amount of material existing about Jesus from the
earliest times is enormous, but it is scattered and frag-
mentary. I viewed the task with mounting apprehension.
Here, it seemed, was a task that could consume half a
decade. It was with great relief that I found that the
work had already been done, and it had taken the
scholar, Dr Robert Eisler, six years and a quarter of a
million words to do it.

His monumental work is not easy to read, and his style
abrasive, but he is a passionate and methodical scholar
of the highest reputation. He states that a 'rich fund' of
historically reliable material once existed about Jesus, but
was systematically revised and altered, indeed changed
so much as to constitute forgery, by the Roman Church.
Fortunately some of this material is still extant, and in
any case it is possible to reconstruct an authentic portrait
by closely examining the shifts of emphasis of material
relating to the reigns of Constantine I and Valentinian
III, AD 477.[1]

Eisler used material published in AD 72 by the Roman
publisher Epaphroditus, written by an influential Jew,
Josephus. The work has come down to us as *The Jewish
War*, but the original appears to have been entitled
Capture of Jerusalem.

Josephus was born in AD 37, took an active part in the
revolt against the Romans, fighting in Galilee, but was
captured, and from then on espoused the Roman cause,
eventually living in Rome in considerable style, a friend
of Vespasian, then Titus. He was therefore in a position
to have known people who knew Jesus, while his know-

ledge of Jewish affairs was very deep, for he was an orthodox Jew even though he bent with the times to survive. Unfortunately his work was not without its enemies, both when he wrote it and later. The form in which it has come to us, via Rome and Eastern Orthodox monasteries, is truncated, there being several passages missing, which might have been lost for ever but for heretical sects who possessed more complete versions.

From this very extensive but scattered material Eisler succeeds in building up a picture of the physical Christ, a short person of some five feet tall. But perhaps his cleverest coup was to realize that since the Romans were very tidy minded, issuing, for example, very precise descriptions of criminals and runaway slaves in public written notices, Josephus would probably have actually had access to documents issued by the Procuratorial Office of Pontius Pilate in Jerusalem, which described Jesus.[2] The result is a vivid picture of Christ, which accords with the tradition of the early Church fathers.[3]

Using a cut-and-paste technique with the sources, Eisler concludes that Josephus wrote the following description of Jesus, a description which was censored by Rome.

Both his nature and his form were human, for he was a man of simple appearance, mature age, dark skin, short growth, three cubits tall, hunchbacked, with a long face, long nose, eyebrows meeting above the nose . . . with scanty hair, but having a line in the middle of the head after the fashion of the Nazareans, and with an underdeveloped beard.[4]

Instead of a human and touching portrait of Christ, the Church opted for a figure depicted more akin to a Greek or Roman God, an Apollo-like figure, a chocolate-box Christ.

Both his nature and form were divine, for he was a man of simple appearance, mature age, ruddy skin, six feet tall, erect, handsome, with a good eye, so that the spectators could love him, with curly hair of the colour of unripe hazelnuts, with a smooth unwrinkled forehead, blue eyes, beautiful mouth, and copious beard of the same colour as the hair, not long, parted in the middle, arms and hands full of grace.

There are several Roman Church texts with different glowing adjectives. Eisler's point is that the descriptions follow the sequence of Josephus' reconstructed text, even using some of the same phrases, but censoring entirely anything appertaining to an ugly, small Christ. Clearly, these scribes either did not know Isaiah's description or did not care to. Particularly impressive is the evidence that the original description of Jesus in official documents gradually undergoes a metamorphosis as time passes. In the eighth century, according to Archbishop Cretensis, Jesus was a possessor of goodly eyes, and is 'long-faced, crooked, well grown'.[5] We can see as time went on the Christian clerics becoming progressively bolder in the changes they made to the original description.

Cretensis was born in Damascus AD *c.*660. He has evidently accepted the hunchback ('crooked') part of the texts coming down to him, but the shortness of stature has become 'well grown'. By the thirteenth century, European idealization had reached full bloom.

Forgeries

'He has a very beautiful face,' as the prophet says: 'more beautiful in shape than all children of men.' In growth and stature he was full seven feet high: his hair was blond and *not very richly developed*; he had beautiful *eyebrows*, not very curved; his eyes were brown and clear (gay), just as it is written that his ancestor David was *dark*, with beautiful eyes, with large nostrils, a reddish beard and long hair, for from the time of his infancy, when his mother had clipped his hair, no razor had touched his head. His head was a *little bending*, since his body was tall ; his hair light blond. His face was round, like that of his mother, kindly, mild, and entirely without anger, in all resembling his mother.[6]

This fantasy was concocted by a Greek monk, Maximos of Vatopaedi, Mt Athos. His literary efforts helped spawn yet another forgery, perhaps the most impudent, for it was passed off as the official description of Christ, and was said to come direct from Pontius Pilate's office. This is the so-called letter of Lentulus. What is remarkable about it is that it has been cobbled together from the sugary description of the Greek monk shown above, and the terse 'police' description which might have come from Pilate's office. However, the forger has mixed them up so badly that it is possible to identify the fantasy parts and the authentic sections, and it is of such interest that I have reproduced it below.

There has appeared in these times and still is at large a man, if it is right to call him **a man of** great **virtue, called Christ whose name is Jesus, who is said by the gentiles to be a prophet of truth**, whom his **disciples call Son of God, raising the dead and healing all diseases: a man of stature** tall, medium, i.e. **fifteen palms and a half** and sightly, having a venerable **face, which beholders might** love and **dread, having hair** of the colour of an unripe hazel and smooth almost to the ears, but from the ears down cork-screw curls somewhat darker-coloured and more glistening, waving downwards from the shoulders, **having a parting on the middle of his head after the manner of the Naza-reans,** a brow smooth and most serene, **with a** face without a wrinkle or spot, beautified by a moderately ruddy colour; **with nose** and mouth there is no fault whatever. **Having a beard** copious but **immature** of the same colour as the hair (and) not long but **parted in the middle. Having a simple and**

mature aspect, with blue eyes of varying hue and bright. In rebuke terrible, in admonition bland and amiable. Cheerful, yet preserving gravity: he sometimes wept, but never laughed. In stature of body tall and erect, having hands and arms delectable to the sight. In converse grave sweet and modest, so that justly according to the prophet was he called beauteous **above the sons of men.**[7]

The heavy type is the original material. However, apart from turning Christ into an idealized physical specimen, there are other misdirections here. For example, it is persuasive that Christ was really short, frail looking, with hair parted in the middle as one would expect of a person coming from Nazareth, but though the forgers have given Christ a beard Jove would not have been ashamed of and Zeus jealous about, it is probable that the original Latin bore the meaning that Jesus had no beard at all. Indeed, from what I can see of the Latin, the term used for facial hair was of immaturity, which can mean anything from a light down to none at all.

However, the most astonishing fact about this notorious forgery is that the text bears the note, in Latin, 'brought from Citeaux'; the significance of this is that the Abbot of Citeaux was Arnold, one of the most fanatical destroyers of the Cathar women priests. It may be noted too that the emergence of the forgery and the unveiling of the Turin Shroud occurred at a time convenient for establishing the athletic male Christ, for adherents of a more human Christ were either being burned to death, or were marked down for destruction. It is also noteworthy how similar the portrait of the Lentulus forgery is to that of the Turin image. Granted, all of this may be sheer coincidence, but it would seem to be that coincidence is remarkably active here.

All these perplexities, however, tend to become cohered in a grave suspicion, for it is a historical fact that the official policy of the Church was censorship, as set out in the *Codex Justinianus*.[8] The reality is that from Constantine on, in the fourth century, books, documents, statues, paintings, any objective material which did not fit in with the Roman Catholic notion of what Christ should be, were censored, mutilated and burned. The Church specifically ordered in AD 449 that books they did not approve of were to be burned, the overt reason being that otherwise they would cause God's anger and scandalize the pious. Yet even at the council of Ephesus, AD 431, an irrecoverable treasure of manuscripts was destroyed. This must be related to the fact that prior to Constantine, the Church was not Roman Catholic, but with the Emperor's military back-up, this Church took precedence, and having once obtained power, began its destruction of records and people. It was a process which escalated as the Popes purloined more and more secular power, and it only came to an end when military force was wrested from the Papacy, not before. Arguably, then, whatever the minutiae may be, the overall thrust of the Papacy was to attain power, keep it, and use it to destroy people who argued with its dogmas. Clearly, if the Roman Church knew of something antithetical to its interests in the south of France, it would act against it if it had the power; at the time of the Cathars the Popes had that power, and they used it to murder them. As soon as the Templars lost their overseas bases and so were no longer able to escape the Pope, they, too, were destroyed.

There were documents, and oral tradition too, which showed Christ to be a small person with no clear masculine features, but this affective figure had been suppressed. Why? Was it just good P. R. to have a tall curly-headed Christ with blue eyes and a rosy skin? Even if the answer is yes, the Church stands guilty of a gross perjury of history, even gainsaying Isaiah's prophecy. But the more persuasive possibility is that the physical descriptions of Christ contained material which threatened the actual dogmas of the Church.

As we have seen, a Pope had actually been brought up with priests who blessed in the Name of the Father, the Daughter and the Holy Ghost. The Cathars said they possessed the flesh and blood of Christ, which seems to have been a head of a small-boned female, some of which came into the possession of the Templars, so they too had to be destroyed. The relics were never seen again, but forgeries of letters said to be from Pilate's own office spoke of a man tall and curly like the man on the fraudulently exposited Shroud of Turin. Do all these facts say one thing: that Jesus was a woman and was not spirited away into heaven as the Creed of the Church insisted? But none of these things say one jot against what Christ taught of love and forgiveness. The conclusion is pertinent: the savagery against Joan, the Cathars and the Templars was not in the defence of Christianity but the dogmatic male-orientated power structure the Roman Church had erected.

Of course this does not mean that the vast majority of the good bishops and priests were privy to deception, fraud or suppression of the truth about Christ, but they were all obedient sons of Rome and did as they were told. However, the position of the Cardinals and the Popes in Rome was very different. They were able to discern what the truth was, and the melancholy conclusion appears hard to escape: they suppressed the truth, distorted history, burned records and killed people for doctrinal ends. The ordinary priest genuinely believed he was fighting for Christ, but the hierarchy knew something else.

The threads were all interconnected, but I had yet to find the extra information which would enable the pattern of the tapestry to be viewed, let alone, as yet, seen the picture that pattern would make. A thread seemed an apposite metaphor, for there were 'holy' cords around each woman Cathar priest, around each Templar.

If we add the evidence together, the following description emerges: Jesus was short, slightly built, dark, with secondary male characteristics of sex so notable by their absence – no beard for example – that he appears to be a boy. He is intensely emotional, and in some strange way his appearance alters when threatened or when in the ecstasy or agony of prayer. He bleeds easily. He looks older than his years, even though he has the androgynous or epicene form of a boy, so it is possible his skin may have been wrinkled.

Clearly this picture is sexually ambivalent. It could be of a girl passing as a boy. However we look at it, this youth is a perplexing figure, for though of mature years there is something unformed about him. The lack of beard is particularly noteworthy.

It was clearly time to look even deeper into the physicality of Christ.

Affliction

We have noted that Jesus had the ability to disappear into crowds when it was convenient, which suggests a smallness of stature, and perhaps a change in appearance. One famous account of this ability is given in the Gospel of St John. Jesus had been claiming an intimacy with God and had uttered the remarkable claim, 'Verily, Verily, I say unto you, Before Abraham was, I am' (John 8:58). In effect, this is a statement of divinity, claiming to be at one with the Godhead, and even more, to be eternal. His questioners in the Temple had already pointed out that Jesus was not yet fifty years of age, and so the claim was not vague but downright. Some of the Jews, rightly from their point of view, considered the statement as blasphemy and took up stones to kill him, but 'Jesus hid himself, and went out of the Temple, going through the midst of them, and so passed by' (John 8:59). How could this have happened? One moment Jesus is a target for stones and the next walking, unseen, through the midst of those who sought to harm him.

A change of appearance is also noted in the transfiguration which, as Matthew tells it, occurred at the top of a mountain: 'and [Jesus] was transfigured before them: and his face did shine as the sun, and his raiment was white as the light' (Matt. 17:2). We may note here that we would not expect raiment to be transfigured, and in that we can perhaps observe some hyperbole, yet clearly something had happened. Jesus had blanched or whitened, at the top of a mountain, and one only reaches the top of a mountain through intense physical effort with blood being concentrated in the muscles for the necessary effort. Some blanching then is understandable, but besides the physical effort, there was something else going on, which, as Matthew puts it, was no less than God speaking from a cloud and saying Jesus was indeed his son. In other words, this was a moment of intense drama for Jesus and a few disciples with him. Again, blanching of the face would be an understandable physiologic reaction, but to such an extent that Matthew regards it as a transfiguration?

A third account of something strange about Christ's appearance is given by Luke, just before the betrayal: 'He took Peter, John and James, and went up into a mountain to pray. And as he prayed, the fashion of his countenance was changed' (Luke 9:28–9). Later in Gethsemane: 'And being in agony, he prayed more earnestly, and his sweat was as if it were great drops of blood falling down to the ground' (Luke 22:44–5). Luke, with medical caution, says 'as if' regarding this sweating of blood. What, then, was reported to him? What had the witness seen? It does seem as if the witness was trying to get over something about the colour of the 'sweat', that the fluid was red. This may or may not be hyperbole, but we do know that certain glands in the skin, particularly under the arms, can produce fluid which varies in colour from person to person, from milky white to reddish. It is not blood but the secretion of one of the two kinds of ordinary sweat glands. The other possibility is that Jesus had a skin condition characterized by weak capillaries, some of which burst under intense excitement.

Is there a medical explanation of 'sweating blood' when in a state of emotional trauma? As we shall see later, there is, and the condition also explains the other two changes in appearance. Hecklers in the crowd are reported as saying 'Physician heal thyself!' (Luke 4:23), and pointing out that although he saved (i.e. healed) others he could not save himself (Luke 23:35 and Matt. 27:42).

Furthermore, we may wonder why Christ died so quickly on the cross, for at most the crucifixion lasted only six hours. Most men would not have died in this time, nor indeed would most women, unless they had lost a great deal of blood and were physically frail. The scourging would mean a loss of blood, but not great amounts, except in certain medical conditions, where blood loss would be severe.

Examination of the historical Jesus now suggests a medical rather than mythical solution, since the physical traits are very clear. What affliction could explain 1) sexual ambivalence, 2) changeable appearance, 3) small stature, 4) compelling beauty yet wrinkles, 5) tendency to bleed easily, 6) youth and age at the same time?

Here is a set of physical characteristics which are so precise that they should be capable of yielding a diagnosis; after all, medical professionals often have much less to go on.

Breaking the material down even further, it is noteworthy how much is surface detail, that is, pertaining to the skin and hair. The question naturally arises: did Christ have a skin affliction? There are traditions which suggest that Jesus may have been leprous, which in some forms gives a whiteness to the skin, but this can be discounted because this form of leprosy does not lead to quick and reversible changes of appearance of the kind we have seen occurred with Christ. But before leaving that aspect, it is pertinent to record that the real reason behind these aspersions may have been more political than medical, for the following reasons. Jesus was referred to as being the son of Panthera. Panthera means lion, and one of the effects of leprosy is to destroy the nose cartilage so that the face becomes flattened and takes on the appearance of a lion, the lion-face syndrome of leprosy. The other link is that in Leviticus leprosy, menstrual blood and reptiles were collected together as items which made a priest ritually impure. This seemed to be so loaded in female imagery and gross hatred of women that it suggested a smear against Jesus to say he was Panthera. As I was to learn later, and which I will discuss, the depths of this particular slur are very deep indeed, pertaining to Christ's birth.

Another important aspect of a skin condition which can lead to changes of appearance, reversible and rapid, is that it might lead to stories of there being two persons. Take this transfiguration for example: Christ blanches so much that he appears white, but in other descriptions he is wrinkled and dark. Oddly, there is a bundle of legends, which Eisler discusses, of Jesus being a twin. This would explain the resurrection, we are told, but there is no evidence the two Marys and the twelve apostles, nor even the soldiers of the High Priest and Caiaphas himself, not to mention

Pontius Pilate, were dealing with two people. There was only one Christ as far as all these persons were concerned. The twins legend arises after the crucifixion, and can be seen as a transparent attempt to throw doubt on the resurrection, an attempt which we shall see is not only gratuitous in a very real sense, but which at the same time supports the view that Christ died on that cross outside Jerusalem's walls.

However, the possibility behind all these canards is that Jesus did suffer from some affliction of the skin, of a kind which so weakened it that the terrible Roman flagellation caused more than usual bleeding, to such an extent that profound weakness resulted, with so precipitous a fall of blood pressure that within six hours of the torture of the cross, life was extinct in that small anguished body.

Smallness of stature and even skin afflictions are sometimes hereditary, but what of the more important attributes of Jesus? Christ was a speaker of uncommon, perhaps unique power, able to hold thousands in thrall, capable of piercing men and women to the heart with words. Indeed, so effective was Christ's speech that he referred to himself as a sword, for in this case the tongue was used like that weapon. Certain abilities are passed on from Mother to child, and I wondered if this was one of them. Mary the Virgin, for example, was extremely religious and that had been passed on to her child. Was it through her milk, that is nurture, or through her blood, that is nature? Or was it, as is the case with most people, through a mixture of the two?

The questions which kept cropping up appeared to have some connection not only with femality but with Christ's mother. I already knew enough about genetics and case histories of various types of skin afflictions to realize that further research in that area was promising, but still the essential and larger issues were to do with femality, the unifying theme which apparently ran though the mysteries so far uncovered. If Mary Magdalene was responsible for the female legends in the south of France, was Mary the Virgin, as the other woman of great importance in Christ's life, the source not only of Christ's flesh and blood, but of much of his or her teaching? It seemed so obvious a question, and yet I could not find anywhere a serious attempt to assess the overwhelming impact a woman, who said she was pregnant by God, that she was the mother of the Chosen One, might have had on her child.

This seemed to be a larger issue, but there was also the problem of heredity. What bodily things had Christ inherited from Mary? And what of those might explain the collection of symptoms enumerated above? Unexpectedly, the centre of the investigation was on Mary the Virgin. I suppose if I had had more insight I would have realized that this was bound to have been the case, for the odyssey I was undertaking had long ago been informed by the mysterious statues of a reformed whore – or so they called her – Mary Magdalene, and another Mary whom they insisted was the Mother of God, which came near to dominating every Catholic Church. The exhilarating question now appeared to be, could the real Mary be made as physically real as her child had been? For if she could, she might be able to tell us about her small, afflicted yet brilliant child, the tiny woman, it seemed, who had changed history and yet for so long has been censored.

— Part II —

The Sacred Temple Girl

— 6 —

Mother and Virgin?

According to Luke, who may have been a Hellenic physician, writing between AD 50 and 100, a young woman, Mary of Nazareth in Galilee, gave birth to a child in about AD 1 in the village of Bethlehem. He tells us further that Mary had a visitation prior to her conception, by the Archangel Gabriel, who announced she would become pregnant. It is her down-to-earth answer which still rings through the centuries, 'How shall this be, seeing I know not a man?' (Luke 1:34).

Unless the Gospel writers were making things up, they could only have got such intimate information about the events surrounding Mary's conception from Mary herself.

Clearly, Mary is no ordinary girl, for she speaks to a messenger of the Hebrew God directly, asking downright questions in a fearless manner. If nothing else had happened but this spiritual exchange, there would be a rich enough field for research, for women were not expected to be in the forefront of Jewish religious life, let alone take initiatives. The altar of God was not ministered to by women. But something else did happen. The Archangel tried to explain to Mary how she could conceive without knowing a man, for God himself would directly intervene and cause the necessary change in her.

Mary then reacted in an entirely different manner from her first response. Gone is the doubt, and instead a strong and courageous acceptance of her religious fate is expressed. She calls herself the Handmaid of the Lord (Luke 1:38) and demands that the conception be done 'unto me according to thy word'. Mary is clearly a woman of deep religious conviction, yet at the same time her willingness to be used by her God carries no false modesty. The Archangel has told her by implication that her child will change history and, being a Jewish woman, Mary would not need to have the word Messiah spelled out to her. Yet she does not balk on the grounds of its frightening implications, social, physiological and theological, rather she embraces it. Clearly, Mary was an uncommon woman long before she met the angel.

For one thing, where did she get her religious courage? Women were even excluded from the inner courts of the Temple. They were subjected to humiliating ablutions, for even after childbirth they were regarded as ritually defiling a man if they came into contact with him. There is in her reaction to the angel more than just *chutzpah*, rather here is a young woman who already knew that she was special in a religious sense. How would she know?

We are told very little about Mary. Neither John nor Mark give her background, and mention her hardly at all, while Luke and Matthew give genealogies. Luke's is an astonishing one, for he traces Joseph's line to prove Jesus is descended from King David, apparently forgetting the Saviour was conceived not by Joseph but the Holy Ghost, and hence it must have been Mary's genealogy which counted.

Luke does not get round to Mary's genealogy until chapter three, but he does persevere to the fount, by tracing the line through the patriarchs back to Adam. This is, of course, scientifically unacceptable, since if Adam were the first man, many thousands of begets would be needed to trace a line to him, and not the few dozen that Luke finds sufficient for his purpose. This genealogy does, however, contain the important emphasis that Mary's distant ancestress was Eve. Why should Luke labour that, since all men and women were thought to be descended from Adam and Eve? Can we discern misogynism here, by bringing up the woman who tempted Adam with the apple? Perhaps, and this suspicion is reinforced by the fact that Mark, upon which much of Matthew may be drawn, barely mentions Mary; he draws attention to an apparent tiff between Jesus and Mary (Mark 3:31), and makes a cold statement of fact that she is Jesus' mother (Mark 6:3). In John, Mary appears twice, at the wedding feast and at the foot of the cross.

This extraordinarily bleak treatment is a problem which has hitherto been unexplained, but the answer may lie partially in the information given by Matthew, for his genealogy of Jesus from Mary contains the names of four women, and is in any case different from Luke's. Mark and John, the first and last Gospels historically, both dispense with genealogies (or were they dispensed with for them?). Taken together these facts are suspicious. Were three of the four Gospel writers ashamed of Mary, Mother of God? Who was there in her lineage who might cause embarrassment? A clue is given by Matthew's mention of four women as Mary's ancestresses, four in forty-two begettings. Perhaps Matthew is trying to tell us something the other three authors do not care to, or did not know. If Mary herself is the source of this information, it goes a long way in explaining why she felt herself so special in the religious sense. Her four ancestresses are Tamar, Ruth, Bathsheba and Rahab.

Tamar's Story

Judah married a gentile called Shuah, and they had three children. In Genesis 38, we are told that Judah named the first born Er, while Shuah named the second born Onan. This identification of the name given is fascinating, for it is Onan who uses his brother Er's wife after Er's death. Curiously Onanism has been thought to be masturbation by many people, but it is clear in context that Onan was supposed to have full generative sexual intercourse with his dead brother's wife and so maintain the family name. But he used the widow, practising *coitus interruptus*. The actual phrase is 'he spilt it [i.e. his semen or seed] on the ground' (Gen. 38:9). The woman in question was Tamar, so we see her widowed, and then abused. However, Onan dies too, and the third son of Judah and Shuah is Shelah. By rights when this youth was of marriageable age he should marry Tamar, for that was the Law. Judah promised Tamar this, but it was quite clear that he was temporizing even though the youth had grown.

Tamar puts away her widow's clothes, puts on a veil, and sits in an 'open place', which could have been a temple, waiting for her father-in-law to pass. When Judah sees this veiled but beautiful woman, he offers her a kid to possess her, which again is redolent of religious significance, the kid being a sacrificial animal for Jews and pagans. She agrees, but as a sign of good faith, since the kid is not at hand to give her, she requires pledges, so he gives her his staff, his ring and his bracelet. Obviously there is much more going on here than a mere one-off sexual transaction, for Judah has, in effect, handed over all the regalia of his status. This is confirmed by the fact that although Tamar becomes pregnant by her father-in-law, we are told archly that he did not know it was Tamar because she wore a veil.

In due course her pregnancy is apparent, and Judah wants her burnt, but she reveals that he is the father, proving her assertion by the regalia. Judah now reverses his decision. They won't burn her after all, for he recognizes, we are told, that she was forced to do what she did because of his initial injustice, namely not giving her to his son Shelah to marry.

It is significant that Judah wanted her to be burned, not stoned. If he thought Tamar was merely guilty of adultery, even for money, stoning would have been the penalty, but fire was reserved for 'witches', that is women who worshipped Goddesses. Tamar was not simply a prostitute, she was an acolyte of the Mother Goddess, in one of her many forms, Astarte, Hecate, Diana, Isis, depending on region and time, who offered her body to strangers who, in return, paid for the service, the money, goods or animals going to the temple of the Goddess. This form of worship is very ancient, older than Judaism itself.

Taking the place of the Great Goddess through offering her body was the common, not unusual experience of women, of high and low degree, for at least 4,000 years BC in western Asia and Asia Minor and much of the Mediterranean. In Cyprus she, the Goddess, was Aphrodite, in Asia Minor she was Astarte, Ishtar, in Egypt and Rome she was Isis. In Syria at Baalbec women offered themselves in the sanctuary of the Temple of Astarte. This custom continued until the fourth century when Constantine abolished it. In Phoenicia, modern Lebanon, women gave their bodies at the temple, believing they would have better lives for it, because they had paid their dues, that is redeemed themselves, to the Goddess. These women were seen to protect the whole community and ensure fruitfulness by their acts. Consequently there were no scruples in anyone about marrying them; indeed the reverse, for a woman who did not do her temple observances was immoral and antisocial.

Sometimes the onus for redemption and purification by sexual sacrifice, that is offering up your body to a divine power, appears to have devolved upon a single or selected group of families. These women were highly

honoured, often having inscriptions in stone made to
them, as in Tralles, Lydia, where Aurelia Aemilia, her
mother, and so on, back into her line, are votively
honoured on white marble in a public place. In Armenia,
the girls of the richest and noblest families served with
their bodies in the Great Goddess temple of Anaitis in
Acilisena. After their temple service was over, they
returned to secular life and married. Ma, the name borne
by the Great Goddess in Pontus, was served by innumerable women at Comana, in the biennial ceremonies, though here it appears that the redemptresses
served for a few days only.

We may discern then, in the wily Tamar's actions, not
the self-seeking stratagem of a wronged woman of Israel
(though that may have entered into it) but the religious
duty of a devotee of the Great Goddess. That Judah
availed himself of this opportunity to possess a young
woman suggests a certain ambivalence on his part, but
the Old Testament abounds in patriarchs straying from
the straight and narrow. The connection seems to have
been very deep, despite the veil of anonymity.

The 'open place which is by the way to Timnath',
where Tamar sat, may have signified a busy communication route, or even the town centre, where a
sanctuary or a temple stood. These edifices to the Great
Goddess were usually the most beautiful and well-made
buildings of any community. Their ceremonies, too, were
full of grace, even though they must have evolved from
simpler ceremonies of the Corn Goddess in distant times.
Isis in Egypt was also called the Lady of Bread, Creatress
of Green Things. The Greeks identified Isis with corn,
for she also appears as Demeter. Isis is also Sochit Isis,
that is, Isis of the Cornfield. These rubrics indicate her
ancient provenance, but in the cities of Alexandria and
Rome her ceremonies were attended by tonsured priests,
who swung incense burners before the altars. Each day

was devoted to her in vespers and matins. There was baptism, holy water, and jewelled images of the great Mother Goddess. Frazer believed that the beautiful religion of Isis with its decorum, dignity and stateliness, was 'well fitted to soothe the troubled mind, to ease the burdened heart'.[1] He thought it probably had a tremendous appeal to women. It had, but it was not just because it eased a fretted mind. Women were not only aware of their political and social power because of the rites of the Mother Goddess, but in the shrines, sanctuaries and temples they were, if only for a fleeting moment, actually the Mother Goddess herself; it was their flesh that brought the Goddess to this earth.

Through her mortal acolytes, that is the temple girls, the Great Goddess mated with strangers, and the assumption was that often amongst these men there would be a God. The implication of divine nexus is clear enough, and through it the fruitfulness of earth, man and beast was ensured.

The Jews, with their idol-less, aggressively male, sky god, were odd men out, surrounded by richer, more powerful, often better educated peoples such as the Egyptians, Syrians, Parthians, Assyrians, Babylonians and Phoenicians. In their long history they only once achieved military hegemony, *c.*1000 BC, over their neighbours, under the short monarchical period of Saul, David and Solomon. Numerically inferior, militarily insignificant (except for the brief flowering under the monarchy) and basically a loose confederation of twelve Semitic tribes, the Jews at nearly every juncture of their history were likely to be swamped culturally, religiously and militarily. Indeed, they never recovered from the Assyrian interdiction, when ten whole tribes, mostly from the south, were forcibly transported to Asia Minor and disappeared from history, giving rise to the legend of the then lost tribes of Israel. Only the tribe of Judah of the remaining two, centred around Jerusalem, really held its own, and without it the Jews might have vanished from the face of the earth as a religious entity. In such a context, Tamar must necessarily be pictured as a 'harlot'. Jewish religious leaders had difficulty enough, without spelling out the fact that some of the patriarchs had leanings to the Great Goddess. If indeed Mary, the real woman, did see herself as a descendant, not only of a royal but a holy line of priestesses, we should expect to find in the stories of the other three women of her line, evidence of the Great Goddess. Extraordinary as it may seem, despite censorship and shifts of emphasis, the links are quite apparent, even in Ruth's story.

Ruth

Ruth was a gentile, the daughter-in-law of Naomi. Ruth has a book, which is named after her, all to herself in the Old Testament. Ruth was a Moabite, a people the tribe of Judah constantly fought against. Unfortunately, Ruth's husband died, and so did Naomi's, so Naomi decided to go to Bethlehem at the time of the harvest, where her kinsman Boaz, a rich man, might help her. Naomi, however, is persuaded to take Ruth with her, after Ruth has eloquently pleaded her case. The two women scratch a living by collecting the corn which falls from the sheaves as the harvesters work, but Boaz notices Ruth and warns his men that they should let her do her gleaning and not reproach or hassle her in any way. He explains his kindness by noting how she has looked after his kinswoman, Naomi.

Naomi, however, is in no doubt about what she wants. She tells Ruth to go and lie at Boaz's feet at night after he has taken the harvest in. This Ruth does, actually in the threshing barn, by the heaped grain. Boaz wakes up and finds at his feet the young woman he had already taken a great interest in. Doubtless Naomi had already read the signs of love in an older man for a young woman. The story develops into a wrangle about land ownership between Boaz and another kinsman, but Boaz saves the day by redeeming the land and taking Ruth to wife. She conceives and gives birth to a son.

This story, like so much in Jewish and Christian literature, is many-valued. Clearly, here we have two redoubtable women making the best of a bad job. The sexual power of Ruth is evident too, and guided by Naomi, this sexual leverage is made socially acceptable. Boaz gets a young wife and Naomi and Ruth a secure future. Not only that, Ruth's son is Obed who is the father of Jesse, who is the father of King David. But Boaz himself is only six generations descended from Phares, one of the twin sons of Tamar. Furthermore, there is no doubt that the community at Bethlehem was sure that Boaz and Ruth were founding a dynasty, for the elders and the people are reported as witnessing the marriage and hoping that the house so founded would be 'like the house of Phares, whom Tamar bare unto Judah' (Ruth 4:12). And yet there is another level, the successful appropriation of a pagan woman, who is introduced into Israel amongst the heavy symbolism of the corn harvest. Boaz must have wondered if she was a 'whore' coming from Moab, but she showed no signs . . . or did she? Why are we told she lay at his feet amongst corn? We are also told that Boaz made sure no one saw Ruth with him that morning, but he gave her a large gift of grain. It is a beautifully wrought story, with overtones of great human interest, yet at the same time firmly rooted in land, grain, marriage, and it ends with joyful fertility.

Bathsheba's Story

David, who became King after Saul, was a distinguished general and seems to have formed confederations with the redoubtable Hittites, for we know from Samuel (2 Samuel 11:3) that Uriah, a soldier of some distinction, lived with his wife Bathsheba in Jerusalem. After a successful expedition against the Syrians, David was resting in Jerusalem, in the palace where, after a nap, he was taking the air on the flat roof and saw in the city, again probably in the courtyard or on the roof of a house, Bathsheba washing herself. He was immediately attracted for, as Samuel says, 'the woman was very beautiful to look upon' (2 Samuel 11:2). David invited her to come to him, which was tantamount to an order, considering his position, not only as King, but supreme military commander. David makes love to Bathsheba and she becomes pregnant. David by this time wanted her for his wife, even sending Uriah to the most dangerous part of the battlefield so that he might die. He did, and Bathsheba was stricken with grief. Her sorrow was not that of an accomplice, for it is clear in the narrative by Samuel that she had nothing to do with these chicaneries; she had become the victim of the King's lust, and through that lust her husband had been destroyed. The fault of course lies with David, but we are told that God was so angry with David's sin that he caused the child Bathsheba bore to die. Again, Bathsheba and her child are the victims, but David made it public that Bathsheba was his wife and so lifted the curse. Their union was fruitful for Bathsheba bore Solomon, the last of the true kings of Israel, of which there had only been three.

Mary then can trace her descent from a queen of Israel, namely Bathsheba, moreover her ancestress was the mother of a king, Solomon. It is noteworthy perhaps that Bathsheba was summoned by David, just as Mary was to be summoned by her God. Also, just as Bathsheba was the mother of a king, a true king of the Jews, anointed by Samuel, so Mary was the mother of a king too, or so everyone thought, but this time the royalty lay in spiritual matters, not temporal.

Although Bathsheba is the wife of a Hittite soldier of some standing, David takes her, eventually marrying her. What is Matthew trying to tell us? Apart from the symmetry of Bathsheba's life and Mary's in their roles as mothers of important children, a symmetry which is remarkably exact, we may also have uncovered the mystery of the three wise men who are said to have visited the child Mary bore. Isaiah prophesies that kings will visit Jesus the baby, 'from Sheba shall they come' (Is. 60:6). Is this a reference to Bathsheba's own ancestral line? If so, then the men who visited Mary were her distant kinsmen.

Mary

That Matthew was concerned with proving Jesus' mother was of the royal house of David is agreed by all competent scholars, but it has been the practice to ignore the fact that he took pains to include four women in the genealogy. The one we have not investigated as yet is Rahab, who was Boaz's mother. She has been referred to as the madam of a brothel,[2] but a better description is High Priestess. In telling us that these four women were Mary's ancestresses, what has Matthew in fact revealed to us? First, we see that Mary can count herself as descended from a priestess (Rahab), an acolyte of Isis (Tamar), a woman of harvests (Ruth), and a queen who was also mother of a king, Bathsheba. Given Mary's pedigree, the silence about her in the Gospels is tantamount to a snubbing. Is this the result of censorship by the Church?

Have these Gospels been tampered with, with only Matthew surviving more intact because it proved impossible to discount its existence? Other books were successfully made into unbooks, like the Book of James. This gospel was condemned by a decreee of Pope Gelasius (492–6) when Popes had secular power, but an earlier Christian, Clement of Alexandria (died AD 215) used the text to support the Virgin Birth. Here we find that Mary is the daughter of a rich and pious man, Joachim, known by the Temple High Priest Zacharias: we also find that she is dedicated to the Temple and actually danced there.[3] But Zacharias warns that she has to leave before puberty, that is, before she has her first menses. Otherwise she may pollute the temple – again that fear of blood and sexuality in women. Joseph then appears to act as a guardian to the consecrated virgin, but is dumbfounded when she is pregnant for he fears he has not fulfilled his duty in protecting her. However, the supernatural cause of her pregnancy is impressed on him, though Mary is in no doubt of it. This story was accepted by many Christians in Asia Minor.

What is this story telling us? It is not the same as the Church's interpretation, for it is impossible to consecrate a virgin to the Jewish temple, impossible that she could have been allowed near the altar there, impossible that she danced in the temple: women were not even allowed in the Inner Court, and as for gentiles, they would be killed for entering. We can only conclude that in Mary's past there is some affiliation with another temple, a temple where women could approach the altar and whose pregnancy would not be a cause of reproach but of joy. A detail may give a clue to this temple, for Joseph is said to have been singled out as guardian of Mary by a dove perching on his head. This has echoes of the dove at the baptism by John of Jesus, and though the dove also symbolizes the story of Noah and the ark, that is to say, peace between man and God, the dove is also sacred to Astarte, one of the names of the Mother Goddess. Clearly, the book is embarrassing to Rome because in it Mary is so like her ancestresses, for in a very deep sense they were all devotees of the Great Goddess. She is married to an old man as was Ruth, is associated with a Great Goddess temple as were Tamar and Rahab, and has aspersions made about her ritual purity just as Bathsheba did.

The Book of James casts light on the character of Joseph, as well as Mary, for they are both, since they are unwed, forced to undergo the test of the bitter waters. This ceremony is described in frightening detail and is called a trial of jealousy. Basically, a woman who is suspected to have committed adultery is taken before the priest and given some noxious drink which, if she is guilty will 'cause thy belly to swell and thy thigh to rot'.[4] It will be observed that the water torture of witches used by the Inquisition is similar, though they forced water into women with a funnel, causing the belly to swell. What the bitter waters 'that causeth the curse' were, is debatable, but judging from the physiological effects, the swelling of the belly and the thigh rotting (the thigh here is a reference to the genitals), it is noxious enough to inflame the intestinal tract and cause severe ulceration of the vulva on passing urine. It may be observed that most healthy women, and men for that matter, being subject to this test will fail. However, Mary and Joseph survive the test, which seems to suggest that Mary knew some pharmacology, a knowledge of herbs and natural antidotes (which would have had her burned in the fourteenth century). Joseph probably knew useful facts too, for doves do not sit on anyone's head.

Joseph, from this story and the canonical Gospels, emerges as a just and decent man, obviously deeply in love with Mary and very protective of her. Though of advanced age he was able to shield her in those dangerous times on long and arduous journeys. Later, as husband, he probably had children by her: James, the brother of Jesus, for example.

The historical Mary who was beginning to emerge from these investigations, is so at variance with the orthodox church tradition, that it became increasingly clear that the early Roman Church preferred to leave her out, and the clues are there in the condemned and barred Book of James. For example, Jerusalem owed its temple not to a Jew, but to Herod, who was the son of Antipar, an Imudean, a race of people who worshipped many gods, certainly not Jewish by religion, and possibly not even semitic, but negro. Herod was a client of Mark Antony; he knew Cleopatra, and with Roman help conquered Jerusalem. He owed his kingship to the Romans. His wife was Mariamme, a Hasamonean princess. Brilliant, physically formidable, as Josephus tells us, Herod was none the less no real King of the Jews at all, racially or religiously. He died in 4 BC, and this gives independent dating of Jesus' birth at this time, because the massacre of the Innocents was thought to have been ordered then. Herod's building of the temple was his sop to the Jews, but it did not earn him their love.[5] His son, Herod Antipas, born of Herod and the Samaritan (loathed by the Jews) woman, Mathace, succeeded him; it was this Herod who beheaded John the Baptist and mocked Jesus during the trial by Pilate.

Given that recent archaeology reveals that the priesthood in Jerusalem lived in sumptuous Hellenistic villas, had slaves, and were extremely rich, and given that Mary grew up under the kingship of Herod the Great, whose religious affiliations were not Jewish, the possibility that there existed in Jerusalem temples other than to the Jewish God is a real one. The usual stance in this is to assert that the Jews were so strict that nothing like that could have happened. But King David killed a man to have his wife; Solomon tricked a foreign queen into bed with him by denying her water after feeding her salted food; Judah went to a temple of the Great Goddess to avail himself of a temple acolyte whom he later found out to be his daughter-in-law (if we are to believe he *later* found out): given these treacheries, perfidies and apostasies by the men of Israel, can we really be sanguine that in Herod's palaces and houses in the city there were not chapels and sanctuaries of divinities to please himself, and his women? The suggestion is that the assumption of Jerusalem being a closed city in religious terms really does not bear close examination. Mark Antony had profaned the Holy of Holies in the Temple, and in about a hundred years from that event, Titus, son of Vespasian, was to steal the ancient treasures from the Temple and take them to Rome. There was a Roman garrison in Antonia, and Herod's palace was his own, entirely outside the influence of the Temple caucus or any other religious group.

Herod had nine wives, and through his children was related to Parthians and Greeks. There were several Greeks in the household, and intrigue between this motley court was festering; it actually led Herod to kill his own sons, and the woman he doted on, Mariamme. The Temple, too, does not appear so pure at this time either, for Josephus tells us that certain young men and Rabbis hacked off the golden eagles from the Great Gate leading to the Sanctuary of the Temple. Herod had these men burned to death, but he himself was dying too.

It is commonly assumed that he died of some tropical disease, but it is not clear which. However, much of the intrigue in Herod's palace centred around a plot to poison him, and involved the torturing and execution of many of the household, including Herod's relatives. Josephus, in his *Jewish War*, tells us that a woman thought to be implicated in the plot threw herself off the palace roof to escape the torture. But she survived, and Herod got a confession from her which revealed that a noxious poison had been obtained from Alexandria, and though the phials of this drug were found, they were not full. The concoction was made of the secretions of asps (the snake that Cleopatra used) and other reptiles. Josephus also tells us that, fearing he was dying, Herod ordered his soldiers to kill Jews so that there would be some genuine mourning at his death, though the tears would be for those who died with him.

Herod died, after a progressive illness, of fever, itchiness over all of his body, inflammation of the abdomen and mortification of the genitals, producing worms. There were also spasms of the limbs and difficulty in breathing. These are classic symptoms of a poison acting on the delicate membranes of the genitalia and the bowel, and on the nerve centres. Such a poison could be related to the venom of snakes, and if taken by draught would attack the intestines, and possibly the genitals after transmission through the blood. The astonishing thing is that I had written the description and analysis of the trial by the waters of bitterness which the Book of James said Mary underwent, before I came across the above account of Herod's sickness. The similarities are amazing. The worms may indeed be worms, for after initial destruction of tissue by the venom, infestation would occur in such a hot climate. As I suggested, no one had a chance of actually passing through a test based on some kind of poison, just as the witches had no chance of passing the swimming test (if they drowned they were innocent, if they floated they were guilty and so they were burned). Unless Mary did have an antidote, we can only surmise that she did not in fact undergo a poison test and that the Syrian writer is confusedly referring to the cause of death of Herod. But why should he connect Mary and Joseph with Herod? In fact, their lives are deeply interwoven with his, for it is he who sent out soldiers to kill babies in Bethlehem. Or is the connection more obvious than this?

Given that Mary's family were rich and influential, it is possible that she knew the court of Herod and perhaps the reference to her dancing is indeed true but that she danced for Herod at the palace. The Syrian writer of James may have confused the Temple with the palace, understandably, since Herod had ornamented it with a golden eagle in flagrant contravention of the rules of the Jews against idols and graven images. To the Syrian, where kingship and divinity were equal, the Temple and the palace were one and the same thing. Let us suppose, then, that Mary did dance for Herod in his palace, not the Temple. There may have been other pressures on Mary, for Herod was a notorious lover of women. Viewed this way, the gospel of James has consistency about it. The palace is full of plots, Herod is already dying, Joseph is asked by Joachim to take Mary to a safe place, and though he finds her pregnant, he still protects her. He takes her to Bethlehem, where she has the child, just as Herod orders the massacre to mark his death, and he dies from the curse of the waters of bitterness. And while Herod's funeral procession is under way with an escort of Gaulish, German and Thracian soldiers and hundreds of slaves and relatives, as Josephus tells us in his *Jewish War*,[6] Joseph takes his wife out of Herod's son's clutches by going to Egypt.

Why Egypt? Why not Syria? There were Jewish communities in both countries, but there may be something in the notion that Mary was somewhat influenced by the Herodian court, for Herod owed his throne to Mark Anthony, who ruled with Cleopatra, Queen of Egypt. Furthermore, Cleopatra's family were descended from Alexander's generals. Alexander's corpse was actually at Alexandria in a casket. Egyptian nobility, and certainly monarchy, were Greek in origin, and there was much Greek influence in Herod's household and army. What bedevils research into this era is the assumption by Christian writers, for 2,000 years now, that only the Christian viewpoint is consonant with a sense of morality and human dignity. Added to this is the incredible parochialism of the then Jewish outlook; priestesses were 'whores' in both Christian and Jewish vernacular, and both burned them.

Since Joachim, Mary's father, was a devout man, giving alms, as told in the Book of James, it has been assumed that he was a devout Jew, but he could have been a devout follower of Isis. Because Herod broke Jewish laws, he comes down to us as a man of evil repute, beyond the pale. Certainly he did terrible things, but no more terrible than a clutch of Popes or a platoon of Christian kings, not to mention Inquisitors: yet if their faith is unimpugned, why should we assume Herod was not religious? He had a great love of women, and though in the latter part of his life, probably crazed by slow poisoning, he killed female and male plotters, he was more lenient towards women, and certainly more understanding of their conditions than were orthodox Jews. He may have executed for reasons of state, but he did not call women out to be burned just because they may have broken some sexual law or taken the role of temple acolyte of Isis. He was much thought of by Mark Antony, and supported by the urbane and brilliantly perceptive Augustus. That Mary was an honoured member of his household is not impossible, and as such she could have been there in some religious capacity. That she danced there is very likely, since dancing is not the kind of thing you invent about somebody. These influences, then, are plausible, and the effects of mixing with so many noblewomen from virtually every part of the Empire would have opened up her mind, and at the same time impressed upon her that her ancestry was the equal of many of the women she mixed with in Herod's palace.

The King had many wives and concubines, and was a keen patron of the arts, being a great builder, not only in Jerusalem but in Greece as well. His lack of snobbery, his eye for beauty, supports the notion that Mary might well have found favour in his eyes, as had Tamar in Judah's, Ruth in Boaz's and Bathsheba in David's. Josephus lists the following women close to Herod:

The king, indeed, had nine wives and children by seven of them. Antipater himself was the son of Doris, Herod of Mariamme, the high priest's daughter, Antipas and Archelaus of Malthace the Samaritan, their sister Olympias being married to Herod's nephew Joseph. By Cleopatra of Jerusalem he had Herod and Philip and by Pallas Phasael. He had other daughters, Roxane and Salome, the first by Phaedra, the second by Elpis. Two wives were childless, a cousin and a niece. Apart from these there were the two sisters of Alexander and Aristobulus, children of Mariamme.[7]

The intrigues in this family were extensive. Mariamme was to die because of them, and perhaps Herod never got over the fact that he executed a woman he loved passionately; torture, death and treachery clouded Herod's last years. It would not have escaped Mary's notice, even if she had been only a peripheral member of the court, that the intrigues revolved around succession, the fertility of women, and the fact that they brought forth heirs and heiresses. These were the central political facts of life in Herod's palace. A mere careless word was enough to put you under suspicion. Is it possible that Mary in girlish enthusiasm had mentioned that she believed she would be the mother of the Redeemer? We cannot tell, but if a careless word escaped her lips, it would explain why she had to leave. Even Herod's wives could be put to death because of his suspicions, well founded or not.

Virginity

Despite these important historical implications, the Book of James, as it has come down to us, is a hodge-podge of different influences, but the central religious core is clear enough. Marina Warner argues persuasively that the Book of James was crucial to the later cult of the Virgin Mary, and that it was the emphasis on virginity which attracted the early Church Fathers.[8] She also suggests that the author was probably Syrian and was aware of the virginity requirements of young female acolytes in the temples of Diana at Ephesus and Aphrodite at Corinth. If this is so, then Mary's pre-puberty life could well have been as a handmaid of the Great Goddess in one of her forms, possibly Astarte, which would explain the confusion with the Jerusalem Temple. That she was related to powerful people may also explain how she survived the results of her pregnancy, though here the crucial figure is Joseph, who seems to have understood the principle of keeping one jump ahead of the opposition. The truth, if we are ever to come to it, is probably found between the lines, free of partisan interpolation, namely that Joseph got Mary away from Jerusalem just in time, and also got her away from Bethlehem too. It must, after all, be remembered that the other baby from her family at this time, John, was to grow up a thorn in the side of both priesthood and monarchy. This family of Mary had always lived dangerously, religiously, and with great courage and, as we may now be sure, they had hardly ever lived conventionally. Mary, it seems, spent her pregnancy in flight from Jerusalem, and the first days of motherhood in flight from Bethlehem.

There has been much controversy about Mary's virginity, but it has centred on the mistranslation of the Hebrew word *lmh*, that is *almah*, which is found in the prophecy of Isaiah: 'Behold a young woman shall conceive and bear a son, and shall call his name Immanuel' (Is. 7:14). Anti-Christian writers have seized on the fact that the Septuagint translation of the Bible, in Greek, uses the word *parthenos* (virgin), not *almah* (young woman). It is therefore argued that the prophecy refers to a young woman of childbearing age, not a virgin, and hence the virgin birth was not virgin at all. This is not altogether convincing. For one thing, the Jews had very strict laws concerning sexuality. Women who committed adultery were stoned to death, and adultery included intercourse outside and before marriage. The point is that in Jewish society a young woman of unimpeachable reputation would *ipso facto* be a virgin; consequently Isaiah, in his prophecy, does not have to spell out the implications of his own words. What, then, had happened? In modern psychological parlance, she dreamed the angel; in religious language she had a mystical experience; in human terms a young and vigorous descendant of acolytes of the Mother Goddess was certain in her own mind that she was singled out to be the mother of the godhead's child, and she knew she was a virgin.

Joseph believed Mary, his betrothed, about her pregnancy. So did her cousin Elizabeth, who was married to Zachariah (Zacharias), who had been a priest. Actually, Zachariah and Joseph are almost superfluous, for it is Elizabeth and Mary who hold the history of their world in their wombs. Elizabeth bears John the Baptist, Mary bears Jesus. The Saviour was to come of the Jewish race as foretold by Isaiah, but this could come about only if a Jewish woman gave birth, for a Jewish father is not enough to make the child Jewish; the mother has to be a Jew. It does not dilute the Jewishness of her offspring if the father is God, a cosmic ray, a Roman soldier or a Greek sophist.

Mary's insistence that she became pregnant by God has, of course, received much hostile comment, but the curious thing about the libels, other than those involving intercourse with a phantom Roman soldier, Panthera, is that they are centred around some supernatural event, thereby adding credence to her story in a roundabout way. There is also the story of the Roman wife, Paulina, which Josephus recounts in his *Antiquities*,[9] and which may have been excised by Christian censors from his *Jewish War*. Paulina was a young married woman of great beauty and noble birth, who was chaste and faithful. A nobleman, Mundus, was inflamed with lust for her, but she would not consort with him. Through the intermediary of a woman called Ide, whom Mundus hired to bribe the priests of the temple of Isis in Rome, Paulina was tricked into spending the night in the sanctuary, where she believed she would consort with a god. The god came, and they spent the night making love, but of course the 'god' was Mundus. He boasted about the trickery some days later to her face, which shocked her greatly, for she was a sincere believer of Isis and had thought one of the Great Goddess's divine consorts had come for her. Outraged, she petitioned Tiberius, who was so incensed that he had the priests and Ide tortured, and then crucified. He razed the temple, and threw the statue of Isis in the Tiber, and at the same time expelled the Jews from Rome. Mundus he exiled.

Josephus tells the tale with glee,[10] noting that a similar thing must have happened with Mary. The Jewish connection is there because mixed up with Paulina's mishap is the story of a Jewish confidence trickster who bilked a Roman woman out of presents for Jerusalem, pocketing the proceeds himself, and it was this that caused Tiberius to act so swiftly against the Jewish community in Rome. This is a far-fetched rendering, since there is no reason whatsoever why a Roman noblewoman would send gifts to the temple in Jerusalem. Unless, of course, the thread running through all these unsatisfactory stories is that there was a temple of Isis, or at least of the Great Goddess, in Jerusalem. The only place where such a temple could survive was the palace of Herod. What Josephus and Eisler both miss is the sincerity with which Paulina submitted to the embraces of a god. In Jewish eyes this would make her a 'harlot'. The very least that comes from these attempts to libel Mary is her sincerity; but there is no hint of an elaborate plot to take her, no mention of a Mundus in the wings, which may suggest there was nothing to traduce, that indeed she was a virgin.

The Roman soldier father hypothesis was first put about to damage not only Mary's reputation, but to suggest Christ's bastardy. Ian Wilson, drawing on many sources in his *Jesus: the Evidence*, refers to a Jewish tradition of identifying Jesus as Yeshu ben Pantera, meaning son of Pantera, which is sometimes spelt Panthera.[11] The story, which dates at least as early as AD 150, says that Mary had an illegitimate child by a Roman soldier, Pantera or Panthera. Wilson is at a loss to make anything of this, save to say it is understandable that Jews hostile to Christianity would fabricate scurrilous stories. Certainly the attempt by Christian commentators to pass off Panthera as a corruption of Parthenos, in which case ben Parthenos would mean son of the virgin, is barely persuasive. However, there is, it appeared to me, a strong case for an altogether new interpretation.

Panthera, pantera, relates to lions, as in *leo panthera*, the common lion. As Messiah Jesus was truly the lion of Judah, and indeed the New Testament traces Jesus through the Davidic line to the house of Judah. In short anyone calling Jesus Pantera, Lion, would be understood to be referring to precisely what Jesus claimed, namely to be the Messiah.

The role of the religion of the Great Goddess in Mary's life, it seems, has been hitherto traduced and then ignored, because it suited patristic prejudice in both Jewish and Roman Catholic camps, but the stark fact is there is nothing in a male monotheism which would lead to any expectation of a virgin conceiving, whereas the Great Goddess tradition expected a priestess to become pregnant. Indeed in Babylon where Astarte ruled, chosen priestesses spent a night at the top of an eight-towered citadel, in a sanctuary, where, it has come down to us, a god was supposed to make them pregnant, but the internal evidence of this is shaky. For one thing, why should a god enter the sanctuary of a goddess? In other words, the notion of virgin fertility is implicit in the more sacred rituals of the Great Goddess. Add to this the need for a rational explanation of why a Jewish girl should consider that she was chosen to carry the Messiah while still a virgin – and special pleading in the usual accounts is noteworthy for its blatancy. To emphasize the point, the last thing a girl was expected to do in the eyes of the Temple priests was to get pregnant as a virgin, while a religious purpose to such an event was anathema to them. So we are left with the question: where did Mary get the strength and the idea? If we see her in the so-called apochrypha picture there is no mystery at all; as an acolyte, a priestess, a descendant of priestesses of the Great Goddess, her vision would be not only natural but directly within the tradition she believed in. The next point is that her character as we have seen it is such that she would not lie about something so sacred to her. In the absence of evidence to the contrary, the position that she was telling the truth has the merits of being consistent with her life, personality, and her beliefs. It is perhaps pertinent to note that the attack on her for her claims was based on traducing her religious observances.

Politics, Power and Pregnancy

As noted earlier, the Great Goddess religion is endemic to humankind, and in Europe and the Middle East artifacts attesting to the tradition are numerous. Figurines of Astarte, for example, are prevalent the length and breadth of Israel. It was certainly a mystical religion, fully aware of the mystery inherent in existence, but it was also a very human one. A virgin would one day become a mother, so virgin birth in that sense is clear enough. That female blood was, in a very real sense, of positive religious significance was proven by the common observation that when it did not flow a birth resulted.

The problem facing the early Church was to demarcate its not very original ideas from the numerous cults of the Great Goddess. It took aboard the virgin birth because no religion could realistically expect to gain any credence in the Greek and Roman world if it forswore its very foundation of human religious experience. One of the demarcations, however, was sinister: that a virgin coming to term in the usual way could still be a virgin afterwards. Now this was a very odd idea, and struck at the very centre of the Great Goddess.

That a woman might conceive without a man was intrinsic to the philosophy of the Great Goddess. That she was a virgin intacta was a technical point, for then clearly the Goddess was with her. Every woman who became a mother shared this creative aspect with the Mother of the Universe, but when she gave birth, her hymen, if intact, was of course ruptured. The real essence, then, of virgin birth was not a hymen but the superfluity of male intervention. This was something the priests of the Jewish Temple religion would not countenance, though priests in every major city found no difficulty in it at all. The Roman Catholic hierarchy certainly could not accept it, because it would make them just like any other cult in this respect, and so the burgeoning theology of that absurd notion of for ever virgin, for ever intacta, was set in motion. Clearly, it was misogynistic, for it scorned motherhood and made it suspect; whereas in the Great Goddess cults, motherhood was seen as part of the divine in every parturition, however humble.

The suppression of women, then, was there in the insistence, for political purposes, that Mary was intact after delivery. Even worse, at the turn of the fourth century that doctor of the Church, Augustine, was actually saying children were being born reeking of sin, and the cause of it was genital congress. This severed Roman Catholicism from its Judaic roots, for even the Temple priests regarded this as blasphemous, while to Christians who saw their obvious roots in the Great Goddess cults, the idea was obscene. To educated Romans and Greeks, the notion was simply unbalanced. But the idea was politically powerful; it put women down in a way which was wholly without precedence in its ugliness. It was a fearful development, but fear can cow, and if you can back psychological terror with military might, the sad fact is that a potent political force is achieved.

In addition, the Roman Catholics, though only a minority of various Christian persuasions in Rome, insisted that they, and they alone could forgive sins. They insisted, too, that Jesus went to Hell, and then to Heaven. Since even babes were born reeking of sin, which could only be remitted by male priests of the Catholic caucus, parents were put in a quandary. If they believed the beautiful teachings of Christ, and were further suborned into believing the claims of the Catholic minority, to save their children from hell-fire, they would bring them up in the Catholic dogmas. Once this happened new Catholics, terrified, over-reliant on their priests, would be nurtured. The juggernaut had begun, and a Roman Emperor, Constantine, who himself did not share the Roman Catholic beliefs, backed the priests who most controlled their flocks, and made it the State religion.

The other Christians were butchered, burned, made into unpersons, for their beliefs were not dogmatic, not dependent upon a central hierarchy. They did not preach hell-fire, nor even original sin, and were not women-haters. Alas, that is not the way to gain power in this world, just as their true leader had proved, for Jesus was undogmatic, was a lover of women, and ended up on a cross. Jesus even warned that his kingdom was not of this earth. It is curious then that those who professed to be his followers did everything they could to make sure they had a king, a court, a city and a state, and were to use the armed forces of suppliant kings to maim and murder anyone who saw things differently.

I am, of course, not unique in seeing the growth of institutional Christianity in this way. Indeed, I am merely following the footsteps of historians of merit, such as Gibbon, who describes very clearly how the Roman Catholic caucus became powerful, in his *Decline and Fall of the Roman Empire*. Nero may have burned any kind of follower of Christ, but it was the Roman kind who burned all the others. What is new here, though, is the tracing of the traducement of a great religious testimony by a religious genius, founded on the widespread expectancies of the Great Goddess cults, into an instrument of terror and politics. To put it very simply, you only have to read what Jesus did, and then compare what was done allegedly in his name, to be struck by an overpowering sense of paradox.

Mary's child was, it appears, a small person of some affliction, capable, though, of exciting the deepest aspirations of man and woman, a genius who has marked the world, a person who came naturally out of the ordinary beliefs of the majority of people, born as Mary said, virginally.

But Jesus was believed to have been a woman by devout Christians in the south of France, descendants, as it were, of the Church of Mary Magdalene. They believed they had her bones. Rome on the other hand insisted that not only had Jesus been a six-foot male, and did so by fraud, but he rose from the dead, and then ascended into Heaven. The two views are not reconcilable, and the lovers of the female Christ were killed for it.

It is one thing to trace the collisions of ideas and to wonder at religious beliefs, but it is another to make categorical statements about natural events. The believers of the female Christ had no need of Ascensions into Heaven, nor mothers who were intacta after giving birth. They did, however, believe that a woman could have a child without the intervention of a man. Indeed, one of the greatest priestesses of the Great Goddess, the Virgin Mary, was certain she was so honoured, and lived her life accordingly, facing danger and dismay by her claims. We know that when a woman gives birth her hymen is bound to be broken and her private parts stretched, but what we do not know with certainty, is that a woman cannot conceive without a male sperm. Since we do not know this, it would be wise, not to mention courteous, to treat Mary's claim, which after all has come out of tens of thousands of years of religious tradition, of her pregnancy with some seriousness. What are the facts of the matter?

I would like to emphasize one point before going into the biology: of the millions of women on this earth who have had children, the vast majority have been in contact with men. It does not follow from this, however, that all conceptions arose through such contact. As we are learning daily, life can emerge in many different ways.

Virgin Birth

From time to time in the popular press there are stories of virgin births. These are usually treated with the same kind of odd mixture of reverence and ribaldry, explicit or implied, that Mary's motherhood has been. However, the matter cannot so easily be dismissed, except in cases of male children of a putative virgin conception, as we shall see later.

The scientific details which reject male but accept female virgin birth are somewhat involved, but well worth persevering with. There are about 100,000,000,000,000 cells in the human body. Many of them are dividing to replace ones that have died. This division is called mitosis, and produces daughter cells, that is cells identical to the parent cell, and is a kind of virgin birth, in that no other cell is involved. Each cell in your body has the same set of chromosomes, spindly chains of nucleic acid, which are made up of nucleic acid building blocks called nucleotides, arranged in a very precise order. This order is called the genetic code, and predetermined lengths of these nucleotides form a gene, which could be responsible, for example, for blue eyes or the production of certain ferments necessary for the functioning of a cell. Each cell contains twenty-three pairs of chromosomes, each chromosome carrying many genes. In the formation of a daughter cell, or rather two daughter cells, these chromosomes divide into halves, separate and then duplicate, so that when the two daughter cells emerge as separate identities, each has twenty-three pairs of chromosomes, just like the parent cell.

In women, there are twenty-three pairs of chromosomes in every cell, each pair being a duo, the members of which are similar. In males there are twenty-two pairs which are like those in the female, but the twenty-third pair consists of a long and a short chromosome. The short one is found only in males and is called Y, the male chromosome, while its partner, the long one, is called the female chromosome and designated X. To use modern jargon, women have the chromosomal complement 46XX, and men 46XY. The possession of two X's makes a female, the possession of one X and one Y makes a male. However, there are thousands of women with the complement 45XO, that is they have only one X chromosome. We will come to know these women very well as our investigation proceeds.

In the testes, male cells divide and so produce two new cells, but this process is not the daughtering process of mitosis, but meiosis, where the pairs of chromosomes separate, producing spermatazoa, 23X and 23Y. Paradoxically, the testicles of a fertile man contain little female animals, the 23X spermatozoa, and an equal number of male sperms, 23Y.

The ovaries of a woman produce, by meiosis, ova of a chromosomal complement 23X. If a sperm of complement 23X meets it and enters it, a cell of 23X (from mother) plus 23X (from father) is produced, that is 46 XX. This fertilized ovum then divides by mitosis under the direction of the genetic code in the chromosomes, and each cell is a 46XX. The life of a woman is beginning. However, if the 23Y sperm meets the 23X ovum, a fertilized ovum of 23X + 23Y is formed, namely 46XY, and the life of a man is beginning.

But what if the ovum of a normal woman, that is a woman who is 46XX, and the overwhelming majority of women are 46XX, were to undergo duplication of its chromosomes, that is the ovum 23X replicates its chromosomal material to form 46XX, and then proceeds to divide in the normal mitotic way? If development did occur to full term, a girl child would be born, with a one in two chance or higher, depending on ancestry, of having the same colour eyes, the same blood group, the same hair colour, even the same fingerprints, as the mother. This would be true virgin birth, and could not produce, from a 46XX woman, any child but a girl. It might be noted that daughters are often very much like their mothers, more so than sons are like their fathers. I have seen no rigorous scientific proof of this, nor statistical analysis, which, of course, is essential if it is to pass from a personal and perhaps subjective impression to hard data, but it is a common enough impression. What, though, are the scientific and medical facts?

The Medical Evidence

Parthenogenesis is a routine fact of biology and experimental embryology. It is common in the natural form in many invertebrates, simple animals and certain reptiles. However, the main point taught by current science is that the ovum contains within it the 'potentiality to form a new being.[1] The stimulus is usually the male sperm, but changes in the chemical environment of the ovum can initiate division, as indeed can sudden shocks, radiation, and mechanical stimulation.

Professor Matthew Kaufman, Professor of Anatomy, University Medical School, Edinburgh, is a leading expert on parthenogenicity. His experimental work has involved the culturing of parthenogenic mouse embryos *in vitro* (test-tube) to the stage nine to eleven days, where they were indistinguishable from normally fertilized mouse ova at nine to eleven days pregnancy *in utero* (natural). The importance of this observation is the length of time these embryos survived and developed normally, a period equivalent to half the full term of a mouse gestation period, namely twenty days. In our species this would amount to four and a half months.[2]

There are many such experiments carried out by other investigators in a wide variety of mammals, but what is their significance? First, they show that an ovum can divide in the normal way which would, if continued, lead to a foetus, without the entry of a male cell. Secondly, though the conditions are artificial, that is, less good for a developing ovum than the womb would be, considerable development does occur. We can, then, safely conclude that spontaneous or virgin development probably occurs in many mammals, and the chances of coming to term are very high.

What, though, is the situation in human beings? Technically there is no difference; the conclusion must apply to human beings too. But have the experiments been done? Indeed they have. Doctors Plachot, Mandelbaum and de Grouchy, of Hôpital Necker, Paris, report *in vitro* parthenogenesis in the human species, in that during the examination of some 800 oocytes (ova) prior to *in vitro* fertilization, twelve showed evidence of parthenogenetic activation. Four of these twelve underwent division, that is cleavage, and the division of one of them was normal.[3]

There are over a billion women on this planet making ova, and they produce active ones every lunar month. The number produced in a year then is a staggering thirteen billion. Even if the chance was one in a million that an ovum would spontaneously begin to divide – and given the stresses, pollution, radiation and medication so many women are subject to, there are stimuli enough – this would result in 13,000 possible virgin births a year. Even taking into the equation the smaller number of people alive 2,000 years ago, and beyond – say another two thousand years – the chances of it happening at least once in human history must be, in horse-racing terms, very favourable indeed. But apart from the anecdotal material of the tabloids, is there any concrete evidence that it happens?

There is, but we must also resign ourselves to the fact that we only know about the unsuccessful virgin concep- tions called teratomas. This arises because the vast majority of women live with men, and so if they conceived virginally, in other words had a developing ovum which went to term, they, their husbands, boy-friends and everyone else would assume it was the result of ordinary ovum–sperm fusion. The point is that scientific virgin birth merely means no sperm is involved, not that the girl is a virgin intacta. Even if she turned up pregnant to her medical examiner with her hymen intact, without exception, I would hazard, most medical men would assume sperm had entered the tiny hole the hymen has. To prove that a girl has never been in contact with a man is extremely difficult, there being so many men and so many opportunities. Even nuns in convents could, arguably, be intimate with trades- men, gardeners and, of course, visiting priests. It would take a woman of the moral courage of Mary to insist she did not, in fact, know a man.

But why are only the failures seized upon as being the result of virgin birth? That interesting question reflects on the state of the medical mind, but, to be fair, the real reason is that they haven't as yet dared to in- vestigate successful virgin births – it is professionally safer to assume normal development, but in the case of some deformed foetuses, investigators have satisfied themselves that no sperm was involved. There is also the important ethical point that to saddle a normal child with a miraculous conception may be thought unwise.

What are teratomas, these putative failures of virgin conception? A teratoma is tissue often found in the ovary, showing developmental organization, to a greater or lesser degree, similar to that of an ordinary foetus. De Grouchy has been investigating this for some years. In May 1980 he published a paper 'Human Parthenogenesis: a fascinating single event' in which he observed that ovarian teratomas are considered to be a form of parthenogenetic development in humans, where the chromosomal complement is of entirely maternal origin.[4] As I earlier emphasized, if development were normal, a girl child would result.

One American team of investigators concludes that:

Many theories have been advanced to explain the origin of ovarian teratomas in general. Early speculation centered on unsatisfied sexual longings, nightmares, intercourse with the devil, witchcraft, and the judgment of the deity on immoral practices. More recent theories have included degeneration of a fertilized ovum, fertilization of a polar body ... The theory considered most tenable at the present time is parthenogenic development of a germ cell.[5]

What, then, is the status on scientific grounds rather than the anecdotal, of conception without a male sperm fertilizing the ovum? Or to put it rather more accurately and objectively, what is the status of the hypothesis that human ova can undergo spontaneous fission as the result of stimulus by something other than a male spermatazoon? The answer is simple and well substantiated. We know for a fact that the ova in a woman's body can undergo such development. We further know that a variety of stimuli can induce such changes, from mechanical to chemical. What we do not know, in the sense of its having still to be proved, is that such cleavage can go to term and produce a healthy child. However, there is no proof against it; rather the evidence is in favour of its possibility. If it should happen, then a healthy foetus will result, and providing there are no extraneous complications, as in any 'normal' conception, a child will be delivered in term.

The evidence of the teratomas is not proof of virgin conception, only that ova can undergo development without the intervention of a male sperm. As I have discussed, the pathological nature of these conceptions causes them to be investigated, whereas if the development proceeded without pathology they would automatically be regarded as having been initiated by ordinary male–female gamete fusion, fertilization. Clearly this is a tantalizing situation. However, it does carry the challenge of clinically determining how many normal conceptions occur without male and female eggs fusing. There are, of course, great technical difficulties in such an investigation, but it does have serious implications for human fertility, and also legitimacy, since if a woman does conceive without the intervention of a man, and comes to term, and is unmarried, then the child is clearly not a bastard, and this may have legal importance, not to mention social significance regarding status.

In summary, the scientific case for virgin birth is not proved, but the pointers are such that it remains a legitimate possibility. Certainly, it would betray ignorance to aver that it could not and does not happen – except in the case of male children, where it is a contradiction in terms since the Y chromosome is not present in normal 46XX women. In the case under consideration, however, it is intriguing to note that the stimulus most often depicted by artists is a ray of light shining on the Virgin Mary. That electromagnetic radiation can induce cleavage in mammalian ova is a matter of routine observation in today's laboratories. The odd thing is that artists innocent of any science opted for this method in their symbols centuries ago. Coincidence is often very diverting.

It would be a mistake, however, to suppose that virgin conception can occur only in one way after the stimulus. The simplest way theoretically is the ordinary replication of a cell which would give rise to a foetus. The result would be a clone of the mother, not only female but identical genetically, and barring the usual changes induced in the developing foetus by mother's illnesses and infections, the baby would be like her mother was when she was born, and would grow up physically like her, with the proviso that they had the same climate, nutrition and medical history. Of course in the real world these aspects are never the same so that there would be differences, not to mention age changes, yet none the less, the daughter would be a kind of clone, having the same genetic component as her mother.

However, if the ovum replicates its genetic material, it will not be replicating the exact complement of the mother. This may seem confusing, but the explanation is relatively simple. The ovum mother cell has twenty-three pairs of chromosomes. When an ovum is formed twenty-three go to one ovum, but clearly there are a lot of ways you can pick these out of twenty-three pairs. If this ovum then replicates, it clearly will not have the same chromosomal set as the mother. It will still be female, but will only have, as it were, half the original different genes the mother had. One would expect this to be the more likely kind of virgin development, in which case mother and daughter will be very similar but not clones.

I was delighted to have found evidence which supported Mary's claim – she has been traduced enough – but then it became transparently clear that Mary's child, conceived in this way, would grow up looking like a girl, with soft voice, and at adolescence would undergo change into a woman. Since Jesus dies at least in the fourth decade of life, my hypothesis and hence the virgin birth itself, encounters what appear to be insurmountable difficulties, because a young woman with rounded hips and normal breasts cannot pass as a man for long, and in Jewish culture the fact of menstruation was, and still is to a lesser extent, a matter of ritual bathing. If Jesus were a woman, she could not have been so obviously female.

The difficulties appeared to be insoluble, and they were increased by the traditions of what Mary looked like, for we have this portrait of her by Epiphanius, Bishop of Cyprus AD *c*.404.

She was grave and dignified in all her actions. She spoke little and only when it was necessary to do so. She listened readily and could be addressed easily. She greeted everyone. She was of medium height, but some say she was slightly taller than that. She would speak to everyone fearlessly and clearly without laughter or agitation, and she was especially slow to anger. Her complexion was of the colour of ripe wheat, and her hair was auburn. Her eyes were bright and keen, and the pupils were of olive green tint. Her eyebrows were arched and deep black. Her nose was long, her lips were red and full and overflowing with the sweetness of her words. Her face was not round but somewhat oval. Her hands were long, and her fingers also.[6]

How can Mary's child be the little Christ figure we encountered? True, there are features here which match, but Mary is unmistakably womanly, while Jesus passed as a man. How could this be? Again, the problem seemed without solution, but I recalled the description I had built up from Josephus and the Gospels. Was 'affliction' the answer? In other words were there women who were small, with some strange wrinkling of the skin, looking like boys, but nevertheless indubitably women? And were these women gifted with extraordinary verbal ability, as

we have seen Jesus had? Did they too have a special gift
regarding the perception of space and time, something
far advanced of the ordinary run-of-the-mill perception?
It seemed impossible that such could be the case, but if
all the other facts stood, then they predicated there must
be such women.

The Bonnevie-Ullrich Syndrome

It seemed impossible that there was a medical condition
to fit all the known facts, but I recalled some pictures I
had used when giving my post-graduate lectures on the
biochemistry of inheritance some ten years earlier. The
details were smudged by time, and I no longer had my
lecture notes. Consequently I undertook fresh research,
starting with general works, hoping to find a lead to the
more specific and contemporary.

In the *Merck Manual*, a standard medical text, I found
a résumé of the Bonnevie-Ullrich Syndrome, also known
as Turner's Syndrome, a form of gonadal dysgenesis
afflicting women only. The characteristics of these women
are short stature, wide chest, absence of breast development, multi-pigmented naevi (or nevi in the US),
strawberry or brown birth marks, juvenile external
genitalia, absence of menstrual bleeding.[7]

These common features are of course not always found
together, but often they are. The condition is caused by
partial or complete absence of one of the female X sex
chromosomes, but these people are indubitably women
and there are many thousands of them. Today they are
regarded not as distinct from other women, but women
with special characteristics. As with 46XX women, these
45XO women are sometimes handicapped, sometimes
not. It is statistically certain that you have met one and
not known about their condition. What do we know
about them?

One group of physicians at the University Hospital, Seattle, and the University of Washington School of Medicine met weekly for some time to pool their findings, publishing the results in 1982. These physicians point out that not all 45XO women are short and not all do not menstruate, but the incidence of these features is about ninety per cent. They feel that hormone replacement therapy is often indicated, so that secondary sexual characteristics, such as genitalia and breasts, can be developed. Absence of menstruation in these women usually results from non-development of ovaries, which implies that most of them will not bear children, but some have. These doctors say, 'We also tell an adolescent 45XO patient that they will be capable of normal and satisfactory sexual relations, interpersonal relations and family life.' Some women will have problems with kidneys and frailty of intestinal organs. The average height is between four and five feet, but taller heights are found, and if the mother is taller than average, then her 45XO daughter will tend to inherit this trait.

There is some tendency for the bones to be weak, and the face is sometimes narrow. One woman in two has narrow hips (fifty per cent incidence of android configuration of the pelvis, confirmed by X-ray study of the bones). There is an elevated chance of problems with the aorta, the main vessel of the heart, compared with the general population. Haemangiomas, that is concentration of blood vessels (which can be extensive, or merely 'blood spots') are also indicated. The skin may have several, or may have none, of the common naevi, or red spiders; there may be keloids (scar-like puckering of the skin), dryness, or oiliness, and hairiness. The authors point out that pigmented naevi are primarily a cosmetic problem. They also note that the skin may be sensitive to scarring, so 45XO girls should be careful about piercing their ears for ear-rings, though they note that most of their patients have little problem in this area. Facial hirsutism, they report, is rarely a problem. 'Axillary and pubic hair is often scanty . . . Reassurance about sexuality and about the normal variation in body hair among women is often important.' There are indications of some 45XO women having hormonal problems, including diabetes.[8]

The Washington University and Seattle group found that of the adult women treated as their patients, eighty per cent had completed at least four years of college. They note that other workers have found evidence to relate a 45XO karyotype with anorexia nervosa, but the risk is only slightly greater than in the general population. In the report by Judith Hall and colleagues are two photographs. A woman of thirty-five is depicted, with no breasts, longish hair, and looking older than her years. Juxtaposed was a picture of a four-year old girl who had appealing jug ears and looks like any other child of four. In neither case is there pronounced webbing of the neck, or feet or hand swelling, sometimes found in 45XO women. In Chamberlain's *Symptoms and Signs in Clinical Medicine* there is a beautiful picture of a twenty-two-year-old woman with the pure and innocent face seen in paintings of the infant Christ.[9]

Frank S. Pidcock of Jefferson Medical College notes that workers in the field have reported normal distribution of intelligence in women with Turner's Syndrome, with some evidence of decreased practical ability in tests,[10] though I wonder if this has any significance in everyday life. However, several authors have noted spatial disability in some 45XO women, but again I would question what this means. People with highly developed imaginations, William Blake for example, have a kind of spatial oddness about them, such as seeing angels in trees. It is a kind of oddness which is akin to genius, especially when related to high verbal skills. The inability to put square objects into square holes when given a choice of oval ones may, in certain individuals, betoken an imaginative response to a three-dimensional world. Reading skills are not lower than average in Turner's Syndrome, which leaves the likelihood that some women have very high reading skills and, given the datum that a vast majority of Judith Hall's patients completed four or more years at college, the supposition is probably a fact. My reading of the literature is that 45XO women are not markedly different intellectually from the 46XX women as a group, but that the curious mix of abilities could produce someone with extraordinary talents, where verbal skills and a new way of looking at the world might be exhibited.

I wrote to Dr Jean de Grouchy at the Hôpital Necker in Paris, concerning Turner's Syndrome, having already referred to de Grouchy's work on parthenogenesis. He reported that he had not noticed that patients had a lower voice and that life expectancy would not be much shortened. He also said that the shortening of the fourth metacarpal, or shortening of the palm, is not in principle connected with the syndrome (which means that not all 45XO women have this condition). He referred me, in response to my questions, to the work of Avery A. Sandberg, Department of Genetics and Endocrinology, Roswell Park Memorial Institute, Buffalo.[11] Sandberg points out that more than ninety per cent of girls with Turner's Syndrome show normal intelligence levels, and because the distribution is normal, I point out that amongst 45XO women there are exceptionally gifted individuals and retarded ones too, just as in 46XX women.

The curious matter of left-hand/right-hand problems in 45XO women is confirmed, and I suspect that this is related to space-form blindness, the inability to match different shapes and contrast them. Sandberg suggests,

'The personality of Turner Syndrome patients is generally pleasant, although they may appear somewhat undifferentiated and unconcerned.' But he then apparently contradicts himself by asserting, 'Emotionally they may be somewhat more unstable and dependent on their social environment than XX females.' This instability suggests a passionate nature, while the ability to be unconcerned, if it is concomitant, describes a personality which, although deeply committed to some issues, can at the same time distance itself from its personal implications. Selflessness combined with passion is a remarkable association, and one thinks, perhaps, of Mother Teresa working in the slums of India, with passionate love for the needy, yet unconcern for her own welfare.

I also wrote to Dr Frank Pidcock of the Children's Heart Hospital, Philadelphia, asking him several precise questions in an effort to complete my picture of 45XO women. Regarding the so-called space blindness, Dr Pidcock told me Turner Syndrome women have difficulty in finding parked cars in the large lots of shopping malls, but he didn't think the voice was lower, rather it was like a young girl's. Physically, these women did not strike him as lacking agility or endurance, and he observed that they have a marked cheerfulness.

If we overview the literature and, most important of all, the personal testimony of physicians who have worked with these women, we see how extraordinarily close is the fit between what we know of Jesus and the characteristics of the syndrome. The enhanced verbal ability, the idiosyncratic response to space and time, the shortness of stature, the inner optimism, the endurance are all there. For such a woman to occur by virgin birth, all that is required is that the formation of the ovum proceeds by incomplete halving. The details are as follows. In the usual production of an ovum, the egg cell in the ovary divides to give two daughter cells, one large and one small, both containing the same number of chromosomes. The large one, called a secondary egg cell, divides again, but without halving this time, giving a cell which matures to give an ovum and a smaller cell, called the polar cell. The diagram below shows only one egg cell, which gives rise to three polar cells and one ovum.[12]

DIAGRAM OF OVUM FORMATION

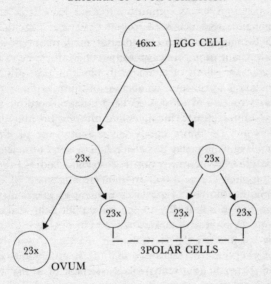

The ovum can be stimulated by various factors, as we have seen, to replicate its chromosomal complement and develop as an embryo. The first step is duplication of all the chromosomes, so 23X becomes 46XX. This is normal or conventional parthenogenesis. After one division there are two cells, two divisions give four cells, 3 give 8, 4 give 16 and so the embryo grows from 16 to 32, 64, 128, 256 . . . until approximately 10,000,000,000,000 cells are grown and differentiated in the new-born child.

But not all women have two X chromosomes, one in 3,000 have only one, (which could occur by the X chromosomes not duplicating in virgin conception, while the other chromosomes do). These women are truly women, and there are approximately 660,000 ($\frac{2}{3}$ million) of them alive today. Naturally one cannot estimate what proportion of them were conceived parthenogenetically, as is the case with all women.

As we have seen, some physicians take the view that 45XO women are women and that modern medicine can help them in many ways. Others take the view that they are not overly handicapped, since many 46XX women are infertile too, while the unusual response to time and space can be viewed very much according to context. It is clearly inconvenient to not be able to locate your car immediately on coming out of the supermarket, but given the general high level of verbal skills of these women, it is not that serious. And I revert to my earlier point, a gift in one circumstance is an affliction in another. To give a homely illustration, a height of 6ft 6in is useful on the basketball field, but it rules out a career as a jockey.

This space-form gift or affliction may very well be one of the roots of Jesus' notion of the Kingdom of Heaven, for though we are accustomed to think of Heaven up there above us, modern astronomy has shown there is nothing up there but a lot of space and a lot of planets. In other words, it was our form of space blindness which had to find a physical 'up-there' for Heaven, while for Jesus it was probably the most natural thing in the world to conceive of another place, so unlike this world, for a truer Kingdom of Heaven.

Transfiguration

But I was still worried about the haemangiomas, the naevi, the strawberry spots, the birthmarks, found in Turner's Syndrome, and still wondering about the tendency found in some women (XO) to scar easily. I found the literature evocative, but I wanted more, for it seemed to me that dermatology was a speciality in its own right, and it was a fair guess that the number of specialists in both XO women and dermatology was small. Accordingly I sought the help of Dr Oliver Scott, one of Britain's leading dermatological physicians, for I surmised that the facts concerning change of appearance might possibly be explained by a condition called pyogenic granuloma, and given the problems associated with skin in some XO women, it seemed a reasonable avenue to explore. Dr Scott supplied me with a summary of what is known about this condition in the form of a paper by P. J. Hare, of the Royal Infirmary, Edinburgh,[13] which, in Dr Scott's words, 'summarizes the situation and there has certainly been no change or increase in our knowledge about pyogenic granuloma since that time [i.e. 1970].'

The clinical description of the condition which alerted me was given by the editors of the *Merck Manual*: 'A bright red, brown or blue-black vascular nodule composed of proliferating capillaries in an edematous stroma.'[14] In other words, puffy areas of skin, highly coloured, with blood vessels underneath and within, rather bigger and more numerous than usual. These stains can be anywhere on the body and can disappear spontaneously. Professor Hare reports that most authors today consider the lesion is primarily a vascular disturbance and not a condition of infection, and is unassociated with any departure from general health.

Some specialists have related the puffy lesions of

granuloma with the port-wine stains, naevus flammeus, which are quite common and are often found on the face. The idea here seems to be that through some insult, injury or imbalance, the superficial port-wine stain becomes more vascular, swollen or puffy, thereby becoming a pyogenic lesion. If this is so, it is clear that the dividing line between port-wine stains and haemangiomas in general, with pyogenic granuloma in particular, is not abrupt. Certainly, the effect of emotional states on the apparent condition of the skin cannot be neglected, for changes in mood are always related to, and concomitant with, changes in hormonal levels. What is particularly characteristic about the pyogenic granuloma areas of the skin is their friability, being much less tough than the surrounding areas and bleeding much more easily. An individual with such areas on the back who was scourged would suffer much more serious damage than a person with ordinary skin. I have speculated that the person whom Pilate had scourged and then crucified may have had some underlying weakness, to have died so quickly on the cross. Given the fragility of haemangiomatous skin, and given its higher incidence in XO women, I suggest it is not unreasonable to relate these facts.

But what of the changed appearance? What of the 'sweating of blood' in the Garden of Gethsemane? We can never really know, but I put forward this hypothesis, based on the medical evidence we have reviewed. Jesus had skin lesions, common to XO women. The colour and condition of these stains, as we have seen, can vary, and their puffiness and hence their fragility can also vary. Blood pressure and heart rate are all functions of activity and hormonal levels. Fear, for example, will increase adrenalin, which can blanch the skin by constriction of blood vessels. Anger can do the same thing. From these facts, I suggest this scenario. When Jesus was threatened in the Temple with death, her emotional condition was adrenalin heightened: a mixture of fear (for death was not to be yet; there was so much to do before death was part of the plan) and anger, for the Scribes were always trying to trip her up. A blanching of the face took place to such an extent that Jesus was no longer recognizable. Given the similarity of clothes people wore, if the face changed colour or a disfiguring mark was less visible, a person could exploit these changes to make an escape, even to the extent of walking through a crowd of people who are looking for a small man with a port-wine stain on his face. I suggest that at the Transfiguration a similar set of events occurred, though this time there was the added stress of physical exertion, climbing to the top of the mountain, plus the ecstasy of exposition, for Jesus was to make an affirmation of status and intent.

Regarding the sweating of blood in the Garden of Gethsemane, I suggest that being in agony, which is the evangelist's term, is a literal statement. Here is this youngish woman, thirty-three years of age, small, strangely ugly-beautiful, knowing she is about to be arrested, beaten and crucified. She was to see her followers scatter, and she already knew Judas Iscariot had gone on his errand. She had worked for this moment, and yet it was sombre and terrible; the steps down from that mountain would lead her to the Judgement Seat and thence to the Cross. The wide and friable capillaries burst under the intense blood pressure, the intense beating of the heart, and the almost catastrophic and sustained high levels of adrenalin combined together to cause blood to flow.

The same hypothesis explains the hitherto inexplicable reports of Matthew and Luke on the insults Jesus often encountered from a hostile crowd, which has led many commentators to conclude that Jesus suffered from an affliction. That affliction, I suggest, was a form of hyperplasia of the subcutaneous blood vessels, hae-mangioma. Jesus, speaking of God, of Heaven, of Judgement and Redemption, was yet so physically imperfect.

Her detractors, knowing full well that no person could be a priest in the Temple who had any spot or blemish in the physical sense, knew they had a point when they called out for him, a male they most certainly thought Jesus to be, to save himself and heal himself. It was, given the Judaic background of priesthood, a bitter and mocking, and ultimately rejecting form of abuse. With 'his' affliction, Jesus could be accepted as a teacher, a Rabbi, but a priest never. Ironically, when the prophets spoke of a perfect victim, an unblemished and unspotted sacrifice, their deeper meaning was not of a physical ideal, but of moral and spiritual perfection.

This stage of the odyssey seemed a good place to ship oars, as it were, and evaluate what had been achieved, and just as importantly, what had not been achieved.

Arguably the hypothesis that Jesus was a woman, or rather was believed to be a woman by certain sects in the south of France, explained the savagery vented on them by the Popes, since they threatened the very structure of papal power. The energy with which the Popes suppressed any cult of a female Christ suggests strongly that they thought the threat was real, not imaginary. This is confirmed by the series of deceptions and forgeries which attended physical liquidation. Outstanding in these developments was the finding and then the 'losing' of the relics of a small-boned woman, Caput 58, believed to be the remains of Jesus Christ.

The broader background is that whereas the Roman Church exploited veneration of the female principle in its cults of the Virgin Mary and Mary Magdalene, there were sinister undertones in that in the hands of Rome these cults were used to suppress women, a conclusion reached by many writers and historians. However, they, the Roman hierarchy, insisted on the Virgin Birth, but traduced it. The historical and scientific evidence is that virgin birth cannot be ruled out as a natural phenomenon, but if it does occur a girl child will result.

The hypothesis, then, is self consistent and does no violence either to science or history, but the odyssey was now perforce to undergo a change, for instead of an aberrant male Christ figure, there was now a small and exceptional woman. This raised a host of questions, hinted at already, but which now must be spelt out. How could this person have become the Christ the Church says Jesus was? And how, at the same time, could she have become the more human figure who seems to stand in the shadows of the legends, folk tales and history of the south of France? In other words, who is this historical personage?

These problems could only be solved by questioning the very foundations of the form of Christianity we call Roman Catholic, and therefore, by implication, its offshoots, the Protestant communions, and its Eastern Orthodox form. Yet the most pressing matter was not an investigation into institutions but a need to see what the implications of the gender of Christ were. Of one thing, however, one could be sure: these are not academic points, for millions have lived by the dogmas of Rome, and by the same token, millions have been murdered because they would not. Yet it is the Christ figure who is the centre of the energy, not any church. It is the human being who died in the Place of the Skull who changed history and the way that human beings look upon themselves. Obviously it is the Nazarene who beckons.

— Part III —

Mary's Messiah

— 8 —

The Inspiration

As I surveyed the scenario which science and long repressed historical facts had ineluctably set before me, the
sense of irony that it was a Catholic dogma of virgin
birth which led to the challenging of its male Christ, was
only surpassed in intensity by the exhilaration of meeting
Jesus Christ for the very first time. Exit the mystic figure
of theology, enter a flesh-and-blood human being with a
real mother and a real set of human problems to overcome. The stuff of drama had at last been reconnected
with the most formidable personality in human history.
And it seemed plausible that this person was a parthenogenetic child of a remarkable woman who was fully
aware of her own religious, not to say cosmic, importance.
Yet, the story is so sympathetic, not something suddenly
appearing in history without antecedents, but an inevitable flowering, as it were, of the tradition of the Great
Goddess.

When Mary left Jerusalem, pregnant with Yeshu, as
she would call Jesus, danger stalked her from the beginning. Herod was out to kill all male children, and Mary
had to go to Bethlehem for the census. But when Mary
looked at her baby in the manger she saw she had a little
girl. As an heiress of the Great Goddess, Mary would
have expected a girl as redeemer, but she also knew that
Herod had set his soldiers the task of killing male children
in Bethlehem, fearing that he would be ousted by the
new Messiah or that his son would be denied his birth-
right. Mary is clearly in a quandary; she knows that no

female redeemer would be taken seriously in Israel, and so her child has to be entered as a boy in the census, an entry which is, in effect, a death warrant unless she leaves immediately. Mary's physical hardiness is a persistent theme in the Christ story, for she has already travelled from Jerusalem on a donkey when near her term.

In the reconstruction of Mary's life, we see the cunning, courage, obstinacy, strength of mind and religious awareness that characterizes the four women whom we have been allowed to know were her ancestresses. Mary is as resourceful as Tamar, gentle but unyielding as Ruth, charming and as beautiful as Bathsheba, and matriarchal as Rahab. She needed to be, for Herod's troops were coming, swords drawn to kill her child. She left for Egypt with Yeshu and Joseph as soon as she could. At this stage two people know that Yeshu is a girl, Mary and Joseph. Was there a midwife? Were there other witnesses to Yeshu's sex?

Jewish children were wrapped in swaddling clothes after birth, so no one less than intimately connected with Mary would know her secret. The Book of James mentions two women, one of whom must have known about Yeshu's sex, a midwife, and a curious character called Salome. The Book of James reveals that the midwife met Salome and told her a virgin birth had occurred. Salome, for reasons best known to her, physically examines Mary. Did she ask? Or did she try to physically force Mary? The story, used in the early Church to prove Mary's virginity, is not only unlikely but offensive. At any rate, Salome's offending hand withers – a warning to anyone disbelieving the dogma of virgin birth? As we have seen, a virgin birth can occur whether a woman is a virgin or not; it simply means the development of an ovum into a baby without a sperm. The hymen can be intact or not. But the Church insists that not only is Mary *intacta* before the birth, but after – hence the point of Salome's story. It is difficult to understand why the dogma asserts *intacta* after birth, when clearly a hymen would be ruptured beyond all repair by the passage of the baby's head through the vaginal canal. This story, then, is sheer figment, but the midwife cannot be so easily dismissed. Women at that time bore children by squatting, but there was usually a midwife present to catch the child.

Salome would not know the child was a girl unless somebody present had told her. Certainly neither Joseph nor Mary would say anything. This leaves us with the probability of a witness to Jesus' sex, the midwife. We may surmise she was a Jewish woman, perhaps of Bethlehem. But would she advertise that not only had she delivered a child of a virgin, but that it was a girl? Given that 'three wise men', probably the kin of Mary, plus shepherds and the star of David shining bright over the town of Bethlehem, all attest to something important happening, and given Isaiah's prophecy of the virgin birth, the midwife may well have understood something of the import of what was going on. She could be reasonably certain of a receptive audience saying that a Messiah had been born, but may have feared for her life in saying that it was a girl. And if she had been interrogated by Herod's murderous soldiers, she could have quietened them by saying she had delivered a girl, but on the other hand might they not have felt she was protecting the child, for Herod's orders were to kill male children? The chances of this midwife convincing anyone of what she had seen are therefore remote, but she would have talked, and the garbled version may very well have come down to us in the Book of James. It contains much important material central to the dogma of the virgin birth, but paradoxically it has been condemned, after several centuries of Christian use, by Rome.

Childhood

The canonical Gospels are remarkably silent about Jesus'
childhood. The only thing we are told is a confrontation
at an early age with Scribes and Pharisees, who are
mesmerized by the boy's scriptural ability. The same
story also suggests a rift between Jesus and his mother
and father, with his petulant response to their worry that
he was about his father's business. Such behaviour,
though introduced by the anecdote of his precocious
ability, seems hardly worthy, just as in a later passage:
the occasion here is when Jesus is told that his mother
wants to see him but asks 'Who is my mother?' The
ostensible point the Gospel writers wish us to take is that
all women are Jesus' mother. Again, this is unattractive,
and simply does not accord with the story of Cana, where
Jesus does as his mother bids, and saves the couple marrying from an embarrassing shortfall of wine.

The problem is worse than unattractiveness in the
child's character at an early age, if we are to believe the
Gospels, for there is no indication of the influences which
shaped Jesus, and surely his redoubtable mother was
crucially instrumental here.

In an attempt to explain or gloss over these gaps, most
Christian apologists have made much of Jesus' Jewishness, hoping to find in that tradition the answer to
natural question of the formative years. But there is cold
comfort for them here, since Jesus appears to have
eschewed Jewishness, at least the Jewishness of the
Temple. Scribes and Pharisees were for ever criticizing
Jesus, and rightly from their point of view, for breaking
the sabbath, consorting with loose women, drinking too
much, mixing with lackeys of the Roman State, such as
Matthew the Tax Collector. Indeed, Jesus actually
visited violence on the Temple, throwing out the sacrificial dove sellers.

But Jesus's anti-establishmentarianism went even further. He healed the centurion's servant, healed Thecla, Pilate's wife, and consorted with women of Samaria, a race which the Jewish priests hated with uncommon venom.

What do we really know about Jesus' childhood? It may be that there were clues in the early works or heretical works which suggested that the break with the Jewish Temple was truly severe, or indeed other clues regarding Jesus's teaching, or even gender. Certainly there appears a strange story in Luke which purports to be of the circumcision, which has misleading details in it.

'And when eight days were accomplished for the circumcising of the child, his name was called Jesus . . . And when the days of her purification according to the law of Moses were accomplished, they brought him to Jerusalem, to present him to the Lord' (Luke 2:21 – 22). In Jerusalem, a man called Simeon had a vision which promised he would not die until he saw the Christ. 'And when the parents brought in the child Jesus, to do for him after the custom of the Law . . .' Simeon recognized Jesus as the Messiah. Not only that, but a prophetess of eighty-four came in and said much the same thing. Luke then says, 'When they had performed all things according to the Law . . .' (Luke 2:39) they went back to Galilee. However, this account ignores Mary's fleeing into Egypt to escape Herod's troops.

I had at first thought that the days of purification must relate to Mary, but the text in Luke does not easily bear this interpretation. The recognition of the child in the Temple by a man and a woman appears far-fetched, as if to prove Jesus was actually there. Significantly, none of the other three Gospels refers to circumcision, so we are left only with Luke's account. Perhaps even more relevant is that Luke is the giver of an entirely male lineage for Joseph, who is not Jesus' father anyway. Luke for some reason appears to be straining to prove Davidic descent of a man who is not Jesus' father, and then trying to prop up a story of the circumcision by two witnesses both of whom miraculously know who Jesus is, though we have no hint that Mary or Joseph told them.

Do these unsubstantiated occurrences suggest some kind of editing, some kind of interpolation, clumsily done? The passage is a case of special pleading to prove Jewishness and male gender, both of which are in question from other sources.

In the apocryphal, that is unacceptable to Rome, gospel of James, there are accounts of Jesus as a head-strong child with magical gifts. The hyperbole and ex-aggeration are at times ridiculous, if taken literally. For example, lions adore the child, and gods in Egyptian cities fall off their plinths. More seriously, Jesus is supposed to strike dead school chums who interfere with his games. What is the author trying to say? In typically Eastern tradition, elliptic and anecdotal, we glimpse behind the symbols a child of uncommon ability, able to impose his personality, and possibly the possessor of cane gifts. Something is better than nothing, and it is the case that behind even the most outrageous story there is some-thing of the truth, if we have the wit to decipher it.

According to Desmond Stewart in his study *The Foreigner*, Jesus spent formative years in Alexandria, and so would have been exposed to Greek, Roman and Egyptian influences in that vast and teeming city. It is a reasonable hypothesis, since it would explain Jesus' familiarity with Hellenic figures of speech so prominent in the Gospels, and which earlier scholars had been perplexed by. Indeed, it appears that Jesus could on occas-ion speak in a mixture of tongues.[1] In Alexandria Mary and Joseph could easily have hidden their child's sex, especially when they had to avoid the rite of circumcision. Had they tried to do so in Judea they would have been thought impious, and severe sanctions would have been imposed upon them. But in Alexandria it was easier, because it was a teeming, sprawling city, cosmopolitan in nature, where one little Jewish child could disappear in the crowd.

There are other important implications in Jesus' upbringing in Alexandria, for we know from the writings of a contemporary of Jesus, Philo, a scholarly Jew at the Imperial Court, that there was a group of Jews who lived on the other side of Alexandria's Lake Mareotis. These people, the Therapeutae, lived like nuns and monks, and were rebels against the secularism of the Jewish Temple cult in Jerusalem. They regarded women as being equal to men, danced together, and used hyssop in their rituals. They began the day with a prayer to the rising sun. However, they were sexually abstemious like the Cathars, whom they resemble in many ways, and had to recruit young people to keep their numbers up. Their stoical philosophy was taught openly, and Jesus may have heard their teachers: if so the seeds of doubt about the Jewish Temple religion may have been sown by the lake shore of Mareotis. Here were no rich priests, fine villas, and the diet was very frugal indeed. Jesus was certainly to practise poverty like these people, and to recruit followers. [2]

In Palestine there was another sect, the Essenes, whom Philo in his *de Vita Contemplativa* described, and his statements have been corroborated by the finding of the Dead Sea Scrolls. The Essenes shared their property, lived communally, but were very misogynist; they too were Jewish to the core, but despised the wealth and show of the establishment of the Temple of Jerusalem. The diet of these people was austere too, and they were very anti-Roman. It is likely that Jesus encountered these people as well, and may have elaborated their notion of communal property into the Christian one of sharing, something that never caught on in the institutional Church, whether Orthodox, Roman or Protestant.

I can see the diminutive but energetic girl, dressed as a Jewish boy, taking in the sights and sounds of Alexandria with those hazel eyes of hers, and that remarkable mind rejecting the false, observing the contradictions. Here was a world rich in learning, religion and commerce. The corn ships left Alexandria and the recruits for the Roman Legions were brought into the harbour from Rome. Greek merchants, Egyptian mystics, Greek mathematicians, the poor and the rich, the downcast and the powerful, they were all here.

But there was something else that may have happened, to Yeshu's mother. Mary would have seen women priests in the temples of Alexandria, and women deities. Freed from the parochialism of Jerusalem, she must have been struck by the diversity of the religions around her, and observed too that the rites of Isis brought to life the things she had heard about her past from her mother, and no doubt grandmother, who passed on the stories of Ruth, Tamar, Bathsheba and Rahab. There was no need to fear, after all, that the promise the angel gave her about her child would not be possible, for here in Egypt women were priests, were goddesses.

Isis the Beautiful

In the temple and rural religions of Egypt, Isis was depicted as a beautiful woman. Sometimes she wore a stone throne motif as head-dress, at other times the crescent of the moon with the sun in it. She also held sway in the mountains and pastoral lands of the Sinai and Syria. Her statues reveal some of her many sides, for she is shown as a mother suckling her child, Horus; as a winged goddess, symbolized as a falcon; she also enticed life into the dead Osiris and bore a child from him. Isis, also

known as Hathor, Astarte, Ashtoreth, always maintained
her hold on the affections of rural people,[3] but in the
towns, especially Alexandria, she became progressively
more important, with an acceleration of her eminence at
about the time Mary was there, an increase which continued well into the third century after the crucifixion.

Isis, as the Great Goddess, was sometimes represented
by the sign of cow's horns, since she could give life-giving
sustenance, symbolized by milk. Her crescent head-dress
doubled as horns. When Moses led the Jews out of Egypt
they took Isis with them, worshipping her as the golden
calf. She also succeeded in dethroning the sun gods, or
rather maintained her position as pre-eminent deity
amongst pastoral peoples – even the Jews when their
leaders were not looking. Clearly she was a sky goddess
too, for the redness of the morning and evening sun was
identified with her life-giving blood. She began the day,
and she finished the day.

The crescent is often assumed to be only a reference to
her allegorical cow horns, when she, as a woman, wears
a head-dress of a crescent with a globe in it. A crescent
and a globe can stand for several things at the same time:
the moon in old and new phases; the moon and the sun;
and horns nestling the sun.

Isis was a great healer, for she was able to restore the
sight of her son, whose eyes had been torn out by a rival
deity, Seth, by bathing them in milk. Isis had the power
to raise from the dead (as she did with Osiris). She
wheedled power out of the Sun God Re, by curing him
of snake bite. This is a very complicated symbolic story,
for Isis herself is capable of very close affiliation with
snakes, and can be identified as a cobra. One wonders,
and the ancient texts are silent on the matter, if Isis
herself stung the Sun God, and so engineered a situation
where her healing could be used as barter for more
power. Since the Great Goddess came before the usurping

male gods, the malicious glee Isis appears to enjoy in her dealings with the upstart Re comes partly from her knowledge that she is only getting back what is hers. Re's having a secret name also has a Hebraic echo, for this tradition was later to be elaborated by the Jewish prophets into a mystery cult, the name of God being secret to the priests and unutterable by all. Such alienation is a far cry from the tender mercies of Isis in her better moments; a goddess who is not above using her own spit to soothe her child when he is burning in the desert sun.[4]

Isis was active and successful for thousands of years before the Jews or the birth of Christ, and enjoyed a phenomenal upsurge of her cult during Christ's ministry. For three centuries, at least, the male Christian priests had great difficulty in expunging her. Only physical repression of her adherents by Christian emperors of both east and western empires was successful. Or was it? Her femininity could not be lost, for the statues we see of the Virgin Mary dandling her child on her knee, or suckling him, are in the same artisitic tradition as the thousands of similar images of Isis and her child. Moreover, the milk of Isis was also celebrated in the medieval cult of the milk of the Virgin Mary.

The Great Goddess in Greece and Egypt went in several guises, one of which was Aphrodite, daughter of Zeus. She had shrines at most major Greek cities but she is the Greek form of the Semitic Astarte and Ashtoreth, Goddess of Love, Beauty and Fertility. The Romans incorporated her into their deities under the name Venus. Like Isis, her husband was physically imperfect, Osiris being castrated by a rival God, Seth, and Aphrodite's husband was the lame smith Hephaestus. Aphrodite's marriage did not stop her having numerous liaisons, and her religious ceremonies were sometimes marked by prolonged sexual congress between male and female devotees. She had many sons and daughters.

Isis was the daughter of two deities, Nut, a sky goddess who is often pictured as a giant bee, and the earth god Geb, provider of green things. Geb taught Isis secrets of healing, especially scorpion stings. The union between Nut and Geb is perhaps one of the most beautiful of symbols, for the dark-skinned Geb lies on the earth, and the graceful form of Nut, now a young woman, arches over him. The Greek–Egyptian origin of the parents of Aphrodite, involving a sky god Zeus and Nione, daughter of the earth goddess, is thus sexually the mirror opposite of the Egyptian one, where the earth god is male and the sky god female.

In her aspect of Minerva the Great Goddess was one of the trinity of official Gods of Rome. Weddings were celebrated with the motifs of male and female generative organs on display, and even children wore lucky charms and amulets celebrating the energy and life-giving strength of sex. They had done so for hundreds of years in Rome, and would continue to do so, until the anti-sex, misogynist Church, elaborated by the all-male hierarchy in Rome, finally obtained secular power and used it to destroy their opponents.

The notion of a healing, loving, mother God, rather than a vengeful Lord of Hosts, is here in the tradition of the Great Goddess. True she could be terrible, but usually she was supportive, certainly towards the weak.

Until the hierarchy of Rome established their brand of misogyny and a male God, the only other group to remove the Great Goddess were the Jewish priests, who solved any theological difficulty by killing off all their female deities and subsuming the rest into one unnamable God. Was much of the hatred of the Great Goddess historical? We recall the Jews were slaves of the Isis-loving Egyptians. Their first anointed king, Saul, along with his three sons, was killed by the victorious Ashtoreth-loving Phillistines on Mount Gilboa. The armour of the fallen royal family was placed in her shrine.

Yeshu, primed by her mother in her role as Redeemer, would not only have been influenced by the overt ideas of the Great Goddess around her in Alexandria but by Jewish literature too.

Yeshu, when reading the Old Testament, as we call it, would surely have seen the confusion in it, the longings, even a sense of guilt, for the Jewish priests who controlled the documents had to develop these ancient texts to fit their conception of religion. Since mankind had worshipped the Great Goddess, the sex change necessary for a male Jewish sky God was bound to leave traces in the texts, which after all came from the Great Goddess tradition of the earlier semitic nomads.

In Genesis Yeshu would have read: 'In the day that God created man, in the likeness of God made he him; male and female created he them; and blessed them, and called their name Adam, in the day they were created' (Gen 5:1–2). Clearly this is saying that Adam means both male and female, while since Adam is made in God's image, God must be at the very least hermaphrodite, though more persuasively, since Genesis speaks of one flesh when Adam and Eve cleave, God is neither male nor female. The intimacy of sex and the Godhead is further elaborated in Genesis, for during sleep Eve is formed from Adam (Gen 2:21), while the act of love makes one flesh: 'Therefore shall a man leave his father and his mother and shall cleave unto his wife: and they shall become one flesh' (Gen 2:24).

At the very least the sex of God is ambiguous in these accounts, but the common humanity of man and woman is emphasized by the idea of one flesh, something perhaps misogynists failed to observe. Obviously the pro 'God the Father' Jewish faction, though they won the day in Israel, had none the less to distort the traditions they had expropriated, mostly from Babylonia, but traces of the Great Goddess and her sacrament of sex are still present.

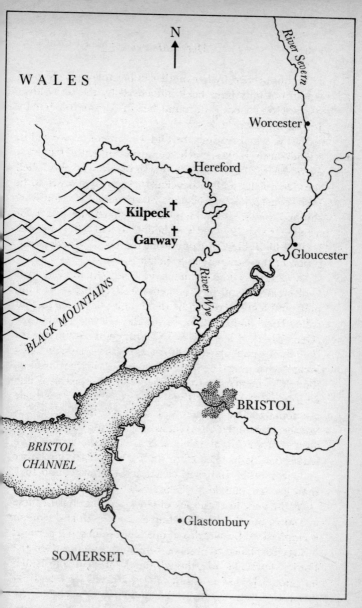

Map of Kilpeck

2 Kilpeck Church, the
round Chancel

3 Romanesque carvings
on door of Kilpeck
Church, featuring
Goddess motif of snake
swallowing its own tail.
These were done by a
master mason, *c.*twelfth
century

4 Lady of Kilpeck,
Kilpeck, Herefordshire

Two mysterious
ures possessing same
atures as the Lady of
ilpeck. Mother and
ild?

6 Aspects of the Great Goddess. *Top*. Central figure is of Qudsh, goddess of sexual energy. *Bottom*. The Great Goddess as Anat receiving worshippers. Dynasty XIX, c.1300 BC

7 The Great Goddess as Nut, she who gives birth to the Gods. Dynasty XXI, c.950 BC

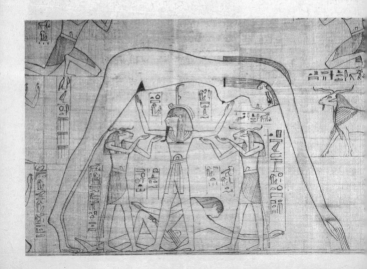

8 The Great Goddess as Isis. Here Isis suckles Horus. Egyptian, at end of first century BC

Isis suckling her child Horus. The Great Goddess was often symbolized by sacred serpents. Here her triple aspect is shown by three cobras. Egypt c.600 BC

10 Great Goddess as Aphrodite tying her hair with a ribbon. *c.*300–100 BC

11 The Great Goddess in the guise of Aphrodite. First century AD. Note the triple head-dress.

12 The Great Goddess
as Aphrodite in Christ's
time, c.AD 20

13 Pope Joan from the
illustration in Lawrence
Durrell's translation of
Emmanuel Royidis's
Pope Joan. The portrait
is of interest because it
shows Joan with a
tonsure, and typical
features of Saxon
English women in
middle age

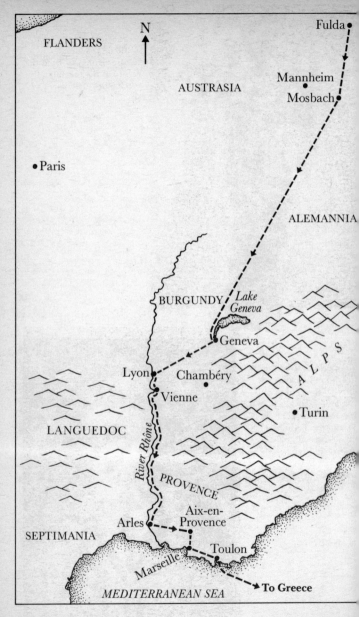

14 Map of Joan's pilgrimage

15 Notre Dame, from Île de la Cité, approximately from the site of the burning of Geoffrey de Charny

16 Eve, on front of Notre Dame, facing Geoffrey de Charny's place of execution

17 Leonardo da Vinci, putative self-portrait

18 Study for the Crown of Thorns? Leonardo da Vinci

19 Da Vinci, Virgin and Child with St Anne and Infant St John (1498–9). Such complexity of drawing would surely not survive in a negative, but see (below)

20 Photo of negative of a Vinci drawing (right). The form has survived, illustrating da Vinci's mastery of light and shade which makes it possible for him to have created the Turin Shroud

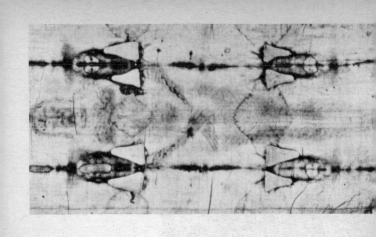

21 (right) Front image of the Turin Shroud. If the markings were made from a real body, the top or crown of the head should also appear. It is absent

22 Back image of the Turin Shroud. The feet are in 'tip-toe' position

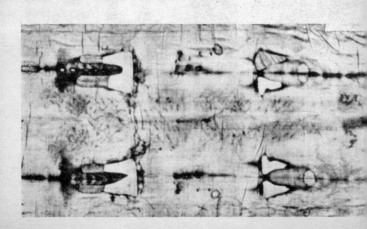

23 Painting by Giovanni Battista della Rovere, sixteenth century. Note the figure in the drape is clearly masculine but the figure above it on the stretched representation of the Shroud has feminine characteristics

24 Della Rovere detail: note that it predicts there would be an image on the linen of the top of the head

25 Gallic Great Goddess motif on Palais de Justice, Paris

26 Gallic Great Goddess motif on Tribunal Correctionel, Paris

Ligurian Shrine Skull Cult, second century BC. Pagan cults were
ropriated and metamorphosed by Christians in the South of France.

28 Crossed thigh bones and thong in Chapel of Christ, Vienne, Provence, France. This motif is often associated with the Knights Templars, but with a skull. The motif with the ribbon display is evocative of Fleurs-de-Lis

The blood of the Goddess, however, was not to be allowed to remain unsullied, for in a series of edicts the new priests proclaimed that a man was made ritually impure by coming into contact with reptiles (Levit. 11:29 –31), lepers (ibid 13:3), and menstruous women (ibid 15:19). In addition to this insult of bundling together two loathsome things with a woman, sex too is calumniated for intercourse with a menstruous woman was forbidden in any case (Levit. 18:19).

It can be argued that avoidance of lepers is prudent, and certainly caution with reptiles is wise, but what justification can there be in classifying a woman's physiology along with reptiles and leprosy? Certainly, in hot climates, risk of infection is greater if blood is not scrupulously bathed away, but that is merely a matter of hygiene, while here we are confronted with a *concept* of ritual impurity, of uncleanliness of a spiritual kind, where mere contact renders that person unfit to handle sacred objects, enter the Temple or even the Synagogue. There is still, even in the Anglican Church, the ritual of 'Churching' for women after they have given birth. Since a priest must be ritually pure, it is obvious that no woman can be a priest, for she becomes ritually impure every time she menstruates.

One might legitimately conjecture that once male priests had removed the Goddess from her temple they had to find reasons for removing women too. By insulting her physiology, the priests seem to have achieved their aim. The wound this attack made was to persist to the present day, and may yet outlast this century.

What passed through Yeshu's mind when she read the Genesis account and observed the stigmata put upon other Jewish women, who unlike her, did menstruate? First, there was nothing in Genesis which made God definitely male. As for the cruelties of misogyny, it could only have bolstered her desire to do something about it. But what?

In the Jewish literature of Jesus' time there is a great yearning for the Messiah, someone who will solve all Israel's problems. This deep yearning can often appear like that of a child who has lost its mother, and Yeshu may have noted the irony, for in matricide of the Great Goddess, the priests may have made the Jews different from everybody else, but they were now bereft of a Mother who, in Isaiahs's words, would dandle them on her knee. It was this yearning that Yeshu recognized, and was to use. The need was there, all she had to do was fulfil it. But again, the practical question is, how?

The great prophet of the Messiah is Isaiah. What would Yeshu find inspirational there?

Mother for the Yearning

Isaiah was brought up in a well-to-do but rural Jewish family, and was active between 740 and 690 BC. Though highly learned, he appears to have kept his distance from the ruling cliques in Jerusalem, and was well thought of by the ordinary person. As such, his country roots are never far absent from his writings, and recent writers have pointed out that even his seraphims, which announce God to him, are actually disguised serpents, suitably modified for the patristic prejudice of the ruling priesthood, echoes indeed of the Mother Goddess.[5]

Much of his book is taken up with the parochial concerns of a small nation being taken over by more powerful neighbours, for the Assyrians, with their formidable army, were to conquer Israel. They actually did so with the help of the priesthood, the northern tribes of Galilee being enslaved, but Judah being set free.[6]

This bitter background of internal Jewish division may explain the terrible images of death and destruction with which Isaiah assails his reader; the chief import apparently was to warn Israel against her own evil. Yet Isaiah also has a message of hope, for a redeemer is promised who will not only save Israel but the whole human race. When Isaiah speaks like this he is obviously not promising a new David, Saul or Solomon, but a spiritual leader who will do away with burnt offerings in the Temple and introduce new ways of worshipping the Almighty.

The remarkable element in the prophet's words is that he makes it clear that the Chosen One is for the whole world, not merely the Jews. This Chosen One is not to be the Messiah of an earthly kingdom of Israel. Furthermore, he is saying that the old sacrifices, particularly burnt offerings, are no longer acceptable to the Creator of the Universe. Not only that but with the coming of the Chosen One, those who thirst will get water, milk and wine without money and price; in addition they will get bread which will satisfy the otherwise insatiable hunger in mankind's soul; this is the bread not obtained by the sweat of the brow to feed the body, but a bread which lets the 'soul delight itself' (Is. 55:1–4).

But how is all this to come about? A redeemer, a sin bearer, the Chosen One will do it all, though the prophet does not know how. But he is entirely clear how the Chosen One will come into the world. 'Behold, a virgin shall conceive and bear a son, and shall call his name Immanuel' (Is. 7:14). This seems to be a direct statement of a male redeemer, but appearances may be deceptive because Isaiah points out that the redeemer will be called, 'the Mighty God, the everlasting Father' (Is. 9:6). As we saw earlier in Genesis, God the Father can equally well be read as God the Mother, and so the redeemer can be seen as 'the everlasting Mother'. What is really more amazing is that the redeemer is God and child, for a child is to be born who is the everlasting deity. This is an unambiguous statement that the redeemer has divine attributes.

Modern scholarship has revealed that the above prophecies were written by Isaiah, but that chapters 40–55 were written by someone else, another prophet, during the time when the Jews were in Babylon. The Babylonians were worshippers of the Great Goddess, and it is fascinating to observe the new prophetic voice repudiating even more the centralist priests of Jerusalem, for it is well to remember that the Temple was not the whole of the nation; indeed the Jerusalem sect had connived with the Assyrians for the downfall of many Jewish tribes.

What do we find the new prophet telling us? The message that the redeemer is for all mankind is reaffirmed, a 'salvation unto the end of the earth' (Is. 49:6), but we are also told many personal details too. The redeemer is very eloquent, 'he hath made my mouth like a sharp sword' (Is. 49:2), but he will be whipped and spat on (Is. 50:6). In words reminiscent of the Song of Solomon, the prophet says the good news will come from the mountains (Is. 52:7), which may be a reference to hilly Galilee, but there is no mention of a beautiful young man of the icons and paintings of Christianity, for 'his visage was so marred more than any man, and his form more than the sons of men' (Is. 52:14). It does not seem hard to conclude that if the Christian position is that the book of Isaiah prophesies Jesus, then there can be no justification whatsoever in portraying the Christ as a tall, beautiful young man.

However, Yeshu was not a man, but a girl who read the prophet, her mind already alive with her mother's personal avowal of being the bearer of the Messiah. She was not a conventionally beautiful girl; as a 45XO woman she was short, with a serious skin affliction, as is borne out by the physical description of Jesus which has come down to us through the scattered documents of

Imperial Rome. Yeshu could have seen herself in the words of Isaiah, because the prophet speaks of the Messiah as having no beauty (53:2) and being afflicted (53:4). But there is more, much more, that the sensitive and rich mind of this young woman could persuasively have applied to herself.

Yeshu knew she would have no children of her body, for she did not menstruate and knew she was barren. Isaiah specifically describes the heartbreak of a barren woman refused marriage (54.1), but also speaks of her Maker as her husband (54:5–6). The point is not what Isaiah may have intended by these allusions, but what a female genius might have made of them.

In a very down-to-earth way Yeshu may have indeed seen herself as the Redeemer, who is spoken of by the prophet, who will suck the milk of the gentiles (60:16), since Mary was not wholly Jewish for one of her ancestresses, Ruth the Moabitess, was gentile. This reference to the milk of her mother naturally fits in with the visions Yeshu already had of the Great Goddess Isis suckling her child. These allusions are developed, for the Redemptress will console even the gentiles with the 'breasts of her consolations', and they will be 'dandled on her knees' (66:12–13). The redemptress, although barren, is to act in the tradition of the Great Goddess by being a mother to all mankind. Yeshu, barren though she was, daughter of a woman who sincerely believed she would bear the Messiah, none the less would have many children.

Commentators have noted the close relationship between what happens to the Messiah in Isaiah, and what happened to Jesus Christ: the spitting, the whipping, the rejection. Some have thought it was all pure mythology, which, as Isaiah and Yeshu certainly lived, seems a little extreme; while others, in the Christian tradition, have

regarded Isaiah as simply prophetic. Now perhaps we
have a much more exciting and down-to-earth explanation: Yeshu through her mother's faith and her own
spiritual genius saw her role spelt out by the Prophet,
and by strength of will, a sublime courage and character,
set out to make it all come true.

The ideas of a blood sacrifice are there in Isaiah, and
they come from an older tradition of the Great Goddess
being healer and helper of mankind, but what is not clear
is the origin of the notion of the Last Supper, where her
body will be divided into twelve pieces. The idea of her
blood being shed is, as I have noted, a Great Goddess
concept, but what of dismemberment? How did Yeshu
obtain that notion, a concept frightening and yet, along
with the blood and the sacrifice, capable of enthralling
billions of people?

There is another theme, the theme of women being
given to men to despoil to prevent someone else being
hurt; that is, women were being used to 'save' someone
else, in the most literal sense. The patriarch Lot, for
example, is confronted by Sodomites who demand he give
to them his two male house guests. Without any hesita-
tion this man offers these rapists his daughters, who are
both virgins. He says he will give them over with a
father's blessing to do what they like to them: 'Do ye
unto them as is good in your eyes' (Gen. 19:8). Isaiah,
therefore, was drawing on a very deep tradition of re-
deemers.

The Levite's Woman

There is in Judges a strange account of a woman who is
offered in sacrifice and her body cut up to be distributed
amongst the twelve tribes of Israel, even though one of
them, that of Benjamin, has played the traitor against

God. It does not make edifying reading and is perhaps
only equalled in savagery by the Gospel accounts of the
crucifixion, which it closely parallels.

The woman is not named, but she is very independent
minded, and leaves her guardian or protector. She is
spoken of as coming from Bethlehem, like Jesus, from the
tribe of Judah (Judges 19:1). The relationship with the
Levite, the man whose actions lead to her death, is not
made clear. She is spoken of as a concubine and as a wife
(Judges 19:1 and 20:4). The Levite, finding she has left
him, sets out in pursuit, for she has gone back to her
father, in Bethlehem. Apparently, he is successful in
persuading her to rejoin him, for she leaves Bethlehem to
go back to the slopes of Ephraim. However, the woman's
father does all he can to make good relations with the
Levite, keeping him entertained for five days, before
letting him go with his daughter, riding on asses. The
writer of Judges makes mention of the Levite and the
woman riding asses several times (Judges 19:10, 19:19,
and 19:28), a significant detail in view of the tradition
of the Messiah being obliged to ride an ass, or donkey,
into Jerusalem, a fact the young Yeshu would have
known.

They were to go into Jerusalem, but at this time those
who resided there were 'not of the children of Israel'
(Judges 19:12) and the Levite decides instead to go to
Gibeah of the tribe of Benjamin, one of the twelve tribes
of Israel. It was a fateful decision. Having decided against
taking his wife into the houses of strangers in Jerusalem,
the Levite lodges in the house of a Benjamite.

In Gibeah, the Levite and the woman are at first
ignored, but then befriended by an old man, who uses a
phrase later to be echoed in the Gospels, 'Whither goest
thou?' *Quo vadis*? (Judges 19:17). The Levite's answer is
that he is going to the House of the Lord (Judges 19:18)

and 'there is no man who receiveth me to house'. The
old man takes them in. At this point in the story, already
clearly not merely an anecdote, so heavily garnished is it
with symbolic allusions, a new note is struck, for the
Levite says he has bread and wine for the old man and
his handmaiden. This is a curious reversal of roles, for
the Levite and the woman are the guests, but we are told
the old man comes from Ephraim.

It is not to be a peaceful night for Benjamite men,
'certain sons of Belial', surround the house, knocking at
the door and asking for the Levite. They have in mind a
sexually explicit purpose, for they say: 'Bring forth the
man that came into thy house, that we may know him'
(Judges 19:22).

These events occurred perhaps a hundred or so years
before the Jews had confederated closely enough to have
a king, Saul, *c.*1000 BC. That the Benjamites have to
some extent apostasized from the strict observances of
the God of Abraham is revealed both by their homo-
sexuality, expressly forbidden, and their affiliations with
eastern deities.

But it is the old man's reaction to the mob outside his
door that reveals the low status of women under Yahweh,
something not to be materially altered in Yeshu's day. It
is worth quoting in full (Judges 19:23–28):

And the man, the master of the house, went out to them and
said to them, 'No, my brethren, do not act so wickedly; seeing
that this man has come into my house, do not do this vile
thing. Behold, here are my virgin daughter and his concubine; let me bring them out now. Ravish them and do with
them what seems good to you; but against this man do not
do so vile a thing.' But the men would not listen to him. So
the man seized his concubine, and put her out to them; and
they knew her, and abused her all night until the morning.
And as the dawn began to break, they let her go. And as

morning appeared, the woman came and fell down at the door of the man's house where her master was, till it was light.

And her master rose up in the morning, and when he opened the doors of the house and went out to go on his way, behold, there was his concubine lying at the door of the house, with her hands on the threshold. He said to her, 'Get up, let us be going.' But there was no answer.

The evidence is that after her ordeal she showed some signs of life, for the Levite speaks to her as if he recognizes she is alive. It is certainly not clear that she is dead at this point, but her demise is certain within a few hours through the actions of the Levite (Judges 19:29–30).

Then he put her upon the ass; and the man rose up and went away to his home. And when he entered his house, he took a knife, and laying hold of his concubine he divided her, limb by limb, into twelve pieces, and sent her throughout all the territory of Israel.

This is a terrible story, a nightmare of cruelty and degradation, but it coheres with the notion of sacrifice. Here a life is given, and the body dismembered into twelve pieces. There is internal evidence that the story itself is a corruption of a Great Goddess myth, which has not survived the patrisitic censor in clear form.[7] But all that is irrelevant, for the electrifying possibility is that Yeshu read this Judges' story and saw in it a means of making her love and her sacrifice the role of the Redemptress, accessible to millions, by which I mean she transformed it into the beautiful rite of the last supper. Here her blood was to be drunk by twelve, and her body eaten by twelve. Her blood was truly to be shed, but it was drunk as wine before that

happened; her body was truly to be destroyed, but
under the Great Goddess symbol 'life from bread', her
body was to be broken into twelve, and eaten by twelve
men, her apostles.

If she drew on one aspect of the Great Goddess tradition, she may have drawn on others, and equally transformed them. What, for instance, was the ritual of sacred
sexuality? Women of the lowest and the highest social
strata performed sacred duties as priestesses and acolytes
of the Great Goddess. The form of service depended very
much on the culture in which it was enacted, for the
Great Goddess herself would be manifest in different
aspects at different epochs. The crucial question is this:
which influences did Yeshu choose to use? It is idle to
suppose she did not know of the sexual aspects of the
Great Goddess traditions; the real problem is to try to
see what she was to make of them.

In Palestine itself, as Frazer tells us in his *Golden Bough*,
'cones of sandstone came to light at the shrine of the
Mistress of Turquoise among the barren hills and
frowning precipices of Sinai.' He tells us that in Meso-
potamia, indeed throughout the eastern Mediterranean
countries, women in the service of the Goddess, be she
called Isis, Astarte, and so on offered themselves in ritual
sexual service, the fees going to the upkeep of the
Temples. At Heliopolis (Baalbec), Syria, maidens offered
themselves to strangers in the Temple of Astarte. This
lasted well into the Christian era, for it was Constantine,
with his new-found Christianity, who abolished the rite
of thousands of years and built a church amidst the
ruined temples. Frazer waxes so scholarly and eloquently
he is worth quoting at length:

In Phoenician temples women prostituted themselves for hire
in the service of religion, believing that by this conduct they

propiatited the goddess and won her favour. 'It was a law of the Amorites, that she who was about to marry should sit in fornication seven days by the gate.' At Byblus the people shaved their heads in the annual mourning for Adonis. Women who refused to sacrifice their hair had to give themselves up to strangers on a certain day of the festival, and the money which they thus earned was devoted to the goddess. A Greek inscription found at Tralles in Lydia proves that the practice of religious prostitution survived in that country as late as the second century of our era. It records of a certain woman, Aurelia Aemilia by name, not only that she herself served the god in the capacity of a harlot at his express command, but that her mother and other female ancestors had done the same before her; and the publicity of the record, engraved on a marble column which supported a votive offering, shows that no stain attached to such a life and such a parentage. In Armenia the noblest families dedicated their daughters to the service of the goddess Anaitis in her temple of Acilisena, where the damsels acted as prostitutes for a long time before they were given in marriage. Nobody scrupled to take one of these girls to wife when her period of service was over. Again, the goddess Ma was served by a multitude of sacred harlots at Comana in Pontus, and crowds of men and women flocked to her sanctuary from the neighbouring cities and country to attend the biennial festivals or to pay their vows to the goddess.

If we survey the whole of the evidence on this subject, some of which has still to be laid before the reader, we may conclude that a great Mother Goddess, the personification of all the reproductive energies of nature, was worshipped under different names but with a substantial similarity of myth and ritual by many peoples of Western Asia; that associated with her was a lover, or rather series of lovers, divine yet mortal, with whom she mated year by year, their commerce being deemed essential to the propagation of animals and plants, each in their several kind; and further, that the fabulous union of the divine pair was simulated and, as it were, multiplied on earth by the real, though temporary, union of the human sexes at the sanctuary of the goddess for the sake of thereby ensuring the fruitfulness of the ground and the increase of man and beast.[9]

There was much to ponder on here. It is clear that the Great Goddess cults placed a premium on motherhood, sexuality, energy, marriage, and all aspects of fertility. Even our English word Ma, for mother, was once a title of the Great Goddess. It is difficult to imagine a more important set of ideas, and they are all centred on the positive source of life, recognized as the Great Goddess. Sometimes her temples were elaborate, as in Greece, Rome and Egypt, or simply rustic. Therefore, how can we call priestesses of this religion prostitutes? How can acolytes of a religion concerned with love, marriage, child-bearing, the rhythms of life and death, have an offensive title? The answer appears simple: they cannot; the title has been forced upon them, their rituals traduced to such an extent that commercial vice is seen as synonymous. This may very well be one of the greatest calumnies ever perpetrated.

Significantly Yeshu was to be a teacher for the first time in the history of Israel who would challenge the law on the stoning of adulterous women:

. . . if the tokens of virginity be not found for the damsel: Then they shall bring out the damsel to the door of her father's house, and the men of the city shall stone her with stones that she die Deut. 22:20–21.

and say to such a girl, after challenging the crowd to stone her if they were without sin, 'I do not condemn you.'[10] Yeshu had added her own unique meaning to the prophecies – love.

The role and promise of the Redeemer are unequivocally made clear by Isaiah:

Come down and sit in the dust, O virgin daughter of Babylon ... thy nakedness shall be uncovered ... I will take ven-
geance, and I will not meet thee as a man ... get thee into
darkness, O daughter of the Chaldeans: for thou shalt no more
be called the Lady of the Kingdoms   (Is. 47:1–5).

This passage can be read plausibly as the end of the Great
Goddess tradition as it was known; not by matricide in
the sense that the priests of Jerusalem believed, but by
the self-immolation of the Mother Goddess herself. The
cross would make the sexual servitude of women in
temples redundant.

If I am correct in my surmise that there existed a
young religious genius who, through the teaching and
example of her mother, came to see herself as the Redeemer, the true Messiah of Israel, then many of the
paradoxes of Christianity as it has come down to us
become resolved. When Yeshu read the song of Solomon,
for example, she was reading literature ostensibly written
by her great ... great grandfather, Solomon, and her
great ... great grandmother Bathsheba. She may have
seen herself in the line, 'I am black but comely,' as a
reference to her own pyogenic skin condition I described
earlier.

There then follows, 'I am the Rose of Sharon, the
Lily of the Valley' (Song of Solomon, 2:1), and the
Rose is described as having no spot, a reference which
Yeshu may have taken to mean that the Redeemer
would have to be morally perfect. But if she got this
far, chapter 5 reveals danger, for there are watchmen
who strike the Rose and even take her veil away (Song
of Solomon, 5:7).

Further details of events to come are seen in verse six
of the same passage, where the Rose says she sought her
beloved: 'I called him, but he gave me no answer.' This

is very much like the terrible cry on the cross, 'My God,
my God, why hast thou forsaken me?'

In Psalm 22 there is the astonishing statement, 'I am a
worm and no man' (verse 6). The grisly details of crucifixion, which Yeshu and Mary would have known all too
well, being members of a subject race in the Roman
Empire, reduce a person to a kind of worm, with the up
and down wriggling in an attempt to catch breath. Again
the question arises: did Yeshu read this and see herself in
this role of the sin bearer?

The details in Psalm 22 are so close to physiological
changes of crucifixion as to be unmistakable. Verses 15
and 17 speak of bones being out of joint and the tongue
cleaving to the jaws, precise anatomical statements of
being stretched out and suffering from thirst. Contemporary texts on crucifixion methods confirm these findings. Even the forsaken cry is mentioned, 'for there is
none to help' (verse 11) and so is the piercing of hands
and feet (verse 16).

It is likely that Yeshu's awareness that she was different
would have begun at her mother's knee. Can we picture
the dynamics between Mary, convinced she had been
singled out as the mother of the Messiah, and Yeshu, a
girl, small and disfavoured, being brought up as a boy?
It would probably take the literary ability of a Macaulay
and the insight of a Freud to truly bring it off, but we
must be content with piecing the story together as best
we can, by observing the plausible forces at work within
and upon this relationship, the most formative, and in a
sense the most fruitful, mother-and-daughter interplay
the world has ever known.

Yeshu has to contend with the difficulties of smallness
of stature and a sexual identity outwardly male but biologi-
cally female. The foundations for the growth of a unique
personality are present, but nothing could have grown

without the love, the conviction and the courage of Mary. The sheer brutality of the misogyny that Yeshu would quickly have witnessed as an onlooker, would have been echoed in the slings and arrows visited upon her as a small and disfavoured boy, and would have helped her in her own development, for she could see that they were visited upon women too simply because they were women.

What made all this bearable? Her mother's love? Love was the greatest force of all, for it was strong enough to wipe away the tears shed on the way home from school after being bullied by larger and more aggressive boys; it was strong enough to sustain an inner truth for a greater good, even though it meant that she had to act like a boy or else give up her mother's dream of saving so many weak and defenceless people.

She learned to be subtle too, clever like Tamar, her ancestress, who sacrificed her body in a temple of her goddess. She learned to be an opportunist like Ruth, and use what forces she had available. Yeshu learned to be patient, when the forces of the world were pushing her this way and that, as had happened to Bathsheba when the king had lusted for her and killed her husband. Yeshu had to learn to be quiet at the right times when she was slandered, like Rahab, a High Priestess, who was called a brothel keeper. She had to learn to listen to her own heart and the voices that came from God, just as Mary had done when the angel announced her own coming into this world.

And yet Yeshu's time was limited; soon she would be a woman, and according to the Temple priests, women were unclean, for blood was unclean, but all women bled.

Except Yeshu. When Yeshu became a woman she did not bleed. It was a miracle; she could still pass as a male.

She did not grow breasts. As she did not bleed, she was never unclean, not even according to the religion of Abraham. She was ritually pure and yet a woman. Now she saw what Mary had meant. She was truly the Anointed One.

We do not know when these ideas cohered in Yeshu's mind, but these notions apart, we have to recognize that as a person Yeshu has no equal. There is not one recorded defeat in verbal debate; she was able to take on the best brains of her time and foil them. Her charisma was such that people followed her in the wilderness. Had she so wished, she could have had great temporal power. Part of her uniqueness comes from her mother, an outstanding personality in her own right, but in addition to the influences already mentioned, there is the potentially corrupting, or ennobling, one of deformity.

Can we take this into account as part of the driving force which was to propel a Jewish girl on to the world stage? Yeshu was a child as other children, but small and afflicted with a skin condition. Would this not have sifted and winnowed her developing personality in a never-ending gale, a tornado of self-doubt, as many people have experienced in this life? Ultimately, we all have to settle out of this wind of change, and become at least comfortable with what and who we are. But painful as this transformation process is for all of us, for Jesus it was much more difficult, just as it was for Byron with his club foot, for Plato with his disfigured back, for Socrates with his terrible ugliness. These three, of the many in history, overcame the bitterness and the pain, indeed in becoming victors of their own fate, they may have found uncommon energies, Byron in his poems, Plato and Socrates in their search for truth. But the process can go the other way, as with the bitter brilliance of Joseph Goebbels, or the dour relentlessness of Joseph Stalin.

Goebbels found energy in overcoming his club foot, but used it for an ignoble purpose. Stalin had a withered arm, and the psyche which overcame that was able to work, even in the seventh decade of life, more than sixteen hours a day, year in year out, controlling the vast Soviet Union, but alas, with great cruelty and repression.

Jesus came through on the side of the angels, but from a purely humanistic view, we have to allow that it could have gone the other way, and what terror that supposition invokes, the thought of such gifts used against, instead of for men, women and children! But for Jesus, the kingdom was not of this world, as she was to tell Pilate. There is in that quiet statement an awareness of great power, as if to say that had she so wished, had her vision been less than the transcendental one she had forged out of her experience, the princes of this world would be bowing down to her, just as Satan had promised, when tempting her in the desert. If nothing else, I think it rather pertinent to emphasize that no personality has shown such magnetism in the history of our race as Jesus, as Yeshu of Nazareth. Everything on this earth could have been hers and yet she renounced it.

In summary Mary's influence on her child is seen as crucial, particularly in regard to teaching by example the power of love to overcome difficulties. Far from eschewing the Great Goddess concepts, Yeshu appears to have imbibed them, and would change them in the sense of making them richer.

As a child growing up in Alexandria, Yeshu was exposed to the full beauty and deep ethical teaching of the Great Goddess, as well as to variants in the Jewish tradition. Orthodox Jewish books must not be discounted for it is in them we find much of the material Yeshu was to use. In short, the evidence of Great Goddess symbolism

and motifs in Christ's passion are arguably evidence of
her realizing her role. Indeed, the often commented on
close relationship between the prophecies and what
Yeshu did is seen now in its most understandable light,
that of a young religious genius making these prophecies
come true by acting them out in her life. There is no
'mystery' here, but a marvel at this person's courage,
conviction, and spiritual force. The other important findings are that misogyny was so strongly entrenched in the
Jewish Temple priests that conflict was inevitable; and
so was Yeshu disguised as a man, for only through that
could she even enter the teaching area of a synagogue, let
alone the Temple itself.

However, though Mary and Yeshu clearly may have
derived much from their stay in Egypt, their next move
was to Nazareth. Why? On the face of it, there was
nothing in Nazareth, especially from the Gospel accounts,
to attract Mary, but there must have been a reason for
the family to go there. A clue is given by de Voragine,
who writes in his *Golden Legend* AD 1217 that Mary
Magdalene had a castle called Magdalo, just two miles
from Nazareth.[11] She was a noblewoman, her father,
Cyrus, being rich. Her mother's name was Eucharis,
which has overtones of Eucharist, so we can legitimately
suspect that the history of de Voragine has more to it
than meets the eye. Acccording to de Voragine Mary
Magdalene has a brother Lazarus and a sister Martha.
Both of them owned very valuable property, Martha in
Bethany, and Lazarus in Jerusalem.

Was there a connection between the Great Goddess
cult and Mary Magdalene? She is said in the Gospels to
be cured of seven devils, but this may merely mean that
she had passed through the seven initiation rites of Isis.
If the construction on Mary the Virgin's early life is only
partially correct, that she had affiliations with the Great
Goddess too, then Nazareth would be the place to go, for

there a rich woman could help them in their quest for a new understanding. This is purely speculative but we can reasonably give some weight to the *Golden Legend*, shorn of the lip service to a dangerous church. What all authors, orthodox or not, agree on is that Jesus left Nazareth to teach.

The First Church

Having satisfied myself that Jesus was a shortish woman of great personality and magnetism, afflicted by a skin condition but strong enough to do the work she had to do, I still had a difficulty. Should I refer to Jesus as she or he? This is not such a minor matter as it may first appear, since all the literature we have on Jesus speaks of he, whereas on the basis of the hypothesis I have put forward for consideration, 'he' should read 'she'. But it is not quite that simple; for one thing, perhaps a hypothesis should not be allowed to remove the traces of the previously accepted ideas until it has been accepted, and as far as I was concerned that stage had not yet been reached. The other inherent difficulty is that Jesus allowed himself, or herself, to be referred to as male. Ordinary common respect suggests we call someone what they call themselves. Accordingly, I decided to use the male pronoun and gender where the sense is not dependent on gender, for example when Jesus heals. Does it matter if the healing was done by a man or a woman, especially to the healed? However, this is also a moot point, and sometimes though not always, a greater feeling of sympathy is attached to the female pronoun. However, when the gender is a crucial point, as in advancing or testing the hypothesis, then the pronoun emerges naturally in the discourse.

We have seen that the description of Jesus having rich auburn hair, meeting eyebrows and a beautiful face is not what our hypothesis suggests, nor what the Church

Fathers in the era before Constantine thought was the case, but there was also the possibility that these features were derived from some source other than imagination.

The description of Mary by Epiphanius, already noted, contains some of the features attributed to Jesus; possibly the auburn hair, the sweetness of mouth and eyes, the eyebrows, the long face, the beautiful hands attributed to Christ in the later iconography of Jesus, owed much to this tradition, and perhaps the curious mixture of uncomeliness and beauty found in some portraits arose from an attempt by their authors to make a composite of the Josephus and Epiphanius descriptions. However, the truth may be more compelling than this, for Jesus need not have inherited all the characteristics of the syndrome of 45XO women, as indeed not all of them do, and though Jesus was short and afflicted, she would certainly have inherited something of her mother's beauty, the eyes and the mouth for example, and the grace of her person. Some 45XO women have a strange and perplexing beauty, quite unlike any notions of glamour, but something more affecting, altogether more poignant. I have known two women with physical defects. One I knew in Hereford while I was in the sixth form. Her hand was withered, but she was a most graceful person, with a hauntingly beautiful face; the other, a model, had a very large port-wine stain of the kind that Jesus may have had. It covered one side of her face and half the front of her body. She was small, delicate, and when one saw her from the left side she seemed unspotted, almost too beautiful to be true, with an inner life that animated everything she did. It was only when she turned and you saw her from the right that her stigma was apparent. The shock was at first strong, but in time one did not see the birthmark, only the beauty of form and bone structure beneath. Women with the Turner Syndrome often have this uncanny beauty, and any defects, which after all are not really defects but departures from the stereotype, seem to heighten their delightfulness.

Jesus could have been afflicted but at the same time extraordinarily beautiful, and this beauty in the flesh, marred though it may have been, would have drawn her disciples to her with a love shot through, not only with wonder but with pity; and given the strength of her message and the power of her personality, the added emotional ingredient would have been awe. This seems to fit well with the picture we get from the Gospels, where the personal power of Jesus is evident in her supremacy over anyone with whom she came into contact, though strangers on first seeing her may have chaffed her about her appearance until they got to know her better, and the power of her teaching and personality had time to work. This analysis throws an intriguing light on the sensibilities of Peter and Matthew, for Jesus told them to follow her, apparently at first meeting, and they did. Some people, as we know from everyday life, can see beneath the skin, as it were. Jesus appears to have known this very early on, and picked out men who had the sensitivity, despite their lack of learning, to see her as beautiful, though of course they believed her to be a man. This insight into the spiritual dimension was put to the test when she called on her disciples to follow her. The kind of man she wanted would have seen what the chaffers took so long to find out. Others were not to see at all.

And yet how could the Saviour of Mankind live out the lie of being a man while she was a woman? First, we must note that Jesus never said she was a man, nor did Mary. Second, there is an irony when she calls herself the Son of Man. Such was the misogyny and mis-understanding of what the Messiah should be, a kind of reincarnated Solomon or David, or even the 6ft 6in Saul, that a woman could not be taken seriously. On finding that she had borne a girl, was Mary to give up her faith? Or should she progress as best she could, and so cast Jesus in the role of a boy? In accepting this supposition, we find that a 'miracle' occurs, for being a 45XO woman, born of virgin birth, Jesus at puberty, a time when Mary thought her child would be discovered as a girl, did not menstruate and did not develop the form of a woman. This surely could have confirmed both of them in their beliefs. There is, it may be legitimately granted, no lie in Jesus' life. Her disciples believed her to be male and she did not disabuse them. Why should she? The central truth is not her gender but her message, and her message is love. The Church was founded by Peter and by Paul, both of whom called Jesus their Lord, and so she was. But there is evidence that one of her disciples, Mary Magdalene, did promulgate, by mistake or by decision, the secret of Yeshu's sex, and that secret became a matter of censorship and violence.

There is in the apocryphal Acts of John this extraordinary passage concerning the Transfiguration, where Jesus has gone to the top of a mountain and John has followed:

I because he loved me drew nigh unto him softly, as though he should not see, and stood looking upon his hinder parts. And I beheld him that he was not in any wise clad in any garments, but was seen of us naked thereof, and not in any wise as a man, and his feet whiter than any snow . . . and his head reaching unto heaven, so that I was afraid and called out and he turned and appeared as a man of small stature.[1]

The whiteness, I have earlier suggested, was blanching of the cavernous blood vessels of Jesus' skin by exertion caused through climbing the mountain, and the Transfiguration is simply this change of appearance. That considerable censorship has occurred is obvious, since in the Gospels the account varies, even the clothes Christ wears being set aglow, and the small stature has been removed. Here, though, there is no mention of the countenance changing, as in later accounts. Clearly, all we can be reasonably sure of is that Christ's appearance did change on that mountain, and for very good medical reasons. I wonder, though, if the 'man of small stature' is an addition, for this passage actually says that Christ was not a man. Did John know Christ's true identity? Probably not. He is, however, mystified by Christ's smallness and appearance. That some credence must be given to the Acts of John may be suggested by the account where John says that when he was close to Jesus, as at supper, and lying across his breast (as in the canonical John), 'sometimes his breast was felt of me to be smooth and tender, and sometimes hard like stones . . .' This passage then goes on to say that the body was sometimes without material foundation.[2] This seems mystic in the extreme, whereas the description of Jesus' chest as soft, but sometimes hard, is a classic description of skin which is damaged very easily, as in pyogenic granuloma. It heals with hard scars or keloids, these latter being a condition of 45XO women quite frequently.

It would seem that the Church Fathers in their drive to the unification of texts and the destruction of what they called apocrypha, have denied generations of Christians a picture of the suffering Christ, who suffered every day of her life. I believe that John, who was this intimate with Jesus, was striving for objectivity in his description. His later reference to the airiness of Jesus' body, as if he were a phantom, sounds very much like the sort of thing a young poetic man, deeply in love with his master (not in a sexual sense either) would write when trying his hand at suggesting extraordinary superhuman qualities.

As for the encounter on the mountain, did John believe what he saw? And what did he see? A small man who was not a small man. It is perplexing, but it can be made clear.

We already know that Jesus was small, and that blanching could be explained as a fall of blood away from peripheral supply to feed deeper muscles. We also know that a 45XO woman has no breasts and usually lacks the roundedness of the female body. Given that Jesus was hardly ever still, but moving from lake shore to synagogue, to healing here and preaching there, her motto being, 'Come, we must be away, there is work to do', we can expect her to have been a little underweight.

Goddess' Children

Jesus' transcendental genius is also shown in her choice of disciples. From what we know about them, they are extraordinary for their ordinariness, prior to Jesus taking them up. After being with her, however, they are transformed into powerful figures, capable of taking on the Jewish authorities and bearding Roman Emperors, and becoming world famous historically. Galilee abounded in mystics, such as Honi the Circle Drawer, who was a shaman of some ability, able to heal and perform 'miracles',[3] but the men Jesus chose were tradesmen; simple fishermen, Peter and his brother, a tax collector, Matthew, and even an agnostic Thomas (the Doubter). One appeared to have zealot tendencies, Simon, though he would have had to curb these parochial views as a follower of Christ, and another, a younger man than the rest, John, appears to have been the nearest to a mystic in this band of twelve. Yet another, Judas Iscariot, showed little religious otherworldliness.

Peter is depicted in Christian art as big and tough, the tall and bearded fisherman. There is no reason to doubt

these icons, since fact and the Church's propaganda needs
were one. But, curiously, Peter was not rocklike; he was
so terrified in Jerusalem that he denied his master. But
he was also a man with an inner gift, able to perceive
that Jesus was no ordinary person, and he saw this earlier
than the other men. Jesus was impressed by this quality
too, saying it was clear that Peter had been picked out
for the revelation by God. This was to set Peter on a new
road as founder of the Church, though he needed Paul to
convince him that much of the old Jewish way of looking
at things would have to go in a new world religion, including the rite of circumcision.

James is often forgotten. He may have been a cousin of
Jesus or a brother. In his epistles he clearly states that
good works are essential; in this, his pragmatism is very
Jewish and very down to earth. The flights of mystical
exultation, as much a part of Christianity as good works,
were left to John, the probable author of the Gospel of St
John in the New Testament, and perhaps the author of
that strange mixture of a book, the Apocalypse, or Revelation. In the Gospels John is shown as a favourite of Jesus,
perhaps because of his mysticism; at any rate he sat next
to Jesus at supper, and was known to be Jesus' confidant,
after Mary Magdalene.

The cast of characters seems full and real enough, the
places still exist today, and there is ample reason for believing we are dealing with historical characters, yet there
have been Christians who actually think the Gospels are
largely myth. Curiously they appear to have become
victim to the move against the Great Goddess cults by
Roman theology, in that in order to bolster their case,
Catholic propagandists have had to leave out so much
valuable material on Jesus Christ that the figure they
present is in many ways difficult to substantiate. None
the less these critics, who have gone so far as to deny a
historical Jesus, have to be examined, for if they are right

then it does not matter whether Christ was a woman or a man, since the person did not exist. Is it really necessary or even reasonable to take this stand? I must add that the weight of modern scholarship, with no theistic axe to grind, is firmly on the side of Jesus being a real character, though they, like me, tend not to see him as institutional churches depict him. But what of the Christians who have spirited Jesus off the pages of history?

Christ Killers

The first concerted attack on the historical Jesus was made by the Protestant theologian, David Friedrich Strauss, a tragic and, it appears, a muddled figure. He was born in 1808 at Ludwigsburg to a middle-class family. He attended seminary, and seemed all set for an academic life of a theologian, but his work, *The Life of Jesus Critically Examined*, was received with such a furore that he was dismissed from his post at Tubingen. He was never again to satisfactorily come to terms with the Protestant Church, and was forced to live on his father's patrimony. He had a miserable marriage, great fame, and inner desolation. He died unrepentant, but had made many concessions to his critics. Viewed from this distance, he appears as an original thinker and, like many pioneers, he had to suffer the consequences of opening up new areas of thought, but also of not being as well informed about the territory he was entering to be entirely safe, for he did not have the knowledge that we do about the archaeology and history of Judea at the time of Jesus, so his methods were hampered by ignorance.

Strauss takes the view that just about everything in the four Gospels is myth, but if that is so, why should Mary Magdalene and the disciples have risked death by openly believing in Jesus? Why should these people, and Paul a little while after them, flout convention, have their lives upset and, in the case of Peter, be killed, if they were just making things up? Furthermore, Stephen, the young Hellenized Jew, was stoned to death in Jerusalem by Paul, before the latter's conversion. Why should this young man die for stories? This central question has not been answered by Strauss, or anyone else.

Strauss' basic technique is to say that wherever the Gospel narratives echo or fulfil any of the biblical prophecies they are myth, but as we have suggested, Jesus set out to fulfil the prophecies. In any case there is a serious logical error in Strauss' method.

Suppose for a moment that the Gospel writers had said to themselves, 'This Jesus was the Messiah so we have to show how the prophecies of Isaiah, Psalm 22 and the Song of Solomon came true in his life.' They then proceeded to invent his healing, his trial, his scourging and his crucifixion, as well as details of the Messiah's donkey ride into Jerusalem. The fact is that Jesus' life as described in the Gospels fits the biblical prophecies so closely that if you take the prophetic element away you are left with almost nothing. In which case, how did the authors know that 'this Jesus is the Messiah'?

Albert Schweitzer makes the same error in his *Quest for the Historical Jesus* published in 1906. One example of his lack of insight can be seen from the following argument when Schweitzer is supporting Strauss. Schweitzer makes much of the saying in Matthew 16:28 where Jesus says, 'There be some standing here, which shall not taste of death, till they see the son of man coming in his kingdom.' The drift of the arguments by Strauss, Schweitzer and innumerable others, is that since the glorious kingdom did not come, Jesus was a mistaken visionary.[4]

What kingdoms are these German and Alsatian theologians expecting for Jesus? Have they forgotten that Christ said the kingdom is within, that is, spiritual? They forget too that the condemned Christ told Pilate, 'My kingdom is not of this world.' They assume Christ knows nothing about Isaiah, or perhaps it is they who do not know, for the sin bearer of that prophet has no glorious kingdom of this earth, only spittings and beatings. Even in the very passage they appear to misread, Jesus says, 'For whosoever shall save his life, shall lose it' (Matt. 16:25). The answer to the coming of the Kingdom is in the text itself. Peter and John were standing there, but it was not until they were middle-aged men that they realized who Jesus was. It was then that they saw the glory of the Kingdom, and they had not tasted death. Jesus had.

Apart from their own errors of logic, the difficulties created by the Christ killers, and there have been thousands of them during the last hundred years, simply melt away on the 'prophecy is script' hypothesis. Of course Jesus' life as described in the Gospels fits the prophecies, what else would you expect if her whole life was lived out to make them come true?

Failure to grasp this childishly simple idea (out of the mouths of babes and sucklings) suggests a deeper problem: patristic Rome, as I have argued, needed centralization to wield power. The Great Goddess religions, fulfilled by Jesus, were never centralized. No one was better than another, and they did not mount holy wars or kill 'heretics'. In other words, power politics negated what really happened in Jesus' life and death: the deeper meaning of the Great Goddess religion was personal rebirth, and it was a gift to everyone from Jesus. The suspicion lingers that the good news has been somewhat obscured in the Gospels that have come down to us.

Gospel Truth

The actual birth year for Jesus can be objectively identified with a fair degree of certainty. Cupitt gives the following timetable, based on Roman records and references to the Passover, the building of the Temple, the reign of Herod (he of Salome's dance) and Tiberius' reign: birth, 9 BC, with a margin of error of five years on or off this date, public ministry two to five years, baptism by John AD 28, crucifixion between AD 30 and 33.[5] These dates fit well into the dating of the Gospels and are consistent with the writings of Josephus.

Traditionally Christ died in AD 33. However, a Syrian monk, Dionysius Exiguus, in the sixth century, gave us this BC–AD system. Unfortunately his base date was out by six years.[6] In other words, in AD 33 Jesus was 39 not 33. There is a problem too with the length of Jesus' public ministry. There was, it appears, only one entry into Jerusalem, Easter of AD 33. Some scholars suggest the ministry lasted four years, others three, and so on down to one. The truth seems to point to two years, in the sense that this would account for the build-up of the ministry in Galilee which had limited success and the sojourns in Sumeria. If we take this view, then the baptism by John may have been a little later than AD 28. However, the remarkable thing is that these historical issues are now matters of pinpointing precise years; there is no longer any doubt that baptism did occur, and against that fundamental fact, the question of whether it was AD 28 or AD 29 can best be left to specialists in these matters. Similarly, if Jesus were crucified on the Passover of AD 30 rather than AD 33, it is of very little significance, the historical impact is that she was crucified.

The doubt that Jesus even existed may indeed have arisen because the Church has censored and condemned so much written material that the story is thin and patchy. However, once the rigid formalism of Rome is side-stepped, we enter a much lusher and more sympathetic terrain. This scenario gives us flesh-and-blood people engaged in a great undertaking, the fulfilling of the ultimate meaning of the Great Goddess religion. Even if all other aspects of the scenario were to be denied, this one is worthy of consideration, if only because it coheres so much historical fact with legend which the orthodox path has damned. Yet, even the four canonical Gospels, suspect though they may be in terms of censorship, may contain an irreducible central core of facts. What are they?

Perhaps an analogy is fruitful here. If you ask members of your family, or your friends, to write down their independent account of some shared experience, the following is likely to occur. The drift will usually be the same in all the descriptions, say, of a film you have all seen or a trip you have all made, or better still of what a particular character known to you all did. What will differ will be times, dates, details. Reported speech will be flavoured not only by the narrator's preferences, but by the imperfection of human memory. Another example may be the statements of witnesses in a court case, all describing the same event. When the Judge sums up he draws the general thread and points out the inconsistencies. The imperfection of human testament is in a curious way one of its marks of genuineness.

Another important point is the sheer weight of written testimony to the career of Jesus. The British Museum has a huge collection of documents; some, such as the Egerton Papyrus, are certainly no later than AD 150. In John Rylands Library, University of Manchester, there are fragments of John 18:37, 38 which date from between AD 100 and 125. The Chester Beatty Collection in Dublin has papyrus texts of John and Luke dated AD c.200. The bibliography is very extensive, and the dating methods are based on a variety of scientific and literary techniques.

The copious allusions to places in the Gospels set them firmly in space and time, and though the details differ in the four accounts, it is generally accepted that Jesus did live in Nazareth, did preach and work in Galilee, did travel through Sumeria, knew Jericho, Caesarea and, of course, Jerusalem. Regarding Jesus' disciples, it is also patent that the men and women who accompanied her were so struck by what she had to say that they memorized much of it. Apart from Mary Magdalene, however, none of the twelve seems sufficiently well educated, with the possible exception of Matthew the tax collector and John, to have put this material down in writing. Was there once a gospel by Mary Magdalene?

Don Cupitt, Dean of Emmanuel College, Cambridge, reports on the massive research carried out by a host of scholars, notably the Q school, which argues from textual similarities that there was a source, the work Q (not extant) from which the authors of Matthew, Mark, Luke and John drew much of their material, and that Q was basically eye-witness material. These scholars, successors to the Oxford cleric, Canon Burnett Streeter, argue very well that the original source may have been in Aramaic, which Mary Magdalene would have used. Many of the infelicities between the Gospels can be explained by the authors trying desperately to make good Greek or Latin from a language they imperfectly understood.

The Q school, if I may so designate them, date Q as having been written AD *c.* 50, Mark AD 65, Matthew and Luke between AD 80 and 90, and John between AD 90 and 100. In a compelling work of scholarship, W. G. Kummel dates the four Gospels as all between AD 50 and 100.[7] On much less persuasive grounds, John Robinson shifts them all back to have been written between just after the crucifixion and the fall of Jerusalem in AD 70. I say on less persuasive grounds because Robinson[8] is virtually alone in biblical scholarship in not giving Mark the earliest date. Mark, it is virtually unanimously agreed, was the first of the four Gospels to be written.

The significant deduction from this Herculean labour on the dating and authorship of the New Testament Gospels is that they were written early enough to have been either by eye-witnesses, or that the events happened within the writers' living memory. Therefore, even though these documents have clearly been censored, rearranged and amended for theological reasons over the centuries, it is only reasonable to give them the same serious respect we would give to Suetonius, Tacitus and Josephus. But who wrote down the original sayings from which even Q was derived? Who better than Mary or Mary Magdalene? If we accept their authorship, we have a means of establishing what Jesus actually said. Anything which is patristic becomes suspect. Curiously, this approach leaves us with all of the prophecies intact, and all the sublime teachings.

But what of the miracles? In his study of the historical Jesus, Ian Wilson tackles this question, pointing out that they have a matter-of-fact quality, occurring in actual locations and buildings, such as the pool of Bethsaida, which survived until the fourth century in Jerusalem.[9] He gathers impressive medical evidence to prove what is now a well-known fact, that skin conditions, blindness, even paralysis and demonic possession, can be hysterical or neurotic in origin. Hypnosis can be used to treat such illnesses, and is used increasingly by the orthodox medical profession. Whether Jesus used hypnosis we do not know, but, like many healers she may have used autosuggestion which can have a great effect. Furthermore the belief, or faith, of the sick person that he can be healed, is a powerful force in recovery.

Besides this approach to understanding miracles, there is also the question of literary style. Jewish literature, which to some extent the Gospels are, uses metaphor a great deal. But if the surmise that Mary Magdalene, or indeed Mary the Virgin, was the source of the authentic parts of the Gospels, there is good reason for seeing the miracles as emanating from the traditions of the Great Goddess. The feeding of the five thousand, for example, is done with loaves and fishes, both bounty of mother earth; although, since Jesus was to offer bread as a symbol of her body, and the fish was to become a cipher for her, the story may be entirely symbolic. The wedding at Cana sees water changed to wine, which again links the purifying properties of water with the blood symbolism of wine. The raising from the dead is similar to Isis reviving her husband Osiris, and there are stories of the blind being healed in pre-Christian myths.

Whatever the ultimate finding on miracles, and it must be said that even the hardest-headed scientist cannot respectably take the position that they cannot happen, the outstanding event concerning Yeshu was her death; it is that which has mesmerized the world. As we have seen, it is plausible to see this young religious genius reading the prophecies in such a way that she felt the need for her own sacrifice. After all the literature exists, and existed, but it is not Jewish in essence; it is founded on the Great Goddess tradition. If Yeshu was a woman, fresh insights should be obtained when the crucifixion is examined in this new light. What, then, is the true story of Yeshu's passion?

Crucifixion

The orthodox account of Jesus' passion is that he was betrayed by Judas Iscariot, was arrested by Caiaphas and crucified by the Romans. Surprisingly all these events contain in their descriptions *non sequiturs*, even contradictions. I had no hope of actually providing an alternative account – too many had tried that – but I was curious to see what illumination, if any, might be cast upon these unsatisfactory accounts by the hypothesis that Jesus was a woman who used her own life, and death, to make the Redeemer prophecies come true.

To attempt this, it was necessary to compare the Gospel accounts with those in suppressed and censored accounts, as well as trying to see beneath the censorship of the Church. There was also a great body of material, some of it vehement, which attacked women and sexuality, sure signs, I felt, that possible affiliations with the Great Goddess were under siege, which might furthermore relate to my central hypothesis.

The Judas Mystery

Judas appears to have had charge of the group's common purse, and in consequence he is mindful as any treasurer about expenditure, but as John tells the story (John 12:3-7), Mary Magdalene's ointment, which she used to anoint Jesus, is hers to give, so when Judas says, 'Why was not this ointment sold for three hundred pence and given to the poor?', it really is none of his business. John's utter contempt for Judas is revealed by the verse, 'This he said [that is, why wasn't the ointment sold?] not that he cared for the poor; but because he was a thief, and had the bag, and bare what was put therein' (John 12:6).

Did John really say this? The problem hinges on the authenticity of the additions to the Gospels, that is additions to the central corpus of work, the Q text, which in the main is a collection of Jesus' more pithy and very down-to-earth sayings, embellished with parables and promises that love does not go unrewarded.

As we shall see, Judas as a figure is totally unconvincing. He is called a thief, but there is no evidence of this, rather the account above seems to suggest he is a pettifogging group treasurer, trying to purloin Mary Magdalene's own money.

Mark and Luke put this scene with the ointment a few days at most before the betrayal. Matthew gives a chilling account of Judas' meeting with Caiaphas directly after Mary has anointed Jesus with the ointment, when he agrees to betray Jesus to the Temple Guard for thirty pieces of silver, many times the cost of the ointment, so it was no mean sum, but it is difficult to understand what this betrayal consisted of. The idea put forward by Matthew (26:5) is that the Caiaphas faction was concerned it should be done in such a way that popular support of Jesus could be circumnavigated, and when Iscariot turned up and offered his services later, no doubt they discussed this aspect. As Jesus went to the Garden of Gethsemane after the Last Supper, at which Judas was present, he must have thought the garden was an ideal place, especially at night, for the arrest to take place. And so it transpired, for Matthew reports (26:49) that Judas identified Christ with a kiss, but this begs at least one question. Were the Temple guards blind? Jesus had, after all, been preaching in the city for some time, and had cleared dove sellers from the temple precincts; surely the guards must have known him? Evidently not. The kiss too is a curious detail, though very cruel in import; one wonders how much kissing went on between Jewish men at this time, very little one presumes, and so there is vindictiveness in Judas' act, but there may be more.

Judas has thirty pieces of silver for his betrayal, but seeing that Jesus is condemned to die, he goes to the priests and tries to give the money back, saying, 'I have sinned . . . I have betrayed innocent blood,' but the priests retort, 'What is that to us?' (Matt. 27:4). Judas throws the money at their feet, then hangs himself. Why? Is this the action of a thief?

The money has come from the Temple and been returned to it, for the priests do not leave it lying on the pavement, but scoop it up and use it for the purchase of a burial place for gentiles, though the word in Matthew is translated as strangers (Matt. 27:7); they do not keep it because it is blood money, but there is no clear embargo on such money; after all they gave the money and they got it back, so they had paid nothing. However, there was a law against using money from a harlot as a temple offering; the reference is Deuteronomy 23:17–18, 'There shall be no whore of the daughters of Israel, nor a sodomite of the sons of Israel. Thou shalt not bring the hire of a whore, or the price of a dog, into the house of the Lord thy God.' The inclusion of the dog is odd, offensive too, since it equates a human being with an animal. However, the import is clear: money from a whore is not welcome. But we must be on our guard about this word 'whore', since it may not mean a woman who sells sexual favours, but could be the Jewish term, used without discrimination, for any woman who served in the temple of her religion, virgin priestess, or one who used her body as a sacrifice in the service of her Goddess, the money going into the temple treasury. This service was also called fornication.

The point is of some import as this discussion between Jewish rabbis in the Talmud shows:

Rabbi Eleazar said to Rabbi Aqiba: 'I once went on the upper street of Sepphoris; there I met one of the disciples of Jesus the Nazorean named Jacob of Kephar Sekhanjah, who said to me: 'In your law (Deut. 23:19) there is written: Thou shalt not bring a whore's hire into the house of thy God. Is it permissible to use such hire to make therewith a privy for the high priest?' I did not know what to answer him. Then he said to me: 'This is what Jesus the Nazorean taught me: She gathered it as the hire of an harlot, and they shall return it to the hire of an harlot (Micah. 1:7): it has come from dirt, and to the place of dirt it shall go.'[1]

This passage is quoted by Eisler, though the Deuteronomy reference should be verses 17–18, not 19.

The passage in Micah cited is informative, though to get its full flavour one has to start at verse 6, 'Therefore I will make Samaria as an heap of the field . . .' which is quintessential Old Testament prophecy of ruin and damnation; then in verse 7 we find why this horrific destruction will be visited on Samaria, 'And all the graven images thereof shall be beaten to pieces . . . for she gathered it of the hire of an harlot, and they shall return to the hire of an harlot.' The context clearly reveals that Samaritans worshipped the Great Goddess through temple prostitution. However, Samaritans loom large in Jesus' life and teaching. There is the famous parable of the good Samaritan who aids a man beset by robbers, even though a Levite, that is a priest's server, passes by on the other side. The point about the story appears to be that everyone is everyone else's neighbour, loving acts being the sign of holiness. Jesus also spent much time talking to a Samaritan woman, something which caused consternation amongst the disciples on two counts – first her nationality, and second, her sex. It is in this meeting at the well that Jesus promises that other nations besides the Jews are to be redeemed. We can perhaps conclude that Jesus was also announcing the end of the old form, not only of the Jewish religion but of the Great Goddess cults too.

In order to carry out her work, Yeshu needed people. We have seen that she chose men with the sensitivity to recognize who she was, although at the beginning they could only have known they were confronted with someone they thought was in the tradition of the prophets, those gifted people whose preoccupations were celestial rather than profane. However, it is clear that she chose with great care. Peter and his brother were men of the people and would be attractive to the common man; Matthew was a representative of the Jews who collaborated with the Romans, so this class, large as it must have been, need not have felt left out; Simon the zealot represented the nationalists, although his ardour was curbed by Yeshu's insistence on non-violence; John was a mystic, so the strain of otherworldliness, found in groups like the Essenes, would see that Yeshu welcomed them too. But what of Judas? He was chosen because Yeshu needed a betrayer, and as we have seen, Judas was close to the Temple priests; indeed he may have been a Temple agent from the beginning, which suggests even more strongly that he was chosen for his role as betrayer.

Strangely, there is a source which connects Jesus with the Temple as well: a forgery quoted by Eisler concocted in AD 640[2]. The motive of the forgery appears to counter Jewish criticism that Jesus was a bastard, the old Panthera story of the Roman soldier, by showing him descended from the Levites. Perhaps there might be a nugget of truth in the forgery, which suggests that Jesus tried to become a priest of the Temple.

It may be that Jesus' ancestresses, being temple

priestesses, which was something abhorrent to Jews and Christians alike, gave him claim to the Temple of Jerusalem. If so, Caiaphas would have hated him the more. Judas then becomes not the counterfeit invention as seen in the Gospels, but the more plausible figure of an agent who saw his beloved Temple under threat by a man who appeared to sweep away the old law. This latter was true, despite what Christian apologists try to say, about Jesus' Jewishness, for Jesus prophesied the destruction of the Temple, insulted its priests (Matt. 23), and physically cleared the sacrificial precincts.

This scenario naturally takes on even more sinister undertones if we assume that Judas had guessed at Jesus' true identity – the fulfiller of the Great Goddess prophecies-for the thirty pieces of silver could be construed as Temple hire. It is possible that Caiaphas also knew Jesus' true identity. In his eyes there could be no more heretical or threatening person than Jesus of Nazareth. From the very beginning Jesus had associated with people such as the Samaritans and Mary Magdalene, and Judas may have been hired early on, simply as a Temple precaution. The reports that Judas might therefore have made to Caiaphas, or to Annanias before him, would have been alarming to say the least.

However, the grip which the Temple priesthood had on the Jewish people was not secure, for Caiaphas was an appointee of the Romans through Herod. An insecure position is not improved by the spectre of the Great Goddess being raised once again, something the priesthood had suppressed with great difficulty. Judas would be enjoined to silence, and steps taken to destroy Jesus. Fascinatingly, the problems Caiaphas had in finding charges against Jesus probably grew out of his fear of actually making the true one. This healer, this prophet, this rabbi, is a woman, in direct line with the Great Goddess priestesses, Rahab, Tamar and the rest. As Jesus was to say, 'they hated me without cause' – true religious cause that is.

Jezebel's Bequest

Yeshu's choosing Judas may seem cold-blooded, and in a sense it was, but only in a minor sense, for if he was a Temple agent, she did not make him so and at any time he could have thrown in his lot with her, but he never took that option. As Yeshu was to say, he was a liar from the first.

The role of men in Yeshu's great quest at this stage is clearly secondary to that of the two women, her mother and Mary Magdalene. Mary was her prophetess, her teacher, her inspiration, and when she was in her teens, Mary took her to Mary Magdalene, the acolyte of the Great Goddess, whose devotion has come down to us in the traduced form we all know so well. As we have seen, both Marys were women of considerable substance, as well as being very powerful religious personalities in their own right. It was this combination of material wealth and know-how which enabled Yeshu to start out on her quest, in her early thirties so well prepared. If our dates are correct, it means that Yeshu was with Magdalene from her mid teens to the very end, and with her mother right from the beginning, which would have given her great confidence despite the dangers ahead, for she had that most awesome of support, a religious conviction in two women who loved her; whoever else might cavil, they would not.

Mary might have believed that her child was the chosen one, but Yeshu still had to live up to it; while Mary Magdalene, sophisticated and well versed in the ways of the world, a priestess privy to the mysteries of the Great Goddess, would have to be convinced who this little Yeshu was. And the only one who could have

convinced her would have been Yeshu herself. That this
formidable woman became Yeshu's greatest lover, after
her mother, is striking testimony to Yeshu's holiness.

It would appear then that there was a central group of
women around which the men revolved, and we know
that most of the time they did not understand what was
happening; perplexity is there even in the synoptic
Gospels, for they are always muttering about not understanding this, and being confused by that. Not once,
however, is there a sign that Mary and Mary Magdalene
were ever unsure; their faith went very deep indeed,
perhaps in a way no man could really understand.

This raises the crucial issue of Yeshu's ancestresses, for
if she was coming to make the old patristic religion
redundant and fulfil the promises inherent in the Great
Goddess tradition of rebirth and love, then her link with
the priestesses of her family, one of blood, had to be made
clear, it could not be done by simply talking about it. As
a woman of action, Yeshu had to symbolize in some
unforgettable way the authenticity of the Great Goddess
priestesses she was descended from. Ultimately it was to
be the shedding of her blood, under the whip, under the
thorns, and beneath the nails, but nothing could be left
to chance; there had to be no mistaking the message, at
least for those with eyes that could see.

It was with some exhilaration, which I hoped would
not be dashed by my further research, that I began to
see at last the real meaning of the allusions to the harlot
and temple hire, and to the symbols of crimson that
abounded in the Gospels. I had instinctively felt there
was something to be discovered, but even at this stage I
did not know what it was. That was to be startlingly
remedied, and yet in a way which was disarmingly
simple.

Yeshu right up to the entry into Jerusalem showed
great conviction. It was apparent from the beginning that

her interests were not for the petty chattels of riches; nor was it the passing victory of a popular revolt, for countless men and women had achieved that and nothing had really changed because of it. She was, in contrast, going to change the thinking of all mankind, and to that end she used history, people, buildings for her purpose. She was the great artist who used a whole culture and a time in history which was expedient to her own ends. In this the Romans were to be used just as everyone else was.

Christ is described as being clothed in a scarlet cloak before the crucifixion. Roman soldiers had scarlet cloaks and presumably one of them had put his around Christ's shoulders. We are told this was done in mockery, but scarlet is the colour of the biblical harlot, the acolytes and priestesses of the Great Goddess. If, as orthodox Christians insist, Christ is living out Jewish prophecies, why the cloak of Jezebel?

Jezebel, Phoenician wife of a ruler over Israel, came to a terrible end at the hands of the victorious Jews, for she was killed (855 BC) at Jezreel, a centre of worship of the Great Goddess, and left in the street for the dogs to eat so that when they came to bury her, all they found was her skull, her hands and her feet (II Kings 9:30–37). However, Jezebel had shown that she was more than a king's wife, for when she heard that her husband Ahab was dead, and was awaiting the victorious Jehu, 'she painted her face, and tied her head, and looked out at a window' (II Kings 9:30). This suggests that she was in a temple of the Great Goddess Ashtoreth (Astarte) with her hair done in Phoenician fashion, though 'tired her head' might also mean she was wearing the veil of a temple priestess. When Jehu saw her he had her thrown out by temple eunuchs, so her blood actually splattered on the temple wall; then this man ground her underfoot with his horse. We know also from the first Book of Kings that Jezebel was a devotee of the Great Goddess (I Kings

18:13). She is mentioned by name (though it is not clear whether as a metaphor or as another woman) by John in Revelation: 'I have a few things against thee [he is talking to a member of the early Church: he puts the words in the mouth of a messenger of God] because thou sufferest that woman Jezebel . . .' (Rev. 2:20). The complaint against Jezebel is that she commits fornication.

The alarming connection here with Jesus, apart from the scarlet apparel, is the saying discussed earlier, that dogs and whores are not fit for the temple. Why dogs and whores? The link is Jezebel – for as we have seen, she was traduced as a whore and eaten by dogs. Only her hands, feet and skull remained. The hands and feet are provocative details, for these members are to be pierced by nails. As for the skull, Jesus is to be crucified in Golgotha, literally the Place of the Skull.

The humiliation of the cross also fits the indignities placed on female saviours in other traditions of the Middle East. Astarte, Queen of Heaven, mentioned in Kings (1 Kings 11:5 and 33) was worshipped in Tyre and Sidon. In summer, when the sun had burned the crops, she would go to the underworld to find her consort Tammuz. On their return in the spring, rain welcomed her, so the crops grew again. The Great Goddesss was known as Innanna, Queen of Heaven, in ancient Sumeria. She left heaven and passed into the underworld, but the judges there, infuriated at her healing and loving ways, condemned her to death, and for three days and nights she was hung naked on a tree. Her father god, also her lover, revived her with celestial food and the sprinkling of water. Alive again, she had temples dedicated to her, as was her right as the Great Goddess. In Babylon, Ishtar is also humiliated in the underworld, but again revives through water and restores the fertility of the earth. These sacred myths are very similar to the Greek cult of Persephone, who is rescued by her mother

Demeter from the underworld, or death. As we have seen in Egypt, it is Isis who is worshipped as the Great Goddess, but here her powers are even greater for, according to Plutarch, she represents wisdom. She is also the maternal goddess *par excellence*, healer and carer of the sick; yet once she was represented by young temple acolytes in Tyre, a city admired by the Jews for its wealth and beauty, but hated for its devotion to the Mother Goddess.

To pose the question again, if Jesus was acting out or fulfilling Judaic patristic prophecies, how is it that these other influences are so blatant? There is simply no male Jewish equivalent. And as for the suggestion, as Christian orthodoxy insists, that Jesus fulfilled Jewish male monotheist prophecies, why is Jesus shown wearing the scarlet of that most hated 'woman' in Christian literature, the Whore of Babylon? The suspicion at this stage may be entertained, and I suggest legitimately, that the true course of events was too close to the enactment of a Great Goddess tradition for a patristic church to countenance – hence the contradictions, caused by attempts at censorship, found in the Gospels.

One of Christ's great . . . great grandmothers was Rahab, as given in the genealogy of Matthew (Matt. 1:5). She helps Joshua conquer Jericho by hiding two spies in her house, which, like Jezebel's temple, was set high in the city walls. Rahab refuses to admit she has the two spies, despite threats from Jericho's ruler. In return for helping them, Rahab exacts a promise from Joshua that she and her sisters, her whole family, will be saved when he attacks. The bargain is struck, and the spies are let down by a scarlet cord from the window. To mark the house for safe treatment, Rahab binds the cord to her window. In the event of Joshua's victory, Rahab and her kin are the only ones spared (Joshua 2–6). However, Isaiah, in an apparent reference to God's power, asks rhetorically, 'Art thou not it, that hath cut Rahab?' (Is. 51:9), and she is further identified with that great Jewish symbol of evil, Babylon, in Psalm 87, and the identification is strengthened in Psalm 89:10, 'Thou hast broken Rahab in pieces, as one that is slain', just as Babylon is defeated in Revelation: 'Alas, alas, that great city Babylon, that mighty city! For in one hour is thy judgment come' (Rev. 18:10), while a few verses previously we have the mystic symbol of a great whore, clothed in precious jewels and scarlet, with a golden cup in her hand full of the results of her fornications. On her forehead is written, MYSTERY BABYLON THE GREAT THE MOTHER OF HARLOTS AND ABOMINATIONS OF THE EARTH. John says he saw this woman drunken with the blood of the saints, and that she was riding a beast. One might observe that if she were riding it, she was in control of it, but still the imagery seems confused, for Rahab is praised by James, the brother of Jesus, in his epistle (2:25) when he points out that she was justified by her good works, and Paul extols her as a model of faith (Heb. 11:31).

This running, festering hatred of women spans two worlds, and appears to have no logical basis, unless one assumes that the Roman Church, like the Jewish Temple priesthood before it, could only retain their power by destroying or demeaning the Great Goddess tradition. It is not so much, perhaps, a matter of theology, but power politics; the opposition has to be annihilated. With the Christian Church, or what passes for it, the problem was infinitely more difficult because, on the hypothesis that Jesus was a woman, the founder of the religion was a fulfiller of the Great Goddess religion. This fact would account for the twisted, confused, self-contradictory annals we have examined.

Anything to do with the Great Goddess was anathema, but scarlet, the symbol of blood, is found in the homely story of Tamar's giving birth to twins. One of Mary's ancestresses was Tamar, a Great Goddess acolyte, whose story we have seen. It says in Genesis, when she was in labour, one of the babies put out its hand, so the midwife, to be sure of precedence, put a scarlet thread around the wrist, saying 'This came out first' (Gen. 38:28). The child withdrew its hand, and the first child to be born, Pharez, had no cord on the wrist; but the second, Zarah, did.

The Great Goddess had red as her colour, in amulets and cords, buckles of women's girdles, and the symbol of life. Here we find the natural, if symbolic, assertion that blood is life. It was Jesus who gave the deeper meaning to this idea, an idea which is found throughout the Bible and the myths it comes from, symbolized by a scarlet thread.

If the flesh-and-blood reality of Jesus and her mother was becoming almost palpable in this quest, then the claims of orthodox Christianity were taking on the quality of phantoms, bolstered by an increasingly unacceptable set of myths; myths, moreover, which in large part, were invented early on to fit the prejudices of a male-ruled Rome, with its divine Emperors and secular priests.

Yeshu was emerging, it seemed, as the daughter of a strong-willed and remarkable person, Mary the Virgin, who believed she was the mother of a saviour. Yeshu, a religious genius, an even more remarkable person, had imbibed the notion of her own messiahship with her mother's milk. As we have seen, the scriptures would bear her assumptions out, even to the sex; 'all' she had to do was make it come true, and then she would be heiress of the religion that all men and women had shared since time immemorial. As we saw earlier, Isaiah was arguably part of her inspiration, and so were other Jewish writings, whose imagery, at least in part, can be traced directly to the Great Goddess tradition. Yeshu took from the past what she wanted and made it hers. Judas' role was to underpin, though perhaps he was never to understand just what momentous events he was part of. His thirty silver pieces, as we have considered, could be construed as Temple Hire; it was paid and then repudiated by Caiaphas, who seems to know exactly why.

Yeshu would have read Isaiah where the prophet speaks of the Harlot of Tyre, whose 'hire' will be dedicated to the Lord (Is. 23:15–18). If Caiaphas had suspected Yeshu was enacting these prophecies with such determination, he may very well have considered himself justified in having her killed, just as Jezebel had been. The danger came not so much from Yeshu's claim to be the Messiah – that was a common enough delusion in Jews, especially if they came from Galilee – rather it was the way she was going about it. She was incorporating elements of the Harlots, and raising them to a sacred level. It may have been at the very moment Judas came back with the silver that Caiaphas knew there was no turning back; his priesthood was threatened by someone apparently intent on reaffirming what the Temple priests had tried to traduce.

Caiaphas had the power to make his hatred stick, for he controlled the Temple Guards, and in trying to understand the events which lead to Christ's crucifixion it is necessary to observe that the Romans did not arrest Yeshu, that was done by the Temple Guards under the direct orders of the High Priest, Caiaphas.

Caiaphas seems to have satisfied himself that Jesus was claiming to be God and, desiring his death, he confronted Pilate. Pilate examined Jesus in Antonia, but found no fault with him. However, the Caiaphas faction was adamant, so seeking to mollify them, Pilate had Jesus scourged.

At this point the story takes on a density of symbolism which hitherto has not been explained, for the Roman

soldiers are said to have crowned Jesus, given him a reed
for his hand, and put a cloak over him. Why would they
do this? Granted, soldiers are given to sadistic pranks,
but their commander had already said the prisoner was
without fault, so it is unlikely that they would have
incurred his displeasure by provocatively maltreating
Jesus. Furthermore, one of their centurions had had a
servant healed by Jesus, and there is also the tradition
that Pilate's wife too had been cured of some ailment.
Their orders in the hall, or dungeons of Antonia, were
simply to scourge. The Romans have never been accused
of excess imagination, yet this business with a crown
and sceptre is very imaginative, or was it the enactment
of something else – something copied, something
ritualistic?

Many Roman soldiers were devotees of the God
Mithras, introduced to Rome, as Plutarch tells it, by
Pompey's captives in 68 B C. He is represented in statuary
in the many shrines dedicated to him as a comely young
man. Initiation was by a baptism of blood, as a triumph
over evil. Originally Persian in origin, the religion had
absorbed elements of the Eleusinian mysteries of the
Greeks. This latter was a variant of the Mother Goddess,
and in this she appears as Demeter in Greek temples,
and Ceres in Roman ones. Demeter is actually the sister
of God, Zeus, and with him had a child, Persephone.

Demeter, in her role of the goddess of renewed life,
wears a garland of corn ears (sometimes a poppy), and
in her hand holds a sceptre of corn, or a poppy. She is
always depicted in full attire.[3]

The Eleusinian mysteries were very beautiful, very
pure, and very serious. Even the fighting during the
Peloponnesian War between Athens and Sparta was
stopped on both sides, so that the Eleusinian procession
could pass out of Athens unmolested. Claudius, the
Roman Emperor, actually wanted the mysteries to be

transferred from Athens to Rome, but the Athenians would not agree, so Roman variants were practised in Rome. In Greece the procession went to the shrine of Demeter at Eleusis, where nearby Demeter was said to have sown the first corn. The sacred precincts have been excavated recently, revealing that they were maintained in Roman times. Those lucky enough to be initiates of the religion were ritually purified, though the cult was so secret that details have not come down to us, but we do know that in a pure and elevated religion, the notion of proselytes needing purification was firmly established in the Latin and the Greek mind, thereby preparing the way for Jesus' teaching of being 'born again'.

As suggested, it is possible to see hints of the Great Goddess in the Gospels, but the confusion, if that is what it was, between Mithras, Isis and the Great Mysteries, enveloped Jesus after her death, even in the 'pagan' mind. Some of the accounts give an authentic whiff of a growing religion in the crowded streets of Rome and the gravid tenements of Corinth.

The soldiers in the Antonia Garrison were in all probability adherents of the Eleusinian mysteries, but it was no longer purely Greek, for it had been subsumed by the Romans in the usual process of interchange between the conquered and the conquering. Add to this the fact these men did not all come from one place in the empire and we have at the centre of Jerusalem a group of tough, brutal, yet religiously inclined men whose ideas came from the four quarters of the globe, and from all quarters the religion of the Great Goddess appeared. But the soldiers came with different names and different details in ritual. What is certain, however, is that these men had no truck with the Jewish male God, whom along with their government they regarded at best as an ignorant superstition, and at worst an insult to the divine Augustus of blessed memory.

But there is one rite of the Great Goddess which was known to the Romans, orgiastic in character, involving water, wine and whipping, and the whipping was done to a girl. Some aspects of this ceremony are portrayed in the Eleusinian mysteries at Pompei, in the Villa of Mysteries, which dated to the first century A D.

What happened in that torture hall of the fortress of Antonia? In carrying out the orders of their chief to scourge Jesus, whom they thought was a man, they would have stripped their prisoner, and there before them Yeshu was revealed. They already knew Pilate was intending to let the prisoner go, for he had said he found no fault in Jesus. What were they to do now? Obviously the officer in charge would have immediately gone to see Pilate, for this was a material change in a vexed case. Actually the Gospels support this possibility, for as John tells the story, Pilate tried to get Jesus released (John 18:38–40) but to no avail, then he had Jesus flogged, and *again* tries to get a release, but Caiaphas demanded Jesus' death, his entourage crying out 'Crucify him' (John 19:6). Then we are told Caiaphas clinches his argument; he says, 'he ought to die because he made himself the Son of God' (John 19:7). But 'When Pilate therefore heard that saying he was the more afraid' (John 19:8).

Why should a Roman Governor be afraid of a Jew calling himself the Son of God? Religious fanatics, as well as lunatics, were common in the Levant. John tells us that he, Pilate, went straight to Jesus after hearing this charge of the Jews. Again, why should he concern himself to release Jesus?

If the Centurion of the Guard had come to him and said what had transpired in the *praetorium*, the hall, how could Pilate react otherwise? If he told the Caiaphas clique they had arrested a woman, even spilt her blood in the priest's house, a riot would ensue. Meanwhile, the redemptive blood had flowed, the soldiers had dressed

Christ as Demeter, with a crown of thorns, a reed for a
sceptre, and in full attire, that is with a scarlet cloak
purloined from one of the soldiers. Yeshu, then, has
undergone the suffering and indignities practised on
priestesses of the Great Goddess, and appears attired like
a Great Goddess.

The allusions would surely not have been lost on
Caiaphas or his clique, but they are far too cunning to
be led along that path; instead they shout out that the
man must be crucified. But Pilate is not to be budged.
We do not know what went through his mind, but at his
back he had soldiers who had with relish enacted a religious
ceremony on a female prisoner, and now sated, were
probably feeling protective towards her. Some no doubt
were thinking of her as a kind of Garrison mascot, others
as someone who would have to die, having gone this far
along the path of ritual; after all in Mithras the Bull was
killed, though prior to bulls, cows were used; others may
have felt that there was a dangerous situation, and if the
Jews wanted a fight they could have it, since the reckon-
ing was long overdue anyway. The ineradicable fact,
however, was that blood had been shed, spattered on the
flagstones, and it was female blood. The bleeding victim
had taught in the synagogue where no woman was
allowed. There is no doubt that now Caiaphas knew it
too, which meant that if he admitted to it, he admitted
to the fact that the Temple in his care had been profaned.
Indeed he himself was ritually impure now, for he had
had Yeshu beaten in his own house and the blood was
on his floor too.

As Pilate and Caiaphas eyed one another the sun was
climbing to its apogee. Whose will would break first? Pilate
was afraid, in that upper class Roman manner, not
of Caiaphas, not the Jews, but of the strangeness of the
prisoner he had in his power. His wife Thecla had warned
him not to harm Yeshu. Then came another stab of fear, for

Caiaphas had found the right note to sound. He shouted out that since this Jesus had made himself king, any man who supported him was guilty of treason to the Emperor. The gall of that remark must have stung Pilate, but the charge of treason was a libel that could stick.

Pilate is at the pinnacle of a great human drama that was to change world history. He had spoken to Yeshu; his wife had been healed by Yeshu. When he heard that Yeshu was calling herself the Son of God, he had talked to her once more, trying to get her released. He thought to satisfy the blood lust of Caiaphas by a scourging, but then had discovered Yeshu was a woman. His soldiers carried out his orders with uncommon detail, a mixture of love and cruelty. He faced Caiaphas again, wondering how much the High Priest knew, and was threatened with treason. If the story of Yeshu's sex got out there would be a riot; if Yeshu was released, there was no real possibility of her being safely guarded. And besides, this strange woman, this haunting person seemed to know the way events would go. The forces on Pilate, material and psychological, had only one possible release. He turned and washed his hands in pure water, probably more than a symbolic act, and told Caiaphas the blood was on him.

The Roman soldiers now had no choice, the Procurator had ordered a crucifixion. By now some of the confused soldiers may have balked at the idea of Yeshu's death; others, however, may have felt it was fitting that the man who had called himself the Light of the World, and had transpired to be a woman, was in some way magical and the magic would be released by her death; others were simply eager to get the day's work done. The crucifixion squad was to say the least ambivalent, but Romans had conquered a world by obeying orders, so they did as Pilate bade them.

The Unnamed Witness

The Gospel accounts of the events leading up to the crucifixion are clearly unsatisfactory. There are several discrepancies between the four accounts, but even where they do agree there is more mystery. Pilate, for example, is obviously deeply implicated in some personal way with Jesus, as are some of his soldiers.

When Jesus was on the cross some kind of drink or potion was offered to him, which Matthew says was vinegar, but it could have been wine for that oxidizes to vinegar, and Judean wine was not the choicest in the Empire. John says that it was 'vinegar' with 'hyssop'. Hyssop was a sacred plant used in ceremonies, but it was also bitter. The confusion in the accounts suggests that something was given to Jesus; it may have been a pain killer, or intended to be, but my speculation on this is based chiefly on the dulling effects of alcohol and the fact that some of the Great Goddess insignias featured poppies. The opium poppy ground with wine would result in an analgesic tincture.

In Matthew's account this interpretation is given some substantiation, for the soldiers get a passer-by, Simon of Cyrene, to carry the cross (Matt. 27:32), as if to relieve some of Jesus' suffering. Also, they offer him the 'vinegar' mingled with gall, that is something bitter (Matt. 27:34), which was not taken, but John states that the vinegar with hyssop was put to his mouth (John 19;29–30).

These ministrations are strongly contrasted by the mocking and reviling made of Christ by the Caiaphas clacque reported by Matthew, 'He saved others, himself he cannot save' (Matt. 27:42). This passage shows that the soldiers had covered Jesus' nakedness, for clearly the mockers still thought of Jesus as male. As did the centurion who saw Jesus die, 'Certainly this was a righteous man' (Luke 23:47).

There is also the question of eyewitnesses. Who saw the 'ceremony' in Antonia? Certainly not any of the male apostles, they were far from the scene. And what of the story about Pilate's wife being healed by Jesus? Certainly the accounts in the four Gospels accepted by Rome have been doctored to take account of Roman sensitivities. To make it easier to convert Romans, the Jews – or to be more precise the Temple Establishment – have been cast in a very unsympathetic light, though given the venality and unpopularity of the Temple professionals with most Judeans, this was not hard to do.

What is worrying is the gradual shift of onus from a clique with vested interests, that is the rich clerics of the Temple, to guilt by implication of the entire Jewish people. It is inconceivable that this represents the true state of affairs existing in *c.* AD 33, since the crowds who loved Jesus were Jews. Stealth by night was necessary to destroy the 'man' they loved. To his credit, Herod was evidently unimpressed by charges of sedition, and appears to think that Jesus was a kind of mountebank at worst. Perhaps memories of Mary's involvement in the palace with his father some thirty-three years before still lingered.

Ostensibly, the only immediately obvious and acceptable feature about this death is that political intrigue and political unrest were cleverly exploited by Caiaphas.

Unfortunately, what happened in accurate detail is probably irrecoverable, though even accepted history of other epochs falls short of absolute proof, dependent as we are on sources, rather than direct experiment, as in the sciences. None the less, even with the records at present available, there does seem ground for supposing that the orthodox explanation of the Gospels leaves much to be desired. There are tantalizing glimpses of something else happening at the Roman mockery and scourging.

That Jesus meant to die appears inescapable as a conclusion: here then was someone not overtaken by events but in control of them, using history, times and places as material for her own drama.

The script hypothesis appears to fit these facts well. Yeshu set out to fulfil the Great Goddess religion and succeeded, purloining even a scarlet cloak from the Roman soldiers as both a symbol of the ever healing blood of the Goddess, and the scarlet thread which linked Yeshu with her ancestresses of the great religion. If this analysis is correct, then Rahab, Tamar, Ruth, Bathsheba and the grossly maligned Jezebel are the fertile founts of Christianity. Christ's blood is no longer the inexplicable theme in a male religion, running on from the blood of a lamb and other animalistic ritual slaughtering, but a vibrant life affirmation, as the Great Goddess tradition always was. In this belief there is no difficulty in seeing that the blood of a Goddess is charged with life. No special arguments or theological conundrums are required.

Yeshu's passion was love. She meant to stamp that message indelibly on human consciousness in a way no one could forget or ignore. Even her detractors cannot gainsay the power of what she did, and although the theology is legitimately difficult, the outcome of my investigation is a unique woman who spoke and acted in such a way that a challenge was thrown down which has yet to be taken up, although a few have taken on the crimson mantle. But contention is not the issue here; we are interested in the flesh and blood actuality of a small woman, graceful, energetic, eloquent beyond anyone before or since, who went to her death when with her ability she could have had anything material or political she had set her mind to. She made claims of her uniqueness which, in some ways still not understood, meant she was divine. This is the stuff of drama; a mystery which strikes at our easy preconceptions, points to an unresolved dilemma in the way we see ourselves. But again, within the compass of this investigation, it is the objective facts that seem to be so tantalizingly realizable.

There was no six-foot muscular Christ bearing blows from fists or tensing under the scourge, or even being nailed to a cross; there was, it seems, a little woman, about five feet tall, with hair parted in the Nazarene fashion, hanging long to her shoulders. Her body was afflicted yet animated with a spirit so strong that for millions she has not truly died. That is the testimony of human experience, but the body died on a cross in AD 33.

Perhaps we can be permitted a vignette contructed from the discoveries unearthed, beginning in Caiaphas' house where she is severely beaten. Caiaphas hates her with a vehemence which still rings through history, yet this High Priest has not even bothered to inform the other members of the Sanhedrin what he is about to do; indeed, he has arrested Yeshu with his own Temple Guard, a night arrest when honest folk are asleep. Although Caiaphas' thugs beat and spit on Yeshu, she will not recant her claims. One man hits her so hard it seems he has killed her. Her blood is spattered on the mosaics of Caiaphas' house. He wants her dead, but is reluctant to take the burden wholly on himself; too many people love Yeshu.

Yeshu is taken to Pilate. He knows of his wife's love of this little man and is reluctant to proceed against him. Thinking the bloodlust of the Caiaphas clique will be sated by the sight of blood, he tries a cruel compromise and orders his guards to scourge Yeshu. In the huge hall of Antonia, Yeshu is stripped, and the flagellation squad make ribald remarks, laced with fear and tinged with awe, for the little man is a woman, with no breasts, her body bruised and bleeding from Caiaphas' thugs. The centurion sends a message to Pilate, who comes down personally to see the prisoner. He is afraid now, for his wife has warned him against hurting this man. But he is still convinced that this is the only way to save Yeshu so he orders the soldiers to continue. He looks up and sees his wife, with Mary Magdalene and Mary the mother of Yeshu, at the head of the stairs. Perplexed, he sees that these women are not afraid; although anguished, they seem to have the same steadfastness that Yeshu shows, certain to the death.

Yeshu is tied by the arms to a pillar and is scourged by two men, one on each side, who each carry a Roman *flagellum*, a two-stranded whip with talons of iron at the end of each cord. The first blow cuts deeply; by the thirteenth, Yeshu's back and chest have been flayed. The whippers look at one another – they have never seen a person bleed like this before – but they continue, supposing that their prisoner will be dead by the thirty-ninth stroke, the thrice times thirteen demanded by Roman Law.

Within the hour Yeshu is carrying her cross along the narrow streets of Jerusalem, attired as she always had been, as a man, for Pilate dare not risk a riot. She is so weak, this scrap of humanity, that it is obvious she cannot continue so the soldiers pick a man from the crowd to help carry the cross. Eventually they get to Golgotha, the Place of the Skull, outside the walls of Jerusalem. The soldiers strip Yeshu but not wholly naked, as Pilate has warned them. One man picks her up with ease and lays her out on the supine cross. Another soldier places a seven-inch rough-hewn nail of iron at the wrist, and smashes it through with one practised blow of a square hammer. On the other arm a soldier is pulling, stretching the victim out. Yeshu is again affixed through the wrist.

Some of the soldiers think Yeshu is dead, but they pull on her legs, stretching her out; then they put one foot on the other and smash a huge iron spike through both feet at the ankles. Yeshu contorts. The cross is lifted and placed into its hole. Yeshu cannot breathe unless she pushes on her pierced feet, but when she does lift herself up the pain is too great to sustain, so she falls again. She knows she will die of suffocation and recalls the words of a Psalm she read as a girl, which said she would wriggle upon the tree.

Through her pain-filled eyes, narrowed by anguish and the sun's glare, she can see Mary Magdalene and Mary as close as the soldiers will let them come. John, her favourite, is there too, but the rest are still in hiding. Yeshu calls out to John that Mary is his mother. Perhaps one day he will understand, perhaps he never will. She is fast sinking, and cries out, 'My God, why have you forsaken me?' Only Mary and Mary Magdalene know what she means. Why had the priests made a God who forsook the priesthood of women? The centurion is astonished that Yeshu could find such force to make such a cry, but as he looks up into her face, he sees not only pain but triumph; he does not know that this little woman has changed the world for ever.

It is fast approaching sunset and the bodies must be buried, for others have been crucified too. The soldiers break the legs of the other victims with hacking sword cuts; the men fall on their arms and cannot breathe any more. The soldiers come to Yeshu, but Mary cries out for them not to break this victim's bones. She has seen how the nails have been pushed through the spaces of the little bones of the wrists and feet, and recalls the prophecy that the Redeemer will have no bones broken. Her cry is taken up by Mary Magdalene. The centurion wonders what the commotion is about, but one of his soldiers intercedes, pointing out that not a few hours before they thought this prisoner special. The centurion relents and thrusts his spear between Yeshu's ribs, a diamond-shaped iron head penetrates the heart and as the *pilum* is withdrawn, blood follows it with the waters of the pericardium. He turns to the women and tells them they can take the body, adding that he is sorry Yeshu had to die for, unlike the rest, Yeshu was righteous. He notes with interest that the little group has been joined by a very rich merchant, a man called Joseph of Arimathea, and is even more astonished when he receives orders direct from Pilate that a Roman guard is to be put over the sepulchre.

Meanwhile, their bodies and hands wet with Yeshu's sweat and blood, the two Marys and John take the body down and wrap a cloth about it; a holy moment, for here in Jerusalem, at the Place of the Skull, on a Friday evening in AD 33, there were two priestesses and one priest of Christ with the reality of sacrifice in their hands, hands wet with real blood. The great adventure had ended; the great adventure was beginning.

Pilate is clearly implicated in some mystery concerning Jesus, for it was he who was fearful, he who used water to wash the blood from his hands, he who put up the notice 'King of the Jews' in Latin, Greek and Hebrew, he who gave leave for a decent burial, and he who ordered the Roman guard at the sepulchre. And it was his wife who loved Jesus. If my scenario is correct, all these difficulties are no longer problems but actions arising from Pilate's knowing who Jesus was. His irony has been commented on often before. Some commentators suppose he is mocking the Jews calling a crucified man a King, but they forget that in the Roman religion Goddesses were humiliated; and besides, would he mock his wife? Now, perhaps, the irony is more clearly seen, and seen to be very biting indeed, for once the Great Goddess was the supreme icon of the Jews until the Temple priests made a cult of the unknown, the unseen and unnameable.

And what of Pilate marvelling that Yeshu was dead so soon upon the cross? We are told this in the Synoptic Gospels. What does it mean? Is it likely that a person, after being so brutally beaten, whipped and nailed, would live longer? Or is it more realistic that a seasoned soldier like Pilate, who would know well enough the frailty of the body, was beginning to believe that Yeshu was someone very special indeed? This question had to be answered.

— 11 —

Love Feast

At this stage I found myself in deep waters, which is a
figurative way of saying I had no intention of becoming
involved in questions of miracles, the supernatural, and
resurrections from the dead. However, the uninvited had
occurred, and I found, in place of an inexplicable and
myth-ridden Roman Christian Christ figure, a small and
remarkable woman, surrounded by flesh-and-blood historical characters whose humanness and naturalness
(wicked though some may appear to be) seemed to span
the gap between their time and the present, so real were
their concerns. These were believable people with
understandable motives and aspirations. Gone was the
neurotically tense mystic of a man who could also be a
sheep and an Apollo at the same time; here instead was a
woman who ate and drank with her friends and promised
always to be with them. For her love and companionship,
it seemed, there was no need of any dogmas, churches
or priests. She was in the fields, at the table, in simple
homely terms. None the less, warm and loving as she
might be, she undoubtedly called herself Goddess and
promised resurrection to all who believed in her
claims.

What do we know about the resurrection as taught by
Yeshu? Again, we find that Mary Magdalene is the key
witness, perhaps even the authoress of Q, the authentic
gospel. But again, there is evidence of tampering with
sources to provide more palatable political fare.

Matthew tells us that Mary Magdalene went to the

tomb at dawn with the 'other Mary' who is not clearly identified. A minor earthquake occurs, an angel moves the stone and then sits on it, showing Mary the empty tomb, and telling her Christ is already risen, and that she should inform the apostles. The women rush off dutifully, but actually meet Jesus. Mary kneels down at his feet, just as she had when she washed them with her tears and dried them with her hair. There is a problem with this story (Matt. 28:1–10) – why did the angel tell Mary Magdalene to go to the apostles, and then she bumps into the risen Christ? Something seems to have been missed out and something interpolated. For one thing, Christ was in no need of angels to work miracles.

Mark tells us that Mary Magdalene, the other Mary, the mother of James (which may mean Mary the mother of Jesus, because Jesus, it seems, had a brother) and yet another woman, Salome, went with spices on the Sunday (the first day of the week for Jews) to the sepulchre, carrying spices to anoint the body. They discussed among themselves the problem of getting into the tomb because they knew it was blocked by a large stone. However, when they arrived they saw the stone was moved, and inside the tomb sat a young man in a long white garment. He told them that Jesus had risen and that they should tell the disciples. Mark also says that Jesus specifically appeared to Mary Magdalene later but that the disciples did not believe her (Mark 16:1–11).

Again, we encounter young men or angels. Why should Mary, this educated and rich young woman, confidante and priestess of Jesus Christ, take any notice of a young man at her Lord's tomb? Perhaps she knew this young man, but he was not an apostle or we would have been told so. Who did Mary know that she trusted so implictly? One candidate springs to mind, Lazarus, her brother, the well beloved of Jesus.

Luke tells the story like this. The women, Mary

Magdalene, Mary, mother of James, a woman called Joanna, and other women from Galilee, saw the body in the tomb when it was laid there. They then came back three days later on the Sunday and found the stone rolled away. Two men in shining garments then appeared and told them that Jesus had risen and that they should tell the disciples. This they did, but they were not believed; however, Peter went to check and found only the linen clothes – note the plural – in the tomb (Luke 24:1–12).

Finally, John relates that Mary Magdalene alone goes to the tomb and sees the stone has been moved, so she goes to tell Peter and John. They run to the tomb, but John gets there first and looks in to see, observing only the linen clothes (again the plural, which seems to scotch the Turin Shroud yet again, since that is but one cloth, and these are strips of cloth). Simon Peter by now has caught up and he looks too, but being made of sterner stuff – he is such a mixture of the brave and the dithering – he actually enters the tomb. Peter observes that the napkin that was about Christ's head is laid by itself, not with the linen strips (this on biblical authority entirely destroys the Turin Shroud, for how could the face of Christ or the head of Christ be on a single piece, when that which covered his head was separate?). The two men leave, but Mary Magdalene stays. She is crying, and looks into the sepulchre, where she sees two angels in white, sitting at each end of where Jesus' body had lain. They ask her why she is weeping and she replies, 'Because they have taken away my Lord'. She then 'turned herself back' and saw Jesus standing, but did not know it was Jesus. And then she does. She tries to embrace Jesus, but John tells us Jesus says, 'Touch me not, for I am not yet ascended to my father' (John 20:1–17).

Two important themes appear here: Mary Magdalene's pre-eminence, and the presence of the young man. This latter figure is plausibly, as I was to discover,

Lazarus, the man Jesus raised from the dead. But there is a discordant note in the account: what did Jesus mean, 'Do not touch me?' Is it possible that this could have happened? According to the gospel of Philip, Jesus kissed Mary on the mouth, and was upbraided for it by Peter, stinging Jesus to say, 'Why do I not love you like her?' This information we owe to the fact that in 1945 scrolls were found near the village of Nag Hammadi in Egypt. These were published in 1977 in English.[1] Some of the works date to pre-AD 150, and may relate to an Alexandrian sect of Gnostic Christians. Even Thomas is said to have put his hands in Jesus' wounds, so why is Mary Magdalene suddenly not to touch her Lord?

The obvious answer seems to be that it did not happen as we are told. Mary Magdalene may have had a vision of Christ risen, just as Paul was to have later. In the great apostle's case the event is clearly internal, an awakening. There are no mentions of a figure before him but an unmistakable presence, the power of a transcendant personality. Is this the true resurrection? Of the spirit? If so, it is Mary Magdalene who experienced it first.

It is significant that Paul's letters, and the Acts, which are on much firmer ground than the Gospels historically, reveal that Paul never met Christ in the flesh, and his conversion occurred not by seeing a risen Christ in a room or on a seashore, but in a vision. Taking this lead, the analysis above, of the true account of the resurrection, is therefore supported by *independent* witness. Moreover, the addition of angels and shining lights appears to be just that, 'addition': supernatural falsehood. The motive of these interpolations appears to be to take away the central importance of Mary Magdalene and bolster the status of the disciples.

Further credence to this idea is found in what we know about James the Great, head of the first church in Jerusalem, for this man, either Jesus' brother or cousin, appears not to have believed in the resurrection, at least not the bodily one. His gospel speaks of keeping the commandments and sharing worldly goods. The transfiguration of Mary's experience into a flesh-and-blood resurrection only became Church dogma at Nicea.

A resurrection certainly occurred – but it appears to have been a spiritual one, of the kind millions of sincere Christians have experienced since then. This is not the place to speculate on what the ultimate meaning of this experience is, but as a fact of human spiritual awareness it seems unshakable.

Much of what is said by Jesus can be traced to the Old Testament, and even further back to the myths of Isis and Osiris. The German school of biblical analysts came erroneously to the conclusion that most of the Gospels were myths. But if we suppose for a moment that Jesus was a woman, then the Isis parts of the Gospel stories would very likely be more genuine, especially if she were consciously acting out the prophecies of the Old Testament. The healings were Isis-like. We know today that many conditions of illness are hysterical, and a person with sufficient charisma, something Yeshu had in abundance, can so gain confidence that paralysis, even blindness, are cured. The rationale is that such illnesses are often psychological in origin. Jesus was not above using spit and rubbing it in the eyes to effect a cure, just as Isis was vigorous enough to cool her son Hourus with saliva.

The feeding miracles appear to be symbolic stories. If Christ is to feed spiritually and is symbolized by a fish, then a single fish is sufficient to feed the world, let alone five thousand. In like vein, the turning of water into wine at Cana can be seen as symbolic of the penultimate step before turning wine into blood, which itself was a symbol of loving kindness in the best tradition of the Goddess religions. Jesus called herself the true vine, and told her friends to drink wine in memory, for the wine was her life-giving blood.

But what of raising from the dead? We know today that people who have seemed so dead that even fifty years ago they would have been put into their graves, can be revived by massage, the kiss of life and electric shock. There is even dispute as to what constitutes death. Provided the organs are all extant and the body not damaged, mere cessation of heartbeat, even for a few minutes, is not sufficient for death to be permanent. With Lazarus, his heartbeat may have been so low and slow that he was really thought dead, and in one sense at least he was dead, for without Yeshu he would have stayed in his tomb.

It would seem then that a naturalistic explanation of the miracles is possible. However, what is significant is the kind of miracles reported. They involve resurrection, water, wine, seeing, and having devils cast out, all part of the repertoire expected of the Great Goddess.

Apostless

The problem for me with Church history and the pre-eminent position of Mary Magdalene with Jesus, is not the scale of importance given to her by the Church, but the smallness of it in comparison with her role in the ministry of Christ. How can this be explained? The Church has 'Magdalene' ceremonies, but just as with Mary the Mother, at first there seems scant gospel textual matter about her; however, the little there is for both women makes the roles of the twelve disciples, even *en masse*, or in summation, appear marginal. This is a very strange literary fact. The central characters are hardly mentioned, yet without them there would be no story! Take away Mary the Mother, and Jesus is not even born, let alone being able to turn water into wine at Cana.

Take away Mary Magdalene and the grandeur of Christ is hardly ever mentioned, and the reportage of many key passages impossible. Take the two Marys from Christ and who will stay with her as the blood flows? Who will take Jesus from the cross? Who will bury Jesus? Who will go to the tomb with spices, and who will see the risen Christ on that Easter morning? It does seem that substantial material may have been left out from the accounts which have come down to us, for otherwise the paradoxes are too great.

Indeed, the roles of these women are so evident even in the truncated Gospels, that the role of men and their claims to be the founders and spiritual descendants of Christ, exclusively so, are very difficult to sustain.

Taking the events in the Garden of Gethsemane for example, who was the witness of Jesus' agonized praying, so passionate that he 'sweated blood'? The apostles can be discounted because they were asleep. Since other important events were witnessed and acted through by Mary Magdalene, she seems an obvious candidate. If this is so, why are we not told? Why has her name been excised from such key Gospel events, and she herself excluded from the priesthood?

The mystery deepens when we find that even Popes are not able to deny Mary Magdalene her importance. No less an authority than Pope Gregory the Great (590–604), a brilliant scholar from a rich family with two Popes before him in it, identified Mary Magdalene as the same woman in three key Gospel accounts: the woman who anointed Jesus, washed her feet with her tears and dried them with her hair; the woman who was at the cross with Mary, Jesus' mother, and who helped bury Jesus; and the person who first saw the risen Christ. Even by her act of washing Jesus' feet, she foreshadowed Christ's own washing of the disciples' feet at the Last Supper. No other person has that kind of intimacy, actual or theological, with the Messiah, and it suggests that Mary Magdalene was at the Last Supper; she certainly seems to have been with Jesus most of the time elsewhere.

Even if the hypothesis that she was a priestess, or at least an acolyte of a Mother Goddess religion is incorrect in some aspects, it seems very probable that Jesus regarded her as a priestess. Jesus allowed her to anoint him, to minister to his physical and emotional needs, to be ever present, an intimacy not afforded to any other person, not even to Mary his mother, and certainly not to any of the disciples in his entourage. Mary Magdalene suffered with Christ, by empathy on the cross. Also Mary Magdalene was privileged to overhear the doubts, and observe the agony on the Mount of Olives in Gethsemane, and to watch the blood drop from Christ's tortured body. It is Mary's hands which hold the naked body of Jesus Christ from the cross, and the other hands are those of Mary the Mother of the crucified teacher. It is Mary's hands which carry the ointment to the tomb. These are holy acts no man shares; in which case is it not reasonable to suppose that the hands of this woman were consecrated in a more fundamental manner than Peter's? The case for her being a pre-eminent priestess of Jesus is found even in the truncated versions of the four Gospels, but there is other evidence too.

The question of Mary Magdalene's central role has pervaded, it seems to me, much of my investigation. Internally the Gospels bear witness, but the Church has ignored, indeed suppressed, the obvious implications. In the Gospel of Mary, found at Nag Hammadi, we see Mary in the central role our quite independent investigation had already placed her. Peter is shown to be continually agitating against Mary, evidently upset that Jesus has loved Mary more and confided in her, so he asks her to tell him what Jesus said. Mary tells him, 'What is hidden from you, I will tell you.'[2] It is difficult to see, on this

witness, how Peter can be regarded as exclusively central.
Significantly or not, the four pages in which Mary is to
reveal the secrets have been lost, and it appears they
were lost in the crucial third century when Roman
dogma was being transformed into secular power. Mary,
however, does tell Peter that there are seven conditions
of the soul, while the Church only recognizes three:
heaven, hell and purgatory. Peter asserts he does not
believe her, even questioning what he himself has said,
that Jesus spoke 'with a woman' rather than openly to
him. His attitude makes Mary unhappy; she weeps, and
asks the unanswerable question, 'Do you think I would
lie about what Jesus said?'

She is rescued, significantly, by a man called Levi, who
points out that it is a fact Jesus loved Mary more than
the disciples, and that since he trusted her, the disciples
should too.[3]

It seems, then, that Mary Magdalene did have her
champions, but Peter, James and the rest did not support
her, while the Roman Church has arguably demeaned her.

Gethsemane

The opinion that the four Gospels, in the form that they
have come down to us, have left something out about the
last night of Jesus' life is expressed by Christian and non-
Christian scholars alike. The mystery pivots about some
kind of ceremony or initiation, something which the
twelve apostles are not privy to.

Dr Morton Smith argues that on the night of the Last
Supper Jesus initiated a young man in certain undisclosed
secrets. Ian Wilson takes this theme up and wonders if
the young man nearly captured in Gethsemane was the
same man who was to be initiated.[4] The young man in
question, as both authors agree, is described by Mark,
when on Jesus' arrest everyone flees, except this enigmatic

character: 'And there followed him a certain young man, having a linen cloth cast about his naked body: and the young men [that is the Temple Guard] laid hold on him; and he left the linen cloth, and fled from them naked' (Mark 14:51–2).

This young man is not mentioned by the other three canonical Gospels but appears in apocrypha. Attempts to explain him on the above lines lack conviction, since new hypotheses have to be created to explain events already mysterious enough. In Morton Smith's case, the novelty is some strange and secret baptism (which the other disciples do not share), while in Wilson's case we are asked to consider Jesus as a hypnotist, about to perform a session which is interrupted by Judas and the Temple guards.

But the story is given a further twist by the discovery of a copy of a letter written by the second century Church Father, Clement of Alexandria, in the Eastern Orthodox Monastery of Mar Saba, near Jerusalem. This momentous find was made by Morton Smith in 1941.[5] The letter alludes to a secret gospel of Mark, containing material that was perhaps best kept hidden. These matters describe a ceremony involving Jesus and Lazarus, where the latter comes to Jesus wearing a linen cloth over his naked body and spends the night with Jesus. There is no mention of this event, or any like it in the canonical Gospels, except for this curious passage in Mark already mentioned, about a young man after the arrest of Jesus in Gethsemane, who followed the Temple Guard and their prisoner wearing nothing but a linen cloth, but who ran away when the soldiers tried to apprehend him. Was this Lazarus? It hardly seems possible it was anyone else. And what was the secret ceremony that Jesus initiated him in, one concerning 'great mysteries' according to Clement of Alexandria? Whatever it was, Clement thought it prudent to suppress the secret gospel, and so it was lost to Christendom.

There is, of course, more here than meets the eye; for one thing, Lazarus was raised from the dead, was Mary Magdalene's brother, was rich, was singled out by Jesus and, according to de Voragine's *Golden Legend*, he accompanied his sister to Marseille. There is also the story of Jesus in the Gospels meeting a young rich man who said that he was obedient to all the orthodox Jewish laws and what did he have to do to be saved? Jesus told him to sell everything, give to the poor and 'follow me'. The young man was downcast and declined, which saddened Jesus because, as the Gospel says, 'he loved him much'. Was this man Lazarus, who later was ill and was raised from the dead? John makes an emphatic point of including Lazarus at the table when Jesus is anointed by Mary Magdalene (John 12:2) and even mentions that the Jews were preparing to kill Lazarus, for Jesus had raised him from the dead, so proving enormous power (John 12:9–11). Clearly, like the women closest to Jesus, the importance of Lazarus in Church history and in Jesus' life has been purposely diminished. A man with this amount of intimacy with the Christ would at least be thought of as a priest of the new religion, but nothing remotely close to that is afforded him. None of the disciples, as far as we know at present, were ever initiated into mysteries as Lazarus was.

In the Gospel of St Thomas we find many statements identical to those in the canonical Gospels, but some which have been left out of them. Indeed, it is only by reading the gospels of Philip, Thomas and Mary, that many of the sayings in the four Gospels can be understood in their full meaning.

Seen against the background of the early Church's loathing of the body, something never evinced by Christ, there is a distinct smell of censorship in the enclaves behind closed doors, in Jerusalem, Alexandria and, of course, Rome, where the disciples were elevated to a patristic élite, and the women demoted, their menfolk with them. This view is supported by the passages in the gospel of Thomas, which has claims to authenticity equalling those of the canonical Gospels, although not accepted by the Church, which reveal that Jesus had, as Ian Wilson points out, a distinctly non-Jewish attitude to nudity.[6] The disciples wanted to know when Jesus would be revealed to them, and Jesus answered, when they disrobed without being ashamed like little children.[7] The touching domestic humanity of this story is typical of Jesus, but the passage is nowhere in the four canonical Gospels.

The gospel of Thomas, for example, contains the famous saying by Jesus that the Kingdom of Heaven is like a mustard seed, small at first, but able to grow large. In the same passage, Mary Magdalene asks Jesus, 'Who are your disciples like?' Jesus speaks of them as children who are in a field which is not theirs. Later, we are told that Jesus, on seeing babies being suckled by their mothers, told his disciples that they were like these babes. So they asked if they had to be children to enter the Kingdom. The answer was in the affirmative. The symbols of nakedness, milk, children, all reinforce the born-again image, which is central to the Great Goddess religion. Shortly after these symbols comes the passage alluded to above, 'When you disrobe without being ashamed, and take up your garments, and place them under your feet like little children and tread on them, then you will see the Son of the Living One and you will not be afraid.' Unmistakably, followers of Christ have to be children before him, trusting, innocent, unadorned. It is difficult to conceive of a more maternal expression of concern and love. Immediately after, Jesus says, 'be as wise as serpents and as innocent as doves.'[8]

This passage is so un-Jewish as to be entirely indecipherable on Jewish theological grounds. For in the Old

Testament the serpent is a figure of evil – but it was not always so. The red serpent of Isis, a guise she takes on from time to time, is the motif of healing power, of wisdom. Doves were sacred, that is innocent, to the Great Goddess in many of her guises, particularly Astarte. Jesus' words, then, could be the legacy of the Great Goddess tradition.

Goddess and Her Consort

Yeshu appears to have fulfilled in great detail, both by symbol and in reality, the traditions of the Great Goddess in its most important aspects – save one, for she had no consort. It must be said that not all aspects of the Great Goddess showed a lover or a consort, but many did. Put like this then, there is one obvious ceremony missing from the tradition, which for the want of a better word, we can call marriage. In the four canonical Gospels there are intriguing hints of a secret ceremony. So what has been omitted? If in ordinary literature there are stories of love between a man and a woman which death cannot break, then clearly it is a fitting theme for Yeshu. As we have seen there is some hint in the received Gospels of a ceremony between Yeshu and a young man. Was that ceremony marriage? If so, fresh light is thrown on the Last Supper because it becomes a Wedding Feast, a true Love Feast.

Naturally this has been turned into a secret, for it would not be something the twelve apostles were privy to, but then we have already seen evidence which consigns them to the outer circle around Yeshu, the inner being peopled by Mary the Virgin Mother, Mary Magdalene and her brother Lazarus. Of this latter person, certainly Yeshu had a role for him, for she would have been told when young by her mother about Isis and her consort Osiris, who died but was raised from the dead by the Goddess. Perhaps this is one of the seminal effects of having been brought up in Egypt.

If this assumption of a marriage feast is correct it completes the Great Goddess tradition, for Yeshu is living her life as the Great Goddess, entire and whole, with acts and stories filled with wine, bread, children. She healed like the Goddess is supposed to, she travelled from place to place, full of energy and love, she fished for men with the same energy with which Diana had hunted; she was the protectress of children and the humble, just as the Great Goddess had always been, an avenger too for the proud, for her tongue cut like a sword. Like the Great Goddess she could be angry, even violent, when she whipped with cords the procurers and sellers of the sacred doves of Astarte in the Jewish Temple, a temple she foretold would come crashing down. And she knew marriage was a great mystery, for we have these words from her mouth, reported by a Christian author probably living in Egypt, that the world would not have existed without marriage.[9]

Perhaps the notion that Jesus had married washes away, as perhaps the waters of Cedron brook washed away the sins of Lazarus before he married Yeshu, the mystery of that night. Certainly, it fits the picture we have of Christ's femininity, fulfilling the promise of the Great Goddess here on earth. Was the marriage ceremony interrupted by Judas with his kiss? If so, we can at last understand the forlorn figure of the young man who followed the stricken Christ taken by the Temple Guard. Lazarus' anguish must have been sorrowful indeed, raised to life and yet, apparently that night, to lose the meaning of his life.

I am not suggesting any romantic attachment in Yeshu, and I am not refuting it either, merely observing that to enter into a marriage which she knew would be physically dismembered even perhaps as the vows were being made, strongly accords with her dramatic nature.

As we have mentioned, this scenario also turns the Last Supper into a marriage feast. In celebrating marriage, Yeshu was saying that the body was good, that love was good; for if the body was not good, how could the sacrifice of her life have any meaning?

Early Christians, before the Church took the ceremony away from them, had what were called love feasts. Here, men and women, and children too, sat around large tables, broke bread and drank wine in memory of their loving Saviour. To say that this bread is my body, this wine is my blood is beautiful, but if Yeshu had also married, she was revealing that she believed the Divine love was possible on this earth too. It is difficult to conceive of a more dramatically clear set of actions by which to show your friends how much you love them.

I accord to these notions, on an objective level, no more than they warrant – namely, they fit facts and illuminate what was once dark. However, on the subjective level, they had a force so powerful that Lazarus and the two Marys were able to survive the terror of the crucifixion. Indeed, such was the power of what Yeshu did, that even those not privy to all her secrets, the twelve apostles, were none the less partakers of her feast as well, although they appear to have been guests in an outside room, loved but known for their lack of imagination.

A plausible reading of the evidence, both literary and historical, of what may have happened at the Last Supper and the events thereafter, suggests that a reconstruction, obviously tentative, certainly provocative, can be attempted, albeit in distressingly bare outline – but then the luxury of embellishment has been eschewed. Furthermore one has not had the benefit of 2,000 years' practice in embellishment of the facts.

Yeshu celebrated her marriage on the night of the Last Supper. Present were Mary her mother, Mary Magdalene and Lazarus. The feast has come down to us as the Last Supper and is obviously authentic in its symbols of loving, the bread and the wine, the promise that Yeshu will always be with those who love her. The disciples, who, of course, are not party to this ceremony but in the reception, as it were, are also honoured with the breaking of the bread and the drinking of the wine. The soldiers come and Yeshu is arrested. Lazarus forlornly follows, but can do nothing. Yeshu is crucified. Yeshu is put in the tomb and stolen later by the same raucous, half-profane, half-devout squad of Roman soldiers, and buried in the earth as a goddess should be.

The women, Mary Magdalene and Mary the mother, perhaps with others, as we have seen, come to the tomb and find it empty. This is historical fact.

But something happened to Mary Magdalene – she saw a vision of Christ. Paul was turned from scourge to protector of the word by a vision. He was convinced Christ lived. Millions of people have encountered the Christ personality without actually seeing a broken and bleeding body. Why could not Peter have been so lucky? The probability is that he was, and all the other disciples too. As Jews they would have understood dreams and visions, their Bible is full of them. If the bodily resurrection is a forgery, who did it? The answer is not hard to find.

The risen Christ is rather like those stories of Nero which Suetonius tells; he was seen alive and well, even though people put flowers on his grave. In Rome, as we have seen, the stories of Paul and Peter were soon appropriated into the myths of the divine Caesars, men who became gods and who lived with Jupiter and the rest, drinking the nectar of the gods and living very much like men and women, despite Jesus' dictum that in the

Kingdom of God there is no marriage; in other words, bodies are not like they are on this earth. In Rome, however, you do as the Romans do.

This explanation helps to solve the internal contradictions of the Gospels. The disciples are shown to have been utterly surprised on seeing the risen Christ. Well they might be; they had been told other things, but not this it seems. Yet how could they be surprised, when Jesus is supposed to have said, 'Destroy this temple and I will build it up in three days'? The inconsistencies are surely too glaring and the naturalistic explanation appears to have an indubitable weight to it. Add to this the fact that Mary the mother and Mary Magdalene were actually carrying spices for the body of their beloved. Does this appear to be the action of women who expect a body to rise from the dead? And yet, as priestesses of Yeshu they would surely have known what the truth was. For them Yeshu still lived, just as the Great God of the Hebrews lived, though for them Yahweh was the Great Goddess.

As a speculation, one might wonder if the bodily resurrection mentioned was actually Lazarus'. Be that as it may as an hypothesis, what emerges from this analysis is Mary Magdalene's pre-eminent position, and as she is seen more clearly, so is her brother. Persuasively, too, the fact remains that if we take out the events in which she is mentioned or implied, there is virtually no story at all.

Was she to be the leader of a new church? De Voragine, when writing about saints, specifically says in his life of St Mary Magdalene, that she:

anointed his head . . . was nigh unto the cross . . . made ready ointments and would anoint his body . . . and would not depart from the monument when his disciples departed. To whom Jesus Christ appeared first after his resurrection, and was fellow to the apostles, and made of our Lord apostolesse of the apostles.[10]

Here she does indeed appear to be at the head of this band of uncertain men, she who never once wavered in courage or devotion.

The simplest explanation seems to be that Mary was not able to overcome the prejudice of her male colleagues. They were in any case blissfully unaware of Christ's true identity.

The first head of the Church in Jerusalem was James the Great, who may actually have been Jesus' brother, at least his cousin. There is no reason to suppose he understood his brother's true identity. Given the embargo on nudity amongst Jews, and the fact that the Messiah-conscious Mary ran the Nazareth household, there is no reason to suppose he ever found out. James was murdered by the Sadducees, AD 62, the clique responsible for Christ's death; they had no intention of sharing religious power with anyone, even a staunch orthodox Jew like James, who preached communal sharing of goods, loving kindness, and did not emphasize Christ's resurrection.

Although there were thirteen 'bishops' of this Church, it was severely depleted when Titus, son of the then Roman Emperor Vespasian, destroyed much of the city of Jerusalem in AD 70. Those who survived death, slavery or deportation, were utterly erased by the piecemeal destruction by the Romans of what remained of Jersualem in AD 134. James' Church was not destined to become a world Church; that was left to Paul and Peter.

Paul was a Hellenized Jew, coming from Tarsus in Turkey, a busy port, a crossroads of the Levant and the West, with much Greek and Roman trade, as well as schools and centres of learning. A Talmudic scholar, and perhaps even something of an athlete, for his letters are replete with 'running the good race', he came to Jerusalem shortly after Christ's crucifixion, and finished his education with Gamaliel, a great humanist Rabbi. Fanatic by nature, Paul wanted to destroy the infant

Church in Jerusalem, and caused so much trouble, even having a deacon of James' Church stoned to death, that he was sent to Damascus to root out Christians there. On the way he saw a vision of Christ and became a Christian. Thereafter, he used the same energy and tenacity to spread the word as he had previously shown in persecuting the bearers of the word. His letters are copious. He travelled over much of the Empire, and had great success in converting Jews, Romans and Greeks.

In summary, he taught that you could be saved your burden of sin if you believed in Christ, and that you would live a personally resurrected life after death, though it is not made clear if this would be a flesh-and-blood life. None the less, the message was electric. Moreover, he did not consider the old Jewish Law as being important any more, so converts did not have to be circumcised, a crucial consideration for Romans and Greeks, who regarded mutilation as beneath contempt, though Syrians and Persians were not so squeamish.

He quarrelled with James and also with Peter, but this fiery little man had created a system of beliefs which suited the moods of the times. He was a master propagandist. He was martyred in Rome, under Nero, probably in the mid-sixties A D. His emphasis on faith, however, and his misogyny, have been stumbling blocks for many, for already he had introduced that other-worldliness into a religion, which James considered to be an extension of Jewish humanism, as a means of pleasing God.

Peter, long dithering between the Jewish Church of James and the global policy of Paul, eventually went to Rome where, as a disciple of Christ, he had a cachet. He had forsworn the need for circumcision, but it would be a mistake to assume any dogmas had emerged at this point. He preached the good news, which to the Roman mind sounded very much like a new way to purification, already firmly ensconced in the religion of Mithras, where the blood of the sacrificial bull removed sin. The fertility ideas present in the cults of Venus, Isis, Vesta and Ceres, the last being a goddess of grain, were now endemic to Rome, while wine was used in many ceremonies, particularly those relating to Bacchus. The ideas were already there.

Certainly, when Jerusalem was destroyed in AD 70, many Jews, Christians amongst them, dispersed throughout the Empire, and they carried with them their own individual interpretation of what Christ had taught. Who can tell at this distance if the first teachings of Christ got to Rome through the soldiers of Antonia, the very men who had crucified Jesus? Perhaps they told the story, on leave, or when they were posted elsewhere, of the strange Persephone they had been forced to kill. Or did they look upon Jesus in much the same way as the women of the Bacchante, who tore to pieces their sacred priest-kings? We do not know, but being a follower of Mithras was but a short step from being a Christian; drinking the wine of purification is, after all, more convenient than killing costly sacrificial bulls.

However these were clerics who wanted power. By the time they had finished with what Peter had to say, it was no longer Jewish property. If Jesus was the son of God, surely he had to be a god as well? If Augustus and Claudius were gods, nothing less could be expected of the son of God. Priests were officials in Rome, having secular and temporal offices at the same time, so closely was religion bound to State. We see here, perhaps, the clue to the Romanization of Christianity in Rome, but it was a see-saw process. While one emperor was lenient, another cracked down on it but all the while the religion grew.

It is impossible to say who the 'true' Christians were,

just as one cannot say who the true worshippers of Isis were. We know that Isis was worshipped in Egypt for 5,000 years, and though the cult changed in ritual as it was appropriated by the priests and priestesses in the great cult centres of Alexandria, the peasant went on praying to Isis as he or she had always done for good crops and the healing of children; just as the Greek peasant prayed to Diana, Athene or Demeter, and the Latin prayed to Venus and Vesta. The religions were not centralized; each village, each hamlet, each house, had its fertility goddess. But in Rome the stakes were very high, the need for dogma pressing. Clearly, this had little to do with the Christian religion. After Christ died, who were the Christians?

Were the ribald, Mithras-loving soldiers Christians? Did Mary, as the mother of the Christ, have a greater claim than Peter? Was Lazarus, as the likely inheritor of words given only to him from Christ's mouth, a special leader? And what of Mary Magdalene, a priestess of Jesus if ever there was one, what of her secrets and her testimony? Clearly, there were rival claims from the very beginning. Just one won out, the Church of Rome, which had no room for priestesses.

The tangled meanings from the beginnings of Christianity are even reflected in the story of Pontius Pilate. Recalled in AD 36, he went to live in Vienne, a French town some twenty miles south of Lyon, an area which is to figure largely in my investigation. Most Christians see him in a bad light, but the Copts, an ancient Church in Egypt, dating back to the crucifixion, venerate Pilate as a saint, and the affiliated Ethiopian Church, as ancient, regards him as a martyr. The western and eastern traditions already diverge.

In the first century orthodox Jews burned churches, and Jewish Christians attacked Jews. We also know that just about any idea about Christ was prevalent. People made of it what they would, giving the new belief a flavour of what they already knew.

However, the imputation put on the Gospels as arguments for a central dogmatic church is now possibly shattered for ever. In its place is a story of a young woman who fulfilled the Great Goddess tradition, lived out the prophecies and made them come true.

Fragments of this interpretation still survive in the Gospels themselves, and in scattered documents which have escaped the censor's knife and flames. The Dead Sea Scrolls were buried to escape the Roman legions; the Nag Hammadi Library was put in earthenware jars, and hidden in a cave above the Nile in Egypt one and a half millennia ago, to escape the heretic hunters of the new Roman dogmatists.

As we have seen the evidence is that Peter did not know Christ's true identity, and his assumption of a patristic base for the new religion was underpinned, not without some arguments concerning purely Jewish rites exclusively for men, such as circumcision, by that arch misogynist, Paul. In Paul's case the notion of a female redeemer is something that would have been repudiated without further analysis. Paul was in agreement with many of the strictest Temple traditions, particularly in regard to women, as his letters reveal in all too painful a detail. His conversion was certainly to a new world view, but strictly within the framework of a male Messiah coming from a Jewish male God. It is remarkable then that he was able to take on board the notion of drinking blood and eating flesh, but his concept of the ingrained sin of mankind was so deep that he had to find a palliative. He, like other patristic Christians was able to convince himself of the notion of sacrifice as that means of palliation. Basically this was to recognize the Christ as a kind of lamb, the paschal lamb, offered up by the Jews. It is astonishing that this demotion of a human being to the level of a sacrificial animal has not been picked up as curious hitherto, but since the thrust of Rome's theology was based on entirely false premises, one more error did not seem over-burdensome.

There is no evidence in the development of papal policy, even to the time of Pope Joan, that Rome was in any way concerned about Christ's gender; as far as the Popes were concerned, Christ was a man, and that justified the hierarchy being totally male, but Joan did make a strange pilgrimage to the south of France and pray at the various shrines of Mary Magdalene. Something happened between her visits in the ninth century and the 'crusade', as it was euphemistically called, against the Cathars.

This something could have been the realization in Rome that the Cathars had a relic which some of them were claiming to be that of Jesus Christ, and others thought was Mary the Virgin. This relic, pieces of the skull of a small woman, was not captured from the Cathars, not even when the last fortress fell, but was spirited away and protected by the Templars. When they were in Palestine, the Templars were untouchable; however, they became vulnerable to the Pope when they lost their fortresses in the Holy Land. The relic was purloined by force from the Templar preceptory in Paris. It has since vanished from history, and is probably in the Vatican. The implication is that Popes, or at least the heads of the Sacred College, which controlled the Inquisition for the Pope, have known since that time that Christ was not bodily assumed into heaven.

This of course could not be made public. It had to be suppressed, and this led to the killings of the Cathars and the Templars, and the suppression of women with a new theological urgency. Some of that has already been touched on, but the important problem facing me at this point was simply this, just how long were the skull bones of this small woman in the south of France?

The answer to this seemed to rest on Mary Magdalene's choice in that she did not go to Rome, and did not stay in Jerusalem. Legendary belief as well as more objective evidence point to the south of France. Why did she go there? And with whom did she go? Clearly Jerusalem was no place for her, not with the patristic though honourable James leading his Church as if it were no more than a special kind of Judaism; but why Marseille? Was there someone there or nearby powerful enough to protect her?

There seemed good reason that these questions could be answered, but their implications were profound. Granted the rise of the Roman Catholic Church could be understood as the gradual traducement of a creed of love into an opportunistic political hierarchy, complete with a set of frightening dogmas and a set of sacraments of which the Church claimed a monopoly, but the attraction of this creed was not Rome's doing; indeed, it was successful despite the corruption of some Popes and the Papal court. Rather it was Yeshu's personality which shone through the darkened veil around her hidden sanctuary in Rome. Yet Rome had been threatened by a truer version which surfaced nearly a millennium after Christ. I did not suppose that it abruptly became apparent, for then Rome would have been in a position to suppress it completely. But many accounts of this censored Church, the Church of Mary Magdalene, did survive in history and legend, and it was reasonable to hope that more could be learned of it.

— Part IV —

Hallows of the Magdalene

— 12 —

The Lost Church of Mary Magdalene

The tradition of Mary at Marseille dates at least to the
eighth century, as we know from the works of the
Archbishop of Mainz, Rabanus (776–856), for he wrote
a *Life of Mary Magdalene*. That his sources were probably
authentic, we may deduce from his reporting the whole-
sale disembarkation of virtually the whole cast of Jesus'
drama at Marseille, which suggests Church friction in
the first century, and Rabanus would not have taken the
risk of publishing such stories if they had not had
foundation.

Jacopus de Voragine in his *Golden Legend*, which dates
from 1207, has Mary Magdalene, her brother Lazarus,
her sister Martha – the woman who had fussed about the
preparation of a meal when Mary Magdalene was
anointing Jesus – and other Marys cast out from Jerusalem and set adrift in a rudderless boat on the Mediterranean.[1] Eventually they land in Marseille, where
Mary Magdalene loses no time in preaching and doing
miracles. But let us examine this placing of Mary Magdalene in the south of France.

The density of shrines, churches and relics of Mary
Magdalene certainly supports the claim of de Voragine
and the Archbishop of Mainz. Some of her relics were
authenticated in 1265 at Vézelay, but her preserved body
is believed to have been found in the crypt of St
Maximin's Church in Aix-en-Provence in 1279. De
Voragine's lives of the saints suggests that relics should
be found, for the boat in which they sailed to Marseille

also carried the skull of James the Less and unidentified bones of 'Holy Innocents'. The mention of these bones is provocative.

Who were the 'Holy Innocents'? Is this vagueness used as a smoke screen? And why should the skull of James the Less be so important to Mary Magdalene and the others? Could it be the skull of another, much more precious to them?

The other Marys on board are celebrated in their eponymous town Les Saintes Maries-de-la-Mer.[2] Mary Magdalene is said to have travelled inland from the shores of Provence to Saint Baume, and worked in the forests there to convert the still heathen Gallo-Romans. This association of Mary Magadalene with forests is interesting for a lady who came from the village of Magda in Palestine, Village of the Doves, and who was, before her mystic union with Christ, an acolyte of the Great Goddess. Did she hunt souls as Diana did harts?

However, the main question is when did Mary Magdalene leave Jerusalem? The most obvious date is at the outbreak of the Jewish War, but there were also troubles in Jerusalem in the early sixties. Both dates would have made Mary an old woman for those times, inconsistent with the notion of an active proselytizer. A more likely time is in the late AD 30s, when Paul was killing Christians in Jerusalem by stoning, before he became converted. Given Paul's fierce misogyny, even after conversion, it is entirely reasonable that Mary Magdalene and Mary the mother would have recognized in him great danger, and we have already seen that there was friction between the disciples and these women. The balance of probabilities is that Mary Magdalene and Jesus' mother left Jerusalem in the AD 30s. But did they really go in a rudderless boat?

If the dating of Mary Magdalene's and other Christians' forced departure from Jerusalem is correct, it coincides with the recall by Tiberius of Pontius Pilate who was in some disfavour. Usually his disgrace is explained by his savage repression of minorities in Judea, but this lacks conviction, since the government in Rome, as well as Tiberius in Capri, were more than passingly aware of the problems in the second-rate province they had parcelled up amongst client kings. They also knew that the Jews would have to be brought to account sooner or later, but there were never enough funds to supply the Procurator with a legion which the strategic importance of Judea, with its Mediterranean coastline, demanded. They were also cognizant that the Jews would always continue to spite the emperors and the gods of Rome. Augustus, Tiberius, and later Caligula, Claudius and Nero, were never able to securely install the Roman State religion in Judea, Galilee or Samaria. This is a curious paradox, for the Jews were not really numerous enough to be a military threat, and yet they held this unique position of chronic insulters of imperial dignity. Truly, that insult was to be wiped out, but it seems that until Nero set the might of Rome in motion in A D 66 to destroy Jersualem, something which was achieved in A D 70 under the armies of Titus working for his father Vespasian, the Roman gullet continued to be clogged with Jewish grit. Pilate, with his sternness, was ideal for Judea, so his rigour can hardly be adduced as a reason for his demotion.

What other reason might there be? It is noteworthy that the Coptic Church, the most ancient of Christian Churches, calls him St Pontius Pilate. There is also the legend that Jesus cured his wife Thecla, a name which was given to a saint, indeed one of Joan the Pope's spiritual mentors. In addition, we have seen how Pilate had a crisis of conscience in the crucifixion. If Pilate had become pro-Yeshu, then this would explain why he was recalled. It would explain also why Mary Magdalene went to Marseille.

Surely it couldn't be just by chance that Pontius Pilate retired in AD 36 to Vienne, a French town near Lyon, where the nearest port of call for the Romans was Marseille?[3]

When I visited the Musée in Marseille, I saw the remains of a boat *Navire de Commerce de Judée*, a type commonly used by merchants in the Mediterranean on the sea routes from Rome, Athens, Caesarea in Palestine, and the ports of Turkey. Eminently seaworthy, this boat type was in use during the Greek and Roman eras and even into the first century AD. Single-sailed, capacious, her sisters and she had been plying the Mediterranean, and docking in the old port of Marseille, day in and day out, for hundreds of years.

Such a boat is the most likely candidate for Mary and her companions to have travelled in from Palestine to Marseille. In the AD 30s the port was a hive of activity, with thousands of boats coming and going in the mercantile year. There would be no need for Mary to come ashore at Les Saintes-Maries-de-la-Mer. For one thing, it could not compete with Marseille, being a place of salt marshes and bogland. The rudderless boat, and the landing at Maries, looks like an interpolation by some censor on a true account of the actual journey to Marseille by Mary Magdalene and Mary the Virgin.

From which port would Mary Magdalene have embarked to travel to Marseille? If she went with Pilate, the most likely one is Caesarea, which was the main Roman commercial and military installation for maritime activities in Judea; but the exhibition in the museum at Marseille, when I was there in early 1986, showed the close connections of over 2,000 years between Marseille and the port of Haifa in Judea. This port would have seen the ships, already discussed, plying to and from Marseille.

If Mary left in AD 36, then Mary the Virgin would

have been still young enough to accompany her on her preaching. Indeed, it is difficult to see anyone stopping her, knowing what we now do of this remarkable woman. However, the chances are that she would have died before Mary Magdalene, being at least a generation older.

When Mary Magdalene landed in Marseille she entered a world more Roman than Hellenic, markedly different from Jerusalem or Judea, for here the Roman and the pagan gods held sway. There are great similarities between the Great Goddess religions and pagan-Roman beliefs, as we have seen, but most importantly, Mary Magdalene would not have had to contend with patristic Judaism.

Did Mary Magdalene as a young woman in the forests of Baume (the word in French means balm, ointment or consolation) ever call her Christ 'My Lady'? Or did she keep her holy secret? She had kept it in Jerusalem; perhaps she was enjoined for ever to keep it a secret. But the evidence is that although she may not have used Christ's gender as the basis of her preaching, the internal female force of the story of Christ would not have been lost on her peasant listeners.

As we have seen, Mary Magdalene was a woman of direct communication, of action rather than rhetoric. We may surmise that she taught what Jesus had told her to teach, love and forgiveness. Certainly this is similar to the preaching of the women of Languedoc, the Cathars, who walked in pairs from village to village, carrying their thongs and their New Testaments, breaking the bread and drinking the wine, recognizing no authority but Jesus. If we trace these Cathar priestesses back to Mary Magdalene, then Provence is a good candidate for Mary's base. She would have travelled, working tirelessly, just as, centuries later, Joan who became a Pope was to do, converting the rough people she encountered, as well as

being more than a match for the sophisticated town
dwellers. However, the milieu made it a religion of the
forests, of nature, the ever creative cycle of life and death.
At this level Mary, like Jesus before her and Joan eight
hundred years later, could not fail, for they were speaking
a language the country people understood, that of the
Great Goddess: refined, made deeper, but recognizable
in the wine and the bread.

The picture is certainly provocative, and at the same
time compelling, for here in the south of France were
Mary Magdalene and Mary the Virgin, two Christian
women, both priestesses of Yeshu, who appeared to have
set the pattern for the Cathar women, working in pairs
and travelling, spreading a message of love and hope for
the future.

But how and why was Yeshu's skull taken to the south
of France? The answer to the first part of the question
springs naturally out of the scenario of Pontius Pilate
helping Mary Magdalene leave Jerusalem.

Yeshu died on the cross, the exact form of which we
do not know, but it could have been the Y form, as much
as the T or 'conventional' form. However, such was the
hatred for Yeshu by the extreme clique of the Temple
faction, that both Marys may have feared that the body
would be desecrated by political vandals. It is noteworthy
that the tomb was guarded by Romans, so the body could
have been taken away by the Marys, aided by Lazarus.
Indeed, this would explain the references to the young
man – Lazarus. This means that Gospel accounts of the
first sighting of Yeshu on Easter morning are correct; it
was done by Mary Magdalene, but not perhaps in the
sense reported.

Yet why would they fear molestation of Yeshu's body?
There was a precedence of this kind, for as we have seen
Jezebel, a Great Goddess acolyte, was thrown down from
a height, trodden on by a horse ridden by a fanatical

supporter of Yahweh, and left to be eaten by dogs. Another scarlet thread connecting Yeshu, through Mary the Virgin, with these priestesses in Jewish history.

Perhaps there was even more foundation for this fear, for Judas, it will be recalled, took money for the murder of Yeshu, and we have seen how this can be construed as a 'hire of a harlot'. It is of course not certain that Judas knew Yeshu's gender, but his hatred of her may have been partially formed by a suspicion in that direction, which may then have been communicated to Caiaphas.

Given that both Mary the Virgin and Mary Magdalene were easily capable of thinking ahead of their enemies, perhaps it was mere prudence to remove Yeshu's body. If so, then the 'skull' referred to by de Voragine as having been taken to Marseille could well have been an allusion to Yeshu's skull.

However, there is no evidence that Mary Magdalene or Mary the mother were relic collectors. On the contrary their only concern was for the body of Yeshu, to ensure its dignity. The great weight of ointments, spices and aloes they took on Easter Sunday was to preserve it for the voyage. Pilate's soldiers would make short shrift of any sized stone, and they would see nothing untoward about veneration of Yeshu's body.

It is important to observe, however, that this does not involve either Mary, Yeshu's mother, or Mary Magdalene in lies or deceits. They told some of the apostles they had seen Yeshu that morning, which was true. Something did happen; for them Christ was still alive, and for Peter so strikingly so, he believed he had seen the physically resurrected Christ. Paul saw Christ as a person who had survived death, in the spiritual sense, and communication with this personality had changed his whole life. Neither Mary, Yeshu's mother, nor Mary Magdalene, ever claimed to see the phantom; they knew that birth followed death, as was always implicit in the Goddess cults. For them, of course, Yeshu would live again; she would be in the wine and in the bread.

The scenario fits what we know of the facts. But we still have the difficulty of finding out why the skull was taken to the south of France and how it was kept through those centuries. There is no evidence of a formal Church of Mary Magdalene, at least not a centralized one where the skull would have been preserved. What was there in the south of France which led to a natural explanation of the keeping of Yeshu's skull? I went to Marseille to find out.

The Ligurians

In the spring and summer of 1986, I travelled in France, visiting the towns which might have seen Mary Magdalene and Mary the mother of Jesus. Standing at the apex of the old port in Marseille, with the lambent rays from the May sun bringing the ancient stones to life, it is easy to forget one is in Europe, for Marseille is redolent with the atmosphere of the East. You can see it in the faces around you, in the tortuous winding passages of the old quarter, where the descendants of Ligurians, Greeks, Romans, Franks, Jews and Arabian Africans live. In this startling medley, fused by French culture and genius, one comes across the blond blue-eyed Franks and the dark-eyed, jet-black-haired Greeks, who came here centuries before Caesar, with their trade and their learning. Overlooking Marseille is the great statue of Mary the Virgin, the Mother of the City; although she used to have other names, Athene in the Greek-Roman period, Artemis of the reassuring breast in the Greek period, and beyond her the Great Goddess of the Ligurians, a people with strong affiliations with the tribes of Britain.

I looked out of my third-storey window of the Hôtel Beauvau, over the old port of Marseille. The evening was warm and the sea air made me look forward to my evening meal. On my way to the restaurant, which specialized in a duck dish, a small gypsy girl began to play her accordion to the diners in the white stuccoed street, where all the shutters were thrown open to enjoy the evening air. An elder sister of this waif was selling white flowers. The girls weren't doing much business. I tossed the girl of eighteen a ten-franc piece, and she caught it. The result was that her sister, all five foot of her, in white floral dress, sandals, long lustrous black hair, gypsy eyes and flashing white teeth, played me a few bars of a song I imagine was made famous by Piaf, another street urchin. I wondered if the gain in social security was a loss to art in countries which have driven music like this from the streets.

At dinner I fell into conversation with a real estate developer, who predicted that soon all the stuccoed streets would disappear. I had already seen several acres of old Marseille flattened to make way for a car park. One has the impression that sometimes you arrive only just in time.

The Musée d'Histoire de Marseille is a new building, with an excellent history of the town told in models, displays and maps, with many statues and artifacts of the people who have lived here for nearly 4,000 years.[4]

The Ligurians were a people of small kingdoms in loose-bound confederacy, hence their name, which comes from the Latin to bind or to tie. The thread that bound them was scarlet, in that they were of the same blood, and they were also bound by intermarriage. It was this hatred of centralized power that made them such enemies of Rome, though they got on better with the Greeks, since these latter had a tradition of free city states. Although the cities of Vienne and Marseille might have been Greek and then Roman, the Ligurians, while using the centres for trade, and no doubt picking up ideas, were not easily

controlled by these foreign powers. This tradition continued right up until the time of the Languedoc mas-
sacres, a millennium after Christ, when Rome, now a
spiritual power, sought to make her wishes obeyed by
terror, just as Julius Caesar had forced Marseille to obey
him.

Most of the ancient Ligurians lived away from the
Greek influenced towns and kept to their old ways. Even
in the Roman period, which began in the fourth century
BC, they were never subdued in the forests or country
districts. However, by Christ's time so much intermarriage had occurred in the towns that Greek-Ligurians
and Roman-Ligurians were to be found in Marseille and
Vienne, as well as Lyon and Avignon. But because of
their old independence, it is reasonable to assume that
some of the Ligurians' customs would have survived, and
this cosmopolitan province of Rome would have seen the
usual modification and intermingling of different religious
beliefs.[5] However, I was unprepared for the astonishing
sight which met me on entering the Musée in Marseille.
I was confronted by skulls set in the stone sides of
gateways, for the Ligurians were relic collectors, skull
collectors, something which the Romans and Greeks,
prior to Christianity, were not. Here was the connection
between the skull cult and Mary Magdalene's landing in
Marseille.

The extraordinary mixing up of different traditions by
the Church in its quasi-official story of this area strongly
suggests deliberate obfuscation, for as we have seen, the
most probable explanation is simple to the point of
bareness, namely, Mary Magdalene and Mary the Virgin
came to Marseille in a Jewish merchant vessel, founded a
Church, and died as priestesses of that Church.[6]

When I say founded a Church, it is not to be understood in the way the Roman Church was founded. Here

were no dogmas, merely what Yeshu had taught, that love was pre-eminent, and forgiveness of one another's wrongdoings crucial. There was also the teaching of a loving Creator, and the electrifying promise, proved by both Marys' experience of Yeshu, of survival of the personality after death. One did not have to depend on others for immortality, only Yeshu, who had left behind her homely methods of maintaining contact. There was prayer, there was the love feast of wine and bread, and there was baptism, in the country streams, of newly born infants. Underpinning this hopeful message of rebirth, the fulfilment of the Great Goddess tradition was a stern, though none the less truthful, warning: suffering it seemed was part of life, and it had to be borne. The example was there for everyone to see, Yeshu's own.

This tradition we can trace to the Cathars a thousand years later, but though they were destroyed by the Pope, the intervening millenium was for the most part free of interference in this region of France from the attentions of the Popes. For one thing, for nearly 400 years there was no central Christian authority. Indeed the Arians, who were mostly Franks and Germans, did not expect Christ to have flown up into heaven. As we have touched on it, the fight against Arianism took several centuries even after the Popes became powerful in Rome. In any case, it was only after Charlemagne, and then only fitfully, that Popes could extend their hand as far as southern France.

The Church of Mary Magdalene, then, would be relatively safe for a long time; its real importance could only be grappled with when the Popes had secular power, and we have seen what they did. But what of Mary Magdalene? Did she marry? We do not know, but it is perhaps pertinent to observe that in the fourth century an independent kingdom was set up in the region that the Cathars would eventually flourish in, which was presided over by long-haired kings about whom there is a great deal of mystery.

Even a sober Oxford academic is moved to note, in his exasperated failure to explain the ceremonial gymnastics which the Pope and the Carolingian kings had to go through in order to convince people these latter were real kings, that: 'This can lead one to fasten upon the magical property of Merovingian blood as the element creating the difficulty: what else could there have been to warrant so much trouble?'[7] He is pointing out that the Merovingians were accepted as kings because of their ancestry. However this cannot be traced back beyond the fourth century, so they must have inherited this magic blood in France. The Popes in the seventh century imprisoned the young sons of the Merovingian line in monasteries in France,[8] forcibly shaved them, letting them out from time to time to bless their people. The kings were said to have a birthmark, a red cross. The author of the best study of the long-haired kings, Wallace Hadrill, confesses impotence on all these problems. In contrast, other writers have assumed that the blood of Jesus Christ flowed in Merovingian veins, which they explain by having Jesus walk away from the crucifixion to Marseille.[9]

The explanation actually appears very simple. Mary Magdalene was a young woman when she got to Marseille. Yeshu, if my scenario is correct, had married Mary's brother, so there was no reason why Mary Magdalene should not marry, indeed the opposite, for it was common for priestesses of the Great Goddess to spend some years in loving care of people, and then retire from the temple to take up the other form of sacrament, marriage. Mary Magdalene, as a prominent personality, would have been an attraction to a Ligurian Prince or even King, and it would have been a theologically sound match, since the Ligurians were steeped in Greek and

Egyptian influences, particularly of Artemis, the mother-breasted aspect of the Great Goddess.

It may have been that as a mark of respect to his new wife, this Ligurian aristocrat wore his hair long, just as his brother-in-law Lazarus did. The custom could have caught on, so that when the Merovingians came to the area in the fourth century and made their alliances with the local people, they found one of the ruling families, perhaps more, distinguished by long hair in the men, and a priestess function in the women. There are other pointers in this direction,[10] and the main thrust of the argument is clearly plausible.

The common people began to ascribe holy powers to these kings of the Merovingians, perhaps in a distorted recognition of their link with Mary Magdalene, though it may also have something to do with the possibility that the royal family had the Caput 58. We know that one of their kings, Dagobert II, married a Visigoth princess of the Languedoc; he was allegedly murdered by papal agents in AD 679. As we have mentioned briefly, soon these princes of the Merovingians were being imprisoned in papal forts, euphemistically called monasteries, and shaved, as if perhaps in some strange insult not only to their long hair but to the cult of the skull.[11]

Whatever the ultimate truth of these strange and beguiling monarchs, they provide a link between Mary Magdalene and the Cathars, in geography and in religious symbol and practice. Indeed the whole area is redolent of motifs of skulls, Madeleines and unsolved mysteries, some of which have now become clear.

Indeed, the notion of a Lost Church pervaded European folklore, and we have come to know of it through the romances of chivalry, of knights and ladies, Holy Grails and forsaken love, of chastity, honour, troths kept sacred unto death. Chivalry died with the destruction of

the Templars, and Jacques de Molay who expired facing
Notre Dame is perhaps the most spectacular example of
a knight dying for love; his lady, it seems, was Yeshu.
The climate which allowed the Cathar women to be
priestesses was a chivalric one, stretching back in less
developed form to the Merovingian kings, for when they
were extirpated, only the ideals of the chivalric Knights
acted as protection for women, imperfectly of course, but
as a brake against the more virulent hatreds of celibate
priests.

Here is a continuous thread from the place of crucifixion in Jerusalem to the Languedoc of the Cathars. In
this region Frankish priests talked of the daughter of God
to the young Joan, who would one day become Pope
and visit where Mary Magdalene taught. Here women
priests were murdered, and after the relic of the small
woman, Yeshu, had been safely hidden by the Inquisition, an incredible forgery was foisted on the laity, an
image of a six-foot Christ, said to be the miraculous imprint
of his body in the Jerusalem Tomb. The sequence of
events is provocative, blatant even, for now the Popes
had proof of the true Christ in their hands, but they
came out with its denial, and it has not been challenged
since, so successful has their arrogation been.

But of course it had not been entirely successful; the
Cathars and the Templars left enough behind them for
the story to be woven together. The head which the
Inquisition had traduced was, it seemed, Jesus Christ's.
Yet there was one little mystery still outstanding which I
had still not understood to my satisfaction, for what I
had missed was the diabolic interpretation the Inquisition
had tried to put on the holy cords and girdles the Cathar
women wore, and which the Templars also took up.[12]
What did this ligature mean?

I was aware of some beautiful allusions. There was a
traceable tradition of a scarlet thread, or cord, snaking

its way through the Bible, which acted as a kind of symbol on many levels connecting the ancestresses of Yeshu with the priestesses of the Great Goddess. At one level it is the closeness of a blood relationship these women shared; at another it is the physical cord that connects them all, the umbilicus. I knew too that Isis was sometimes depicted as a scarlet serpent. Viewed in this way, the motif is maternal, not threatening, as the story of Genesis would have us believe.

But this went only some of the way to providing a foundation, as it were, of understanding the importance of the Cathar and Templar cords. Could it be associated, in a very intimate way, with the motif of the skull they both shared, and the legend of life coming from the grave, of love so strong that a Templar embraced the dead body of his lover, and was bequeathed her skull and cross-bones? This was the story of the Lady of Maraclea which has come down to us traduced, but even calumnies cannot destroy the power of the tale.

For the moment I had to admit defeat, and in any case I had an appointment to keep. I wanted to walk where I believed Mary the Virgin, Mary Magdalene and perhaps even Joan had walked, the town where Pontius Pilate, that saint of the ancient Coptic Church, had retired – Vienne. And on the way I wanted to stand where those two lovers of Christ had died, in front of Nôtre Dame – their special Lady.

A Pilgrimage

I flew to Paris on a bright spring day and stayed at the Hotel Louvre Concorde, facing the Louvre, not far from the site of the Templar Preceptory, Villeneuve, the last clearly identified site of the silver reliquary, the woman's head, Caput 58. I spent the afternoon in various leading bookshops, but for some reason the Parisian booksellers were neither able nor apparently keen to produce books on Mary Magdalene. There seems to be an odd reticence, so at variance with Paris *hauteur*, to admit that Madeleine is almost the patron saint of France, so abundant are her shrines, her churches and, indeed, her relics.

I walked to Notre Dame, along the Seine, in the glistening sunshine. It cascaded off the huge Rose window of the façade of the cathedral like iced gold. I stood near the place, now built over, where Jacques de Molay and Geoffrey de Charney were murdered. I too faced the façade, as they had done. High up, there was a figure of Eve, Gallic in her beauty and her roundedness. I wondered if she was the same Eve who had looked down on these two men as finally their heads fell forward.

But it was Notre Dame they were dying for, 'Our Lady', their Lady of the Kingdoms, the Lady of Maraclea. I recalled the legend of Maraclea, how a Templar Lord had loved a woman so desperately that he had tried to embrace her in the grave, and had been promised a great mystery. He returned after nine months and found a skull and crossbones. The skull became Caput 58, for the legend refers to the death of Christ, but had been traduced by Roman scribes. Where was the skull now? In the Vatican? Tragic as the two Templars were, they, it seemed, had kept faith.

Back at the hotel I found myself in sombre mood. It was difficult to shake off the sense of loss, of pain, these Templars must have felt, as if it still lingered where tourists and pigeons go about their seemingly aimless ways. As I broke my bread and sipped my Côtes du Rhône in the Brasserie des Tuileries, I did not feel I dined alone.

I also had the sense the odyssey was over, at least this aspect of it, though so resonant had the journey been that it seemed impossible it could ever end in any real sense. Yet after the pilgrimage to Notre Dame I still felt that I must go to Pontius Pilate's Vienne, although I did not expect to find anything there; it was just a necessary journey.

Next day the high-speed TVG express from Paris to Lyon averaged well over a hundred miles an hour, getting me to Lyon in less than two hours. As the train accelerated from Paris, it was obvious that the day was going to be cloudy and drizzly. I was facing in the direction of movement, well aware that to my left, across those neat French fields and small hamlets, lay Lirey, source of the notorious painting which had so upset the bishops, but which had given a della Rovere who was to be Pope, an idea of a relic to outdo all relics. To my right lay Cloux, where Leonardo da Vinci had died, a broken and dispirited man. Ahead lay Lyon, and ten miles to the north of it was Vienne. What would I find there? I had no great expectations, or rather my hopes were high but scepticism dampened them, just as the April rains were wetting the French fields, glistening on so many churches that one lost count. And so many of them named after Our Lady, and Madeleine.

It was a pleasant journey, curiously silent, a passage through space and time, rapid but less so than my own reflections. I knew that Vienne was very ancient, stretching back far beyond the Christian era. To the Ligurians it was a mystic place, for these Celtic peoples even had a sanctuary there of circled stones. They adopted the Great Goddess Artemis, from the Greeks, but did not lose their cult of the skull. And then the Romans came, and it was with a Roman I had an appointment.

When I arrived in Vienne the Rhône was in flood, recalling to mind the flood waters of the Nile, the Tigris and Euphrates, the great rivers of the Great Goddess, who, as Isis in Alexandria, watched over the Nile, and, as Astarte in Babylon, saw the twin rivers break their banks to moisten the parched earth. Here in Vienne, she was called Cybele, Great Mother of the Gods. Her festivals in Rome were originally begun on 4 April, and I had come just a little late to her sanctuary in Vienne. There is not much to see now of this once proud temple, but as the rain came from the luminous sky, soft and gentle, the Goddess did not seem far away.

I looked around, wondering where Pilate might have had his villa. High above the river and the town is an escarpment, now flanking the railway. Up there the air would be cool and fresh even in summer, where one could see the serpentine Rhône threading its way through the valley. Atop the escarpment seemed a good place for Pilate to live, after the heat and dryness of Jerusalem. No doubt he grumbled to his wife Thecla about the rains, but they come only just enough to swell the river and plump up the grapes. That would be a bonus, good Rhône wine, so different from the lesser grades he had to endure as Procurator in Antonia, Jerusalem. It was of course pure speculation on my part, in the sense that no one knew where Pilate had built his villa in this town.

In the forum a Christian church had been built on the Great Goddess shrines, the church was called Notre-Dame-de-la-Vie, Our Lady of Life. There had been a Christian church here in Vienne since AD 361, but there had been Christians living here long before the official church came. One of them was Pontius Pilate, recognized as such by the Christian Coptic Church in Egypt which reveres him as a saint. Then there was his wife Thecla, healed by Yeshu, the mystic namesake of Joan the Pope's favourite saint. And there were the legends, which now seemed more than that, of Mary Magdalene and Mary the Virgin here in the south of France. Did Pilate, Thecla and the two Marys drink Rhône wine and break bread in Pilate's house? I did not know, but it could have been possible.

It was beginning to rain more heavily, and as I had kept my appointment I went into the Cathedral,[13] St

Maurice's, dedicated to a chivalric saint. There was no one inside except a woman, with a scarf about her head, who was cleaning down the flagstones in front of a chapel which showed a huge painting of a male Christ, fading fast. The woman moved on with her bucket and mop to clean the rest of the church.

In the gloom I saw the ghostly white of crossed thigh bones on the wall of this Christ's chapel. By the side of the bones were white tear-drops, and then I realized that they were meant to be drops of blood, bleached by time to the colour of bones. I bent close and saw that the bones were tied by a cord. The mason had taken away the skull of the Lady of Maraclea, and left the thigh bones tied together by a cord. It was an eerie moment, but I had no evidence that the artist meant anything by these Templar motifs: the bones, the cord, but the skull was missing. Perhaps he, like the writers of the Grail romances of something lost from Christendom, was merely describing a legend he did not understand. Perhaps.

What it meant to the mason remains problematical, but legends hardly ever seem to die; they transmute, they change, and usually enough of the central core survives for the factual basis to be discerned. In this region Gallic people had a cult of the skull long before the Greeks came to found Marseille. And these Greeks came with Egyptian influences.[14]

The amulets of Isis are derived from the knotted girdle, which itself is the amulet of life. They are red, signifying the blood of Isis, symbol of life.[15]

Here in Vienne was a cross made of the thigh bones, tied by a cord, and the cord was as much a symbol of life as the cross. Indeed the *ankh* itself is a kind of cross. Curiously the ligature is fashioned in a manner similar to Egyptian amulets, similar to the fleurs-de-lis, and that flower is equated with the Rose of Sharon. The rose is five-petalled in chivalry, and irrespective of the botanical nature of the Palestinian Rose of Sharon, the symbolism is female, for five is the cipher of the Great Goddess, the five-pointed star of a woman – stretched out.

These thoughts passed rapidly through my mind in that gloomy church. It was a matter of astonishment to me that so much could be seen in what was objectively so little, but that is the nature of symbol and image. The mason may or may not have been aware of some or even all of the illusions of what he was carving, but he was drawing on very ancient sources, timeless motifs of fertility, gender, death and hope. His ignorance or knowledge was immaterial, as armed with the research I had done, the implications were apparent to me, and the conclusions legitimate. The ultimate fate of such informed speculation of course rests with the future, with further investigation, but that can be said of any human knowledge.

It was time to go. I took a photograph of the motif of cord and bones. As I left the church, the sun was coming out from behind the clouds, making it rather more pleasant than the drizzle to walk to the café by the railway station. There I had a huge *café au lait*, as the children were coming out of school, passing in small throngs by the window, beneath the escarpment.

They were just ordinary French school-children, the same kind of children that had been here for thousands of years. The blood which flowed in their veins would be testimony to the Ligurians, Greeks, Romans, Franks who had all lived here. Perhaps there was a trace too of the Merovingians in that street, even a descendant of the Roman who might have lived on the hill, even Mary Magdalene. Oddly, it struck me that the confluence was also in me, being English, for we share the French vitality, and have done so from 1066. None the less I felt a sense of loss, for we, the writer in the café and the children in the street, had all descended from people who had women at the altar, who had no virulent misogyny; we were all children of the Goddess, but she had been hidden and her shrines taken over or desecrated. The loss was real, for with the rise of patristic Rome had come a dark shadow over the length and breadth of Europe, the shadow of being born in sin, with sin; of an ideal of love cut off from its roots. That we were coming out of the shadow owed no thanks to the Church, which had resisted science and rational thought with a palisade of dogmas, backed up by military force. The physical force had been taken away by enlightened men and women, and the Church, unable to accommodate the new discoveries of an evolving age, was loosing its grip. This could never have happened to a church of the Great Goddess, for that was a natural religion; its ceremonies, its teachings, its sacraments were founded on fact, illuminated by vision, and that vision had been clarified by the life and teaching of Yeshu, and by her death, a once and for all sacrifice, the riches of which have yet to be garnered.

These were weighty thoughts to have over a cup of delicious coffee, but it was unarguably the case that the progress of science, of medicine, of the concepts of human freedom to decide, had been attained in the teeth of opposition from dogmatic churches. Indeed, the churches were seen as so retrograde that some people in despair became atheists and equated progress with a disbelief in spiritual sources of energy. However, I was no longer persuaded that the aridity of atheism had to be embraced because one would not be clutched by a church.

I took a pencil and a pad, and drew out the achievements and the failures of the odyssey so far, or to be more accurate, enumerated the main elements of a hypothesis which had taken me to Vienne.

1) Jesus Christ was the logical development of the Great Goddess tradition. She was crucified and her body taken, with Pontius Pilate's help, by Mary her mother, and Mary Magdalene, to the south of France, where the Ligurians, with their skull cult, preserved the head.

2) Mary Magdalene probably married into the Ligurian aristocracy and the custom of growing hair long was adopted as a mark of respect to both her and her brother Lazarus.

3) This line was eventually absorbed by the Merovingian kings, who maintained both the skull and the tradition of long hair, and have come down to us as the Long-haired Kings.

4) Meanwhile the patristic Roman Church, with great difficulty, had claimed universal monopoly of things Christian, backed up by military and fiscal power. The rumours of what was happening in the Languedoc led to papal intervention and the extinction of the Merovingian monarchy, done with great cruelty. But the skull was not found by papal agents.

5) The traditions of the Magdalene Church were kept alive in the south of France, sufficiently well for a woman Pope to make the pilgrimages to Mary Magdalene's shrines, in an area which saw the rise from this Church of the Cathar priestesses.

6) The Papacy, alarmed by the claims of the Cathars that Christ was female and that they had her relics, attacked these women and their families in the Languedoc, killing and burning as many as they could, following this up with the Inquisition.

7) The relics were preserved by the Templars, many of whom were blood relations of the Cathars. When this Order's military strength was at a low ebb, they too were destroyed by the Papacy, and the relics, Caput 58, bones of a small woman's skull, were secreted away, and probably reside to this day in the Vatican.

8) With the destruction of the Templars, chivalry died and this cleared the way for the murderous witch hunts, which amounted to 'gendercide'. Meanwhile a blatantly male image of Christ was created by an outstanding artist, on a linen, and fraudulently exposited as the burial cloth of Jesus Christ. It is called the Turin Shroud.
9) The gendercide of witches was so pre-emptive, that no living trace of the traditions of the Magdalene Church survived.

If all this was indeed so, a light had gone out over Europe. But women were reclaiming their rights to be priestesses so something might be salvaged in this regard. And how could I be so sure, I wondered, that the Magdalene Church had been wiped clean from the face of the Earth? Logically I could not be certain, for there must have existed material, and living witness too, after the trials of the Templars? However, nothing had been allowed, except by mistake, to emerge from the torture chambers of the Inquisition for several centuries as they tore women to pieces.

It was this last point which gave me pause, for I had seen documents which had all the signs of being spurious, yet as I sat in the café that afternoon in Vienne it seemed to me that I had been making a rash judgement, for what I had reckoned to be false I could perceive in a different light. The way in which the messages were couched had the same atmosphere of pain and anguish that I had encountered only in the transcripts of the torture of Templars and witches. Who could it be who were so tortured in spirit that they would produce documents like those I had so brusquely rejected? I got up; there was something to be done.

The Vatican Witness

Back in England I was in a more sceptical mood. London has a way of bringing you down to earth, and has never been accused of being a mystical city, but this was probably an appropriate atmosphere to work in, because as I sifted through the pile of documents and reports I had previously rejected as spurious, the impoverishment of the material was striking. Several times I was tempted to jettison the lot into the waste-paper basket. But there was another reaction besides distaste – a curiosity, for someone had penned these documents and there was, I felt sure, something to be gleaned from them. The problem was of relevance.

What, for example, can one make of *Le Serpent Rouge*? It is a privately produced work, consisting of genealogies of Merovingians, maps pertaining to them, and thirteen paragraphs. It is lodged at the Bibliothèque Nationale, Paris, published date 1967. Bibliothèque number: 41k 7 50490. The cited place of publication is Pontoise, and the putative authors: P. Feugère, L. Saint-Maxent, G. de Koker, all three of whom are dead, and there is no obvious connection between them. It has been suggested that someone may have simply taken their stories from French newspapers (dead men tell no tales) and purloined their names, and then put a date of origin on *Le Serpent Rouge* prior to their deaths.

Furthermore there is nothing remarkable in *Le Serpent Rouge* being in the archives of the Bibliothèque. The British Museum Library, to some extent like the Nationale, is a copyright library, in that a copy of each work published in the UK is lodged there. The onus is on the publisher to provide such copies, something most houses regard as a bit of book tax, since they are provided free. But any crank who wants some kind of recognition can claim to be a publisher, mimeograph a few copies and send one to the Library. The Nationale and the British Museum have thousands of such works.

In any real sense, these works are not published at all, but the libraries have to fulfil their statutory duty, so they file them, bogus with the real. However *Le Serpent Rouge* has been the object of ardent speculation since 1967, and so cannot be dismissed, for its impact has been considerable, giving rise to a plethora of even weirder private publications.

Propaganda of Despair

The genealogies in *Le Serpent Rouge* are traceable if one has the patience, but Europeans are all inter-related to some extent anyway. What struck me was the atmosphere of the thirteen paragraphs under the twelve signs of the Zodiac and an additional sign, that of Ophiuchus. This latter refers to a star constellation, and is depicted as a man holding a serpent.

I translated the thirteen paragraphs, and some extra-ordinary statements emerged, albeit hedged in by assertions and riddles which have the air of derangement about them. In fact I was intrigued by the general atmosphere of this work, for it reads like the confessions the Inquisition tortured out of the last Cathars. They were lonely and isolated people who, although genuinely affiliated with the Cathar Church, had lived in hiding, in exile, hounded by the armed forces of the Church. By the time they were caught they had the Cathar creed hopelessly garbled and distorted. Was I looking at something similar, perhaps even the thirteen creeds of the Magdalene Church? But the allusions were twisted, deformed, tenuous; they seemed a mish-mash of half-remembered notions, with a very loose grip on imagery or symbol. Indeed, some of the references are comic, strident in their inappropriateness.

For example, under Aries, we find the figure of a quester cutting his way through a forest, trying to find the Sleeping Beauty who is the Queen of a Lost Kingdom. Lost Kingdom? Lost Church? Clearly, I could force this to be a reference to Yeshu's lost Church, but – Sleeping Beauty?

Under Cancer, we are told the Sleeping Beauty is connected with an idea, 'By this sign you will conquer'. Again, one could suppose the Sign of the Cross was implied.

Scorpio carried the question, 'What extraordinary mystery or secret has the New Temple of Solomon embezzled?' The French suggests a secret being received, but the verb *receler* carries the meaning of receiving something stolen or fraudulently acquired. Again one can be seduced and see this as an assertion that the Church knows more about Jesus Christ than has been revealed, equating the New Temple of Solomon with the Church of Rome. It was beginning to seem all too pat, but none the less the similarities were legitimate. I had the feeling someone knew more than they would say, but were doing it in so bizarre a manner that the ideas themselves were being tainted.

Under Ophiuchus the writer mentions that he has plunged into an abyss, and then sees, under Sagittarius a red serpent, which is described as *salée et amère*, pungent and bitter – but these are the feminine forms of these adjectives, and the serpent is rendered as the masculine. Bad grammar by our unknown author? Mental stress? Or has he or she got information they do not understand? Or was there another motive?

The Red Serpent is arguably Isis. The other name of Ophiuchus is Serpentarius, while in French *serpentaire* is a serpent-eater. I went back and read what our unknown author (or authors) said under the Serpent-eater. He speaks of a queen with masked abodes (the Church?) and that he understands the secret meaning of the Seal of Solomon.

If we follow the clue that the new Temple of Solomon is none other than the Catholic Church, what is the seal of this Church? The Keys of the Kingdom, perhaps, the claim to be the sole arbiter of Christ on this Earth. The new Judge, Solomon, is perhaps the Pope?

Earlier we discussed the name *Panthera*, Lion, for Christ. Curiously, under Leo there is an entry in *Le Serpent Rouge* which reads like a kind of poetry, but with such dissonance and clumsiness the effect is nullified. Here is my translation:

From her whom I wish to free, arises the scent of perfume which imbues the sepulchre. Formerly, some have called her Isis, Queen of beneficent waters [the French is literally springs or sources]. Come unto me all you who suffer and are afflicted and I will give you rest. To others, she is Magdalene, of the celebrated vase full with healing balm. The initiated know her true name: Our Lady of the Cross[es]. [Notre Dame des Cross (*sic*)]

The passage equates Mary Magdalene with Isis, but who is Our Lady of the Crosses? Again the grammar is faulty. Is the implication that Mary Magdalene, Isis and Our Lady are aspects of one and the same thing?

As we have seen, the Great Goddess Isis, in various guises, is deeply implicated in the life of Mary the Virgin and Mary Magdalene, and that in many senses we have seen that Jesus took the Isis legend and fulfilled it. In this sense Jesus is Isis. Furthermore, we have seen that the

word Magdalene has been used to denote whore, harlot
or prostitute, but that the original temple usage had none
of these meanings. It is a patristic Jewish and Christian
tradition, and the real meaning is that Mary Magdalene
was an acolyte of Isis. However, as such she may well
have enacted ritual love with male worshippers of Isis, in
which case, during that moment, in a 3,000-year-old
tradition, she was Isis, just as all the acolytes of the Great
Goddess temples were. Our Lady of the Cross is equated
with these two figures, but the quotation 'Come unto
me . . .' is a saying of Yeshu. It would seem that the
import we are expected to make, *if we know all this*, is
that Jesus was Isis, was a Virgin, was a Magdalene, is
Our Lady. But the author has so mixed up these aspects
that it is as if he or she had stumbled on the truth of
Jesus' gender, and then tried to obscure it; to symbolize
it in such a way that it appears rejectable. The technique
is a well-known one in propaganda: distort the truth by
quoting out of context and make false analogies. Yeshu,
for example, is not the Lady of the healing balm, Mary
Magdalene is.

Does the author know? I have not been able to contact
him or her, for I believe the use of three names of dead
men on the document in the Bibliothèque Nationale, as
author, to be spurious. The evidence before us is that he
or she is in contact with an underground source of truth
about the Church of Mary Magdalene. In these hands it
is a now shattered piece of truth, containing some
gleaming shards, but the vessel, the grail so to speak, has
been broken. It has taken scientific research, travel and
patient reading of millions of words to uncover what was
lost. If the author of *Le Serpent Rouge* really wished to
liberate Jesus from a 2,000-year-old lie, why do it in so
strange a fashion? The answer may be that for him or
her it may not be strange. They may not be able to
develop an argument persuasively; they may be mystic

not demonstrative, verbal rather than articulate – a thousand and one reasons. Indeed, they may have some other motive in mind; to be mysterious satisfies some people. But the quality of the words and the coherence of the images suggests very strongly that there exists, probably in fragments, documentary material which is traceable directly to the mouth of Mary Magdalene, and from her mouth, which Jesus used to kiss as sister to sister, to the mouth of Jesus herself, but it has been sorely, almost obscenely, traduced and impoverished. With sadness I observed that this is what had happened to the words and stories of the Templars, but with a jolt I realized that the words said to be of the Templars were actually written by the Inquisition, by the Holy Office, which of course in essence still exists.

The Broken Priest

Le Serpent Rouge is decidedly odd, and I tentatively concluded that if there was anything genuine about it, then its air of derangement was the key to any ulterior purpose, if such there be, behind its publication. Even odder, a number of authors have connected the document with Rennes-le-Château[1] by a variety of entertaining but speculative tales, most of which have the effect, though perhaps not intended by these commercial writers, of digging the grave of the Great Goddess even deeper.

According to the French author de Sède,[2] a Roman Catholic priest, Saunière, took up his post in 1885 at Rennes-le-Château and began refurbishing the Church of Madeleine, the village chapel dedicated to Mary Magdalene. He found some parchments in a Visigoth column, left by his eighteenth-century predecessor, Abbé Bigou. Copies of some of the parchments exist, but others are probably in the Vatican, for Saunière, as a good son of the Church, took his finds to St Sulpice in Paris, but when he returned he had only two of the several parchments he had found. He then began to spend lavishly, putting up a tower to Mary Magdalene, and decorating his church expensively and very oddly. Where did the money come from? Theories range from treasure trove to being paid off by Rome so that he would keep silent. What is the truth of this astonishing tale?

Saunière took two lines quoted in the Bigou parchments, and put them under a painting of Mary Magdalene which he commissioned. The inscription reads:

JÉSUS MEDÈLA VULNÉRUM + SPES UNA POENITENTIUM
PER MAGDALENAE LACHRÝMAS + PECCATA NOSTRA DILUAS

which may be translated: 'Jesus healer of the wounds, hope of sinners (penitents) whose sins are diluted (washed away) by Magdalene's tears'. However, it must be noted that Latin does not have accents, and the words *medela* and *vulnerum* may not be declined in case properly, and so another feasible rendering would be 'Jesus of the healing wounds', a reference to the redemptive power of the blood that flowed from them.

Over the Y of *lachrymas* and the P of *peccata* are dots, as if to bring attention to them. Y, as earlier discussed is a sign of the Cross, as well as a cipher for femality. P is rho in Greek, and may or may not allude to the rho cross[3] of Constantine which is not dissimilar to the sign of Isis. I was not sanguine about this analysis but had to face the fact that these two symbols are apparently enshrined in the inscription by Saunière, and if it was done by chance the odds against it are very long.

Another oddity in this catalogue of strange events is that Saunière erased the tombstone heading of a local Marquise (d'Haupoul) in his churchyard, but fortunately copies of it exist. The tombstone was in fact inscribed by none other than Abbé Bigou.[4] Its interest is considerable, for commentators have felt it to be written in a code, but have failed to persuasively crack it. However, it does seem to contain unmistakable references to Great Goddess legends and the Templar skull, which may explain why the Abbé Bigou was prudent enough to hide the documentary evidence.

Given all these leads, I felt sure that Bigou was trying to impart something, but was it relevant? After all, country parsons often have bizarre predilections, and Bigou may have dabbled in Egyptology, but then dismissal was not wholly acceptable, because the Church found his parchments of sufficient interest to change Saunière's life when he brought Bigou's cache to St Sulpice.

Had Abbé Bigou been so exercised by his discoveries that he felt he had to codify them and, fearing for his own safety, then put the proof in the Visigoth column, to be found a little more than a hundred years later by the tragic and obsessed Saunière? Prudence on Bigou's part is understandable; the Church was still very powerful, especially for country priests. The crucial point is that there is no evidence that Saunière ever understood what he had found, but the ecclesiastical authorities at St Sulpice, Paris, appear to have grasped the significance of what he brought them. They let him have back Scrolls I and II, but the rest of Bigou's message is lost to us.

The assumption could be that Saunière was paid by the Church the large sums of money he dispersed. However, when he died payments stopped. His housekeeper left no money either. This suggests that Saunière had no written or objective proof of the Abbé Bigou's momentous discovery. Why, then, was he paid in the first place?

It seems most plausibly to be a case of spreading francs on the waters, as it were, so that waves would not be made – so payments were made. First, because he had been a good son of the Church and that deserves reward.

Second, payment was made to keep him at Rennes-le-Château. Better the unworldly Curé, than to replace him with someone else, leaving Saunière to wander the world arousing interest in matters Rome wished to keep quiet. Third, a simple man such as Saunière could be expected to indulge, with the money from the Vatican, in priestly schemes – new roads for the villagers, a refurbished church – which he duly did.

Short of permanently silencing a man who has stumbled across a deadly secret, those who fear the secret getting out are probably best advised to 'smother' dangerous sources of unrest such as Saunière. However, such treatment is bound to have an unsettling effect, indeed to be psychologically damaging. If one had been paid large sums of money for something one did not understand, it might become an obsession, as the years rolled by, to find out what there was to know. The suspicion might also cross one's mind that it would be safer to leave well alone. These two emotions, curiosity and fear, are the classic ingredients required to destabilize a man's mind. Perhaps it takes 2,000 years to become this subtle.

From what we know of Saunière, he apparently spent the rest of his life trying to work out what the secret was. He came down, almost bereft of reason by this time, on the side of some occult relationship of the Church and Isis, a sin which only Magdalene, his patron saint, could wash away. He had the inscription 'This place is terrible' put on his church, and a devil figure ensconced at the door. He also built a separate tower for St Mary Magdalene. The clever man-managers of the Vatican had succeeded: Saunière was obviously unbalanced; he believed the Church was evil, paid undue attention to the Magdalene, and spent his life trying to decipher inscriptions to no avail.[5] Anything Saunière had to say by this time would be dismissed as the delusions of a crank.

Dangerous Secret

What then could have been the nature of the material Saunière took to St Sulpice, which was then taken to Rome? Abbé Bigou's cache in the Visigoth column, we know, included genealogies, and there were two other parchments which were never returned to Saunière. Was this perhaps an authentic trace of Mary Magdalene's or her brother Lazarus' line, through Visigoths to Merovingians, through Franks, right up to the Marquise d'Haupoul? Possibly, but this would hardly warrant the secrecy and mystery which surrounded the Abbé's historical studies. Did his cache contain something that both he and the Church believed to be material evidence of the true gender of Jesus Christ? If so, in what form was the proof? Authentic documents of a previous priest who had pieced the history together?

A letter or codicil of a bishop, notary, or even nobleman, citing sources, names, dates and locations pertaining to the true story of Jesus or Mary the Virgin would be sufficiently alarming for the Church to have taken the action it seems was taken. It seems reasonable to conclude that the destination of Bigou's cache, after St Sulpice, was the Vatican. If so, perhaps only the Pope has access to them, or might the head of the Sacred Congregation, or the Holy Office, be privy too? It might be remembered, that the Inquisition in effect still exists, but is no longer a secular power. Furthermore, the possibility remains that copies of the documents, or the information in another form, may be waiting outside the Vatican to be discovered.

Electrifying as these legitimate speculations are, there remains the historical fact of the burial ceremony of the unshriven priest of the Church, Bérenger Saunière. When dead, he sat in a high chair on the terrace of the Magdalene Tower, with a robe about him of many scarlet tassels. These were, on the morning of 23 January 1917, pulled off by numerous mourners.[6] The scarlet thread, the thread of Rahab, of Tamar, the cord of the Cathars and the Templars, the girdle of Isis? Saunière may not have made the right deductions on what he found, but he wore the cloak of Isis, the scarlet robe of Christ. His buildings show he adored Isis and Mary Magdalene, and perhaps he knew no more, but the unnamed people who took the tassels appear to have known what to do.

But why did they do it? Were they confused and bewildered occultists who, eschewing the constraints of Rome, had found some reassurance in enacting rites which were possibly traceable to those of Isis? It is not an easy question to answer, and I was very sceptical about digging deeper. Occultism is a murky subject in that very few adherents have any real idea of what their actions represent; they suppose their rites are in some special sense anti-Christian, whereas the paradox is that they are not. This confusion and lack of real knowledge concerning the true nature of the ancient rites, demonstrably not diabolic or satanic, has led to a free-for-all, with little substance.

An example of this is the plethora of films about the occult which, if they mention Isis at all, do so in loaded terms: she is an embodiment of evil, as are witches. The truth of the matter would appear to be the direct converse: these legitimate ancient religions have been savagely repressed by Rome, and traduced as satanic, and the mud has stuck. Yet, as we have seen, the majority of the allusions and symbols used by Yeshu owe their origin to the Great Goddess religion.

Saunière stumbled on sufficient evidence to lead him to conclude that the Church was frightening, and advertised the fact by putting up a notice to that effect on his parish church and erecting a statue of a devil at the door.

As we have speculated, he was by this time very disturbed, and so his claims could be discounted. That he understood the real import of what he found is extremely unlikely, though his eighteenth-century predecessor, Antoine Bigou, apparently went much further.

However, the objective problem was to try to assess what these mysterious happenings in the south of France mean in terms of the present investigation. It would seem helpful to summarize the facts pertaining to them. A country cleric in the Languedoc came across documents which he hid in a column of his church at Rennes-le-Château. He also erected a tombstone to a local aristocratic lady which has been the centre of numerous, sometimes not persuasive, speculations concerning buried treasures in the area, even that the treasure looted from Jerusalem by Titus and taken to Rome had somehow found its way to the Languedoc (if so, it has yet to be found, but given the spendthrift ways of Roman emperors, it is unlikely that it survived long).

In summary, a muddled and not very bright scholarly parish priest found the documents and let his Church superiors know. Afterwards he became increasingly eccentric and had more money to spend than could be accounted for. He died, and his body was bedecked in a robe with scarlet tassels, which people plucked off, in the foreground of a tower built to Mary Magdalene by this priest. A reasonable explanation of Saunière's decline has already been considered, but the cord ceremony has not been explained at all, despite the plethora of books written on the subject here and in France.

Privately printed and suspicious documents, tenuously but tellingly connected with Rennes-le-Château legends, with an atmosphere of either mental illness or deep spiritual affliction about them, for some decades past have been circulated in France with no apparent motive. These documents use the motif of the red serpent, and can be seen as stating that Jesus was a woman, and is in some way connected with Isis.

Presented in this way, a legitimate explanation should be discoverable. First, as we have argued, there is a real connection between Jesus Christ and Isis, for the latter is an aspect of the Great Goddess and the former the fulfiller of the religion; indeed by her testimony she was the incarnation of the Great Goddess. The red serpent is a well-known symbol of Isis herself, for in her role as protectress of the dead, Isis showed her power against serpents of the tomb and underworld through her amulet of this serpent, which was sometimes the head, sometimes the whole snake. This was placed on the dead, and a beautiful prayer recited, which directly referred to Isis: 'I am the flame which shineth upon the opener of hundreds of thousands of years . . . the standard of young plants and flowers.' The Goddess herself was often represented by a red serpent, a symbolic way of revealing her total power, for the serpent was not only regarded as wise, but also a generative principle. However this is not a symbol of the phallus, for the serpent is often looped to form a girdle so that the tail is being swallowed. The significance of this is that it portrays graphically the fact that a woman is born through the vagina and she herself will give birth through the vagina, a succession which is circular. Men, of course, are also born through the vagina but they do not give birth, and so are excluded from the implicit continuity of the red serpent swallowing her own tail. In some mythologies, the snake encircles the globe to stop it falling apart.

The colour for Isis was red, the blood colour, and so her emblems and amulets were always fashioned in red by her priestesses and, of course, by her worshippers. There are many of these emblems still extant; those from Cleopatra's time are very ornate, with gold and precious jewels emblazoning them. The Egyptians might well say

'Who can find a virtuous woman, for her price is far above the ruby,' for indeed Isis was more than precious stones. The saying is found in the Old Testament, which again was innocent of its origin in the Great Goddess religion. The poorer people would show their veneration by making motifs for Isis, using paste or red paint, the calxes and sulphides of mercury, iron and lead all being pressed into service to colour the paste. Blood was also used, especially menstrual, although this darkened rather rapidly, and was used for acute symbolism rather than long-term artifacts. Wine, of course, with its red colour, was unmistakably the draught of Isis, though white wine was used to symbolize the first stage of the Goddess, the girl before her menarche.

Isis had a girdle and a buckle, and either or both were symbolized in glyph form by the *ankh* or symbol of life.[7] It is not immediately apparent what development has occurred here, but its origins are very simple and down to earth, as most things are in the Great Goddess religion, for they spring from the most basic themes of human life, birth, love and death.

When a child is born it is connected with its mother by the umbilicus, the cord of life, which is naturally smeared with blood and is red. Women used to be attended only by other women in childbirth, and the position was squatting. After delivery, the umbilicus would eventually be severed, by the teeth if necessary. This cord has obvious similarities to the red serpent, and has no overtones other than maternal and life enhancing, just as the red serpent motif is entirely positive. We can also see another reason now why the red serpent when swallowing its own tail is a powerful birth motif, for unattended women would bite the umbilicus, and in so doing the child would be starting, for the first time, its independent life.

A red cord, worn around the waist, either tied simply

with a knot or with a buckle, is the girdle of Isis, with its many shades of meaning. Earlier, when considering the tragic but beautiful stories of the ladies of the chivalric knights, evidence was examined which revealed the meaning which could be imputed to the Y girdle, a chivalric form of the girdle of Isis. It may also be recalled that Mary the Virgin left her girdle behind, according to legend.

Yeshu's ancestresses are virtually all referred to in the Bible as having connections with a scarlet or red cord, and if not the cord, then the scarlet cloak. Rahab let two men escape by lowering them down a scarlet linen sash from the battlements of Jericho and then tied the sash in a conspicuous place so Joshua would know all was well. For this she and her family were spared when Jericho fell. Another ancestress, Tamar, had twins, the firstborn being identified by a scarlet cord tied around its wrist as it thrust its arm out. The arm was then retracted and the first baby delivered had no wrist cord; the child with the cord was delivered second, but was indubitably the one who could claim precedence. Did Yeshu, with her intimate knowledge of her ancestors, gently remind her listeners of this domestic tale when she said, 'The first will be last and the last first'? The link between Yeshu and her ancestresses, as with all women, is the red cord of birth, and the worshippers of Isis wore its symbol as amulets of jasper, red glass, crimson pastes, as well as a buckled belt.[8]

Here was the answer to the mystery of the 'holy' cords the Cathars and the Templars wore. It is the cord of life, symbolizing the Great Goddess. Yeshu used a cord to free the doves of Astarte from the Temple in Jerusalem, and a cord was used on her to make her bleed, the scourging. When measured up to these awesome symbols and the power behind them, the pathetic documents privately printed and distributed which, in distorted fashion, attempt to use them, are sad indeed; so impoverished in fact that they do a disservice to them. And it was that thought which electrified me.

Had this private publishing industry been set up not by confused and vulnerable people but by an organization whose sole aim was to traduce the rituals, the emblems, even the very ideas of the Great Goddess religions? Had Saunière been a dupe of misinformation, and the sad spectacle of people plucking at his unshriven body been yet another blow at the beauty of Isis? In other words, had the materials hidden by the scholarly Abbé Antoine Bigou in Rennes-le-Château been exactly what I suspected: documents asserting the femininity of Christ and the existence of her bones as Caput 58? If so, not only must Saunière be discredited by this organization, but the very idea itself – hence the garbled *Serpent Rouge* and related detritus, a collection of bogus papers and annals which, like the fraudulent exhibits at a witch's trial, were designed to impugn and malign. Who was behind this ugly propaganda? The answer could be obtained if one asked the simple and disarming question: who would benefit by traducing the Great Goddess religion? The response seemed glaringly obvious – the same organization which had always fought the Triple Goddess, the topmost echelons of the hierarchy of the Roman Church.

If this were the case, the existence of an organization in the Vatican dedicated to the spreading of disinformation, it would not be something new. The melancholy facts are that with the first official history of the Church by Eusebius there was much disinformation, as we have seen. Then there was the traducement of Cathar and Templar, the débâcle of the witch trials for several centuries. In these, physical force was combined with mental cruelty. There seemed, sadly, no reason why the Vatican would not use psychological warfare now it no longer had Inquisitors who could call upon armed men to take citizens out of their homes at night and put them in torture chambers. Every means of coercion and repression known to man has been categorically employed by the Papacy, and that is a simple matter of blunt historical record. The question of forgery too has cropped up monotonously throughout its history, and many egregious examples have been examined in this investigation.

The dates of publication of this cache of odds and ends relating to Merovingians, Templars, Rennes-le-Château, Red Serpents and much else besides are clustered together between 1956 and 1978, with citations of place of origin predominantly Paris, Toulouse and Geneva. Oddly, the most active exhibiting and examination of the Turin Shroud falls into the same epoch, there being an exposition on television in 1973, with a preliminary examination by art experts in 1969. There was a further flurry in 1978, which, with the first in 1933, makes four to date this century. The latter was by the express wish of Pius XI, whose eponymous successsor, Pius XII, was also a devotee, and proclaimed the bodily assumption of Mary the Virgin into heaven as required dogma.

Of course, these relationships may be merely coincidence, but there exists a particularly sinister piece of history in 1978, when a Pope, John Paul I, reigned for less than the time the Turin Shroud was being exposited. Indeed, as we have discussed, John Paul I was elected, reigned and died within the exposition period. The significance of this Pope is that he was making a move towards the relaxation of the birth control decrees of the Church.

Perhaps it is illuminating to see birth control in a rather wider context in order to trawl in the full implications of what John Paul was doing, or rather proposed to do, before he was discovered dead in his bed in the Vatican.

Birth control, like birth itself, has in Europe and the Middle East been traditionally the concern of women. The theology was that since the Triple Goddess was mother of all, from which all came and to which all would return, her incarnations, women, had the right to control their births in the sense of not becoming pregnant by a man. This point is perhaps remarkably apposite in view of the discoveries reported earlier about our ignorance of virgin birth. Birth control of such conceptions was of course impossible, no precautions could be taken against becoming pregnant by some inner change. But pregnancies arising from sperm–ovum fusion were an altogether different matter. Various techniques were used, squatting down and coughing after intercourse, douches and, of course, no reception of sperm. This latter was effected by removing the penis at the point of ejaculation, or 'stopping up the womb' by a variety of barriers, some herbal, others domestic, like half a lemon (natural Dutch Cap). The Cathars and Templars are alleged to have known several spermicides. The intestines of lambs could be pulled thin enough for condoms. There was also abortion, but the doctrines of interest to John Paul I, the thirty-three-days Pope, were those to prevent conception.

If he had been successful, then some power would have been restored to women. He was not. In fact a contemporary historian, David Yallop,[9] in a very lengthy and painstaking research, found evidence that John Paul had been murdered. The evidence is factual, categorized, and involves an examination of that other method of wielding power used by Popes throughout the centuries, financial control of vast resources. I have analysed his evidence, and suffice it to say at this point that I concur with other commentators, that his proposition that John Paul was killed for reasons of internal policy cannot be dismissed.

I differ, however, in identifying the motive, for though fiscal consideration no doubt played a part, for John Paul was very critical of the capitalist caucus in the Vatican hierarchy, his real crime appears to have been to try to reassert what women had lost during 2,000 years of Roman hegemony. The Vatican can exist without being an arch investor, but it cannot survive in its present form if power begins to flow back to its religious fount. Since the dawn of time women have controlled fertility, for 2,000 years the men at the head of the Roman Church have increasingly abrogated this, one of the most ancient of prerogatives. John Paul was the first to reverse the trend, or try to, and he died as millions of eyes were being concentrated on the muscular torso of the painter on the Turin linen.

Against Women

I had hoped before this last phase of the odyssey to find evidence of a change, an evolution, in the Church, but without much success, until a gleam of promise seemed possible in the stance the Church was taking on the admission of women into the priesthood. If this revealed potential for change, one could be sanguine for women in the future. But what I have found is the reverse – there is no hope, not for the devout women who yearn, as only religious people can, to do service. For them, the gates of Rome are closed for ever, just as the inner courts of the Jerusalem Temple were.

I suppose it was unreasonable to be optimistic because from Rome's point of view there can be no question of women ever becoming priests for the following reason. If my hypothesis is correct, and there exists in the Vatican material, and perhaps even documentary evidence on the gender of Christ, the most likely material being Caput 58 and the most likely documents we know about being the parchments of Abbé Bigou, then should there be even one woman priest, she could one day become Pope. And if so, she would eventually be privy to the truth. How could she play traitor to all her sex? The possibility would be that she would proclaim the truth, and the enormous façade which men had built would crumble down. Of course, there had been a Pope; her name was Joan, and she was murdered. Indeed her name thereafter was used by Inquisitors as synonymous with witch. They burned hundreds of thousands of Joans. Clearly, for men whose sole reason for living was their power, wealth and prestige in a rigid dogmatic hierarchical church, women could never be allowed in.

What then is the Pope's position? Pope Paul VI confirmed ten years ago that women were *persona non grata*, in his acceptance of the report from the Sacred Congregation for the Doctrine of the Faith, *Declaration on the question of the admission of women to the Ministerial Priesthood.*[10]

This polemic begins by asserting that sexual discrimination is wrong, but then says women cannot be priests. The assumption is 'that the priest represents Christ;[11] but where is the scriptural justification for this? Jesus told the disciples to perform the Last Supper, and that the bread was the body and the wine the blood. Also, Jesus said, 'Where two or three pray together, I am there also.' These enjoinders carried no force of gender whatsoever. In any case, which is the greater, the bread and wine which denote the body, or the body itself? Clearly, the real is greater than the symbol, yet who was it who held the body? It was not Peter, it was Mary the Mother and Mary Magdalene. They saw the death, they held the body, they saw the resurrected Christ first. Who then is the priest?

Curious as the Church's arguments are, they become even more curious, for after the claim that only a man can represent Christ comes the admission that in heaven, as Christ taught, no one is given or taken in marriage; that is, the risen body is sexless (Matt. 22:30). Christ is saying that spirit is neither male nor female; gender is a material condition. In any case, there are tens of thousands of human beings who have no clear organs of one sex or the other – their bodies are neuter; and yet again there are human beings with a perfect set of both male and female organs. Do they have their own separate hermaphrodite heaven? Their own hermaphrodite souls?

'The priesthood,' the *Declaration* says, 'is not conferred for the honour or advantage of the recipient, but for the service of God and the Church.'[12] If by the Church were meant the communion of all Christians, how could one disagree? But who shall do the conferring? Suppose a pagan community found a copy of the Gospels and one of the people read it and, seeing the beauty and power of it, baptized him or herself, imagining John the Baptist were doing it. Would this not be a true baptism? And then, would not that person be able to baptize all others? And to the Eucharist: would not it be done right at a table with bread and wine, and would not a member of the community who, in leading a life blameless of sin inasmuch as a human being can attain such, who by example is patient, courageous, kind and forgiving, who has taken to poverty, make a true and fitting priest, be they man or woman? And would not all the words of the four canonical Gospels be fulfilled? For if Paul can find Christ on the road to Damascus, why cannot a man or woman, before the sands of time run out, find Christ in some place where none has even heard of the Pope?

Significantly, Archbishop Runcie of Canterbury exchanged letters with Pope John Paul II in the summer of 1986, and the latter warned, in no uncertain terms, that a condition of communion between the two churches would be a clear understanding of the non-acceptance of women for ordination. The saving grace, it appears, of the Anglican Communion is its breadth of vision. A majority of the bishops see no doctrinal reason for the inadmission of women, which suggests that some of them may have been reading history more closely than they sometimes appear to. Others, although negative, are prepared to accept women. None the less, I was haunted by a television image of a Church of England priest asserting that only a man could offer the Eucharist. Again, apart from the debate on how many times an all-embracing sacrifice has to be made, the priest appears not to have grasped a point made earlier: what is greater, the symbol or the body? Women's hands held Christ's body; are not they to hold the bread? Their hands were stained with Christ's blood; are they not to hold the chalice?

There is real cruelty here, and to their credit, some Anglican bishops are well aware of it, and are earnestly seeking what they call a whole communion, that is one which does not exclude women. As in the case of the witch trials, cruelty produces hurt, and the sense of dismay and pain is borne by devout women in their tens of thousands.

But there is an even deeper issue, for if women are not to take their rightful place after an aberration in human history of 2,000 years, when mankind began to be cut off from the true tradition from which Yeshu stems, the institutional Church will probably bleed to death. Already the Anglican communion is shrunk to a dry segment of what it was, while the Catholic Church is caught between its dogmas and a new demand in its laity for a more natural religion. What Yeshu taught, as she said herself, was all things to all people, which implies an inner relevance to the human family anywhere and at any time. Yeshu developed the Great Goddess tradition; it would seem strange then that other people feel they have the right to fossilize it.

Ultimately, perhaps, all we have is the Communion of
the saints (many of whom as I have shown are not even
recognized by Rome, because it was Rome that killed
them) and the sacraments Yeshu gave us.

I say all we have, but it is a plenitude, for baptism can
be done by any Christian on a child or adult in an un-
broken succession of 2,000 years from John's baptism of
Yeshu on the banks of the Jordan. We have her promise
that where two or three gather together in her name she
will be there. She broke the bread and drank the wine,
but it was her mother who bore the child in her body
and fed her at her breasts, and it was Mary Magdalene
and Mary the Virgin who had her blood on their bodies
as they took Yeshu from the cross. The continuity is there
in the fact that we are joined, since Yeshu is our sister.
Bread broken and wine drunk by a lover of Yeshu is
valid in itself, for who should stand between her and
you? In short, I for my part, perhaps idiosyncratically
Protestant, see as much reason for an institutional Church
as Yeshu did for the Temple. At base, the altar of Yeshu
is this earth, which grows the bread and feeds the vine.

Postscript

I am unprepared for looking into the future, but there do seem certain obvious implications of the discovery suggested in my investigation. The ultimate status of the hypothesis of Christ's gender rests with further research and the balance of time. I am sanguine that there is a great deal more to unearth, probably literally, yet whatever the final analysis, one great theme emerges: the doctrine of the exclusively male Church has been shown, through the very violence it has caused, to be an aberration, both in history and the development of western thought.

For at least 8,000 years prior to the foundation of the Roman Church, mankind worshipped the Triple Goddess; the Great Goddess came in many forms and many aspects. Then suddenly, abruptly, in historical terms instantaneously, a male sky God was on this earth. So abrupt was this emergence that it was impossible to square with human development. There was, so to speak, no logic in it, either religious or psychological; above all there was no sense of development. For this reason alone it boded ill for the future, for the Church had to hedge itself around with dogmas, which soon became fossils.

The problems the Church has encountered have often been of its own making. By taking a defensive and then very aggressive stance, it tried to obliterate the past and control the present, while the future was to be pre-cast, a whole globe controlled by Rome. This incredible scenario is merely a sober description of the stated aims of Rome through a succession of Popes. It would seem that the Popes thought of themselves as super Roman Emperors, but the latter were well aware of their limitations, since it was clear that Rome could not be extended materially from the boundaries set by Augustus.

Curiously, the forces which made larger empires possible, namely the development in technical knowledge which improved communications, transport, and utilized sources of power other than animal and human muscle, had to be kept at arm's length by the Vatican. I am, of course, speaking of the liberating forces of human reason, an energy which was once recognized in the naturalness of the Great Goddess cults. Nothing, it seems, illustrates the constrained and ultimately unworkable nature of the dogmatic Roman Church better than this inability, for deeply intrinsic reasons, to avail itself of the productions of human insight and endeavour. Basically this is the same thing as saying that the Roman Church cannot cope with progress, but is doomed to retreat for ever into its own dogmas.

As I said, and as has been recognized by many commentators, there is greater and greater difficulty for the ordinary person to take on board the arbitrary dogmas of the Catholic Church. People find it difficult to believe in a body rising into the air into heaven. They do not understand why the Virgin Mary, after she had had a child, must be believed to have the private parts of a virgin. In addition, although the notion of Original Sin is a very important one in the obvious sense that we human beings do appear to have great difficulty in doing much right, that this difficulty is passed on from women is utterly unacceptable. One could go on with the litany of Vatican impossibilities, but the important issue is simply this: once the femality of Christ is accepted, once the great truths of rebirth and development, in other words those of the Great Goddess tradition, are accepted, there is no need to fear science, because the Great Goddess religion is a natural one.

But natural does not mean superstitious, or scientific in the sense of a mechanical view of the universe or ourselves. This is perhaps so obvious a point that I do not need to make it, but none the less simplicity was enjoined on us by Yeshu, and her insight was so wonderful, so beautiful and unique it is prudent to trust her. Yeshu believed she had something very important to say and do. She said it, and she did it. She left us with unforgettable images of loving kindness, but she did not leave us entirely, for there is her love feast of wine and bread which, by the way, is her gift to us, not the bequest of a church. She also gave us a warning about being too concerned with material things, for, according to her, there is so much more for us than the chattels of house and business, war and politics. Her message is very deep, so deep indeed that we have not got to the depths of it yet, but the thrust of what she said was intensely personal for all of us.

We know that Mary Magdalene, Mary the Virgin, and Paul, to mention just a few of the uncountable many, believed that Yeshu transcended death, not perhaps by walking after the crucifixion, but by being personally contactable. This appears to be a fact of human experience, mysterious though it is. At the very least, there is this persuasive evidence of Yeshu's continuing presence. Resurrection, clearly, has a very important meaning.

All these ideas and more are contained, in embyro as it were, in the Great Goddess tradition; it is natural then that Yeshu should have taken these ideas and developed them. Hers was a vision of growth, of regeneration. It would appear that this process must continue despite the 2,000-year interdiction of the Roman Church. Yeshu, the first Christian, was her own priestess, and there may be something important in that, but for now I think it may be best observed that Yeshu was not only a catalyst to human thought, but a dynamic so powerful that there is probably much more to know than is already discovered, but only if we recognize that it is through growth and development that her richness can be perceived. In fine, there is something in mankind which is evolving, it grew through the Great Goddess, was fulfilled in a personal way by Yeshu, and she left us with new insights for new life and new understandings. Try to constrain her teachings in dogmas, and she is crucified yet again.

In an odd way, it is the progress of science which has begun to illuminate the limitations of our own perceptions, just as Yeshu said. In this sense we have learned, if we read the achievements of pure science aright, of our own incapacity to stand still. We are developing creatures, and our understanding, though rooted in the past, has tendrils pushing into the future. When Leonardo began to see men as machines it was, in one sense, a step forward, for there is little doubt that we are in many ways physico-chemical bio-machines, but that is not all we are. In Victorian times, the fashion was to suppose measurements had no lower limit, that precision was infinite, but the revolution in physics some eight decades ago has shattered that complacency.

There are limits to what we can do in this universe because of the nature of the universe itself, and we are of course limited as well – except in the spiritual sphere. We, as human beings, actually think and believe things which have no obvious value in any mechanical or biological sense, and this ethical aspect of us Yeshu held dear. Of all the sages that have appeared in human history, Yeshu stands head and shoulders, despite her small physical frame, above them all. She is simultaneously, as she said, human and divine. We still do not know what she

meant by this latter claim, but it would be prudent to
listen to what she had to say, and much of that is, fortunately, in the four Gospels.

Much of what she did and said is mysterious, but not
in any bad sense. She felt she was helping us in some
way, and since she was not mad, but creative and
powerful, there is clearly something to be learned here.
She insisted that our very natures are such that self love
is harmful, while selfless love is not. It is a counsel far
removed from the market place. Then there is the fact
that she put great store by simple acts, baptism, sharing
a meal, remembering her, prayer, monogamy, eschewing
hate and embracing love. She was vehement about the
need to protect the innocence of children, and the
dangers of loving material things. And beneath her
actions and her words there is the unmistakable message
that the life we have on this planet is not the only one.
But she is in no sense vague. She taught that she was the
literal way to a life after death; not a diffuse existence in
the absolute, but a specifically personal one. This is a
challenge to all of us, and we have to see it from our
standpoint.

The Greeks and the Romans wanted their bodies to be
reborn, just as they pictured their gods and goddesses,
which alone probably explains their amendations to the
tradition they received from the Jewish Christians. It is
understandable; after all they really did believe there was
a physical heaven and that they could ascend to it. But
Yeshu never said this; she said that her kingdom was not
of this world, and that it was within each person.

I think it is not unreasonable to suggest that Yeshu
knew what she was talking about. Human experience,
according to her, does not end with the death of the
body. Beyond this material universe, she said, there was
something else where the self existed, and could be in a
variety of states of self awareness, some of them distinctly

unpleasant, but only if you wanted it that way. Who knows what form our 'bodies' may take in this brave new world? Her mother, Mary Magdalene, and all the apostles knew she was still alive. So did Paul, and he had never met the physical Christ, let alone a phantom of her. If anything is a fact of human experience it is this: billions of men, women and children have been touched by this presence and have borne witness to it. There is less reason for dismissing her today than there was when Caiaphas hated her. I suspect as the days roll by there will be less and less comfort for those who would wish to dismiss her, even in the bosom of science.

Clearly, there is much more to discover, but as I confessed, I am not prepared to go much further into it in this work. Yet I think it reasonable to elaborate on some of the implications of rediscovering our religious human roots.

First, Yeshu did live, did teach and did heal. The mystification of this real person by the conventional churches has led many people to reject Yeshu's teachings because they have been repelled by dogma, and so they have lost contact with a person unique in human history. If nothing else, it should be clear by now that Christ does not belong to any church or any hierarchy. There is no reason for anyone to feel they have to accept dogmas. As we have seen, there are very good reasons why these dogmas should be ignored.

Second, the process of reappraisal has been going on for some centuries. The Protestant Reformation occurred largely because Europeans could no longer stomach the abuses of Rome, and these were central issues, not mere corruption. The notion of anyone taking unto themselves the forgiveness of sins for money, for example, is theologically as well as morally repugnant. Unfortunately, the Protestant revolution soon made the same kinds of mistakes concerning power in a church as the Romans did. There is no evidence that is persuasive that Yeshu wanted her followers to become members of tiny, or for that matter large, empires. As she said, the kingdom was within. Perhaps this is best summed up when she renounced the claims of government over the sovereignty of human conscience; the teaching is contained in the incident when she was asked to decide on priorities between the demands of Caesar and God. She had already taught that obsession with wealth was a hindrance, and so when she said, 'Give to Caesar what is Caesar's and to God what is God's', she clearly meant that the claims of the spirit were infinitely greater. Powerful institutions, then, are not in Yeshu's style.

As a fulfiller of the great natural religions Yeshu contradicted the notion that this world and its animals and plants were for exploitation; rather it was a question of harmony. It is only now, it seems, that the partnership between mankind and the natural order, so central to Great Goddess cults, is at last again being recognized. There is no contradiction between true Christianity and an awareness of what we are doing to this planet.

Yeshu would not countenance killing; even when her own life was in danger she told Peter to put down the sword. She was determined to make her dream and vision actual, and she knew that squabbling with weapons was something that had gone on for millennia and settled nothing. Yeshu is the peace advocate, as befitted one who came after Astarte with her doves. Oddly, then, it is curious to observe that institutional churches have blessed the weapons of war, when Yeshu repudiated them without qualification.

Regarding sexuality, it has been obvious for centuries that institutional Christianity has been wrong in its teachings. Based on misogyny and the elevation of virginity to a mystic symbol, much spiritual and mental mischief has been done. The religious use of sexuality was central to the Great Goddess cults, and though there were excesses, in the main the body and its functions were seen to be fitting for service of the Goddess. Overwhelmingly, the concepts of the Great Goddess cults were to cohere heterosexuality as a joy, energy and worship, with its unquestionable function of maintaining the human race; the gift of children was the gift of sex, and sex was the gift of the Great Goddess. Rome spurned these down-to-earth and beautiful ideas and, with obscene edicts, backed by armed force, extirpated the last remnants of the natural religion, even seducing millions of men and women to cloister themselves without experience of heterosexual love in monosex institutions, which caused great psychological damage. It perhaps should be remembered that most of the men and women whom Yeshu chose for her work were married. Chastity, then, had some very real meaning for Peter and Mary the Virgin. They were not naïve youngsters.

Yeshu herself, as we have seen, probably married Lazarus, raising him from the dead, as it were. Moreover, the union of man and woman was given a new meaning by her, for they became one flesh. Clearly, in our culture sex has been devalued almost in the mirror image of the devaluation given it by Rome. It may be mere factual observation to note that misogyny implies hatred of the body, and that has spilled over to men's bodies as well. The symbols of sex were once the motifs of a religious appreciation of energy and regeneration, none the less spiritual for that. However, the pleasures of sex were inseparable from the bond of heterosexuality. Today, words like obscene and pornographic are used for these very same motifs. I take this as partial evidence of the evil that has been done to the minds of people by the killing of the Great Goddess and the desecration of her shrines by a sex-hating church and by the demands of commerce.

This last point concerning Mammon may appear rather quaint, but in actuality is one of the problems we face. In the vacuum created by the Church all manner of strange gods have entered to fill it up. Commerce accentuates the anxiety by titillation. Lately, western civilization repudiated the notion that sex was evil, but had nothing to put in its place. The gulf is spanned by the teachings of Yeshu: the natural acceptance of sex, the love between men and women. But that was excised by the dogmas of Rome. Perhaps if we recognize this sleight of hand, we can begin to see just what is wrong with a culture which uses a woman's body in countless impoverished ways to sell things, often to people who do not even need them. It may help us to start to question the idea that promiscuous sexuality is some kind of crusade, and that any deviation is acceptable.

If I am right that Yeshu was the natural outcome of a worldwide Great Goddess tradition, which is another way of saying that mankind yearns for a natural religion, one that does not strain credulity nor insult intelligence, then it may be high time we recognize the fact. Religious hunger appears to be as natural to men and women as hunger of the body or the heart. An unnatural religion has queered the pitch, has led to unbalanced idolatry of things material, and thoughts profane. By this I simply mean it is understandable that we felt scientific rationalism and a mechanical view of mankind was preferable to the unbelievable, and often terror laden, dogmas of orthodox religion. I think what the rediscovery of Yeshu has meant for me, at least, is that I no longer believe that these impoverished choices are the only options open to us.

There is, after all, so much we do not know. The great experiences of religion are not confined to any one creed, but on the contrary appear to be something that comes from our very nature. Yeshu clearly recognized this. This is the beginning of seeing that we neither have to choose dogmas nor the emptiness of a mechanical and random universe as promulgated by science. There is a lot more going on. I do not know what it is, but if ever anyone did know, it was a small and afflicted woman, who was born in Bethlehem and died in Jerusalem 2,000 years ago. The power of her teachings and personality is so great that it has survived misrepresentation and down-right forgery.

I have expanded on these ideas to some extent, though clearly not even fractionally as they deserve, not because I think I have any message to give but to emphasize that the richness of what Yeshu did and said is not dim-inishable by anything we may find out about her. She becomes more, not less, the more we know of science, as befits a Great Goddess; for the tradition is a natural one, of the here and now, with a spiritual dimension. She cannot be contained in dogmas, but her teachings, I feel sure, can liberate us from the parochial constraints of a material universe. I am sure, for example, as Christians are, that she did 'ascend to heaven', that she conquered death. No doubt if I had been a Roman soldier hearing her story for the first time in Rome, probably in a tavern near the Circus Maximus, I would have expected her to have physically ascended. Why not? I would not have known about the emptiness of physical space, for all I could reasonably tell there was a heaven beyond the blue sky. But I know now that there are millions of miles beyond that blue sky, and there is no heaven there, not of the stuff of this universe. Then why should I be con-strained by dogmas of a mistaken philosophy? After all, Yeshu, to reiterate, said her life was not of this universe, not of the stuff we see, feel and hear, not even in what we understand as time.

Christians need never fear anything factual; the only danger is if Yeshu is identified with any institution or any set of currently fashionable dogmas. The fashions of Greece and Rome formed the Catholic Church. Only Yeshu's sacraments really give it power, only Yeshu; the rest will pass away, as we are seeing now; fewer men for the priesthood, fewer girls for the convents, fewer laity. The unreal formulations of institutional Christianity are being overrun by history, and the walls of these churches will surely come crumbling down. But Yeshu will survive, just as she did the fall of the Jerusalem Temple in AD 70, some thirty-seven years after her death of the body. She will survive on this earth as long as two or three gather in her name – and if two, then one.

Notes and References

Introduction: Fertile Ground

1 The quote is from Graves, R., *The Greek Myths*, Part I, Penguin, Harmondsworth, 1960, p. 13. His theories of the Triple Goddess are contained in his *The White Goddess*; Faber and Faber, London, 1961.

2 Eusebius, *The History of the Church*, translated by G. A. Williamson, Penguin, 1965. For Eusebius' mistake on the first person to see the risen Christ see op. cit. pp. 64–5; for the letter allegedly written by Christ, ib. pp. 64–70; his attack on Simon and Helen, ib. pp. 86–7.

3 Warner, M., *Alone of All Her Sex*, Weidenfeld and Nicholson, London, 1976, p. 191.

4 Harrison, M., *The Roots of Witchcraft*, Tandem, London, 1978, p. 121.

5 Augustine, *Treatise against Julian*, 3.14. The Sermon 151 is 'Of Marriage and Sexual Desire'; see Ayerst, D. and Fisher, A.S.T., *Records of Christianity*, Vol. I, Blackwell, Oxford, 1971, p. 285.

6 Jerome, *Letters*. He wrote many between AD 384–99; they are translated in Ayerst and Fisher, op. cit.; of particular interest in revealing the importance of women in the early church are Jerome's letters concerning the Christian women Blessilla, Fabiola and Principia.

7 Cheetham, N., *Keepers of the Keys*, MacDonald, London, 1982, pp. 18–19, 59. Rome was still a great city in the sixth

century; the public baths still operated, the granaries were well stocked by the Pope, the slave markets thrived and much of the architectural magnificence remained. The decline into the Dark Ages was gradual rather than precipitous. After Gregory, a succession of Popes had to deal with the demands of the Emperor, the problems of the Arabs and continuing bickering about dogma, the latter being much their doing. Popes were condemned for heresy, imprisoned and maltreated by Constans, and there was constant oscillation between Rome and Constantinople of the centre of gravity of Christian authority. Constans came to Rome in A D 664 to fight the Lombards, and was the first Emperor for two and a half centuries to visit the city. The Emperor died and was succeeded by Constantine IV, aided by Pope Vitalian (657–72), who was also carrying on Gregory I's evangelizing of Britain, from whence would come the missionaries to evangelize the pagan tribes in Germany.

Meanwhile the Arabs, as Islam, failed to capture Constantinople, and Constantine in delight at this victory, tried to reconcile his Greek Orthodox believers with his Latin believers, in the Council of the Church, the Sixth, 680–681. The Eastern Church emerged with recognition of their Patriarch, and the Latin Church with recognition of their Pope. The seeds were sown for the great split between Rome and Byzantium. Indeed, for a time Greek Popes reigned, there being nine Greeks and only one Roman of the ten between 680 and 715. In Agatho's Papacy (678–81) Dagobert, a Merovingian King, was murdered on 23 December, in the forests of Wöevres, abutting the Ardennes.

The Greek influence in Rome continued, and although public amenities were allowed to fall into disrepair, many new churches were built with great richness, as the fabric of ancient secular and pagan buildings was used for the new Roman churches. The Church was now a proved secular force, and John VII had a new palace built for himself, where he lived in luxury. So important had the Papacy become after Paul I's death in 767 that the Roman nobles used force to scare the Bishops into electing a layman Pope, who was not yet even a clergyman. He was deposed by force and Stephen III (767–772) was properly elected, but he proceeded to blind and mutilate rivals, political or religious, though the two were indeed now indistinguishable.

It is at this stage that Charlemagne the Great enters history as the new Emperor. Stephen III elicited his support but then ditched him in favour of the Lombards. The result was bloody violence, with clerics being torn out of the sanctuary of St Peter's, blinded and strangled. The blame for all this was firmly put at Stephen's door. He died leaving Rome confused, and Charlemagne determined to restore and, if possible, enlarge, at least the European part of Constantine's Empire. He was not above humiliating Popes, even convening his own councils of bishops to ratify or countermand Roman edicts, though in general he used the Papacy to unify his realms. But he was upstaged by one Pope, Leo III, who assumed that it was the papal right to crown him emperor, thereby taking on a function of recognizing kings and emperors which was really not the Pope's right to do. This papal 'recognition' of true kingship was to prove very useful.

Charles was to die in 814, and we will take up his descendants' story soon, but already it was clear that the Papacy had become more the centre of power than anything else, often cynically using religion to secure temporal ends. The Papacy was a target and a source of violence, it not being uncommon for Popes to be waylaid and hurt, as Stephen III was. The stories of the Church and the Merovingian Kings are not really separable, nor is that of the Carolingians, for it was Charlemagne's predecessors who took over the Merovingian Kingdoms.

The word squalid seems to fit these stories as easily as any other. One legitimately wonders what had happened to the teachings of Christ, and how the vast secular apparatus in Byzantium, as well as Rome, is in any real way related to Jesus at all. It is not an original thought, but one worth noting.

The empire of Charlemagne, tied by the umbilicus of the Pyrenees to Rome, was not to survive. The Papacy had used a forged document, purportedly of Constantine, and probably written in the papal chancery (see Cheetham op. cit. pp. 18–19, 59) just before Pope Stephen II (752–7) went to see King Pippin, Charlemagne's predecessor, to lay claim to spiritual authority over the Franks' lands. It speaks, as no other story does, of the depths the power-obsessed Papacy were willing to go to (not only destroying documents but manufacturing them) in the pursuit of this power. The Franks agreed to recognize, and Pippin was re-anointed. This unholy alliance of secular and spiritual power boded ill for Europe, but the Church could afford to see dynasties come and go. The Charlemagne Empire had served its purpose, for the Pope was supreme Pontiff in the Latin world, 'authenticator' of kings.

Chapter 1 Mystery of the Priestesses

1 Compare the penitent Magdalene with the woman described by J. de Voragine, *The Golden Legend*, trans. W. Caxton, 1470. Dent 1900.

2 Joan's annalist was Bartolomeo Platina. He was born in Piadena in 1421, and died in Rome on 21 September 1481. He was a man of some considerable importance through his connections, for he knew Popes intimately and had solderied with Francesco Sforza, patron of Leonardo da Vinci. Platina was a survivor, for though Pope Paul II arrested him on a charge of 'neopagan impiety', a singe away from heresy, it was later changed to 'conspiracy' and he was actually hired by the Borgia Pope, Sixtus IV, as his Vatican Librarian. Platina seems to have learned his lesson from his brush with Paul II, for he now toed the line, or appeared to do so. His position as librarian meant that in effect he had access to the official and unofficial history of the Roman Church. One would expect that any books emanating from him would studiously adhere to papal precept. It is therefore the more astonishing that in his well received lives of the Popes, *Liber de vita Christi ac omnium pontificum*, published in Venice 1479 and dedicated to Sixtus, we find Joan's entry.

Platina's entry on Joan reads as follows:

'POPE JOHN VIII: John, of English extraction, was born at Mentz and
is said to have arrived at Popedom by evil art; for disguising herself
like a man, whereas she was a woman, she went when young with
her paramour, a learned man, to Athens, and made such progress
in learning under the professors there, that, coming to Rome, she
met with few that could equal, much less go beyond her, even in
the knowledge of the scriptures; and by her learned and ingenious
readings and disputations, she acquired so great respect and authority that upon the death of Leo (as Martin says) by common
consent she was chosen Pope in his room. As she was going to the
Lateran Church between the Colossean Theatre (so called from
Nero's Colossus) and St Clement's her travail came upon her, and
she died upon the place, having sat two years, one month, and four
days, and was buried there without any pomp. This story is vulgarly
told, but by very uncertain and obscure authors, and therefore I
have related it barely and in short, lest I should seem obstinate and
pertinacious if I had admitted what is so generally talked; I had
better mistake with the rest of the world; though it be certain,
that what I have related may be thought not altogether incredible.'

[From Royidis, E., *Pope Joan*, trans. L. Durrell, André Deutsch,
1960, the Preface. Platina is cited in the *New Catholic Encyclopaedia*,
Vol. II, p. 430.]

How can a person so scholarly and so well versed in
scripture and so commanding of respect – secretary to Pope
Leo IV as Joan was before becoming Pope herself – be
regarded as coming to the Papacy by evil art? Perhaps the
only evil that Joan was guilty of was her sex.

Platina tells us she was in the company of a learned man,
but why is he called her paramour? If Joan were so easily
mistaken as male, might not this scholar be merely her tutor?
After all, she was a scriptural scholar, a speaker of uncommon ability. This interpretation rings true, for her
patron Leo IV was said by Platina himself to be 'a person of
so much prudence and courage that, as the Gospel directs,
he could, when it was necessary, imitate either the wisdom
of the serpent or the innocence of the dove'; obviously not
the sort of person to be taken in (quote from Royidis, op.
cit., p. 163, note 47).

As we read the rest of Platina's entry on Joan, we

observe the curious use of the word 'travail', literally labour from the French sense, or it could also be task, or even agony. It certainly does not have to be the labour of birth, but Platina is drawing on sources which state this, so he has hedged his allegiance and used a word which is ambivalent in stress.

Joan's name is a derivative of Johannes or John. The form Joan is listed in OED as being first used in 1588, for prior to that the form is Joanna or Johanna; the male equivalent can also be found with an 'h' as Johannes. Joan is also a generic name for a female 'rustic', as well as a close-fitting cap worn by women about 1750. That Joan is associated with rural women is not immaterial for during the Persecution of Witches we find that Joan and its derivative Jane are used to denote a woman of witchery. However, Pope Joan impressed herself on the common mind from the ninth century well into the sixteenth, for we find a card game, Pope Joan, in 1590, which was named after her. It is a game played by three or more persons with a pack from which the eight of diamonds has been taken. This datum is from the OED, but we may add to it by observing that Joan was John VIII, the eighth.

3 Royidis, op. cit., p. 20.

4 Royidis turns this part of Joan's story into a strange farcical romp, pp. 4–42, which has some curious symbols, and abortive rape by three monks. Royidis has one of his monks, Brother Roleig, making a blessing in the Latin, '*In nomine Patris, et Filii et Spiritus Sancti.*' He puts this 'blasphemy' in the mouth of a monk who is later to attempt to rape Joan. Royidis introduces a note of farce, by having these Christian men eat goose on a 'fish' day. The fish is a symbol of Christ; the goose motif appears earlier, for Judith, Joan's mother, is a goose girl. Moreover, the goose features in Egyptian myth, as ancient or even more so, as the belief in Isis, the Great Goddess, as a kind of progenitor of creation, a Godhead in our language (see Rundle Clark, R.T., *Myth and Symbol in Ancient Egypt*, Thames and Hudson, London, 1978, p. 213). There are times like these when it might appear that

Royidis is writing a kind of anagram, or a coded message.

The initial reason for taking Royidis seriously as a writer is not his turgid prose style or his doubtful wit, but the fact that he spent many years researching all extant documents on the story of John VIII. There is, on the surface of his book, *Pope Joan*, much ornation, much detail, and a melancholy sense of repressed sexuality, but beneath there is a narrative line which is as strong and tense as the hawser on a suspension bridge. The woman Royidis is enamoured of seems to float between the real historical Joan and the Joan of his imagination. The latter is an unbelievable figure, for we are asked to accept that she went against all the precepts of Christianity and at the same time had the spiritual gifts of a saint; the historical Joan, the gifted stateswoman, the outstanding scholar, the mystic, Pope Joan I, is perhaps too real for him. However, Royidis, if nothing else, was an astonishing rarity in the late nineteenth century; he actually felt that a Pope could be a woman or a man, as long as they did the job. For his liberality and the publication of his book, in Athens 1886, he suffered excommunication for his beliefs.

5 Royidis, op. cit. p. 57.

St Thecla is described by Butler in his *Lives of the Saints* as of charming disposition and very learned. She had an early vocation to the service of God, and broke off her engagement. The young man, with the hatred of one spurned, denounced her to anti-Christian authorities and she was cast naked into a den of lions. Like Daniel, she went unharmed. St Thecla's association with lions also links her to Jesus, for he was called Panthera, which is Latin for lion. We may speculate that the rich and original mind of Joan did not miss the allusions either, and her attachment to St Thecla may suggest that Joan herself saw her life as totally dedicated to the service of God. Her sister in faith, Thecla, may have given her courage to undertake the next important step in her already eventful life, for she left the Abbey for St Fulda's, with Frumentius. Joan was dressed as a man, in the habit of a priest. In this she followed a Christian tradition, for St Margaret the Pelogian, who is mentioned in Butler's *Lives of the Saints* and in de Voragine's *Golden Legend*, broke off her engagement and dressed as a monk, eventually becoming an Abbot.

6 There is a note of Frumentius to Joan:

Frumentius to his Sister Joanna rejoicing in the All Highest

> As the hart panteth after the water-brooks
> so panteth my soul after thee, my sister – Psalms

> The hungry dream of bread but I saw thee
> asleep, Joanna, yet waking found thee not – Isaiah

[Royidis, op. cit. p. 54–5]

7 Indeed, there appears ground for suspicion that Royidis has some deeper motive in writing his *Pope Joan*, for note this sentence, the context being the happiness of Joan with her co-worker, Frumentius, at Fulda, op. cit. p. 66: 'Such was Joanna for her Frumentius, a rose without thorns, a fish without bones, a cat without claws.' Might not the rose without thorns be the Rose of Sharon, in the Song of Solomon, and that Rose is Jesus? The thorns did not come before the crucifixion: 'rose without thorns'. The fish symbol for Christ dates back to the Roman catacombs and also comes from the Greek 'Jesus Christ, God, Saviour of the World', for in Greek the initial letters of this phrase spell Ictheus, fish. Christ is a fish in this sense, but without bones. A cat without claws is again Jesus, for Jesus was known as *Panthera*, or lion, yet if Jesus were a lion then the lion had no claws. The stringing together of three symbols of Christ in an otherwise banal, even profane, piece of prose may be thought beyond the realms of mere coincidence. Was Royidis quoting another author?

8 With what appears to be in unbelievable bad taste, Royidis has the ass that Joan has used to utter the prophecy. Had Royidis come across a source of Joan's religious experience traduced in this way, and done the best he could with it? Curiously too, Royidis is not far off the mark when he includes the donkey in his story, for the earliest known portrait of Christ is that of a crucified donkey, a graffiti A D *c*.30 (see Harrison, M., *The Roots of Witchcraft*, Tandem, London, 1978, p. 38).

9 Warner, M., *Alone of All Her Sex*, Weidenfeld and Nicolson, London, 1976, p. 88.

10 Cheetham, N., *Keepers of the Keys*, MacDonald, London, 1982, pp. 313–14.

11 Support for this view is given by the records which still exist on Nicholas I (858–67), Joan's successor, for they were penned by none other than Anastasius, who now held the position of Lateran Librarian, supervising the official papal biographies, *Liber Pontificalis*. Given that Nicholas was a stern patriarchal Churchman, any hope of Joan surviving this supervision of history is slight, and moreover Anastasius, whose record to date has been appalling, was in the perfect position to improve his image for posterity. That he had offered violence to a Pope was retained as historical fact, but it is possible that the identity of that Pope has undergone a gender transformation. This would suit Nicholas's strategy, for he was engaged in asserting the supremacy of the Papacy, and had no use at all for the scandal that a woman Pope would bring about. At one time, 864, Nicholas had actually to lock himself in St Peter's in a contest of wills with Lewis II. He won, and went on to a bout of excommunications, wranglings with Byzantium (the patriarchs routinely excommunicated each other – a tit of the east for a tat of the west). When Nicholas died the Duke of Spoleto sacked Rome, Lewis II restored order and Hadrian II was elected Pope, just as his relatives Stephen IV and Sergius II had been. Hadrian's daughter added further disgrace by running off with a cousin of Anastasius, the Librarian. Hadrian ordered that his daughter and Eleutherius, this cousin of the Librarian, should be pursued, but fearing capture, Eleutherius stabbed the girl and her mother (Hadrian's wife before he became Pope) to death. Anastasius was, as form demanded, excommunicated, but he survived this second cutting off from God by becoming personal representative of Lewis II at important councils of the Church in Constantinople. It may be an excusable response to feel that this is a period of history when charlatans and dynasts, as well as saints and fools, occupied the

chair of Peter. To suggest that a learned and brilliant woman of great piety wore the slippers of Peter, comes in this heady atmosphere as a breath of calming air.

The revised Papal succession appears to be – Leo IV (847–55), Joan (855–8) = Benedict III (?), Anastasius (Pope for a few hours but never consecrated) (855), Nicholas I (858–67), Hadrian II (867–72) and then John VIII (872–82). This last Pope died in mysterious circumstances. Cheetham remarks on his great ability, which alone would be a distinguishing feature from the likes of Hadrian II and Sergius II (relatives), and then tells us, 'Yet doubt obscures the circumstances of his death.' A German annalist reports that he was attacked with a hammer, after attempts to poison him failed.

None of this prevented Joan being called a witch (see Royidis, op. cit., p. 137). Consult Cheetham, op. cit. for details of papal succession.

12 Warner, op. cit. p. 143

13 Sumption, J., *The Albigensian Crusade*, Faber and Faber, London, 1978, pp. 256, 47.

14 ib., p. 58.

15 ib., p. 198.

16 ib., p. 227.

17 See Picar, M., *Les Cathares*, M.A. Editions, Paris, 1986, pp. 81–3, 90, 162–3 and Baigent, M., Leigh, R., and Lincoln, H., *The Holy Blood and the Holy Grail*, Corgi, London, 1983, p. 53; and pp. 54–8, for speculation; and Sumption, op. cit., pp. 238–41, for a factual analysis.

No one has been able to explain this strange truce given by Henri d'Arcis, the French King's Captain at Montségur. Curiously, he appears to have been the ancestor of a certain Bishop d'Arcis, who some one hundred years later was to speak of the grave danger to souls occasioned by a false relic of the de Charny family, a so-called shroud showing a male Christ, purportedly from the actual tomb of Jesus.

Chapter 2 Knights of a Special Lady

1 A standard work on these events is by S. Runciman, *A History of the Crusades*, in three volumes, Penguin, Harmondsworth, London, 1978.

2 The history of the Knights Templar has a copious literature. In addition to Runciman's work cited above, there is an earlier important work by C. G. Addison, *The History of the Knights Templar*, London, 1842. An unorthodox account is given by A. Daraul, *A history of Secret Societies*, Pocket Books, N.Y., 1962.

3 Baigent, M., Leigh, R., and Lincoln, H., *The Holy Blood and the Holy Grail*, Corgi, London, 1983, pp. 484–5.

4 Michelet, M., *Procès des Templiers*, Paris, 1841–51, Vol. II. p. 364. Translation given quoted by I. Wilson, *The Turin Shroud*, Gollancz, 1978, p. 156.

5 Wilson, op. cit. above, p. 154.

6 ib., p. 154.

7 ib., p. 160; the Abbot of Lagny quote, ib. p. 158.

8 ib., p. 157.

9 Addison, C. G., *The Knights Templar*, London, 1842, p. 473.

10 Michelet, op. cit., p. 192, Vol. I.

11 From Raynouard, *Monuments historiques relatifs à la condemnation des Templiers*, Paris, 1813, p. 73.

12 From Langlois, *Revue des Deux Mondes*, Vol. CIII, 1891, p. 411.

13 Wilson, op. cit., p. 159.

14 Oursel, R., *Le Procès des Templiers*, Paris, 1959, p. 208.

15 Michelet, op. cit., p. 192, Vol. I.

16 Finke, H., *Papsttum und Untergang des Templerordens*, Munster, 1907, Vol. II, p. 334.

17 Graves, R., *The White Goddess*, Faber and Faber, London, 1961.

18 Gautier, L., *Chivalry*, trans. by D.C. Dunning, Phoenix House, London, 1965.

 The girdle worn by the ladies of chivalry was a fashion that persisted for some time. For example the Y girdle is shown very clearly in the miniature paintings of a fifteenth-century manuscript in the Bibliothèque de l'Arsenal, Paris, illustrating Boccaccio's Decameron, serving a story of a girl who dressed as a priest. (Bibliothèque de l'Arsenal, Paris, MS 5070 II–3.)

 A girdle also figures provocatively in the legends of the bodily ascent, called the Assumption, of the Virgin Mary into heaven. Her girdle fell to earth as she flew skyward. If indeed the Y girdle was what it appeared to be, a statement of feminine gender, then the legend maker was saying Mary had left her body behind on Earth. In fine, within the legend itself was its own demolition; the legend maker while appearing to accede to the Assumption was in fact saying that it was untrue by including the detail of the girdle. For the legend see Warner, M., *Alone of All Her Sex*, Weidenfeld and Nicholson, London, 1976, p. 292.

19 The scholarly work of A.E. Waite, whose huge (nigh on a quarter of a million words) study of the Grail, *The Hidden Church of the Holy Graal* (Rebman, London, 1909), reviews the literature. His conclusions are remarkable, for he suggests that a secret Graal Church, part of which predates Christ, exists secretly in the Catholic Church.

 Waite summarizes his findings under several headings which suggest the existence of a hidden sanctuary which possesses a great mystery that cannot be communicated except under certain circumstances, and which has healing powers. Despite his scholarship, however, he does not a) identify the Graal, b) explain how it can be all the things he mentions in the headings above, or c) disentangle it from myth and legend.

 The odd thing about the Grail Romances is that they

emerged from the late twelfth century, flourished for about a century, and then enjoyed little new publishing until Malory's *Morte d'Arthur*.

The other equally significant fact is that most Christian countries once part of the Roman Empire, with the possible exception of Italy, produced their own versions (see Waite, op. cit., pp. 689–709). In all, there is a pathos, a pervading sense of loss, as if something had been taken away from Christendom, something stolen and hidden. Waite expresses this fact poignantly:

The same story of loss is therefore everywhere . . . Now it is a despoiled sanctuary; now a withdrawn sacramental mystery; now the abandonment of a great military and religious order [he is speaking of the Templars] . . . now the vacancy of the most holy of all sepulchres.

(op. cit., p. 607)

He even seriously considers there was a book of the Graal, predating the romances, which contained:

. . . the greatest secret of the world, a minute volume which would lie in the hollow of a hermit's hand . . . which the Count of Flanders gave to Chrétien de Troyes with instructions to retell it.

(op. cit., p. 499)

It is Waite's passionately held view that the Graal romances are actually symbolic statements of what was lost, but apart from suggesting that there exist in the Church guardians of the inner mysteries, none of which are named, nor are the mysteries delineated, he adds little more. Indeed the value of his monumental work is to prove there is a mystery and that it is intimately associated with something the Catholic Church has hidden, though he is not sure why.

Some priests were worried about Rome's claims, as Waite strongly writes:

That before 1000 A.D Claudius, Archbishop of Turin, characterised the censure pronounced on his anti-papal writings as the voice of the members of Satan; that Arnulph, the Bishop of Orleans, at the Council of Rheims pointed to the Roman Pontiff saying: 'Who is that seated upon a high throne and radiant with purple and gold?'

Waite notes that chivalric writers too were concerned:

These were the accusations of prelates and with them may be compared the opinion of Figueiras the troubadour, who described Rome as an immoral and faithless city, having its seat fixed in the depths of hell ... So also St Bridget termed Rome the whirlpool of hell and the house of mammon, wherein the devil barters the patrimony of Christ.
(op. cit., pp. 623–4)

His mistake was one shared by most writers before and after him, for in assuming they were dealing with an inanimate object which had to be found, they then forgot it and concentrated on mystic symbolism alone. This split in concentration has been fatal for the Grail literature.

20 The alchemists combined several traditions; the native European herbal lore, and also Arabic chemistry, introduced by the Templars into Europe from their close contacts with the Saracens who understood many processes which today we call chemical. Many alchemists were known to one another, not so much by writing but by the master and apprentice relationship; curiously, they often made a practice of burning their notes, and so the alchemical tradition is largely oral. Their link with the Great Goddess tradition is found in their herbal lore, but they also regarded Isis as the greatest of alchemists, and included in their pantheon Cleopatra (who was the daughter of Isis in some cults, and the incarnation in others) and the remarkable Mary the Jewess.

They studied Egyptian and Hebraic magic, and used the Hebrew script, transferring to their own language and Latin the habit of leaving out vowels. Much of their work centred on materials they called calxes; a calx in their script was CLX. This finding is remarkable, for even such sober scholars as Sherwood Taylor (*The Alchemist*, Paladin, 1976), late of the Science Museum, was convinced the alchemists knew an important secret. It would appear that they knew something about the Grail, and hence the femality of Christ.

But is there any other evidence, in addition to this odd cipher link? Curiously, the richness of the meaning of CLX goes even deeper. It is well known that the alchemists tried to transmit what was base into what was incorruptible. This has been symbolized as the transmutation of lead into gold. Doubtless many practitioners were out to make a fortune, but the vast majority were reclusive people, obsessed by their arcane art. What, then, is the hidden meaning?

The word Calx refers to oxides of metals. One of these, lead oxide, is red. So is another, Mercuric oxide. Lead as a metal when heated will give a silver liquid, while mercury itself is a silver liquid. Here, then, is a connection between silveriness and redness. The moon is the silver orb, and its cycles are those of menstruation. The moon is also the crescent of Isis, and red is the colour she wears and is symbolized by. This is a direct alchemical link between the blood of Isis and alchemical practices. The occult powers attributed to the calxes, the red calxes of metals, is a distortion of the fertility elements of the Isis cult.

Vermilion, the dye used by the 'scarlet lady', that is, the priestess of Isis, can by alchemical processes, be changed into a silvery liquid. Actually there is nothing mysterious in this, since it is routinely done in O-level chemistry to this very day when studying mercury. It can also be changed back to the red powder. A more telling symbolism is difficult to find, for in his cloistered laboratory, the alchemist was able to mimic the changes of the moon and the cycles of menstruation. But why the search for gold? The answer seems very clear; the adept could change the silver of the moon into the blood of Isis, but Isis had between her crescent the orb of the sun, which was gold. When the sun went down the sky turned blood red, so the alchemist reasoned that he should be able to mimic this as well. He couldn't, because nature has not provided a convenient Calx.

Isis then presides over the alchemist, and Jesus wore her scarlet cloak to the crucifixion, which was given to her by a Roman soldier. Isis presides, too, over the moon and the sun; both affiliated to blood, one in the red sky and the other in timing menstruation. The Great Goddess can transmute red to silver, silver to gold, and is the source of all life. Isis, however, sometimes wore a stone throne as a fetching headgear, when she was not wearing the sun. It is curious, then, that the magic ingredient which the alchemists sought was called the philosopher's stone. What they were really trying to find (it seems, somehow, such an attractive idea) was the Throne of Isis. Some of them appeared to know this, and would not pass on their secrets. As true devotees of the Great Goddess, they would rather stay in her good graces than be profaned by traffic with the world, particularly a church which had killed their Goddess.

The sign for Isis (and Venus) is $\frac{\varphi}{}$, while the moon sign is $\cup$. We know these glyphs go back to those great lovers of the Goddess, the Babylonians. The sign for Mercury is a $\frac{\varphi}{}$ combination of the Isis sign and the moon sign. (See Shah, I., *The Secret Love of Magic*, Abacus, 1972, p. 17.)

21 According to the Church no one could have the bones of the Virgin Mary because she had been assumed into heaven bodily, directly, and without corruption. Her bones, like those of Jesus, could not be on the face of this Earth. This belief grew out of the Dormition, that is the falling asleep without corruption of Mary the Virgin, but Pope Leo IV (847–55), he who was to make Joan a Pope, gave the feast of the Assumption solemnity by adding a vigil to it, while Nicholas I (858–77), the Pope who succeeded Joan (John VIII) equated the Assumption with Christmas and Easter which, as Marina Warner points out, makes the Assumption as central in the Church's belief as the birth of Christ and the Resurrection (Warner, op. cit., p. 88.) Despite this, St Bernard of Clairvaux, although passionate in his love for Mary the Virgin, 'never commits himself to her mortal death or her corporeal ascent to heaven'.

Why was Bernard so cool on the Assumption? A clue is perhaps found in his close links with the Templars. Bernard was the nephew of André de Montbard, a French nobleman and one of the co-founders of the Order of the Knights Templar.

Given these connections Bernard may have heard of the sacred relic, Caput 58, Virgo. For Bernard, committed to the resurrection, these bones could not have been those of Christ, and so he took the less inflammatory line of assuming that they were of the Virgin Mary, Virgo; what he forgot was that the Church also insisted Christ was a virgin too. A drawing of the sign after Caput 58 is found in H. Lobineau's *Dossiers secrets d'Henri Lobineau*, Paris, 1967. This is a privately published document, and can be viewed in the Biliothèque Nationale, Paris. The Virgo sign, if that is what it is, has letters written in the M. See also Baigent et al, op. cit. above, p. 486, note 21; pp. 80–81, p. 123; and Fol.–LM 3 4122 in the Bibliothèque Nationale.

It is perhaps understandable why the Assumption took so long to be ratified, for the problems inherent in the Roman Mariology were very deep indeed.

Indeed, the point was not pressed, for it was not until 1950 that the Assumption was made a required article of faith for Catholics by Pius XII.

As the fires burned to embers in the Languedoc, chivalry died, or rather it was transformed into Church preoccupations, the new Knight was Christ, the Apollo, tall, chestnut-haired, muscular, the great lover; at the same time Mary was made into an increasing cult, the new Lady. Obviously this left real women rather a long way behind, for the new ideal did not make love. Yet, because her son was also God, and God was the father of the son, then in a sense Mary was married to God; and since God was the son, she was married to her son! The intricacies of these ideas speak for themselves. Only against this florid background of incestuous dogma of the Church of Rome, courtly love transformed into the new liturgy of Knight and Lady of Heaven, burnings of heretics, and slaughtering of hundreds of thousands in crusades, can we perhaps even begin to grasp the depths of paranoia and confusion that permeated the intellectual climate of France.

22 Ward, J.S.M., *Freemasonry and the Ancient Gods*, 2nd ed., London, 1926, p. 305.

Chapter 3 Mary's Child?

1 Justin Martyr: 'He appeared without beauty as the Scripture proclaimed.' Dial c. Tryph. 14, 36, 85, 88;

Clement of Alexandria: 'not displaying the beauty of the flesh, but manifesting the beauty of the soul in his beneficence, and that of the flesh in his immortality.' Paedagogus, III, p. 1.

2 I have somatotyped him as 253, which at 5ft. 11in. gives a weight of between 170 and 175 pounds. (See Sheldon, W., *Atlas of Men*, Hafner, 1970, and Harris, A., *Human Measurement*, Heinemann, 1979, for this classifying technique.)

3 Wilson, I., *The Turin Shroud*, Gollancz, London, 1978. Scientific evidence is reviewed in Chapters I through to IX. Contact Hypothesis p. 41.

4 Ib. Wilson reproduces a picture of a scorch shadow of a tap caused by a nuclear explosion, p. 147.

5 The lack of blood should be contrasted with the profuse bleeding expected from scalp wounds, see Nickell, J., *Inquest on the Shroud of Turin*, Prometheus, 1983, pp. 60–61. Further forensic data is examined by I. Wilson; see photographs following p. 50, op. cit. for details of excavated crucifixion victim.

6 Fox, L. D. *The Holy Shroud*, Catholic Truth Society, 1984, p. 11.

7 Nickell, J., op. cit., p. 29.

8 Yallop, D., *In God's Name*, Corgi, 1985.

9 Nickell, J., op. cit., pp. 111–12.

10 Ib., p. 116.

11 McChrone, W. C., *Light Microscopical Study of the Turin Shroud*, II, The Microscope, 1980, 28, pp. 115–28.

12 Nickell, J., op. cit., p. 141 et seq.

13 Ib., pp. 133–40.

14 Wilson, I., op. cit., p. 78 et seq.

15 QED TV Programme, *Shroud of Jesus: Fact or Fake?* Available from BBC Enterprises Ltd. AEFS262Y.

16 Wilson, I., op. cit., p. 54.

17 Froissart, *Les Chroniques*, p. 202, in the trans. Buchon, 1835, Vol. 1.

18 Wilson, I., op. cit., p. 164.

19 The letter to Clement VII by d'Arcis is lodged in Bibliothèque Nationale, Collection de Champagne, Vol. 154, Fol. 138, Paris, trans. H. Thurston, 'The Holy Shroud and the Verdict of History', *The Month*, CI, 1903, pp. 17–29.

20 Ib.

21 Fox, L. D., op. cit., p. 11.

22 Humber, T., Pocket Books, N.Y., 1978, p. 103.

23 Quoted by Wilson, op. cit., p. 189, from U. Chevalier, *Le Saint Suaire de Turin: Histoire d'une Relique*, A. Picard, Paris, 1902, p. 16.

24 Wilson, I., op. cit., p. 188.

25 Ib., p. 189.

26 See Johnson, M., *The Borgias*, MacDonald Futura, 1981, p. 75, et seq.

27 We owe much of our knowledge on the Lirey Scandal to the French priest, Cyr Ulysse Chevalier. In 1900 he published his Critical Study, *Étude Critique sur l'origine du Saint Suaire de Lirey-Chambéry-Turin*. He has been heavily drawn on by opponents of the shroud: John Walsh (*The Shroud*, Random House, 1963), who believes the Turin Shroud is not the same as the Lirey Shroud; also by Thomas Humber (op. cit.), who noted that most scholars on Chevalier's work concluded that the shroud was a 'bizarre episode' in the Church's history (p. 113) while Chevalier (see Humber, p. 106) himself deprecated the deceits and trickeries associated with the relic, or relics, when with the de Charnys. Humber,

who has examined the shroud, is convinced that the Turin Shroud is not the Lirey Shroud, and is in any case an artist's work, op. cit., p. 179.

28 Johnson, M., op. cit., p. 136.

29 Ib., p. 147.

30 Ib., p. 165.

31 Library of the Inst. de France, H137(6r)V.

32 Codice Atlantico, 120 r.d.

33 Library of the Inst. de France, LIV.

34 Ib., I 65(17)V.

35 Goldscheider, L., *Leonardo*, Phaidon, 8th edition, 1967, p. 38.

36 Library of the Inst. de France, L (72) V.

37 Bibliothèque Nationale Ms 2038 34V (Italian MSS).

38 McCurdy, E., *The Notebooks of Leonardo da Vinci*, Reprint Society, 1954, Vol. 1., p. 44.

39 Ib., p. 53. Draws heavily on H. Ludwig's work (*Leonardo da Vinci, Das Buch von der Malerei*, Vienna, 1882, Stuttgart, 1885).

40 McCurdy, op. cit., p. 54.

41 Popham, A.E., *The Drawings of Leonardo da Vinci*, Reprint Society, 1952; first quote p. 21, second quote p. 24.

42 Royal Library, Windsor, Quaderni d'Anatomia VIIIv.

43 Codice Atlantico 358, r.a.

44 First quote Library of the Inst. de France, A 23 R; second quote British Museum, Arundel MSS 44r.

45 See Goldscheider, op. cit. Introduction, et seq., pp. 28–32 for a good review of da Vinci's life, and bibliographers.

46 Royal Library, Windsor, Number 12, 425; a branch of blackberry, red chalk on pink prepared surface heightened with white (RLW 12, 419); spray of blackberry, red chalk on pink prepared surface (RLW 12, 420). These drawings are dated 1505–8. Flowering rushes and a bullrush was done with red chalk, the flowering rushes done on a pink prepared surface, Windsor Library nos. 12,430, recto and verso.

47 Library of the Inst. de France, G 3 V.

48 Codice Atlantico, 360 r.c.

49 Library of the Inst. de France, E 15 R.

50 Crawley, G., *British Journal of Photography*, 24 March 1967, pp. 228–32. Astonishingly, after this paragraph was written, there was a furore in the world press over evidence that Leonardo had used himself as model for *Mona Lisa*. See *Daily Telegraph*, 19 Dec. 1986.

Chapter 4 Shaven Women

1 Hope Robbins, R., *The Encyclopaedia of Witchcraft and Demonology*, Spring Books, London, 1967, p. 331. The following references and quotes in the text are from Hope Robbins' monumental work, compiled over several years with a professional historian's accuracy, with many original transcripts. Bartolo the jurist, p. 500; de Cauzon, disgust at the trials, p. 271; quote by Lord Acton, p. 274; stripping to pudenda, p. 502; 'nameless' sexual parts, p. 468; the story of Madelaine de Demandda, p. 20.

An easy to read study of witchcraft is M. Harrison's *The Roots of Witchcraft*, Tandem, 1978.

2 *Malleus Maleficarum*, Part I, Qr.6. Trans. M. Summers. Arrow Editions, 1971, p. 114.

Chapter 5 What Did the Real Jesus Look Like?

1 Eisler, R., *The Messiah Jesus and John the Baptist* according to Flavius Josephus' recently discovered *Capture of Jerusalem*

and the other Jewish and Christian sources, trans. A.H. Krappe, Methuen, London, 1931, Preface.

We have a fine translation of the 'Roman' version, which has become the modern standard in many ways, by the Oxford scholar G. A. Williamson. The other texts can be referred to as Slavonic. Eisler claims that Josephus wrote a first draft in Aramaic, called *The Capture of Jerusalem*, which contained material on the early Christians and Jesus. Williamson considers that it is entirely plausible that this may have occurred, and that the Greek texts he worked with were extended versions of the Aramaic, but with certain deletions, namely the material relating to Christians and Christ (see Josephus, *The Jewish War*, trans. G.A. Williamson, Penguin, London, 1977, Introduction).

From this scattered material, Eisler does succeed in reconstructing a physical description of Jesus of Nazareth that bears no resemblance to the Turin image. In this he supports the early Christian Fathers and writers, who were convinced that Jesus was of no commanding physical presence; indeed they rightly pointed out that God, in taking on human form, had inherited all its frailties. Thus Tertullian, Celsus and the *Acta Johannis Leucii* all aver this. There is also some internal evidence in the Gospels, Matthew 6:27 and Luke 12:25, where Jesus pointedly asks 'Which of you by taking thought can add one cubit unto his stature?' Eisler also quotes Ephrem Syrus, a Syrian author (AD 320–79): 'God took human form and appeared in a form of three human ells; he came down to us small of stature.' Three ells gives a height of approximately five feet. (Eisler, op. cit., p. 415) Eisler suggests that Josephus actually had access to documents, originals or copies, from Pontius Pilate's Procuratorial Office in Jerusalem.

According to Eisler, Josephus wrote:

At that time also there appeared a certain man of magic power – if it is meet to call him a man, whom certain Greeks call a son of (a) god but his disciples the true prophet who is supposed to have raised dead persons and to have cured all diseases.

In texts accepted by the Church of Rome, the passage reads:

> At that time there appeared a certain man of great powers, if it is meet to call him a man, whom his disciples call a son of (a) god, but he was the only born son of God who raised dead persons and cured all diseases.

It is significant that the Roman Church version has removed the uncertainty about raising from the dead.

2 Certainly it is an indisputable fact that physical descriptions of slaves and prisoners were meticulously noted down by the Romans in civil and criminal proceedings, as this manuscript proves, being a writ for the recapture of two slaves of Alexandria AD 145.

> On the 25th of *Epiphi* a servant of Aristogenes (son) of Chrysippus, delegate of Alexandria, has escaped (2nd hand: in Alexandria). His name is Hermon, otherwise Nilus: by race a Syrian of Bambyce: age about eighteen years: of medium height, beardless, straight-legged, with a dimple in the chin, a mole to the left of his nose, a scar above the left angle of his mouth, tattooed on the right wrist with foreign characters . . . Information may be given by any one to the chief magistrate's officers. His companion in flight is Bion, a slave of Callicrates, one of the chief ministers at court: short of stature, broad-shouldered, bow-legged, grey-eyed . . . Papyr. Par 10 (Graec.2333) in the Louvre, P. M. Meyer, Jurist. Papyr. no. 50.

3 Thus Tertullian, Celsus and the Acta Johannis Leucii all aver this. See note 1.

4 Eisler, op. cit. p. 424 et seq.

5 ib., p. 393.

6 ib., p. 401; this text was cited by Gaster, *Literatura Populara Romana*, Bucharest, 1883, p. 351.

7 ib., p. 404, where full references are given.

8 ib., p. 594.

Chapter 6 Mother and Virgin?

1 Frazer, J.G., *The Golden Bough*, MacMillan, London, 1947, p. 383.

2 Wilson, I., *Jesus The Evidence*, Pan, London, 1985, p. 56.

3 Book of James, 6:2 in the Apochryphal New Testament, Oxford, 1926.

4 Ib., 5:22.

5 *Everyman Classical Dictionary*, Ed. J. Warrington, Dent and Dutton, 1970, p. 273.

6 Josephus, *The Jewish War*, trans. G.A. Williamson, Penguin, 1977, p. 112; The story of the poison vials, pp. 101–103.

7 ib., p. 97.

8 Warner, M., *Alone of All Her Sex*, Weidenfeld and Nicholson, London, 1976, p. 32.

9 Josephus, *Antiquities*, xviii, 3, 4.

10 Eisler, R., *The Messiah Jesus*, Methuen, London, 1931, p. 90.

11 Wilson, I., op. cit., p. 55.

Chapter 7 Virgin Birth

1 *Gray's Anatomy*, Churchill Livingstone, 1980, p. 100–101, 36th ed.

2 Kaufman, M.H., *Jnl. Expt. Zoo.*, 1982, vol. 224, pp. 277–82.

3 Plachot, M., Mandelbaum, J., and Grouchy, J. de, *Ann. Genet.*, Paris, 1984, vol. 27(3), p. 158.

4 Grouchy, J. de, *Biomedicine*, 1980, May, vol. 32(2). p. 51.

5 Abbott, T.M., Hermann, W.J. and Scully, R.E., *Int. Jnl.*

They had studied the case of a nine-year-old girl who, otherwise medically unremarkable, was found to have a well-developed teratoma or, as the authors call it, homunculus, after complaining of abdominal pains and reporting to Memorial City General Hospital, Houston, Texas.

The homunculus had dark hair, limb buds, though the lower limbs had feet and toenails. X-rays revealed skull bone portions and other skeletal bones, including spinal column indications, and other nervous tissue. This case is amongst the most well-developed teratoma found, and the mother may be the youngest case on record.

Although the tissues of the teratomas are of maternal origin, and are hence female, some women are chromosomally abnormal, and have tissues which contain Y chromosomes. However, these are very rare, and statistically can be disregarded, though when teratomas have male tissues, this would be one of the explanations; another would be that the teratoma is simply a deformed foetus conceived in the normal way.

If indeed an ovum divided in the normal way due to some stimulus, and it is remarkable that ultraviolet light so well represented in sunlight can do this (a favourite theme of the conception and annunciation of Mary by painters being a beam of light), then the child would be female. There are no other 'normal' possibilities, but there does remain one area to be investigated, that of chromosomal abnormality.

The vast majority of women have 46XX chromosomal complementation in every cell, but there are variations. In Down's Syndrome, for example, marked by somewhat lowered general intelligence than average, and smaller stature, there is an extra chromosome. It is in fact chromosome 21, which is not a sex chromosome, and so Down's Syndrome can exist in males and females. These have karyotypes 47XY, 21+ for the male, and 47XX, 21+ for the female. One live birth in 700 is a child with Down's Syndrome. Another variation is found in Mosaic phenomena where, instead of the body having one kind of cell, there are two 'lines'. Some cases of Down's Syndrome, marked, usually, by less retardation of intelligence, have normal cells in the body, that is 46XY or 46XX, depending whether male or female, along with the cells possessing 47 chromosomes. The mechanism for this is still not fully understood, but it is thought that the fertilized ovum has developed without full separation of the pairs of chromosomes during division.

There are many differing states of chromosomal defects, because basically there are, after all, twenty-two pairs of chromosomes, not counting the sex chromosomes which have their own peculiarities. Most of these aberrations are either totally innocuous, or fatal, often bringing about spontaneous abortion, still birth, or death within weeks or a few months of live birth. However, where survival is common, as with Down's Syndrome, the personality and general energy level is such that a restricted life-style, with much support, is needed. We conclude then that Mary, the mother of Jesus Christ, could not have had any of the chromosomal defects so far discussed, for she had, if anything, a higher level of intelligence, physical strength and force of character than is found in most people.

On similar grounds we can reject the possibility that Mary was hermaphrodite, and so must conclude that Mary was a normal 46XX woman, though of uncommon hardiness, vitality, strength of mind and physical attractiveness. She would, therefore, in a normal virgin birth, be the mother of a little girl very similar to her.

6 Quoted by M. Nassan SJ, CTS, London, 1982, 'More Meditations on Mary', p. 16.

7 *Merck Manual*, 13th ed., 1977, p. 1107.

8 Hall, J. D., MD, et al., 'Turner's Syndrome', *The Western Journal of Medicine*, 1982, vol. 137(1), p. 32.

9 Olgivie, C., in Chamberlain's *Symptoms and Signs in Clinical Medicine*, Wright & Sons, 1980, 10th ed. p. 450.

10 Pidcock, F.S., 'Intellectual functioning in Turner Syndrome', *Devel. Med. and Child Neur.*, 1984, vol. 26, p. 539.

11 Sandberg, A.A., 'X Chromosome Anomalies and their clinical manifestation', in *Cytogenetics of the Mammalian X Chromosome*, Liss, N.Y., 1985.

12 *Gray's Anatomy*, op. cit., p. 94.

13 Hare, P.J., *Brit. Jnl. Dermat.*, 1970, vol. 83, p. 513.

14 *Merck Manual*, op. cit., p. 1611.

Chapter 8 The Inspiration

1 Stewart, D., *The Foreigner*, Hamish Hamilton, 1981, p. 37.

2 ib., p. 46.

3 Rundle Clark, R.T., *Myth and Symbol in Ancient Egypt*, Thames and Hudson, London, 1978; provides an easy to read background to this section.

4 The stories of Egyptian Gods are clearly set out in *A Dictionary of Egyptian Gods and Goddesses*, G. Hart, Routledge and Keagan Paul, London, 1986.

5 Beltz, W., *God and the Gods*, Penguin, London, 1983, p. 161.

6 Ausbel, N., *Pictorial History of the Jewish People*, Robson, London, 1984, p. 62.
    There is also evidence that even the monotheism of the Jews was not exact, for a temple near Aswan has been excavated which shows a five-aspected god, one gate dedicated to Yahweh alone. Who were the four other gods of the Jews? Here they were Aneth, Bethel, Ishua and Herem. One or more of these may have been female. There is a question mark against the facile assumption of what Jews believed; it is clear that Isaiah and other prophets did not share views held so stringently by the priests of the Jerusalem Temple in the time of Jesus. (For polytheism see Stewart, D., *The Foreigner*, Hamish Hamilton, London, 1981, p. 42.

7 The story does not hold together, or rather it seems to have been altered to prove some point appropriate for a patristic society. The woman 'played the harlot' (Judges 19:2) and

was punished for it, but what had she done? Is the story actually one of a priestess visited, not abused, by Great Goddess worshippers, and then killed by the Levite?

8 Fraser, J.G., *The Golden Bough*, Macmillan, 1947, London, p. 330.

Whatever its motive, the practice was clearly regarded, not as an orgy of lust, but as a solemn religious duty performed in the service of that great Mother Goddess of Western Asia whose name varied, while her type remained constant, from place to place. Thus at Babylon every woman, whether rich or poor, had once in her life to submit to the embraces of a stranger at the temple of Mylitta, that is, of Ishtar or Astarte, and to dedicate to the goddess the wages earned by this sanctified harlotry. The sacred precinct was crowded with women waiting to observe the custom. Some of them had to wait there for years.

9 ib. Frazer refers specifically to Babylon:

At Babylon the imposing sanctuary of Bel rose like a pyramid above the city in a series of eight towers or stories, planted one on the top of the other. On the highest tower, reached by an ascent which wound about all the rest, there stood a spacious temple, and in the temple a great bed, magnificently draped and cushioned, with a golden table beside it. In the temple no image was to be seen, and no human being passed the night there, save a single woman, whom, according to the Chaldean priests, the god chose from among all the women of Babylon. They said that the deity himself came into the temple at night and slept in the great bed; and the woman, as a consort of the god, might have no intercourse with mortal man.

(op. cit., p. 142)

10 Jerusalem Bible, John 8: 3–11.

11 Voragine, J. de, *The Golden Legend*, trans. by W. Caxton, 1470, Dent, London, 1900.

Chapter 9 The First Church

1 Eisler, R., *The Messiah Jesus*, Methuen, London, 1931, p. 441.

2 ib., p. 440.

3 Wilson, I., *Jesus: the Evidence*, Pan, 1985, p. 69.

4 Schweitzer, A., *Quest for the Historical Jesus*, A. & C. Black, 1910, trans. W. Montgomery, p. 93.

5 Cupitt, D., and Armstrong, P., *Who Was Jesus?*, BBC Publications, London, 1977, p. 30.

6 ib., p. 30.

7 Kummel, W. G., *Introduction to the New Testament*, London, 1970.

8 Robinson, J. A. T., *Redating the New Testament*, SCM, 1976.

9 Wilson, I., *Jesus: the Evidence*, Pan, 1985, p. 85.

Chapter 10 The Crucifixion

1 Eisler, R., *The Messiah Jesus*, Methuen, London, 1931, p. 593.

2 ib., p. 621.

3 See under Mithras, Demeter, Persephone Mysteries, *Everyman's Classical Dictionary*, Dent and Dutton, 1970. And *Oxford Classical Dictionary*, 2nd ed., Eds. N. G. L. Hammond and H. H. Scullard, OUP, 1970.
    That Christ was crucified at Golgotha, the Place of the Skull, may have resonances other than the obvious one of death. Throughout Europe, culminating in the twelfth-century legends of a woman who was buried, but so loved by her paramour that he dug her up and made love to her, were common. The stories suggest love goes beyond corruption. The Free Masons, who claim descent from the Templars, used the skull and crossbones as their motif in the eighteenth century, an emblem found on their graves. In the Lady of Maraclea version of the 'resurrection' story, the lover is a Templar, at any rate a Lord of Sidon (Zion?). After his nexus with his dead beloved, a voice tells him to return in nine months, for he will then find a talisman and protection; he returns, and finds a skull and crossbones. Oddly, at a chapel of Christ in Vienne, there exists, as I was to find, just

the crossed thigh bones; the skull is missing. Curiously too, the story actually says the Templars kept the skull, and it is also alleged that Free Masons may have retained it. If they did, these all-male societies were venerating a female skull. See M. Warner, op. cit., p. 51, and J. S. M. Ward, *Freemasonry and the Ancient Gods*, 2nd ed., London, 1926, p. 305.

Chapter 11 Love Feast

1 *The Nag Hammadi Library*, trans. Members of the Coptic Gnostic Library Project of the Inst. for Antiquity and Christianity, Director J. M. Robinson, Harper & Row, 1977, p. 138.

2 ib., p. 472.

3 ib., p. 473.

4 Wilson, I., *Jesus The Evidence*, Pan, 1985, p. 101.

5 ib., p. 24.

6 ib., p. 25.

7 *Nag Hammadi library*, op. cit., p. 120.

8 Quotes from *Nag Hammadi Library*, pp. 120–122.

9 ib., p. 139.

10 Voragine, J. de, *The Golden Legend*, trans. W. Caxton, 1470, Dent, London, 1900, p. 75.

Chapter 12 The Lost Church of Mary Magdalene

1 Voragine, J. de, *The Golden Legend*, trans. W. Caxton, 1470, Dent, London, 1900, p. 76.

2 Warner, M., *Alone of All Her Sex*, Weidenfeld and Nicolson, 1976, p. 229.

3 *Everyman's Classical Dictionary*, Ed. J. Warrington, Dent and Dutton, 1961, p. 420.

4 Much of this section, and sequence, is derived from the

exhibits in the Musée d'Histoire, Marseille, and library; significant authors are Justin, Strabon, Diodore, and *Caesar's Gallic Wars*.

5 *Everyman's Classical Dictionary*, op. cit., p. 242.

6 The Caput 58 Virgo was never claimed to be the mortal remains of Mary Magdalene by the Inquisition, and its subsequent disappearance rests on two factors. It would have been less embarrassing to assume that it was Mary Magdalene, but her bones have been claimed by no less than three locations, Les Saintes Maries, Aix-en-Provence and Besançon (which has figured largely in our story as a resting place of a disputed and rival shroud to that of Turin). The relics of Aix-en-Provence have been accorded greater authenticity than the other two shrines to the Magdalene; at the time the Inquisitors probably felt that to make a fourth claim was to stretch their case too thinly, but they could not draw the obvious conclusion and declare the skull Mary the Virgin's because of the papal development of the bodily assumption of Yeshu's mother into heaven, thereby leaving no bones behind. There is an even more dangerous supposition, however, that of the apocryphal legends of Yeshu surviving the cross and going to Marseille; in which case there may have been in the Church camp the realization that, according to that account, the Caput 58 Virgo was no less than the mortal remains of Jesus Christ. The more blatantly careerist in the Inquisition may have seriously considered this possibility; but it would have been unthinkable, for sincere Christians, for Yeshu died on the cross. Indeed, our reconstruction of the last days of Yeshu and her physical condition, as well as the evidence we have reviewed at length, simply do not allow, on any rational grounds, for the trickery this hypothesis demands – not to say casting Yeshu and the two Marys as liars, which does not square with any evidence. None the less, there remains the reasonable assumption that atheists in the Church interested only in their power, the kind of person Jerome spoke about, would have seen the implications, and acted even more savagely. Their power depended on their inter-

pretation of the Gospels, and nothing would be allowed to stand in their way, a head of Christ included.

Isis in Provence   Curiously, in 1078 at Les Saintes Maries, on the site of a sixth-century chapel, monks were given a church which was called Notre Dame de la Mer. In the crypt, in 1488, two skeletons were found, one with arms crossed. Nicolas de Branças, Bishop of Marseille, officially recorded this event. Speculation was rife, and the bones were said to be those of Mary Jacob, the Virgin Mary's sister, and Mary Salome, the mother of James. This latter attestation would make Mary, James' mother, the mother of Yeshu, since James was her brother. As for Mary Salome, the clues are tenuous but very suggestive. The original Salome danced, which led to John the Baptist having his head cut off, and this would fit neatly into the lore of skull-gathering Ligurians. The story seems to suggest other than what is accepted about it, since the Church taught that Yeshu had no brothers. To add confusion to this misty tale is the legend that Mary Magdalene, in about AD 40, brought a black woman with her, Sara. She has since been subsumed in local festivals, 22 October and 25 May, both with 'gypsy' traditions.

The suspicion arose that this Sara never existed, but was introduced to render Mary the Virgin's landing in Marseille implausible. The black Mother Goddess, as depicted by the statues of Isis and her child, are found all over the Mediterranean. Many of these have been appropriated in Christian iconography as 'Black Madonnas'. They most certainly are; however the woman was not the Virgin Mary, but an aspect of the Great Goddess, most commonly Isis.

7 Hadrill, W., *The Long-Haired Kings*, Methuen, 1962, pp. 245–8.

8 ib., pp. 231–5.

9 Baigent, M., Leigh, R., and Lincoln, H., *The Holy Blood and Holy Grail*, Corgi, 1983, pp. 421 et seq.

10 The Merovingians wore their hair long, like Samson. In the grave of one of their Kings, Childeric, was found 300 golden

bees (Hadrill op. cit., p. 162), appropriately enough for a man copying Samson's belief that in long hair is strength. Samson is author of the riddle – out of the strong comes forth sweetness. He was of course referring to the carcass of a lion in which wild bees had made their nests. But we might note that Jesus was referred to as Panthera, lion, and from the death of Jesus came the sweetness of redemption, the words of salvation, like so many honey bees. Hadrill clearly is no entomologist, for he calls them cicadas; flies they may be, for these devour a carcass, and then bees make their nest in the bones.

11 It is significant that historians of this period, such as Gregory of Tours, Rome's man, sixth century, who knew Vienne well but also did not mention his visit there, provides scholars with no answers to Merovingian puzzles, while other Churchmen are guilty of forgery, like Hincmar, Bishop of Rheims late ninth century. This period of history is often referred to as the Dark Age, the reason for its opacity may be simply censorship, not barbarism, illiteracy or fecklessness (see Hadrill, p. 96).

Certainly at this time the Roman Church had a monopoly on writing and most libraries, and later when the Cathars were destroyed, so were authentic records of the Merovingian period. What we do have on the Merovingians has been coloured by Rome; none the less we know that these kings used to have their skulls trepanned. Was this so that they would never be confused with their most precious relic, Caput 58?

12 Michelet, M., *Procès de Templiers*, Paris, 1881, Vol. II, p. 208.

13 Pelletier, A., *Histoire de Vienne*, Horvath-Roanne Collection, Histoire des Villes de France, 1980.

Plans for the present church, now Cathedral, on the site of the Church of the Resurrection, were drawn up in the twelfth century. The cathedral was consecrated on 20 April 1251 by Innocent IV. By 1312 the cathedral was the focal point of a Church meeting convened by Clement V. Embellishments were added to the church by Clement VII, whom we met earlier in connection with the Lirey Shroud.

Over the door is a mysterious sculpting of La Vierge d'Aaron, the Virgin of Aaron. Mysterious, because Aaron as a priest of Yahweh, has no connection with Virgins. Again, an example of ambivalence, which is reinforced by Exodus, with this astonishing mix-up of female and male symbols: '. . . and thou shalt gird them with girdles, Aaron and his sons' (Ex. 29:9), while earlier the symbol of the scarlet is introduced in connection with priestly vestments having embroidered scarlet fruits (Ex. 28:33). This passage reveals the novelty of having male priests, but the female echoes are still there.

Mary Magdalene is there too, in the church, anointing Christ's feet with precious ointment, which is a derivative of oil, technically a suspension of water droplets in oil. We may recall that she also anointed Jesus head, just as it says in Exodus, 'take the anointing oil, and pour it upon his head' (Ex. 29:7), with reference to the consecration of Aaron. Here the symbols are direct: Mary Magdalene is a priestess of Jesus Christ, but who had the power to make Aaron and his sons priests? Mary the Virgin and Mary Magdalene trace their priestly role back to the beginning of time.

14 Marseille was founded through the marriage, as legend has it, of Gyptis, a Ligurian Princess, and Protis, a Greek. Gyptis may very well have been a real person, and so might Protis; certainly some kind of alliance between the Greeks from Phocea and the Ligurians would have been beneficial to both sides, and marriage was the time-honoured method, not always successful, of cementing such agreements. (See Philiparie, S., *Les Fondateurs*, c.1986, Marseille (an edition for education by the history museum, Marseille, and very beautifully done). On the other hand, the legend has all the signs of being conveniently used to describe much later events. Alexander's conquests of the fourth century BC included Egypt. The Greek god Proteus, son of the sea god, Poseidon, had the gift of prophecy, but would-be gainers of his knowledge had the problem of his turning into different animal shapes – he was, in other words, Protean. This process

of metamorphosis is intrinsic to myth and legend; changes are brought about according to circumstances and to the ruling power. Current notions of gypsies being the cultists of Les Saintes Maries are convenient to the Church, and were probably fostered by them as early as the discovery of the bones in the crypt of Notre Dame de la Mer at Les Saintes Maries, since it obscured rumours, false though they were, that here were the bones of Mary Magdalene and Mary the Virgin.

In truth, gypsies probably had nothing to do with the cults at all, the real connection being much more matter of fact. Alexander's generals were rewarded by being given thrones in conquered lands. In this way Greeks became the Pharaonic class in Egypt. Cleopatra, born 69 BC, was Greek, and used her guile to temper the rapacity of Julius Caesar. It was he who brought Marseille firmly under Roman dominion in the sixth decade BC, when the city sided with his rival Pompey. As heirs to Greek conquests, the Romans added another slice to the rich cake of Marseille's influences, though Marseille had actually aided the Romans in the destruction of Carthage, for reasons of trade, much earlier. The Egyptian connection then, was actually through the Greek ruling class, and continued not only through trade but through Rome too. Mark Antony, Caesar's supporter, ruled Egypt with Cleopatra, and it was he who supported Herod in Jerusalem. With the death of Antony and Cleopatra in Alexandria in AD 31, Augustus became master of the Roman world, with all its interlocking, serpentine influences, and as we have seen, these were the formative influences on Marseille and the Rhône valley.

The south of France was, therefore, Roman with Greek undertones, with all that meant in Egyptian influence and affiliations, while in the pastures, forests and hills of the Rhône valley and beyond, the ancient cults of the Ligurians held sway.

When viewed as a result of dynamic interplay, cultural identification automatically becomes less a matter of central authority but more a mixture of breezes, as it were, some prevailing, others languishing, so that the ship of civilization is first blown one way and then another

15 The thongs have never been satisfactorily explained but in the light of the hypothesis that Christ was a woman and fulfiller of the Great Goddess tradition, they are emblems of her gender and that tradition.

The symbol of life, the *ankh*, is related to the *tyet* 'a girdle or loop, with a knot on the front' (G. Hart, *A Dictionary of Egyptian Gods and Goddesses*, Routledge and Keagan Paul, 1986, p. 101), but there is some confusion in the literature of the *ankh*'s relationship with another amulet, called a *tet*, which is a tree, from which the *ankh* arises (E. A. Wallis Budge, *Egyptian Magic*, Dover, 1971, p. 58). R. T. Rundle Clark (*Myth and Symbol in Ancient Egypt*, Thames and Hudson, 1978, p. 237) is also in no doubt of the central feminine importance of, '*Tit*, a knot of cloth or leather'. The Vienne Cord around the thigh bones is therefore a significant motif. The knot symbol, however, if seen in the Great Goddess tradition, signifies life.(See note 7, chapter 13, below).

Chapter 13 The Vatican Witness

1 The clearest account of the facts of the mystery of Rennes-le-Château is given by Gérard de Sède, who wrote *Signé: Rose Croix*, Plon, 1977. This has been adumbrated by M. Baigent, R. Leigh and H. Lincoln, in *The Holy Blood and the Holy Grail*, Cape, 1982. However, these latter authors assume Christ's survival of crucifixion and involve him in a lie, since his teaching was based on dying to save many. Furthermore, they ignore the effect of being arrested in the early hours, beaten and interrogated, then scourged, and then crucified, not to mention being lanced through the heart. That Christ died on that cross is unambiguous. The authors make no factual counter-claim.

2 De Sède, op. cit., gives considerable detail on genealogies, and refers to *Le Serpent Rouge*.

3 The Constantine Cross is $\cancel{\times}$, which is not dissimilar to the ankh, $\top$ the sign of Isis.

4 In one sense the inscription is incompetent, letters are put in

capitals, then in lower case, names are broken up, and the P in 'SEPT', seven, is dropped below the other letters.

However there is, perhaps, a pattern in these apparent mistakes. The date of death for the Marquiese is given as MDCOLXXXI. Usually O is not present in Roman numerals, and the sequence spells 'COLX'. Is it reasonable to see this as a play on CLX? If so, both without the vowel give the cipher CALX (Notes: Ch. 2, no. 20), standing for Chalice, as well as the red oxides of lead and mercury, used to colour emblems of Isis. Following this train of thought, the dropping of P in SEPT gives SET, the name of the homosexual rival to Osiris. Set was an eye-gouging and otherwise disreputable deity of the Egyptians, and an enemy of Isis.

The original inscription has been copied by Languedoc antiquarians, and is displayed by de Sède, op. cit., p. 33. It is reproduced below.

```
        ✝
  CT GIT NOBLe M
  ARIE DE NEGRᴱ
  DARLES DAME
  DHAUPOUL Dᴱ
  BLANCHEFORT
  AGEE DE SOIX
  ANTE SET ANS
          P
  DECEDEE LE
  XVII JANVIER
  MDCOLXXXI
  REQUIES CATIN
  PACE
```

Some of the odd numerical relationships are as follows. The sequence of the number of capitals in the first four lines is 10, 10, 10, 9, giving 39. The second four lines give 11, 10, 10, 10, adding to 41. Numerologists might observe that 39 = 3 x 13, where 3 is the Triple Goddess cipher, and 13 the sacred coven, whose numerals add to 4. 41 has no apparent significance, except that its numerals add to 5, the female cipher of Isis. The first two sets of four lines give 80 capitals, 8 being the Sybilline number of the Great Goddess. There are twelve lines in all, in three sets of four. The last four lines give this sequence for the number of capitals, 11, 9, 12, 4, which adds to 36, of which no clear significance can be observed other than that its numerals add to 9, which is the triple triple (3 x 3) of the Great Goddess. So far all we have are the commonplaces of Great Goddess numerology. Why put them on a tombstone of a woman called Haupoul?

Perhaps the clue lies in MDCOLXXXI, which could be read as MD followed by the cipher COLX, followed by XXI, that is 15–21. This adds to 36. Bigou is apparently laboriously hinting at 36 again. And again the question is why? Are we to read CLX–36, as CLX–9? If so the message is being hammered home, for CLX is the cipher of the blood of the Goddess, and 9 her tripled cipher.

It is however very dangerous to assume too much in numerology, for two basic reasons. First, as is very evident, the numbers used in reference to the Great Goddess are 3, 5, 8 and 9; in other words four out of the ten digits, so they are bound to occur in a set of numbers. Against this must be weighed the chances of their appearing in a unified non-random manner. On balance, the Goddess numbers in Bigou's inscriptions appear to present a pattern allied with the names, which is beyond mere chance. The second ground for caution, is that the ciphers for the Great Goddess have become tainted by their misuse in Satanism and by people who call themselves occultists but have no real knowledge. Bigou, however, is clearly not in this category.

Why did he choose this particular Marquise when there are dozens he could have erected tombstones to? Perhaps he was paid, but then why all these mystic clues? Perhaps there is something in her name. The first four lines contain broken names, Marie for example is broken up, to no apparent purpose, except that the words Noble, Negre, and Dame fall under one another as a result. Noble negre dame. Noble black woman? This contrasts very strongly with the name Blanchefort: white strength might be a literal translation. How can white be strong? In the sense of purity being a powerful virtue. Yeshu had such virtue, being spotless in thought, word and deed. She was, according to my investigations, also afflicted with a skin condition which darkened her skin, although she also blanched. Did Abbé Bigou know this? Possibly, but the inscription, and others in the Languedoc might provide material for deeper study. Oddly, this particular Marquise for whom Bigou chose to set so enigmatic an inscription, died at 67, the number of the psalm the Templars used in their ceremonies when they worshipped the 'head'. Perhaps even more remarkable a chance, if that is what it is, the number of capitals in total is 116, exactly twice the number of the Templar reliquary containing the bones of a small woman, Caput 58.

5 De Sède, op. cit., p. 59.

6 ib., p. 49.

7 The *ankh* is ☥ . Its evocative, if nothing more, similarity to ✖ referred to above possibly has deeper connotations. The forms of the cross include ┼ , which is Phoenician for *tau*, ⊤ , which is again another form of the cross. Badly written, *tau* is Υ , or *upsilon*. The handwritten form of Y, *gamma*, is ʃ which is the Christian fish symbol for Christ. Υ and ʃ are easily confused in poor script. *Tau* in its Phoenician form is plausibly related to three forms of the cross ┼ , ⊤ and Υ , and there is also the variant, Ψ the tree of life.

The Y sign may then be a silent witness to the femality of Christ, which may explain why the fashion-conscious ladies

of chivalry adopted it. At the most basic level, the sign
is an ideogram of the female groin; it is also the form of the
cross seen on the back of robes of Catholic priests. Upside
down, it is the familiar Tree of Life sign, appropriated by
the CND movement though they are innocent of its deeper
meanings. The fleur-de-lis is then the Lily of the Valley,
which is equated with the Rose of Sharon, in the Song of
Solomon. Hebrew poetry makes the same statement twice.
A rose is of course a motif, symbolic and allusive, not only
of love, but the female parts of sex, but so is the fleur-de-lis,

which can be glyphed as ⅄ . By the time of Thomas

Aquinas, Y was used to denote a doubt about gender. (See
the engraving by Michael Maier, Frankfurt, 1617, depicted
in E. Zolla's *The Androgyne*, Thames and Hudson, 1981,
p. 42.) Oddly enough in the Magdalene Church at Rennes-
le-Château there are fleur-de-lis motifs, accompanied by
other patterns, which one writer (D. Wood, *Genisis* [*sic*]
Baton Press, 1985, p. 67) has painstakingly counted, and
found that the pattern is separated into 14 and 35. It
occurred to me that these numbers add to 5 and to 8 re-
spectively. The oddness lies in the fact that these numbers
are part of the church decorations, which include Mary
Magdalene and a skull by a cross in a painting; as well as a
statue of the Magdalene with a skull. It is curious that
Caput 58 is the relic which featured in Cathar history and
Templar trials.

8 Wallis Budge, E. A., *Egyptian Magic*, Dover, 1971; buckle,
   p. 43; Serpent, p. 58.

9 Yallop, D., *In God's Name*, Cape, 1984.

10 *Women and the Priesthood, Publication of the Declaration of*,
   Catholic Truth Society, 15 Oct. 1976.

11 ib., p. 12.

12 ib. p. 17.

Acknowledgements for Illustrations

Illustrations 2–6: A. Harris, London; 7: British Museum; 8: A. Harris, London – reproduced by courtesy of the Trustees, British Museum; 9: British Museum; 10–12: A. Harris, London – courtesy of British Museum; 13: Lawrence Durrell's translation of Emmanuel Royidis's *Pope Joan* published by Derek Verschoyle, London, 1954; 15–16: A. Harris, London; 17–18: the Royal Library, Windsor – reproduced with gracious permission of H M the Queen; 19–20: reproduced by courtesy of the Trustees, the National Gallery, London; 21–2: reproduced by permission of Don Bosco, Silesians; 23–4: by courtesy of Ian Wilson, from Don Bosco, Silesians; 25–6: A. Harris, London; 27: A. Harris, by permission of Musée de Marseille; 28: A. Harris, London.

Index